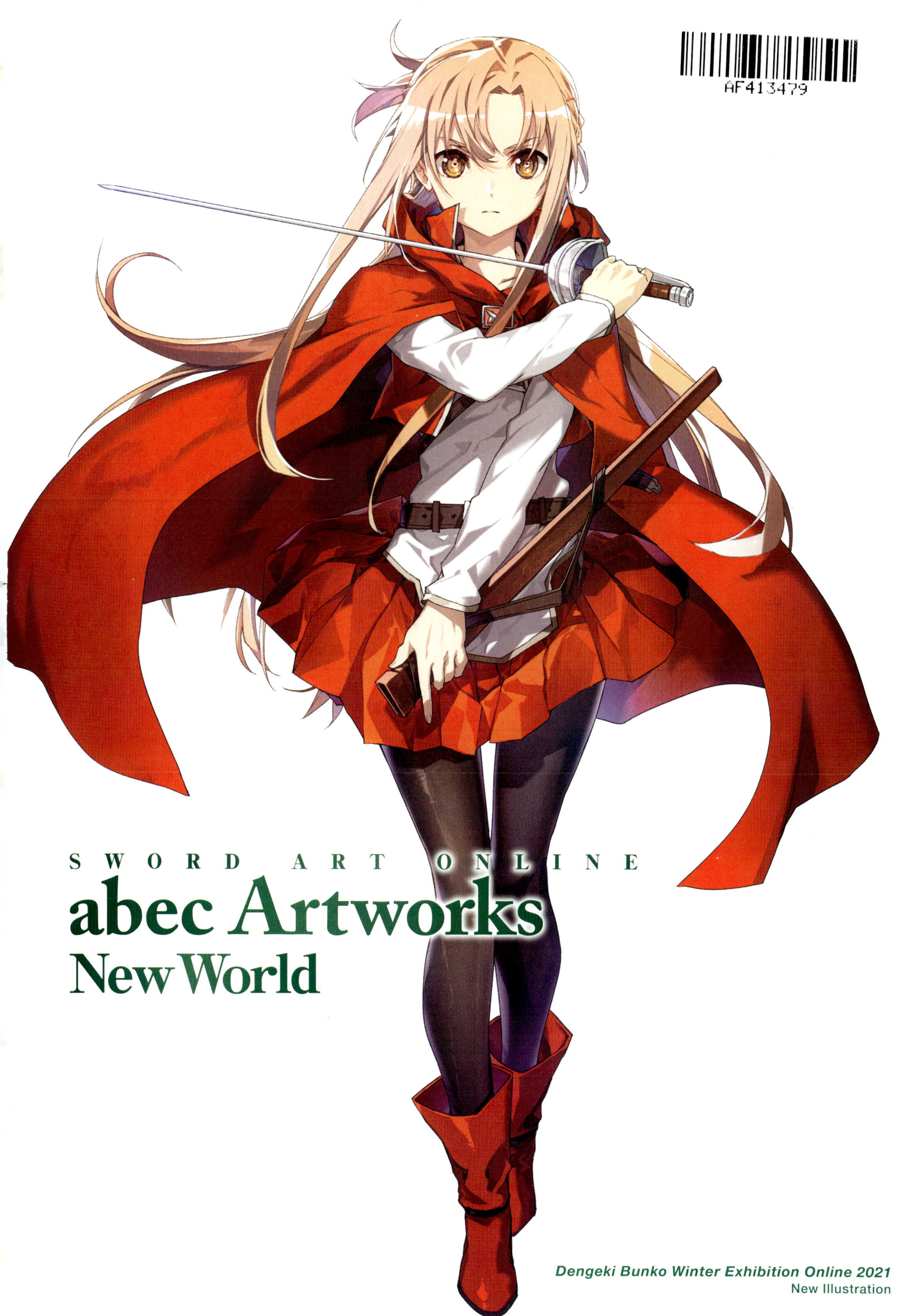
AF413479
SWORD ART ONLINE
abec Artworks
New World
Dengeki Bunko Winter Exhibition Online 2021
New Illustration

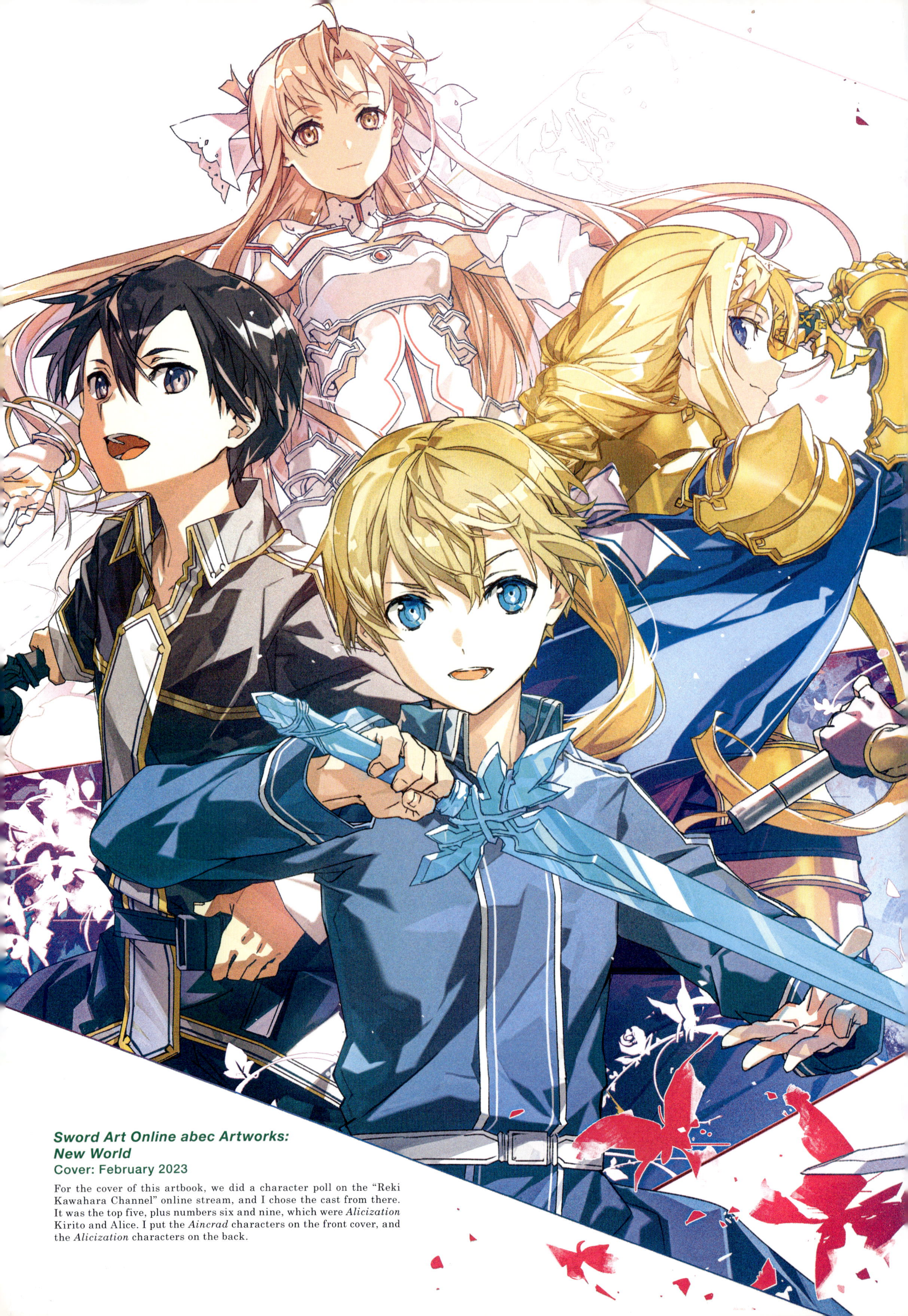

**Sword Art Online abec Artworks:
New World**
Cover: February 2023

For the cover of this artbook, we did a character poll on the "Reki Kawahara Channel" online stream, and I chose the cast from there. It was the top five, plus numbers six and nine, which were *Alicization* Kirito and Alice. I put the *Aincrad* characters on the front cover, and the *Alicization* characters on the back.

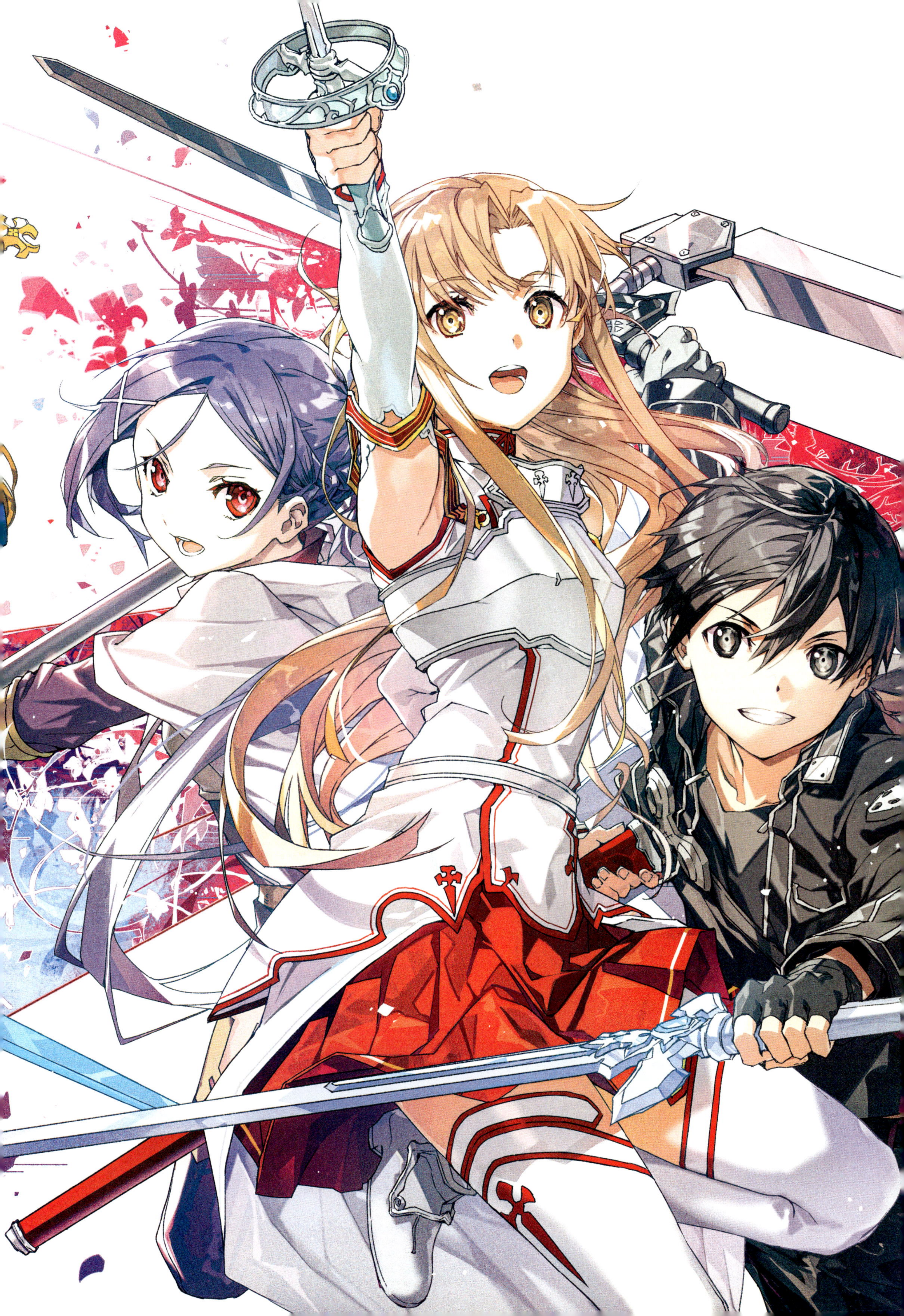

SWORD ART ONLINE
Alicization Exploding

In this volume, the final stress test begins, and a huge war breaks out in the Underworld, which meant there were many dense illustrations to put together this time.

Dengeki Bunko
Sword Art Online 16:
Alicization Exploding
Cover: August 2015

The main draw is Asuna's Stacia outfit, followed by the army of invaders, and then my painful attempt to fulfill the quota of one Kirito on every cover. Get back on your feet soon, Kirito!!!

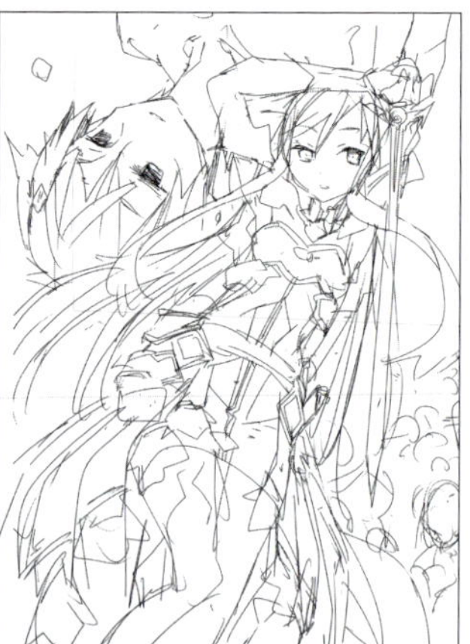

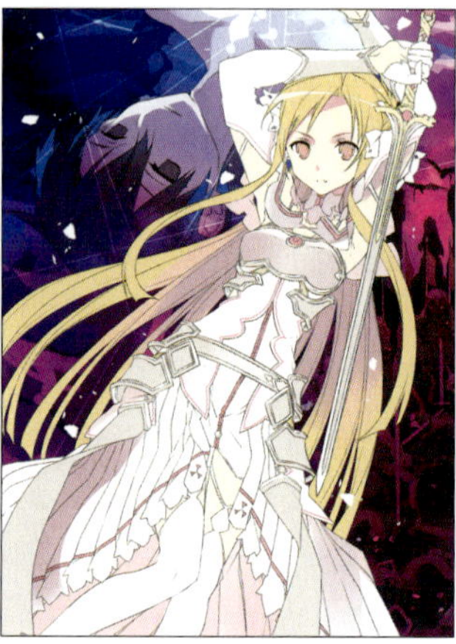

Rough Cover Sketch

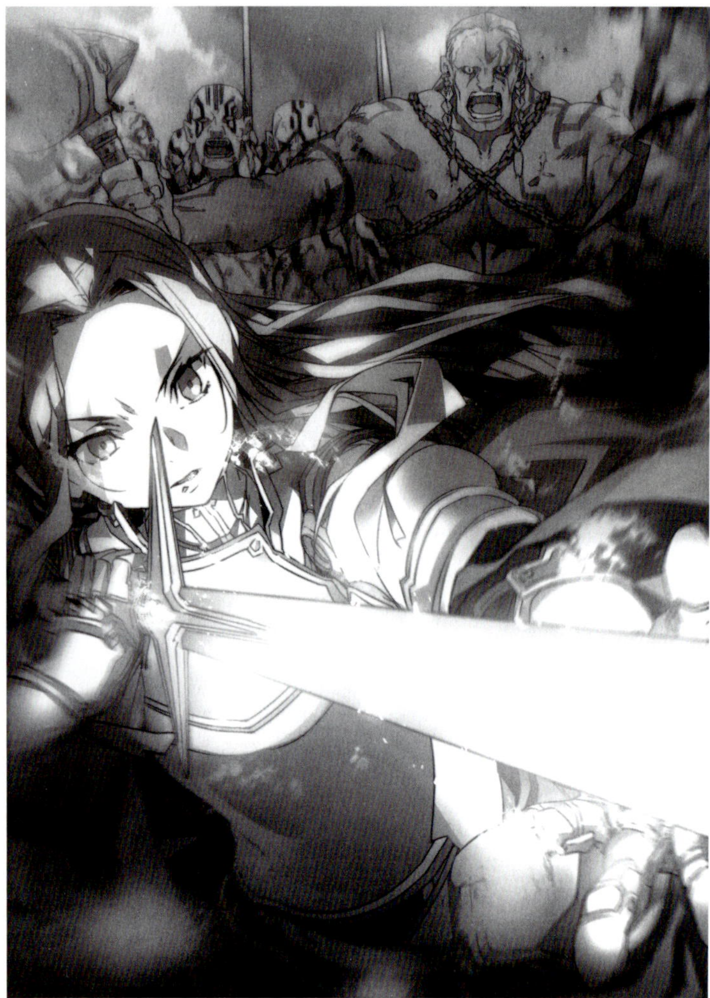

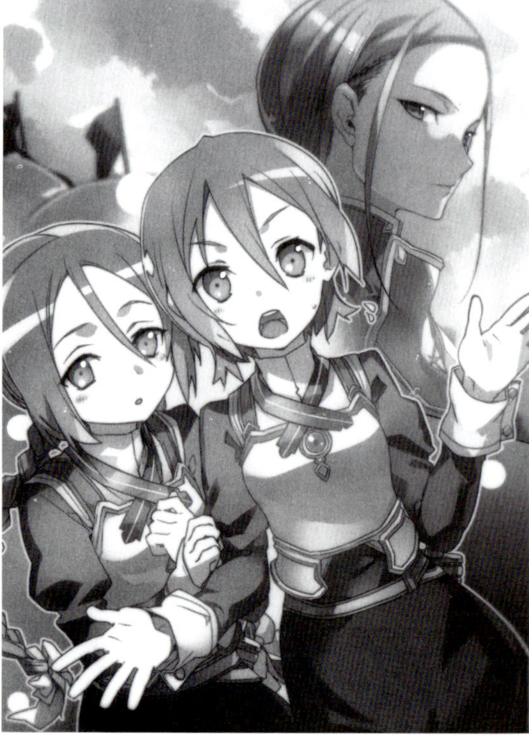

Dengeki Bunko
Sword Art Online 16: Alicization Exploding
Illustration: August 2015

The story illustrations were mostly battle scenes, so I remember that drawing Fizel and Linel was a real treat.

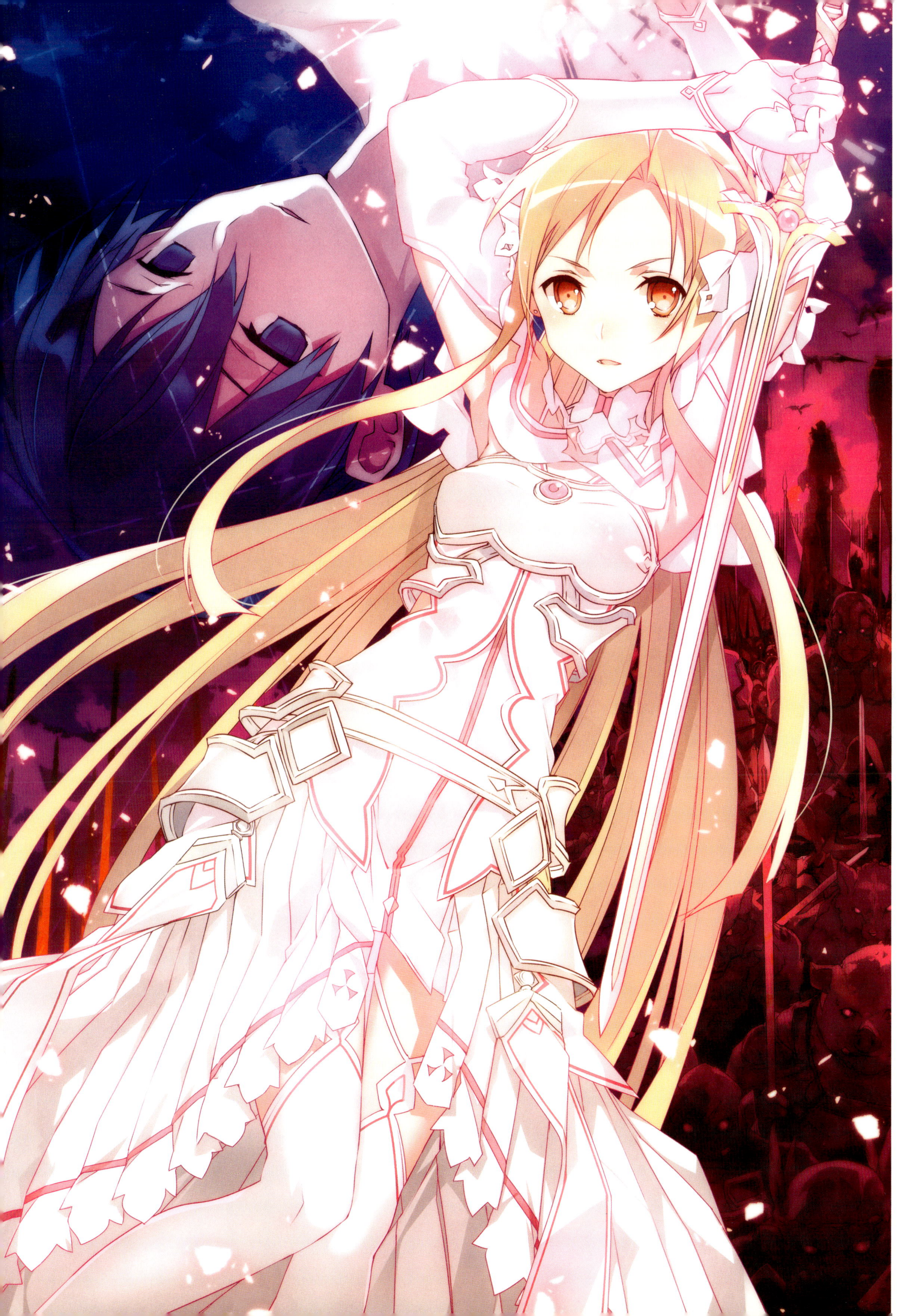

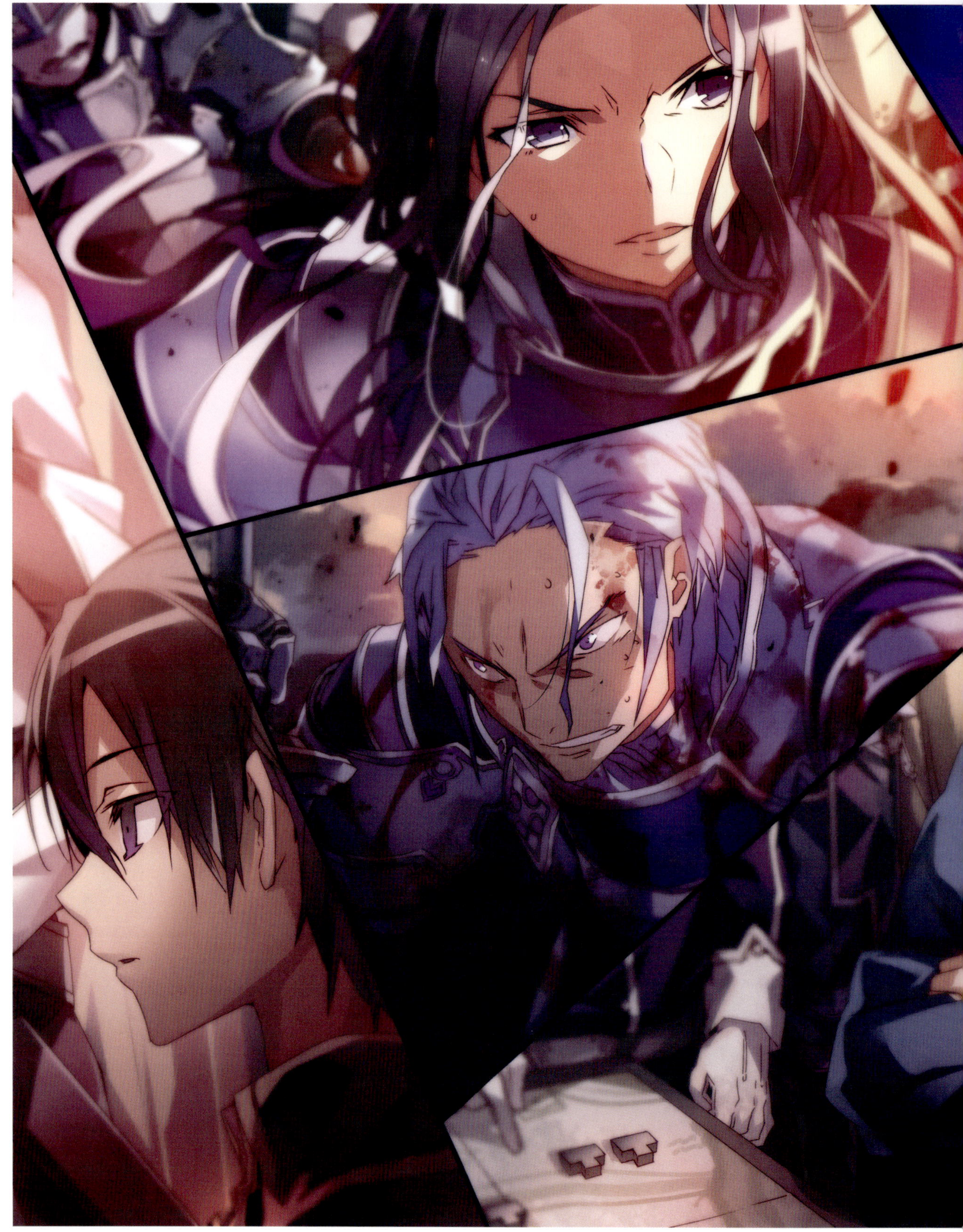

Dengeki Bunko
Sword Art Online 16: Alicization Exploding
Frontispiece: August 2015

This is a colorized version of a preview illustration that ran at the end of Volume 18 of *Accel World*. It shows the Integrity Knights on the battlefield, each in their own individual cut. I've always liked drawing battle scenes, and I find ensemble battle pieces to be quite fun.

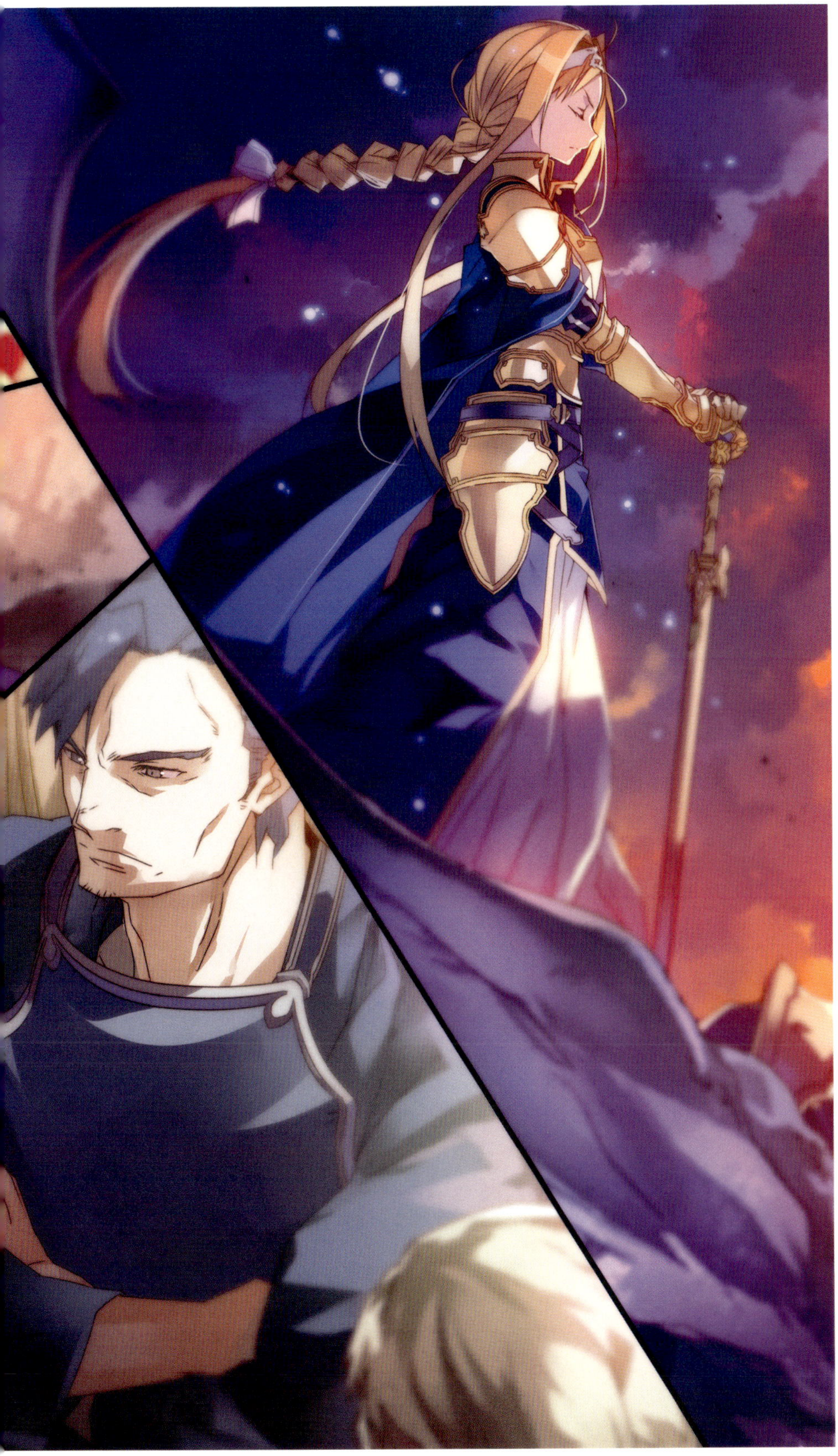

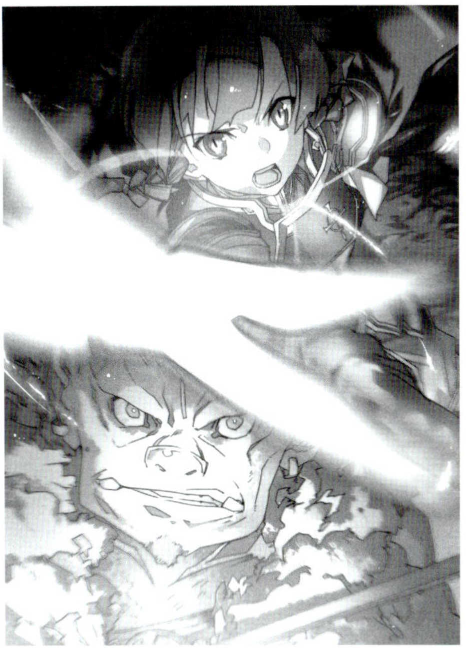

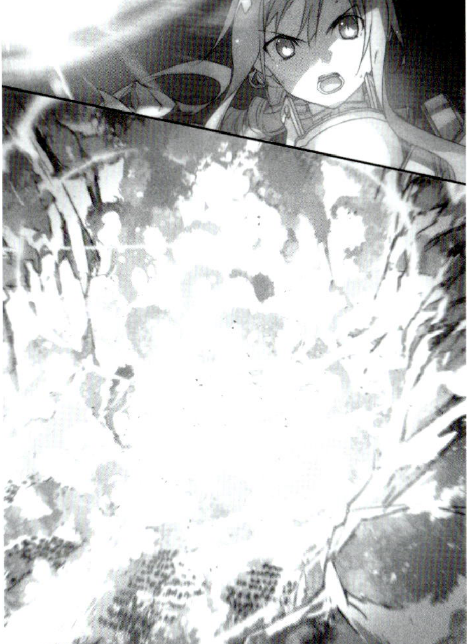

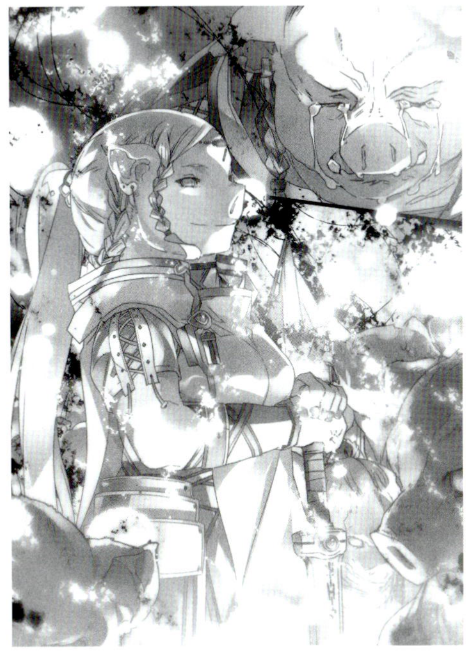

Dengeki Bunko
Sword Art Online 16: Alicization Exploding
Illustration: August 2015

Battle scenes have more to show off, so I naturally end
up splitting them into more panels. Lots of them have
fancy effects applied. It's a lot of work, but you can tell
that I get more excited as the story ramps up.

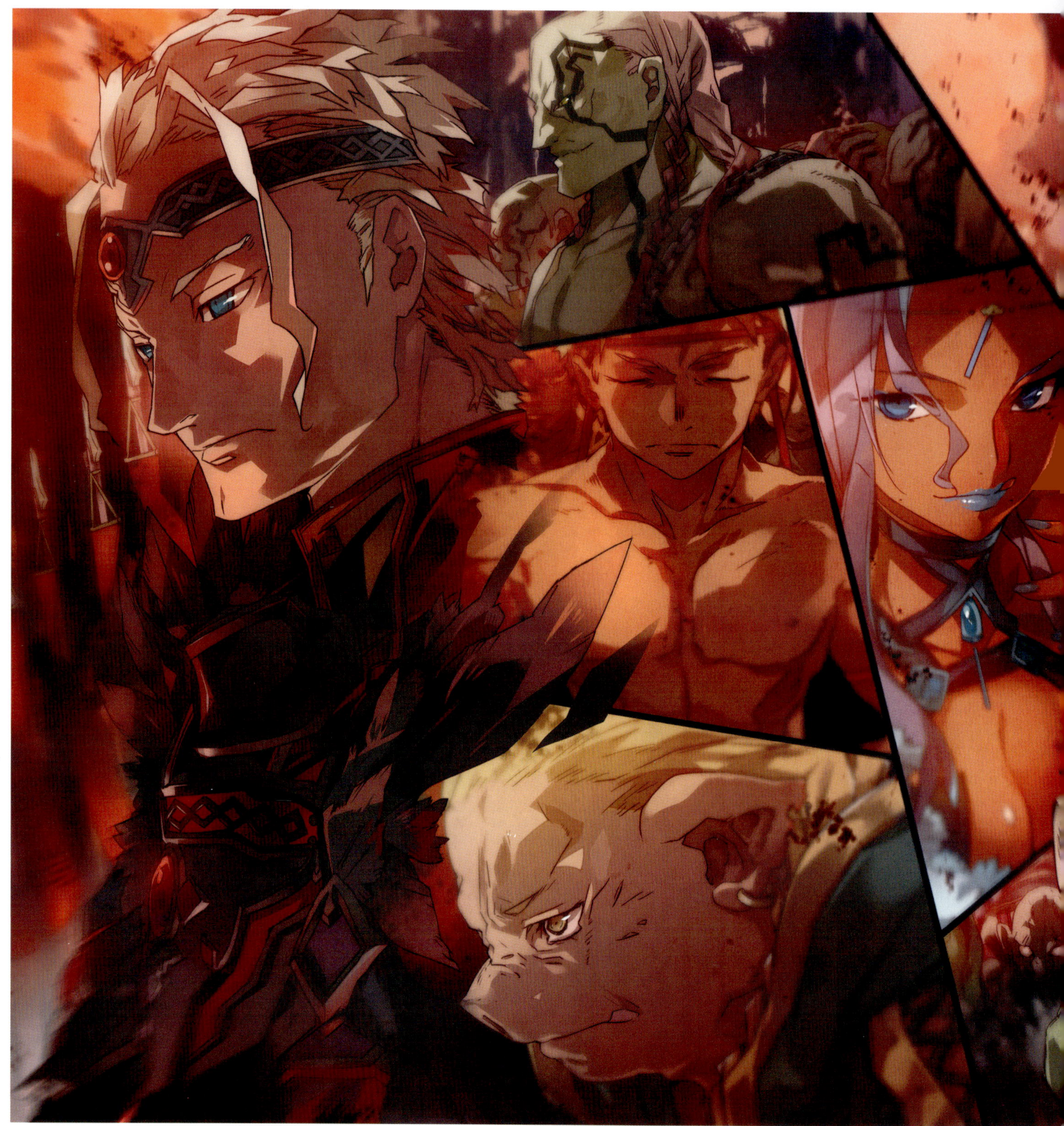

Dengeki Bunko
Sword Art Online 16: Alicization Exploding
Frontispiece: August 2015

This is a Dark Territory piece to match the one of the Integrity Knights.
Ordinarily, each of these would be its own illustration with more of a
full-body focus, but since the Japanese trim size is pretty small, I made
sure you could see their faces in detail.

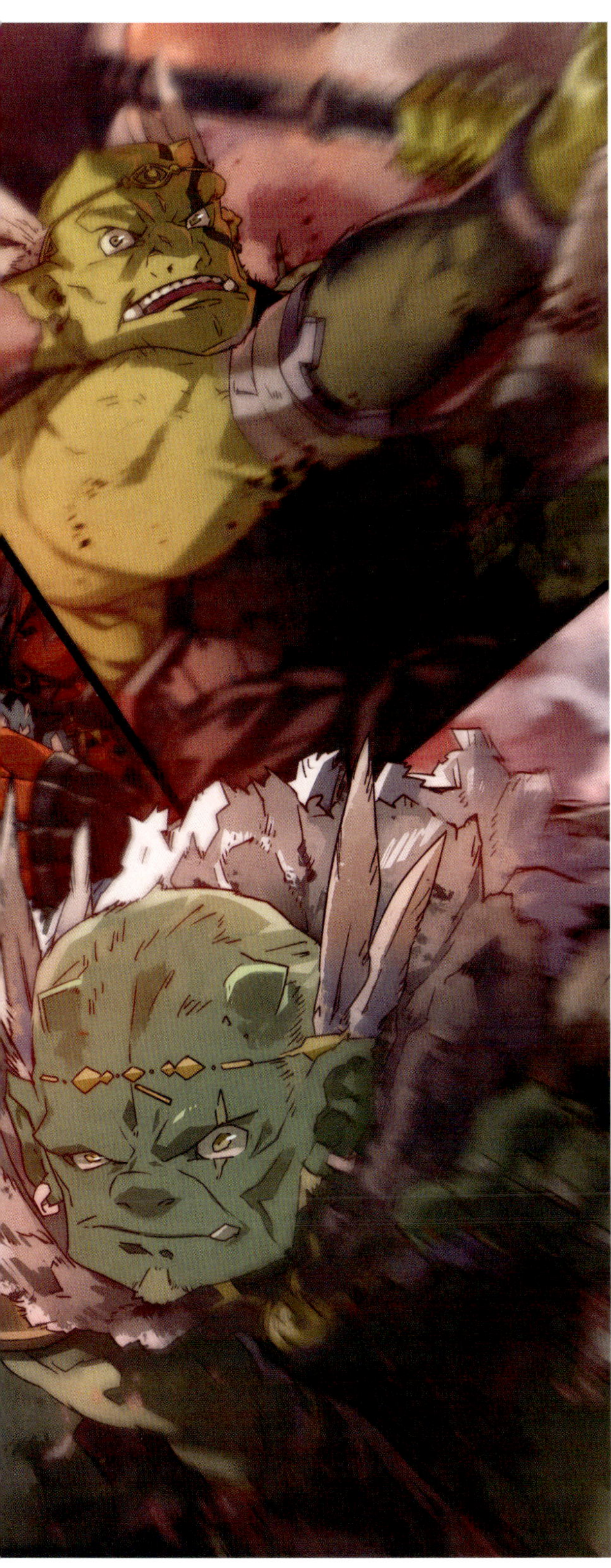

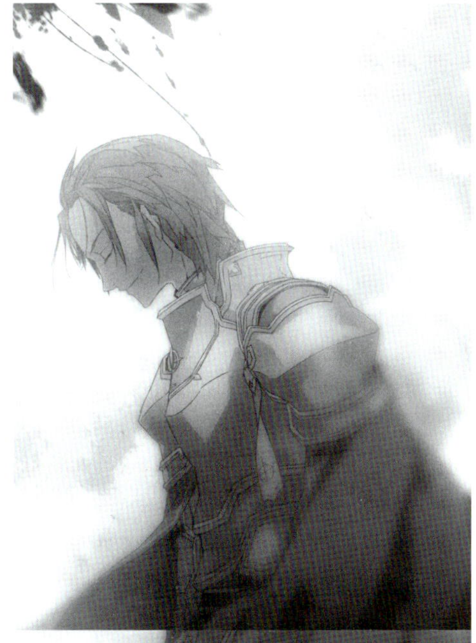

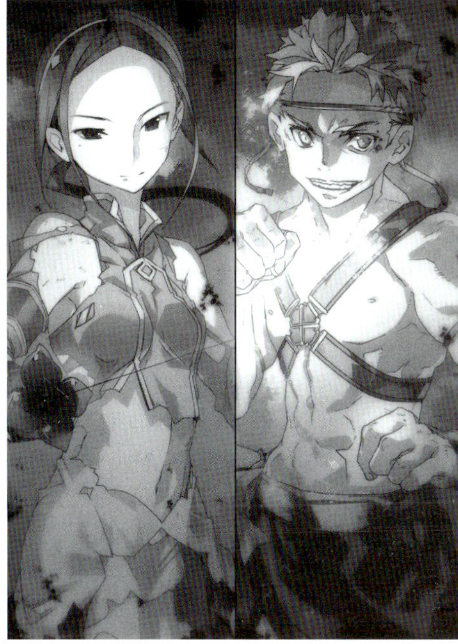

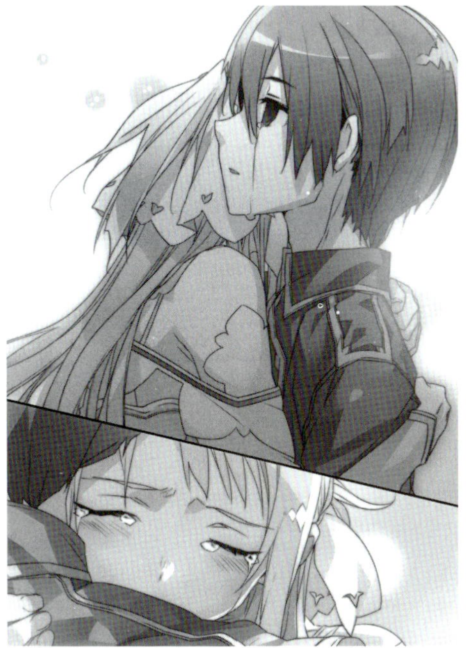

Dengeki Bunko
Sword Art Online 16: Alicization Exploding
Illustration: August 2015

Illustrations of quiet and still moments might seem easy to draw, but
I second-guess myself the most with them. It's actually much easier
to set up a motion scene. It's just more work to do all the detail.

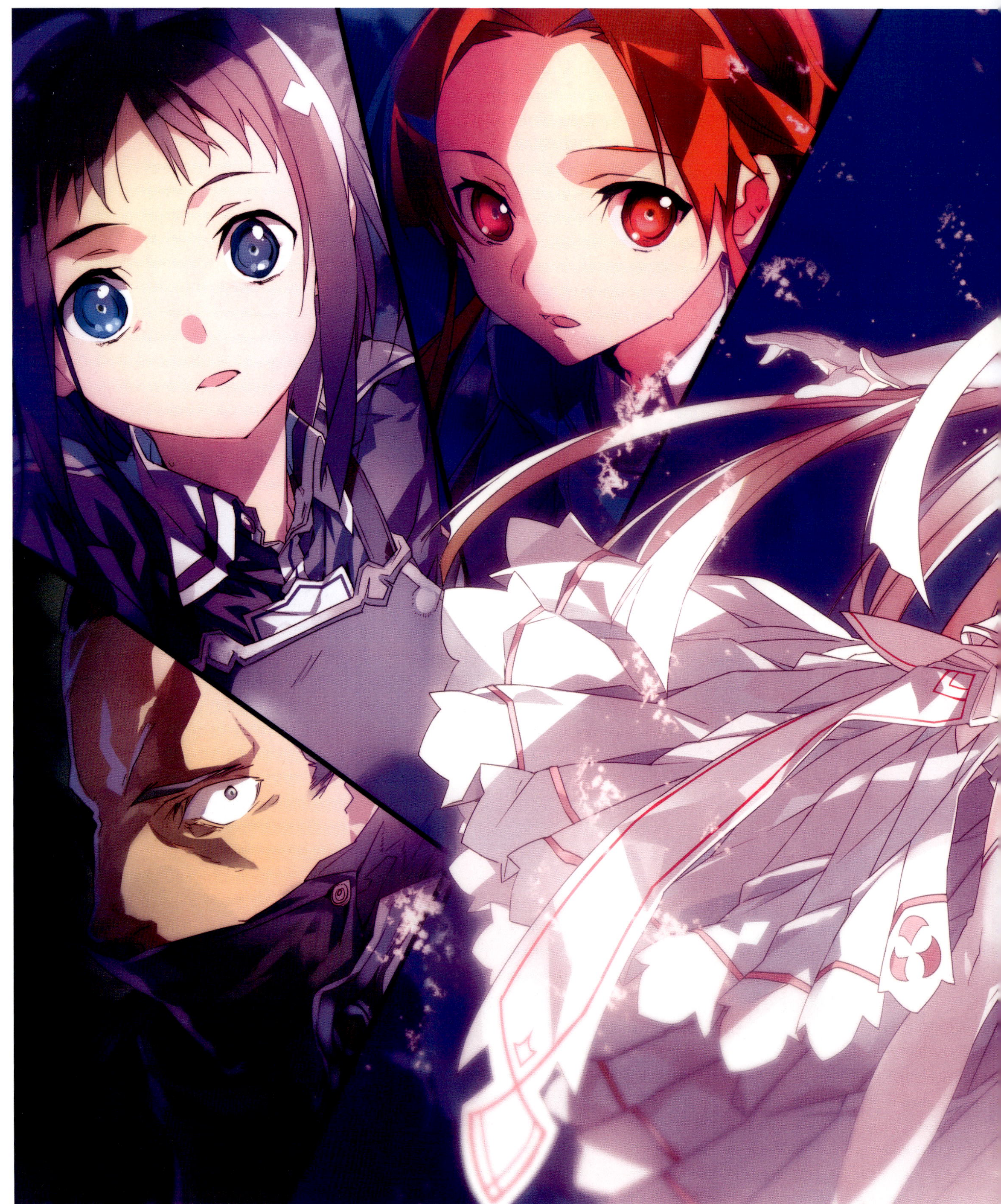

Dengeki Bunko
Sword Art Online 16: Alicization Exploding
Frontispiece: August 2015

The second detailed illustration of Stacia Asuna's clothing. When I'm expressing holy symbology during character design, I tend to go white, with parallel lines and circles. That's a common set of visual motifs you'll see repeated with Terraria and Solus in the next volume.

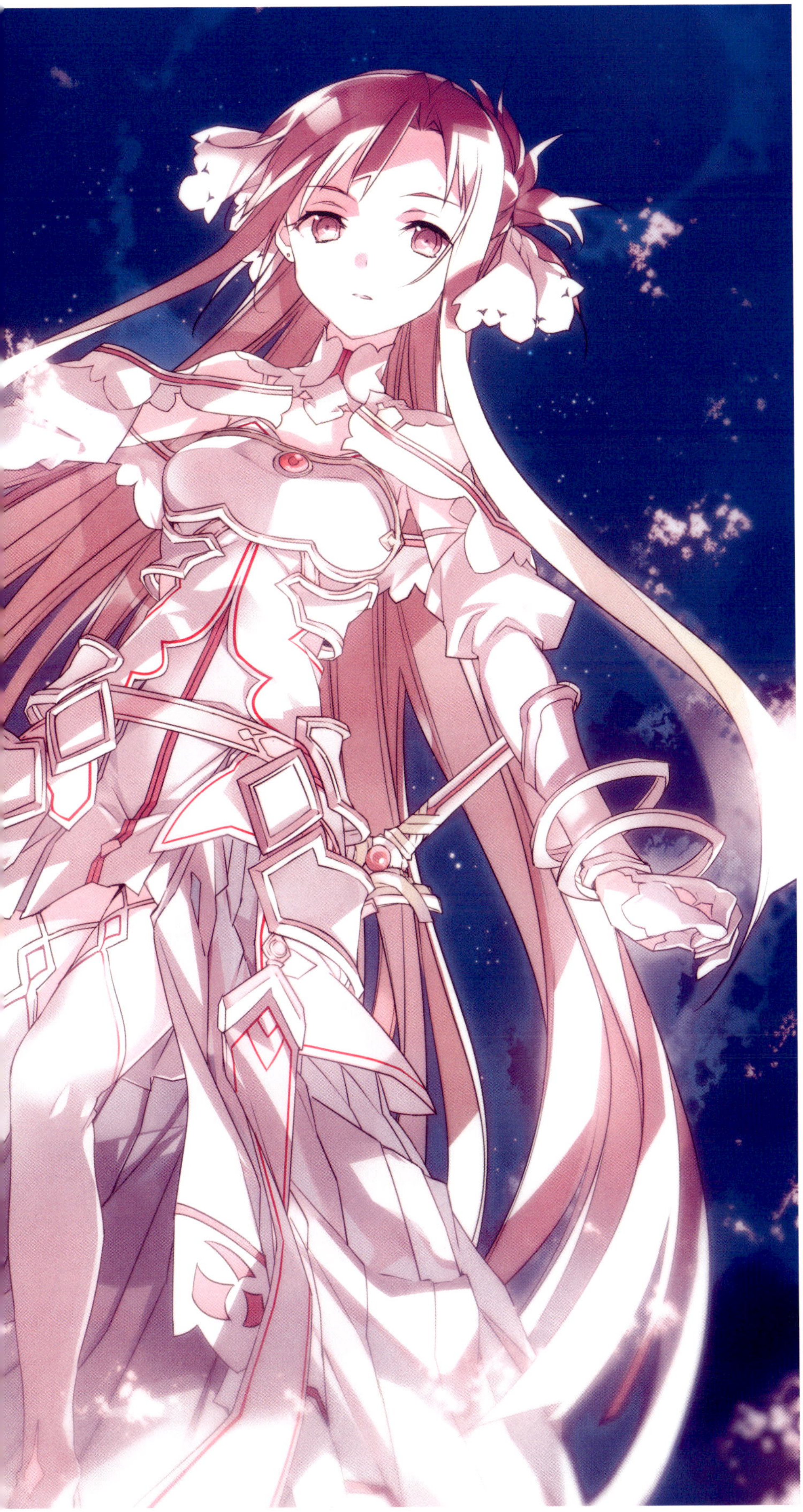

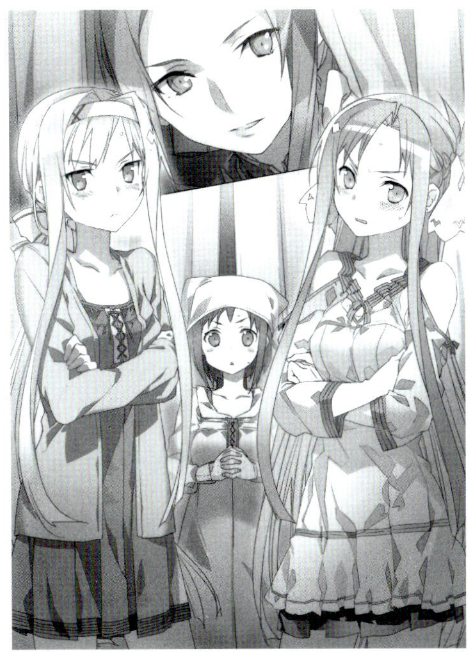

A comical scene. The man who can move the story even when he's just sitting in a chair doing nothing. That's our Kirito.

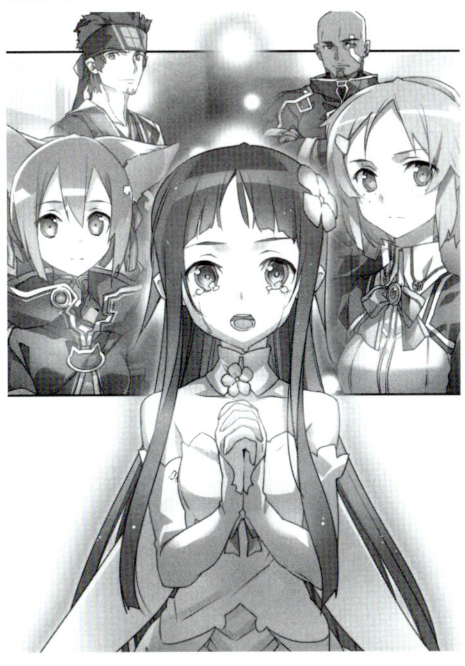

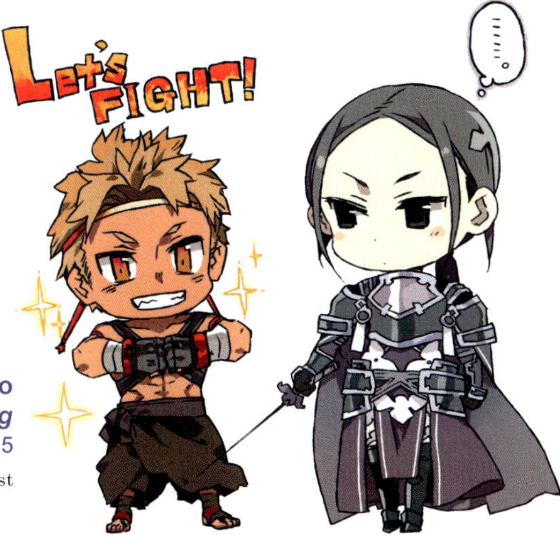

I've always loved Iskahn and Sheyta since I first read about them in the novel ten years ago.

SWORD ART ONLINE Alicization Awakening

Friends from the real world come to join the fight in this volume. It's the kind of thing you can only pull off in a really long story arc, and I love that stuff.

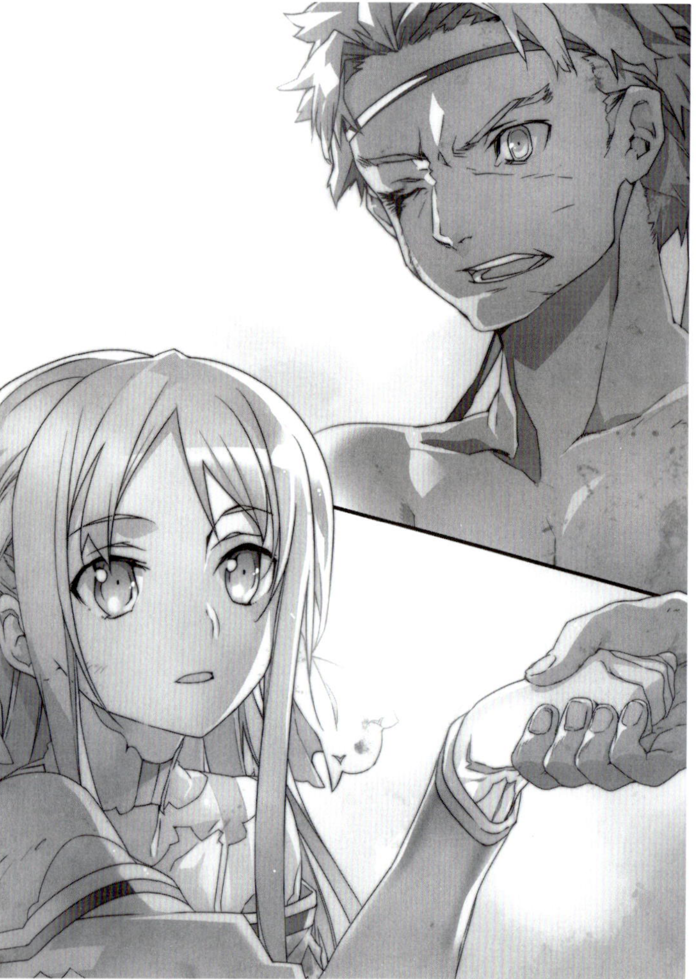

Dengeki Bunko
Sword Art Online 17: Alicization Awakening
Illustration: April 2016

Dengeki Bunko
Sword Art Online 17:
Alicization Awakening
Cover: April 2016

I wanted people to be excited for this. The message was, "After Asuna, you get these two as well!" And the subtitle of *Awakening*. Yes, Kirito is awake! But…not on the cover yet! The painful fulfillment of my quota that began in Volume 15 ends here.

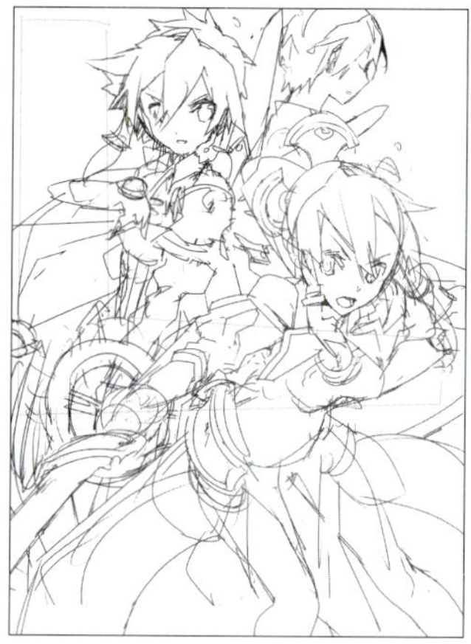

Rough Cover Sketch

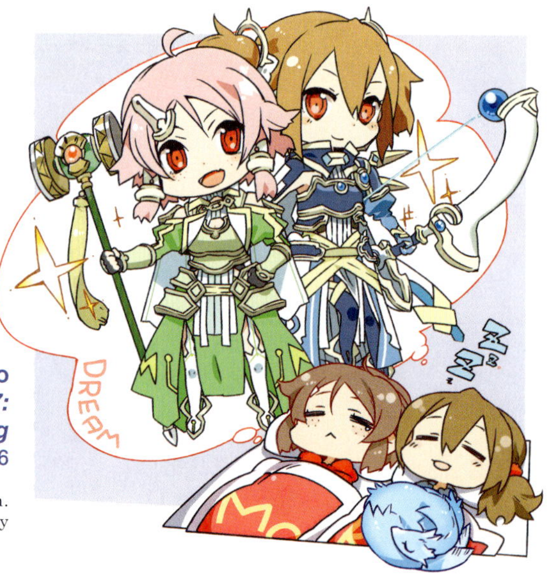

Dengeki Bunko
Sword Art Online 17:
Alicization Awakening
Rear Cover: April 2016

A world that could have been. Well, probably not. As usual, they get no scenes.

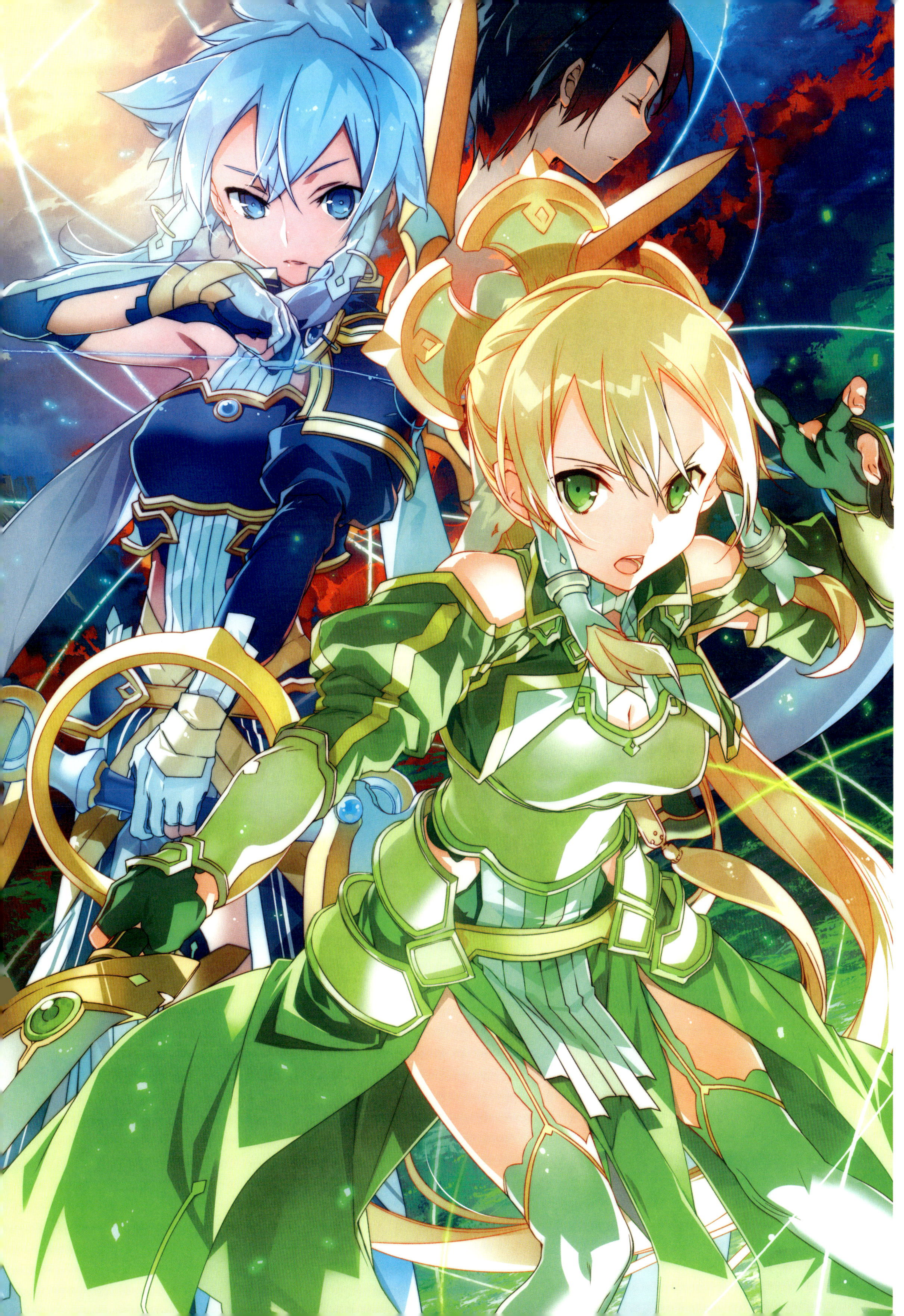

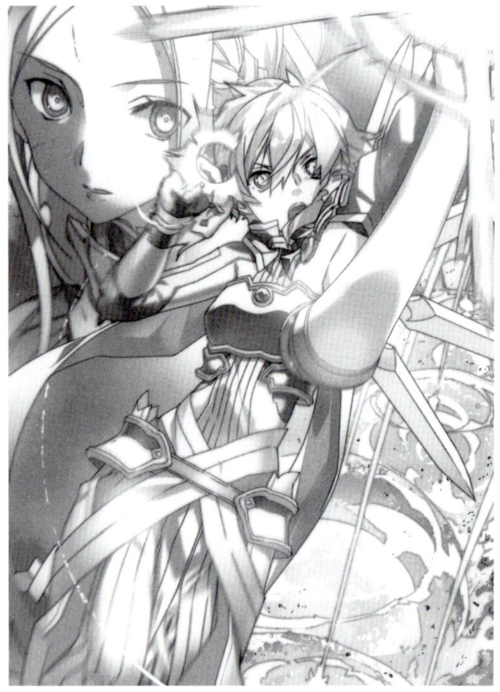

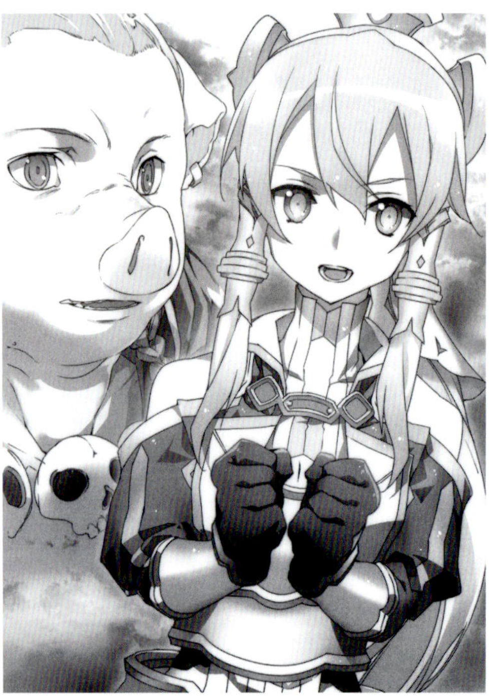

Dengeki Bunko
Sword Art Online 17:
Alicization Awakening
Illustration: April 2016

Scenes of Terraria Leafa and Solus Sinon getting into the action. I love the combination of Lilpilin and Leafa.

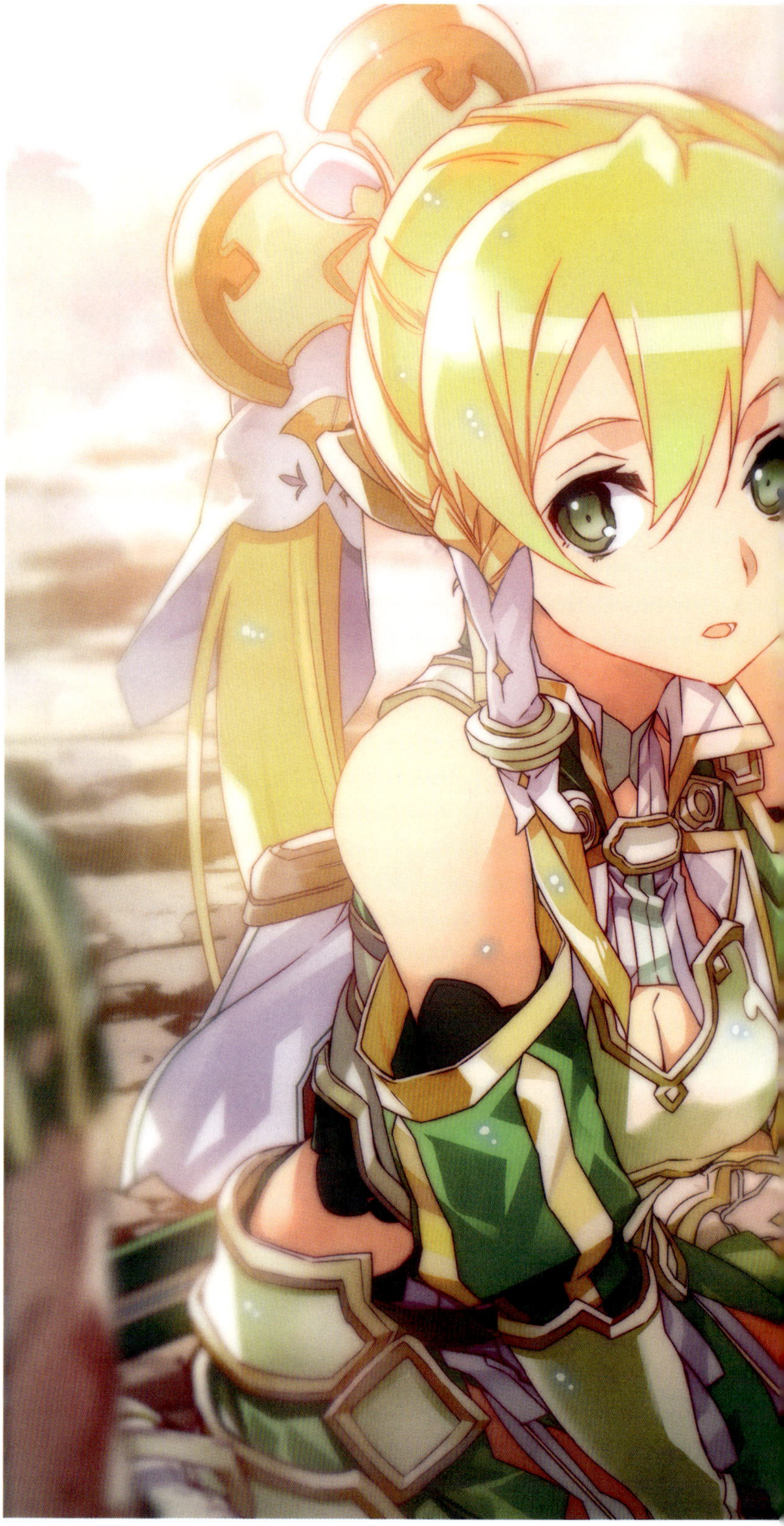

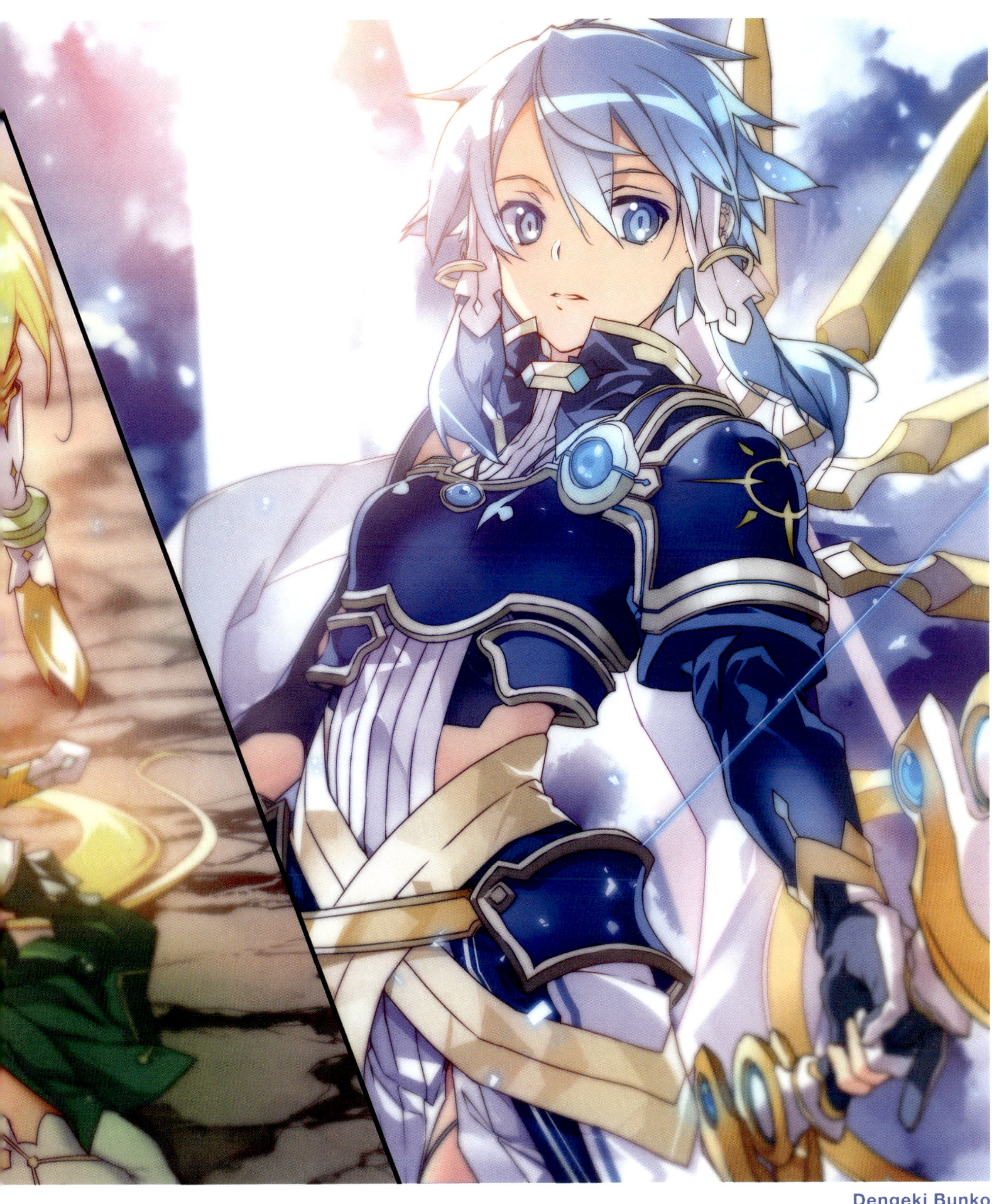

The introductory image of the pair who graced the cover.
Sinon has a very straightforward and active scene, which
makes it easier to come up with something to draw.

Vecta versus Bercouli. The anime was incredible for this scene. I felt like it wasn't even fair that you could pause any frame of the anime, and it would still look better than my illustration.

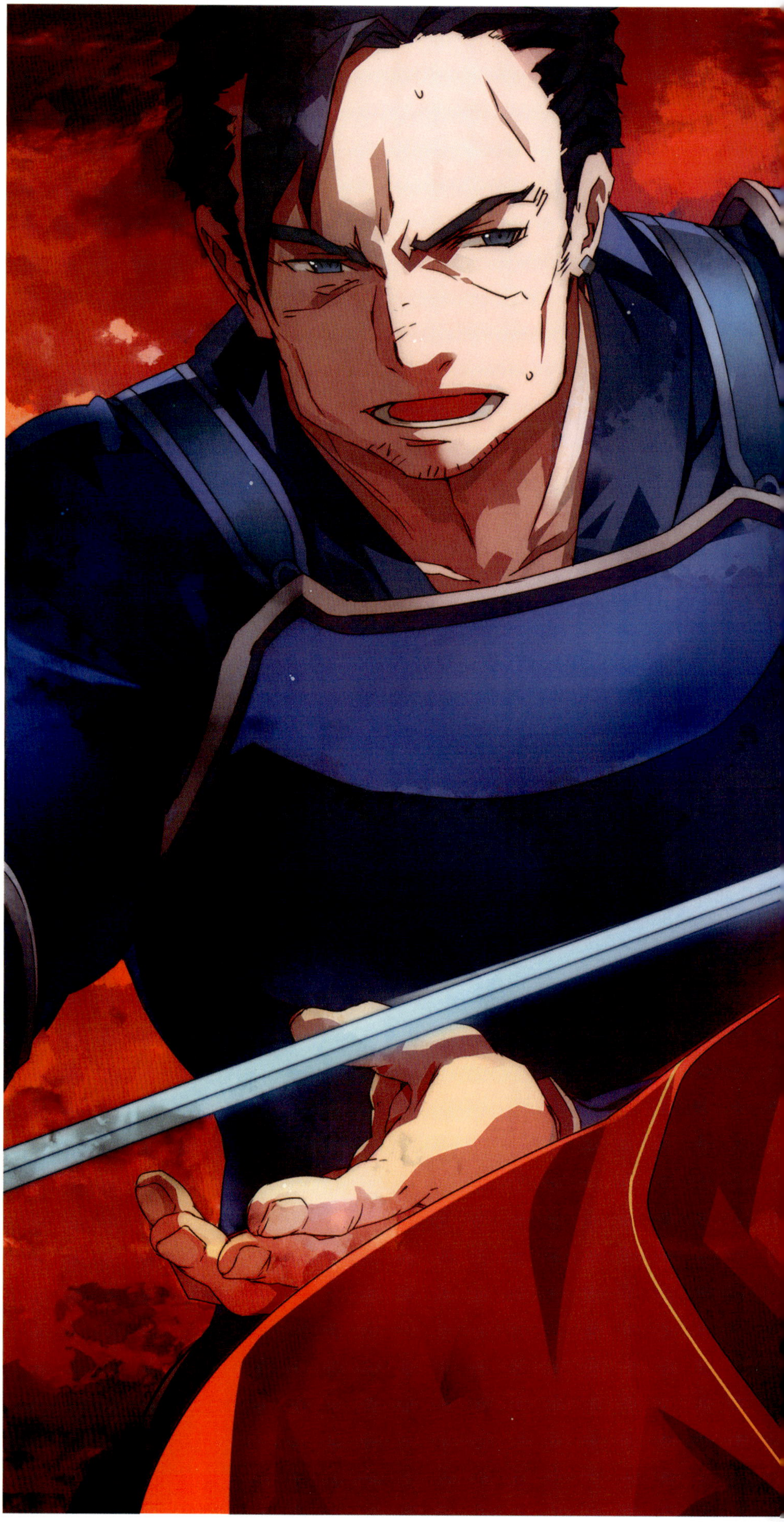

Dengeki Bunko
Sword Art Online 17:
Alicization Awakening
Illustration: April 2016

I like the expressions in both of these story illustrations.

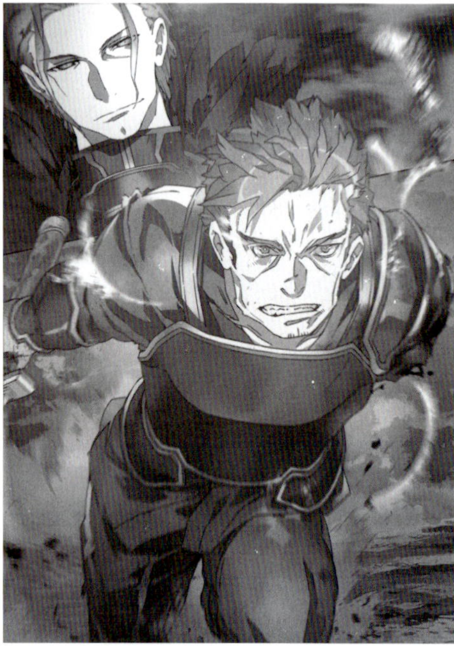

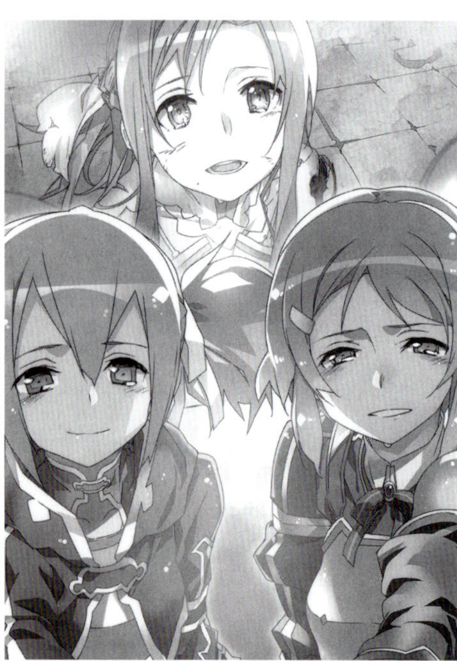

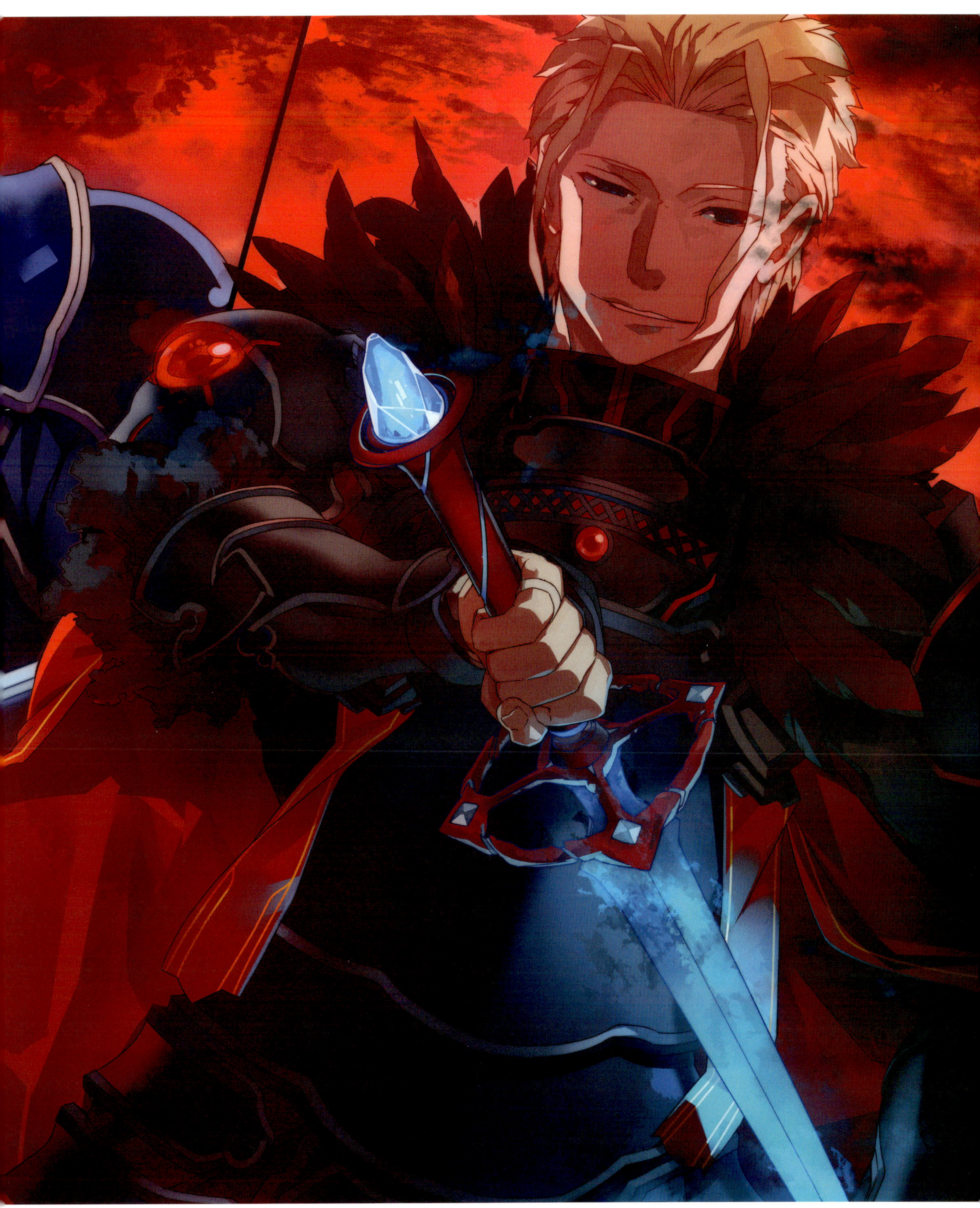

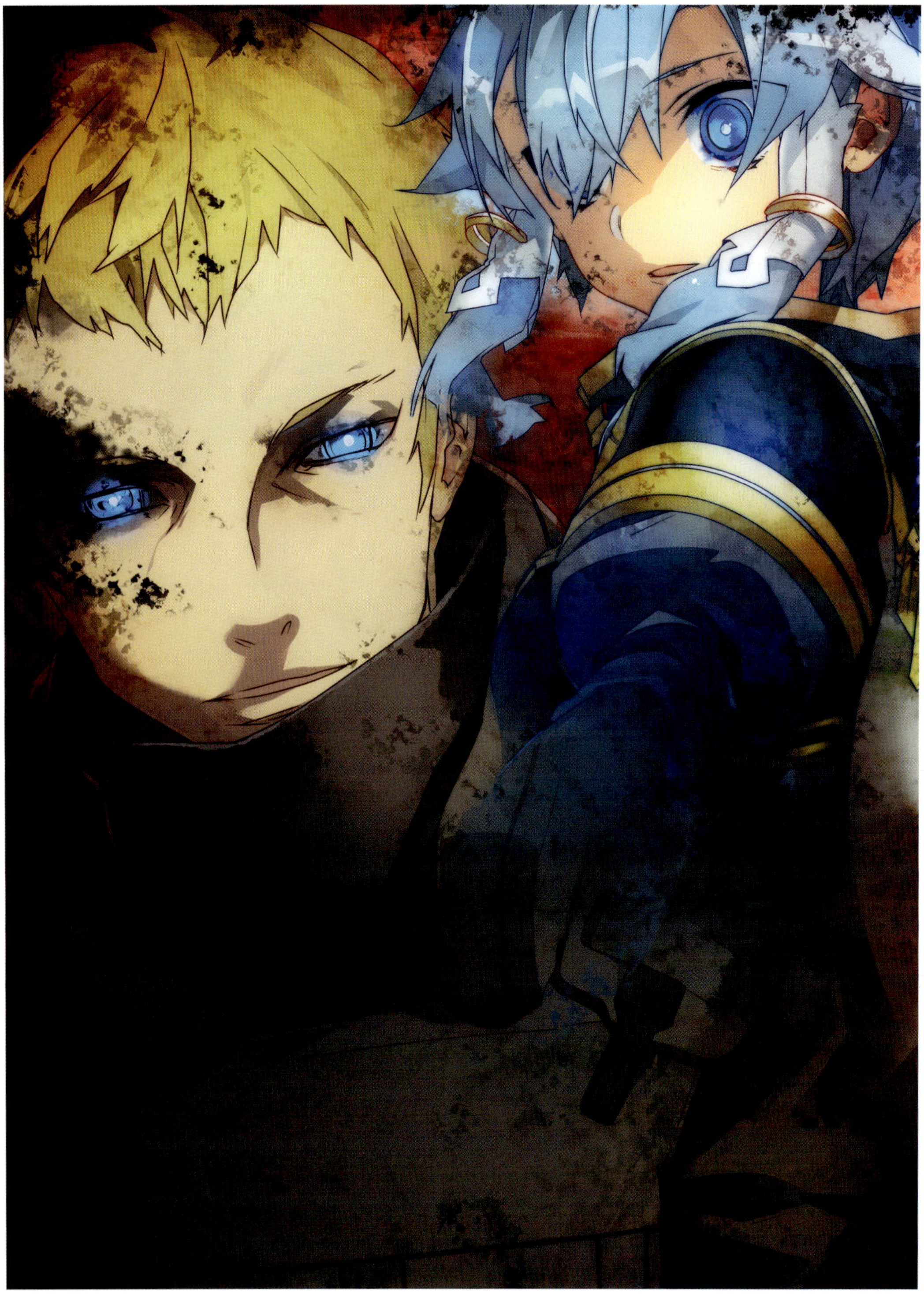

Solus Sinon versus Subtilizer. There's a Sinon-centric illustration after this, so if anything, it's meant to show off Subtilizer more.

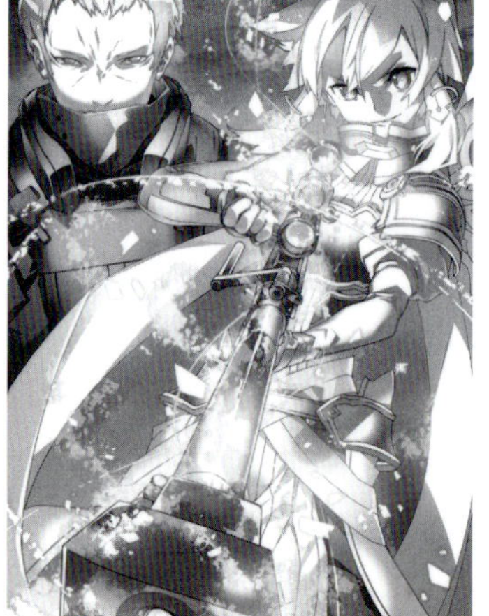

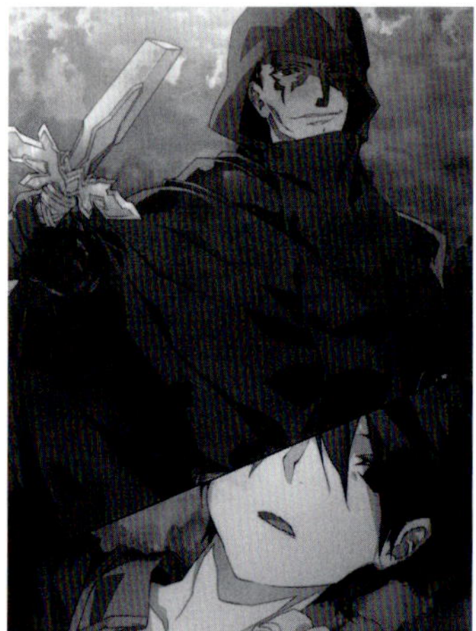

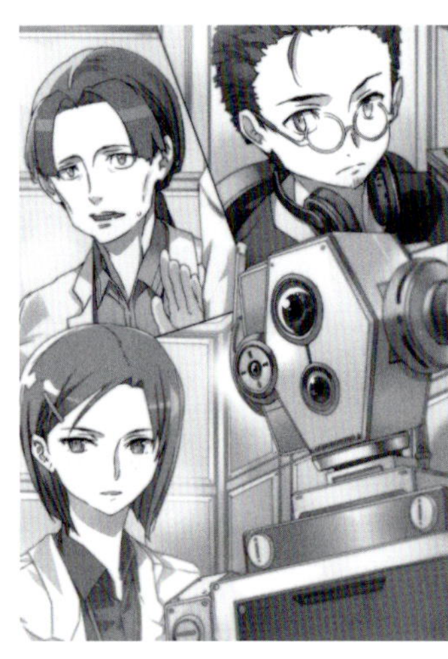

I drew PoH a bunch, but I keep his face hidden for the most part, so even when you do see it, it doesn't often sink in. If you walked right past him, you'd never even notice him. I hope I never walk past him.

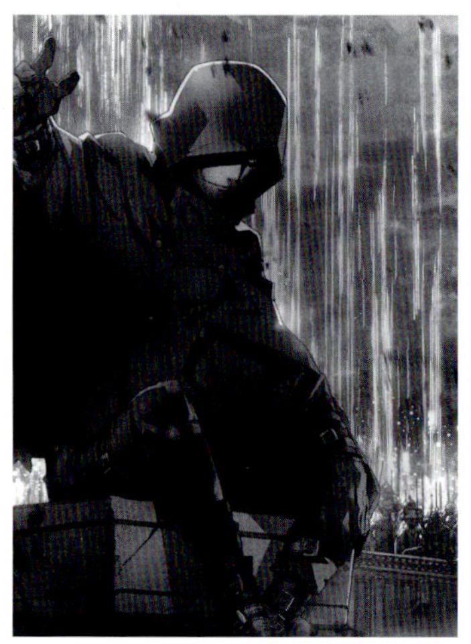

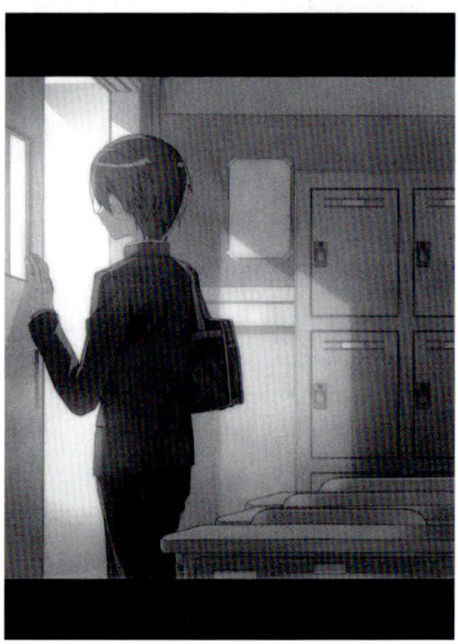

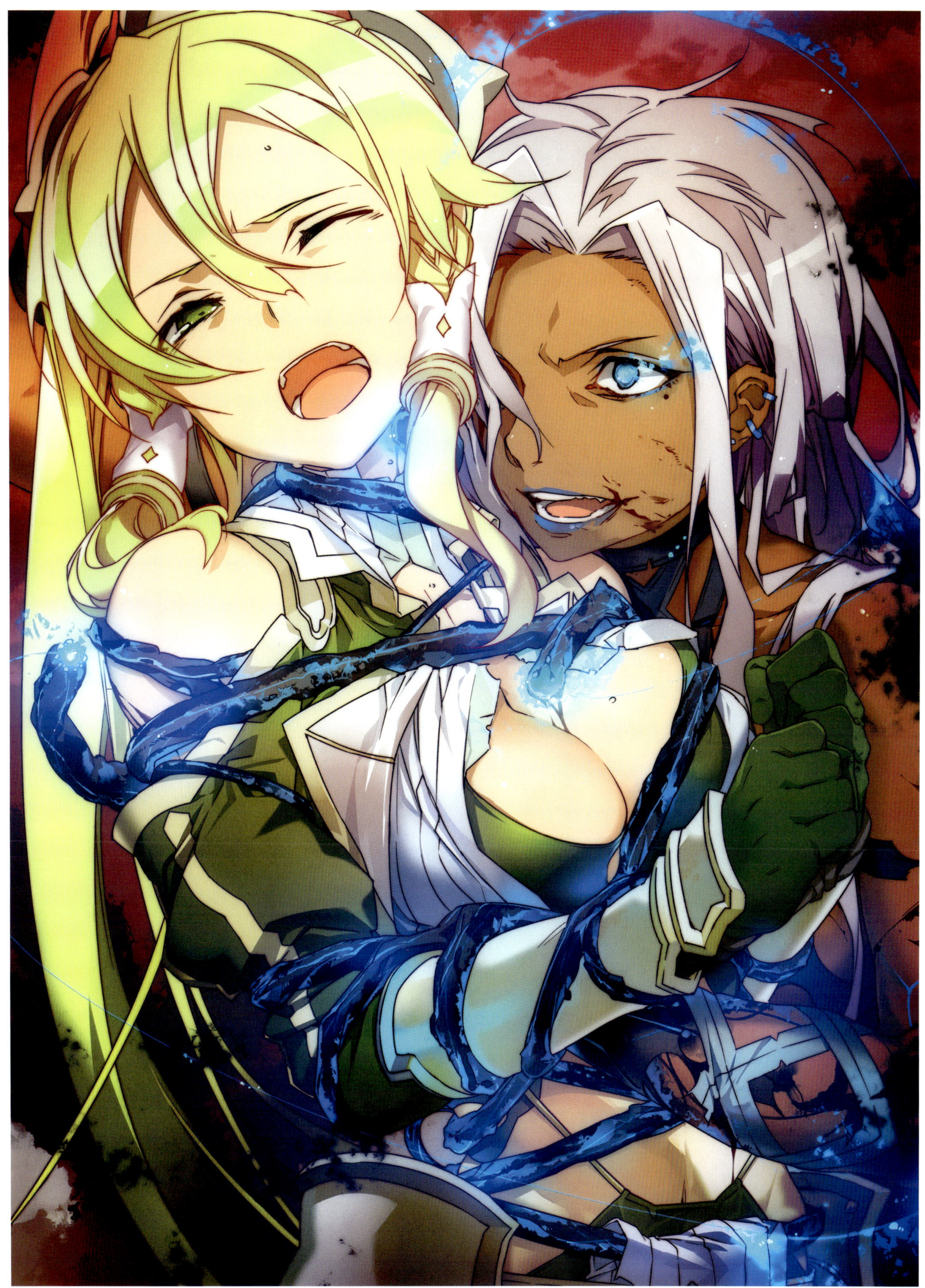

Dengeki Bunko
Sword Art Online 17: Alicization Awakening
Frontispiece: April 2016

No, you don't understand. Kawahara-sensei wrote this scene, and the editor asked for it to be drawn. It wasn't me. In fact, I'll include an excerpt of the request: "Make Leafa's heaving buzzoms [sic] the focus of the piece." And if there's one thing abec does, it's follow directions. I drew the focus of the piece as requested. Simple as that. Boy howdy, though, Leafa's body looks great all tied up like that! (^q^)

SWORD ART ONLINE
Alicization Lasting

When I first got contracted to illustrate this series, this volume was the latest material that had been written. The final arc of the *Alicization* series. A very long battle finally comes to an end.

Dengeki Bunko
Sword Art Online 18:
Alicization Lasting
Cover: August 2016

Kirito is back!!! And he's got a sharper pose than usual. Personally, I think that because Kirito's missing fluctlight fragments were filled in from the memories of his friends, he probably came back more idealized than he was originally. So some of that idea is contained in this illustration.

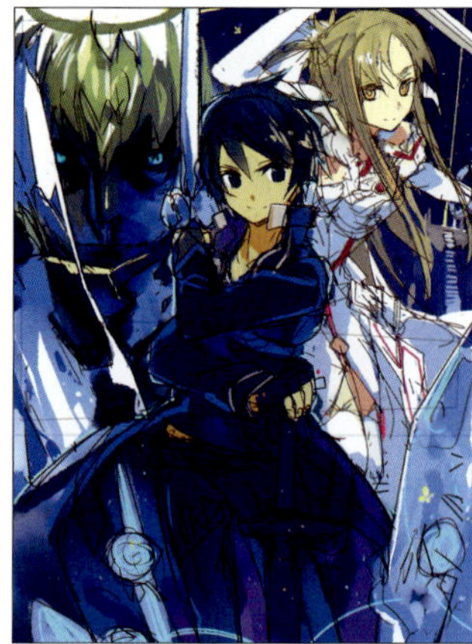

Rough Cover Sketch

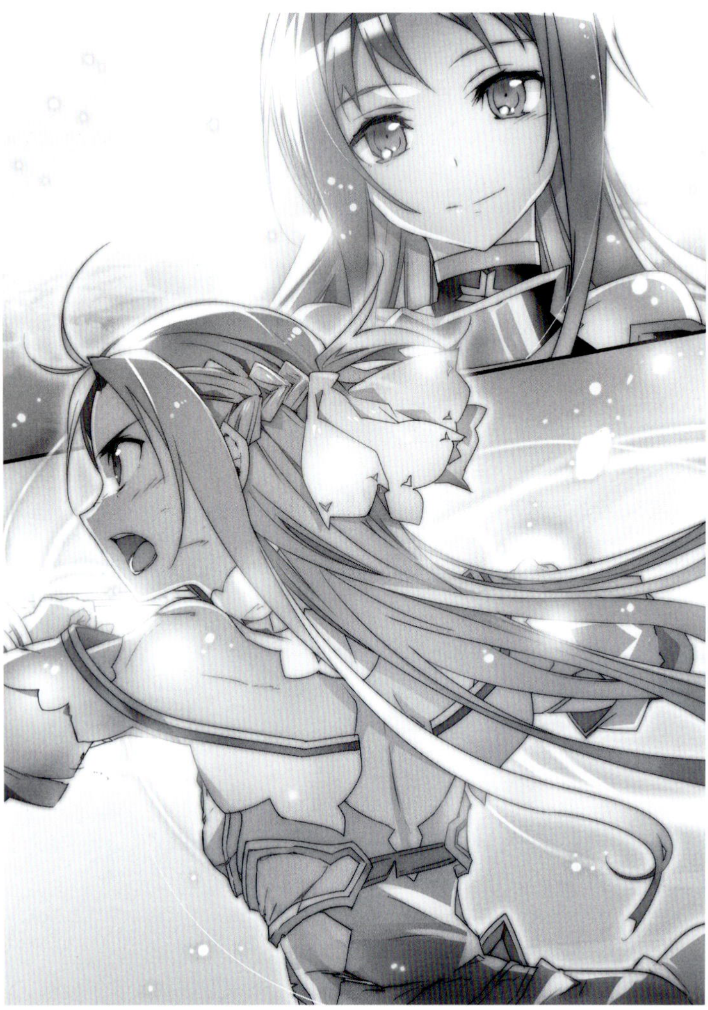

Dengeki Bunko
Sword Art Online 18:
Alicization Lasting
Illustration: August 2016

The showdown scenes. The sword skill scenes based on big finishers are easy to draw, but the regular swordfighting battle scenes are actually pretty tough.

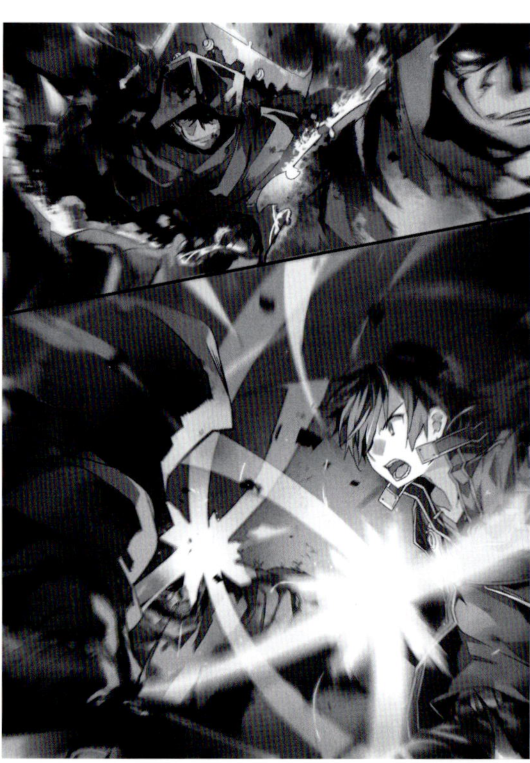

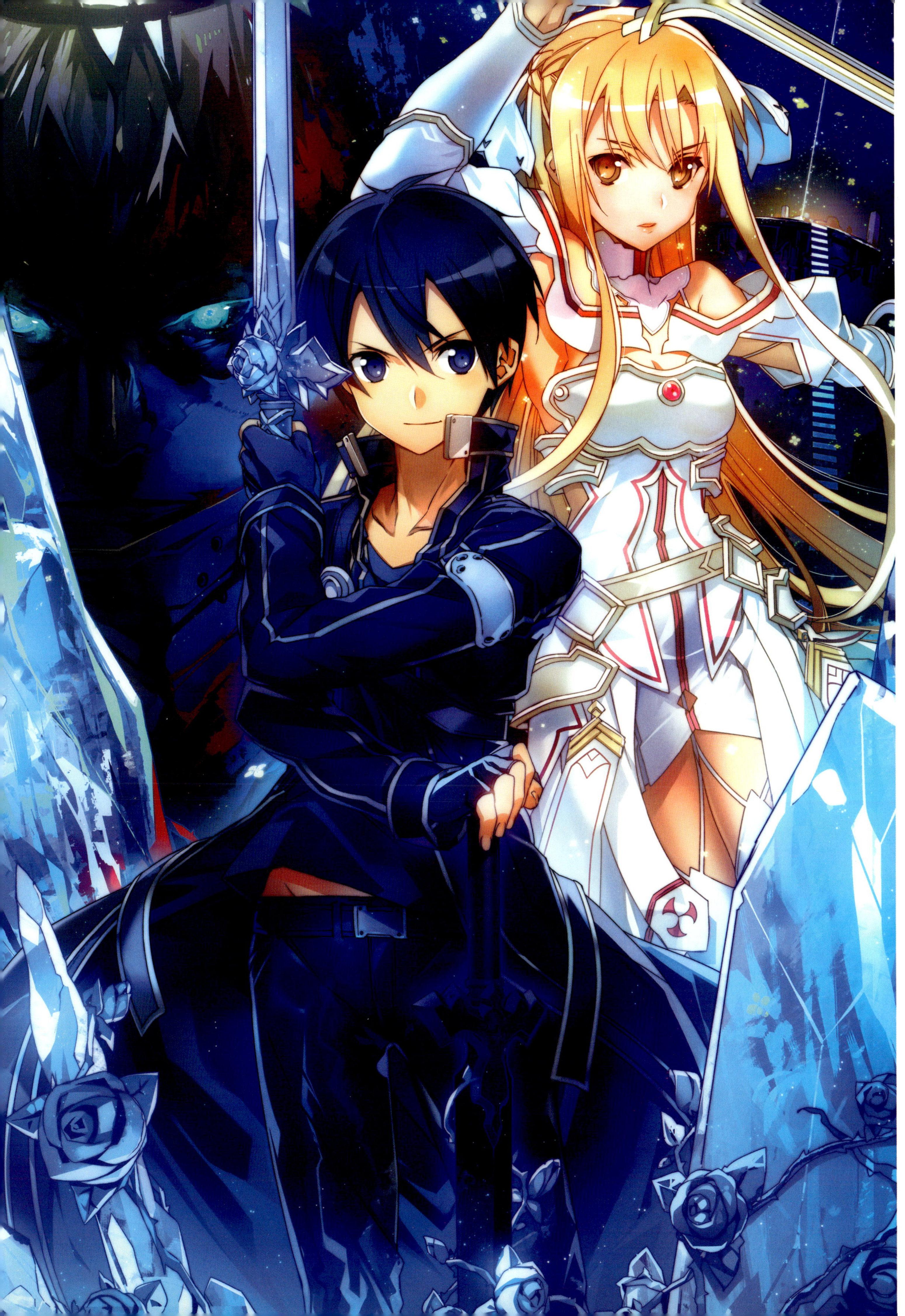

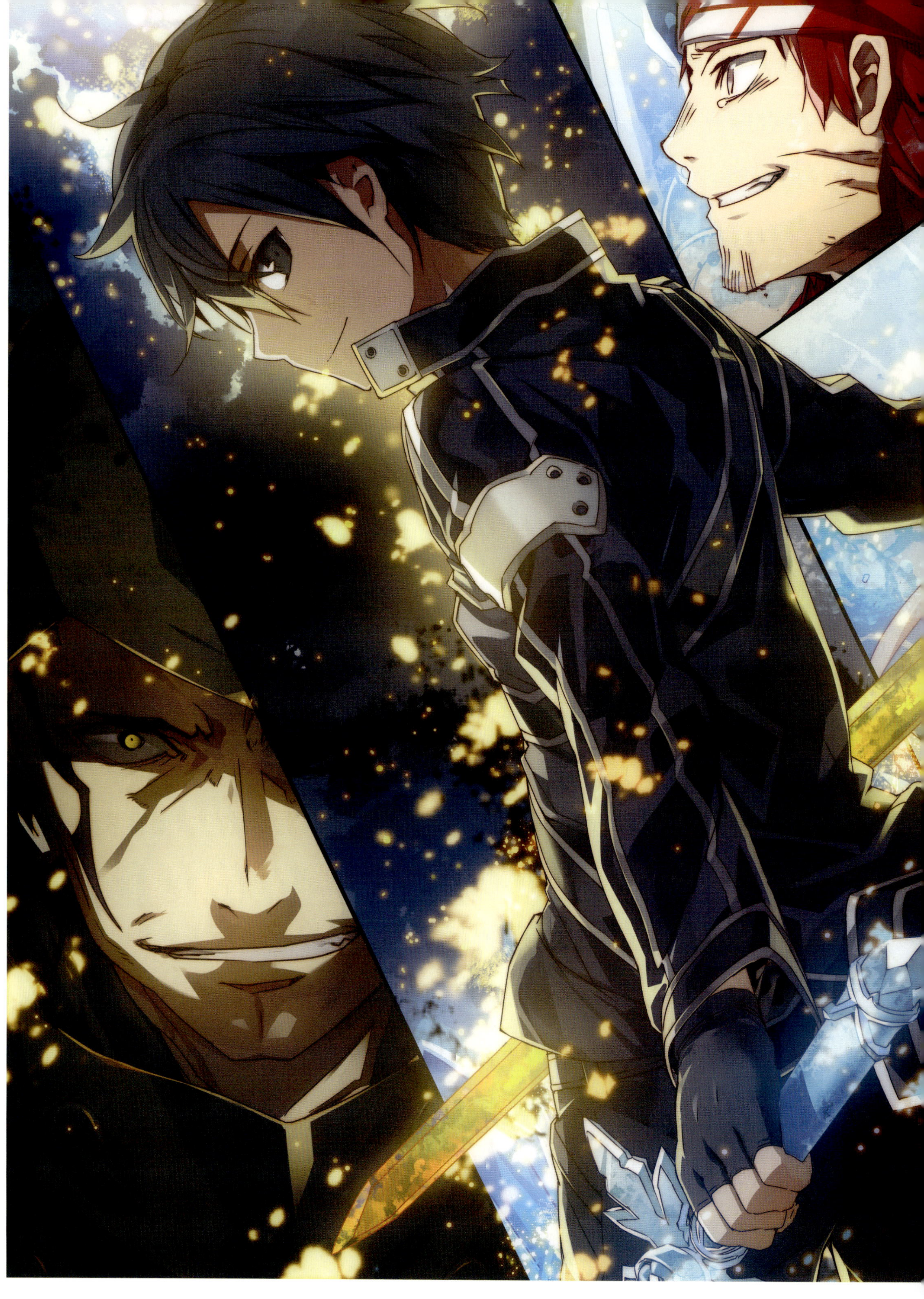

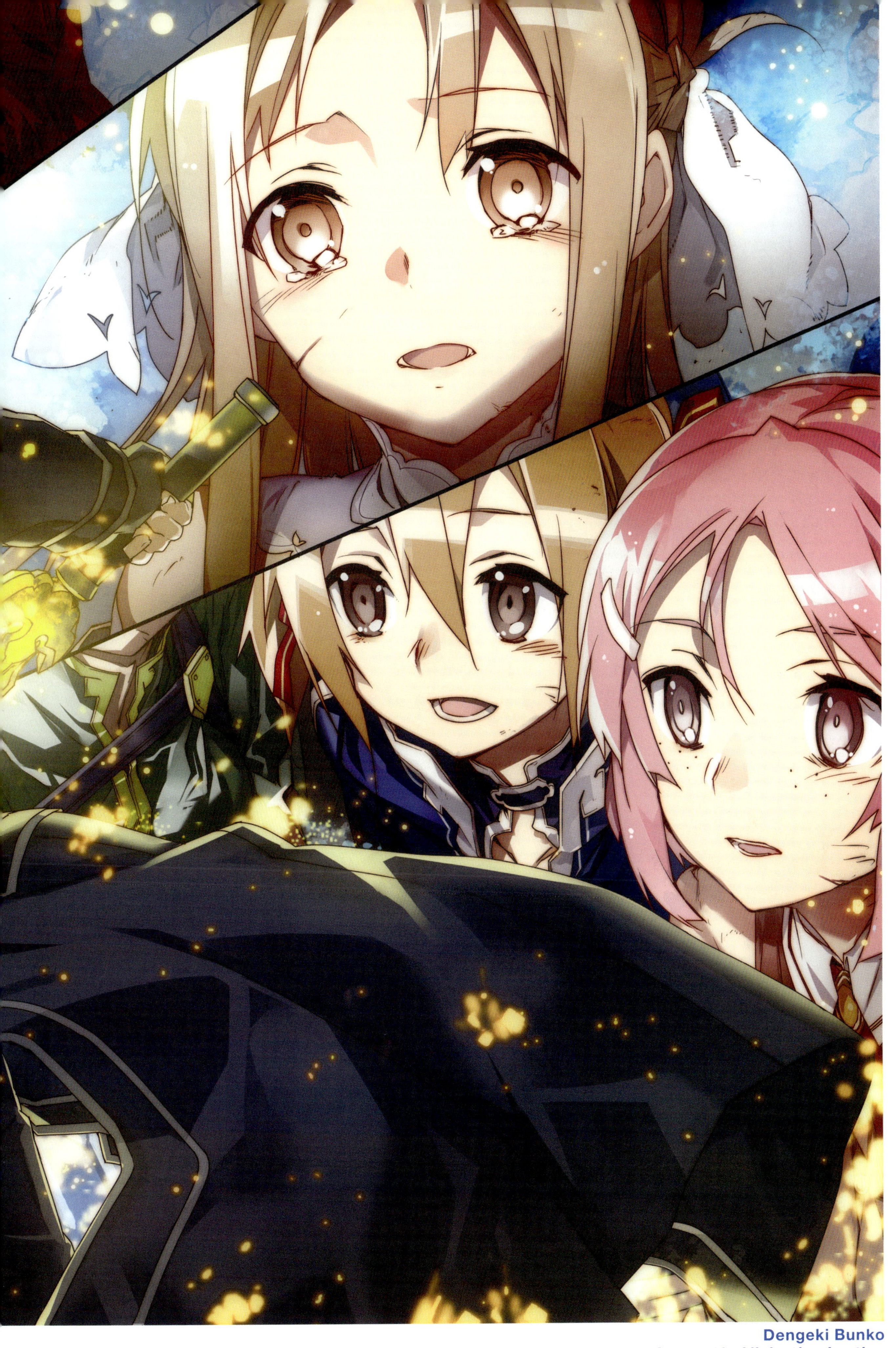

Dengeki Bunko
Sword Art Online 18: Alicization Lasting
Frontispiece: August 2016

Kirito's triumphant comeback scene. The moment everyone's been waiting for. Like I wrote on the previous page, this moment is especially heroic for Kirito, so I imparted a little extra smugness in his expression.

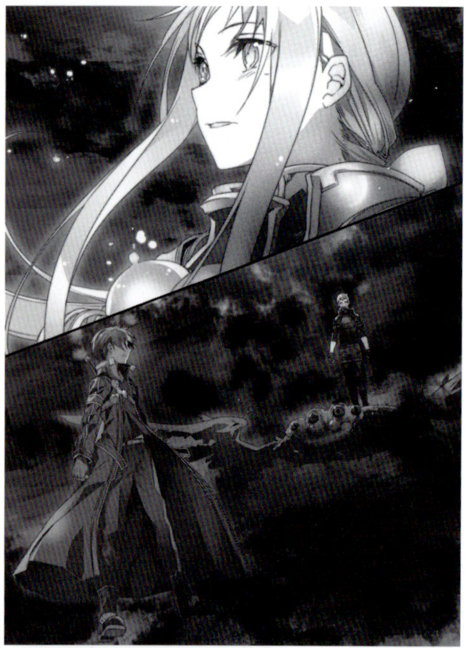

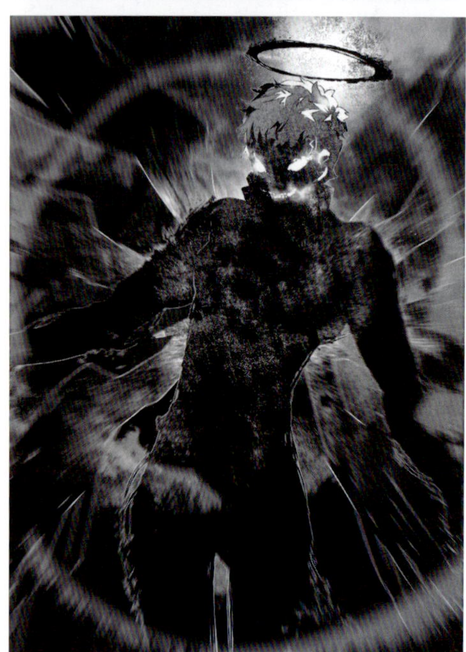

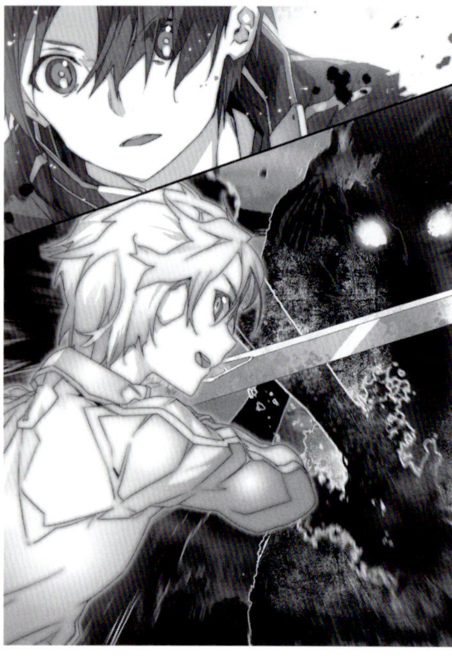

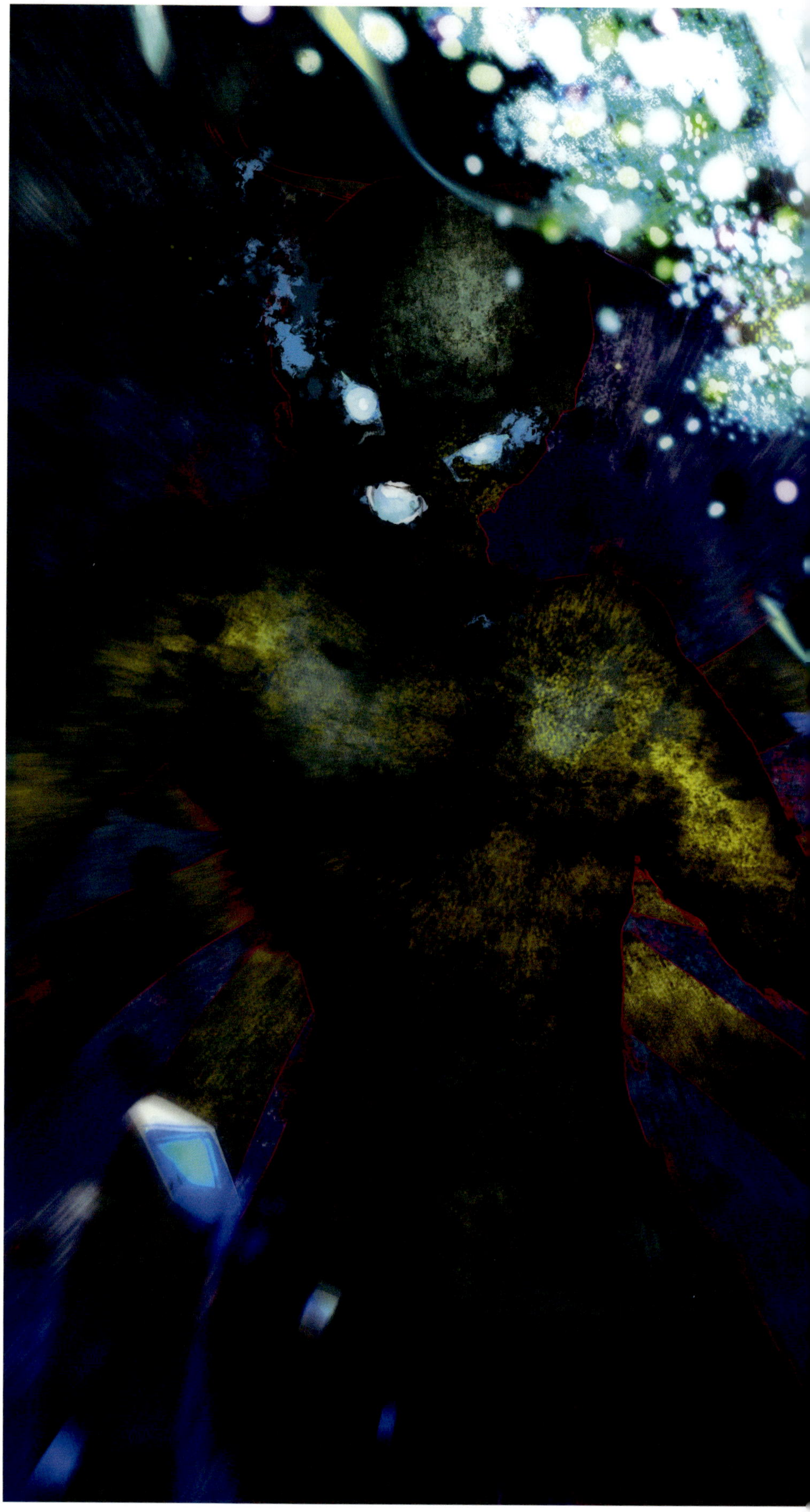

Dengeki Bunko
Sword Art Online 18: Alicization Lasting
Illustration: August 2016

It occurs to me now that the illustration of Gabriel was already depicted in the frontispiece, so I should have drawn him smaller, from further out. Then again, when you're reading the story, maybe this size is proper for setting the scene. These considerations are tricky.

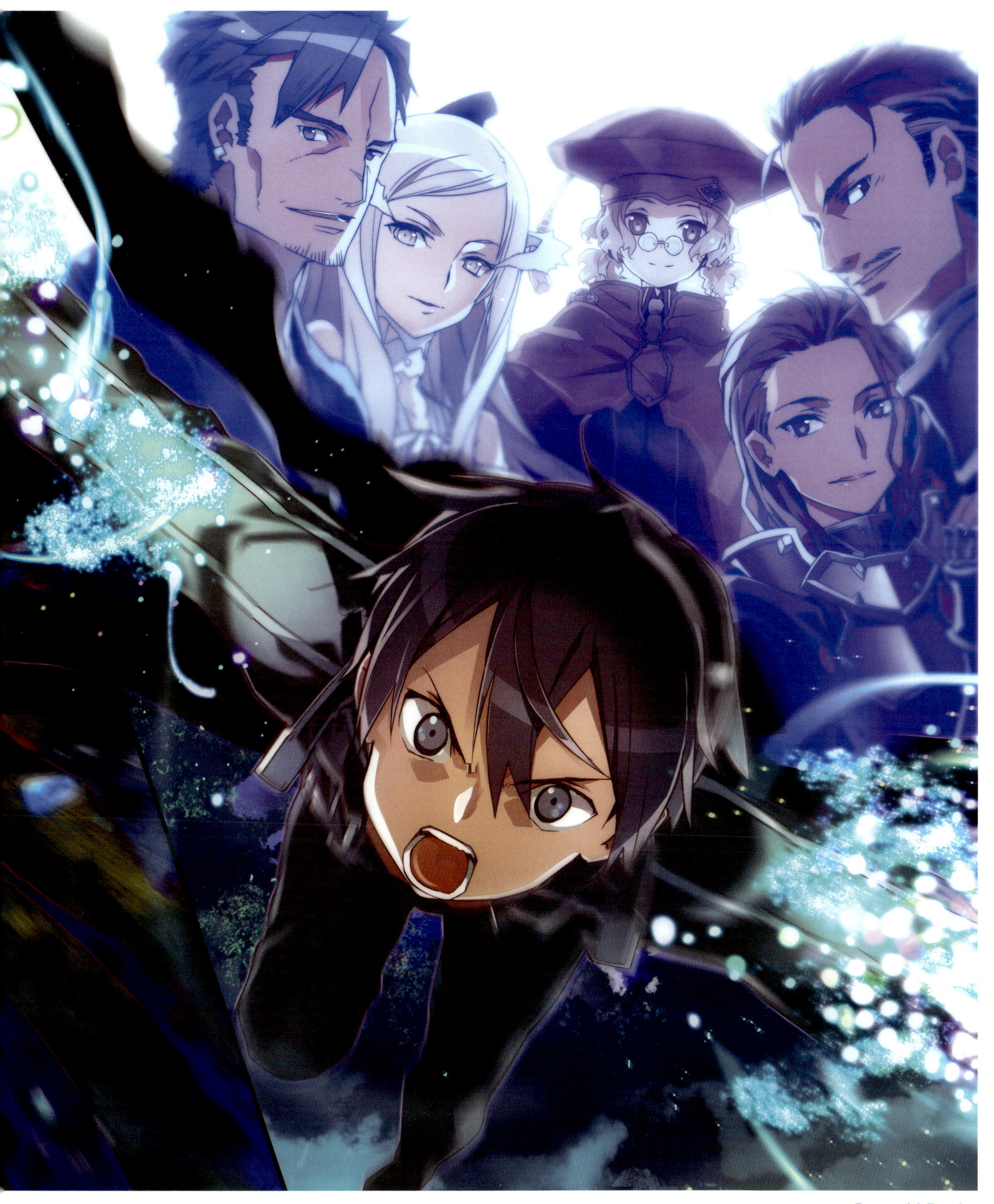

Dengeki Bunko
Sword Art Online 18: Alicization Lasting
Frontispiece: August 2016

In retrospect, this color version of Gabriel is so heavily processed that it's harder to tell what you're looking at.

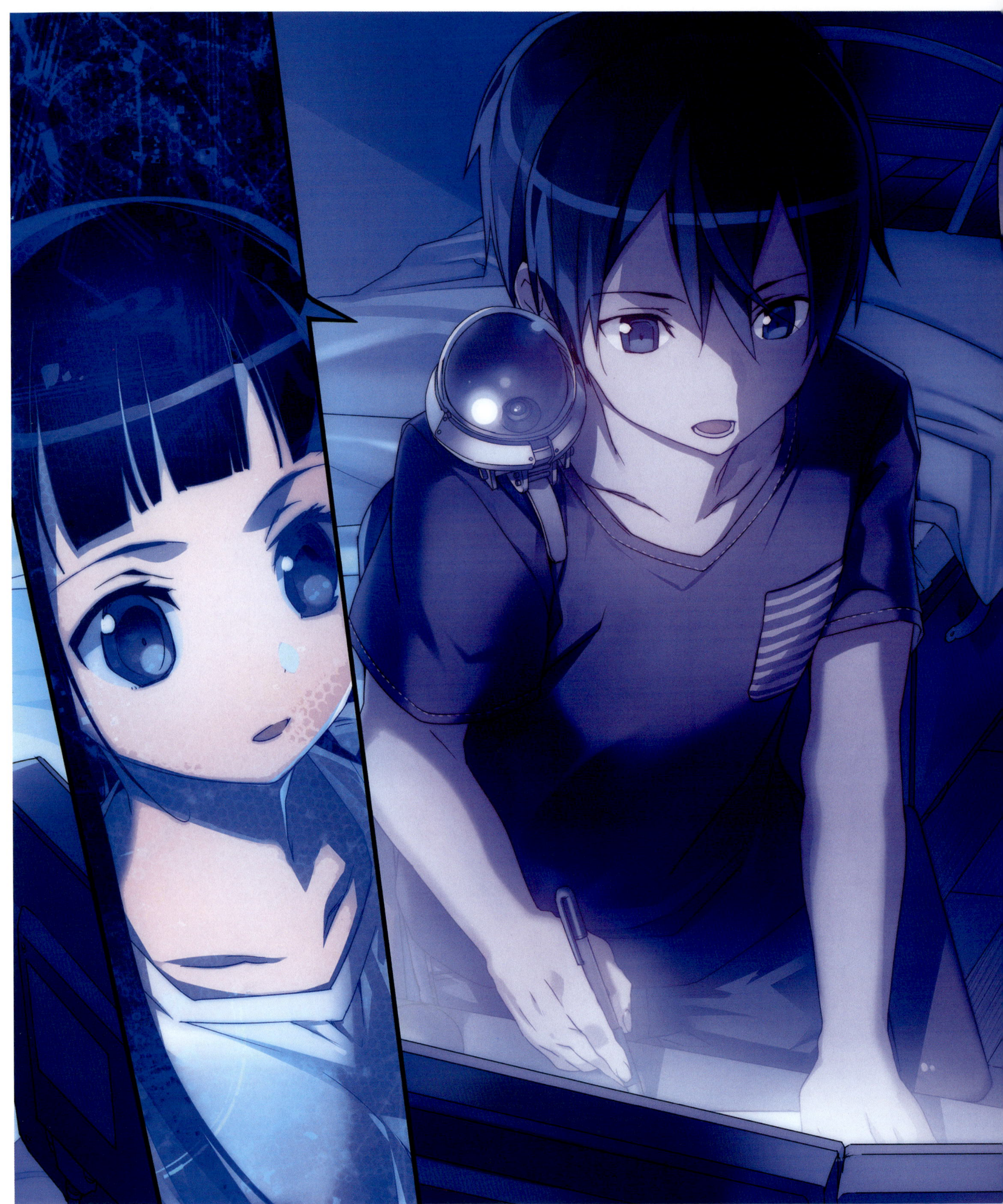

Dengeki Bunko
Sword Art Online 18: Alicization Lasting
Frontispiece: August 2016

The problem-solving scene. The part in Alice's hair is a bit off from usual,
but I wanted to show that this was a more casual side of her coming out.

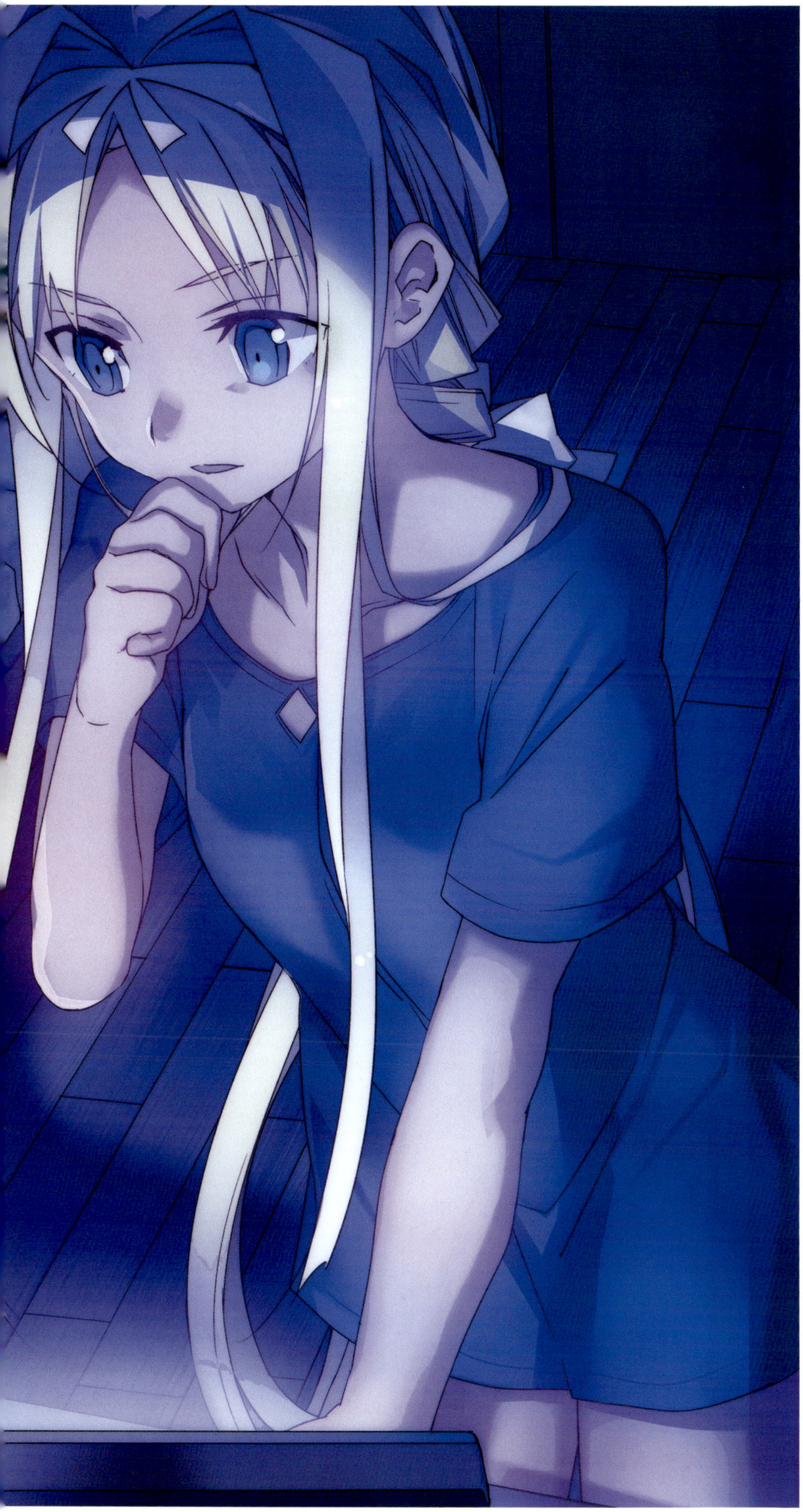

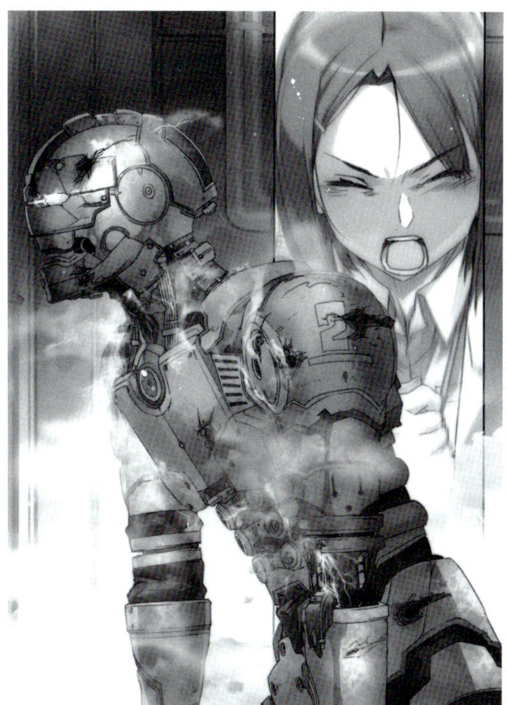

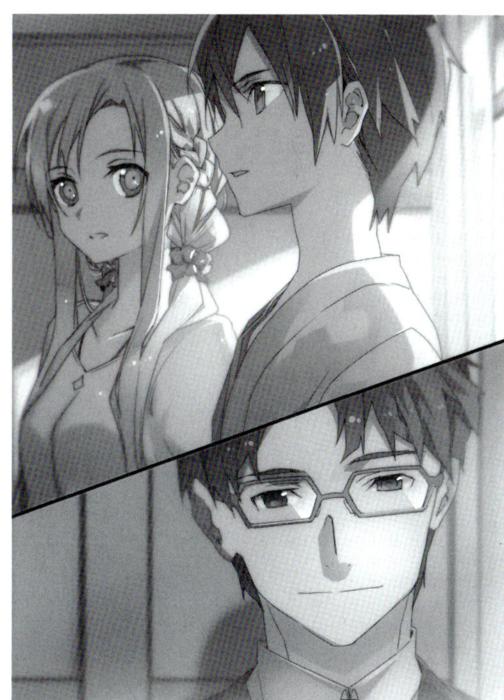

Dengeki Bunko
Sword Art Online 18: Alicization Lasting
Illustration: August 2016

Looking back at the request, they asked that Niemon's scene be superimposed with Kayaba, but I didn't draw that. I don't recall what I was thinking at the time, but I do think that it's more powerful if your mind fills in that blank on its own.

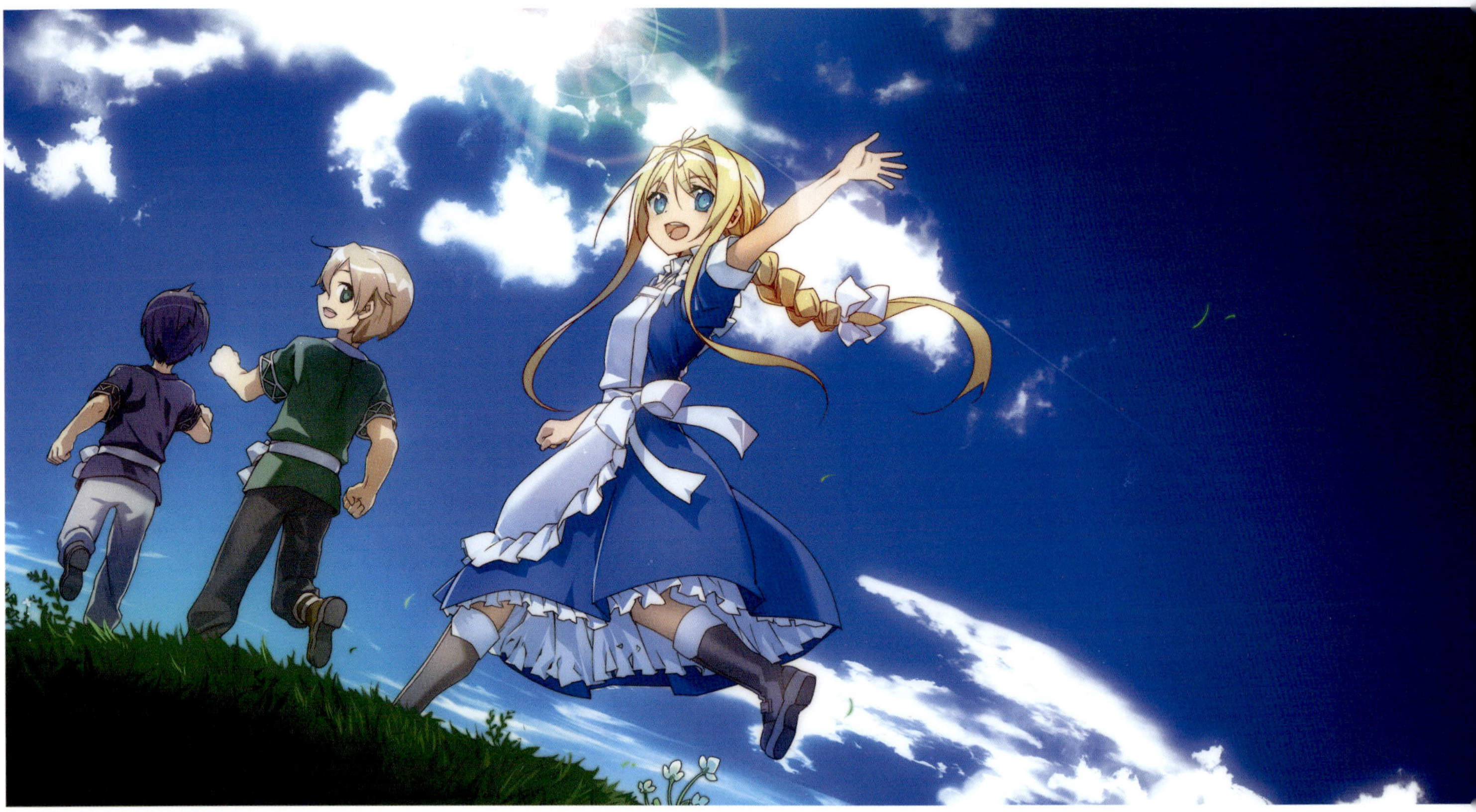

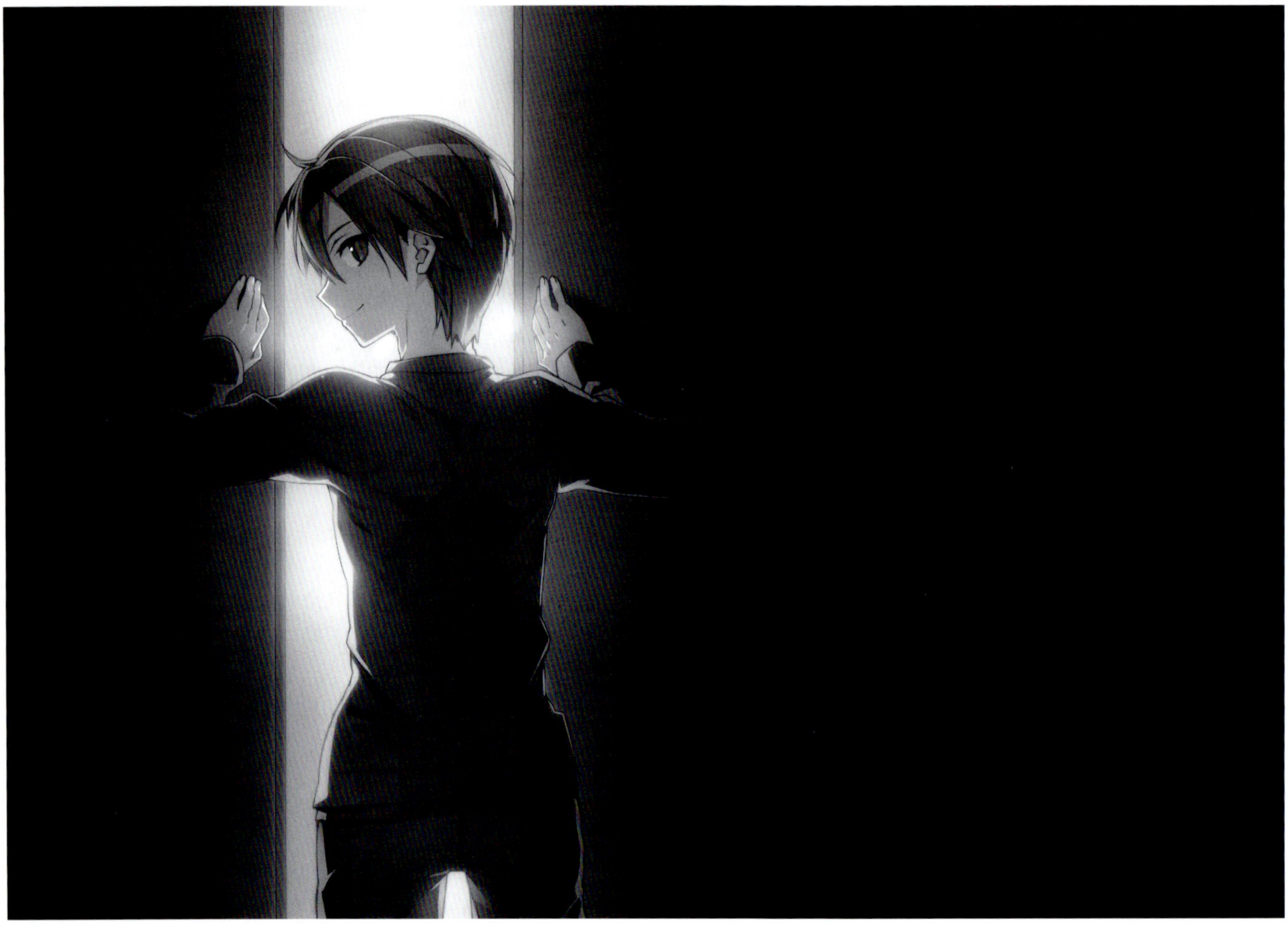

Dengeki Bunko
Sword Art Online 18: Alicization Lasting
Illustration: August 2016

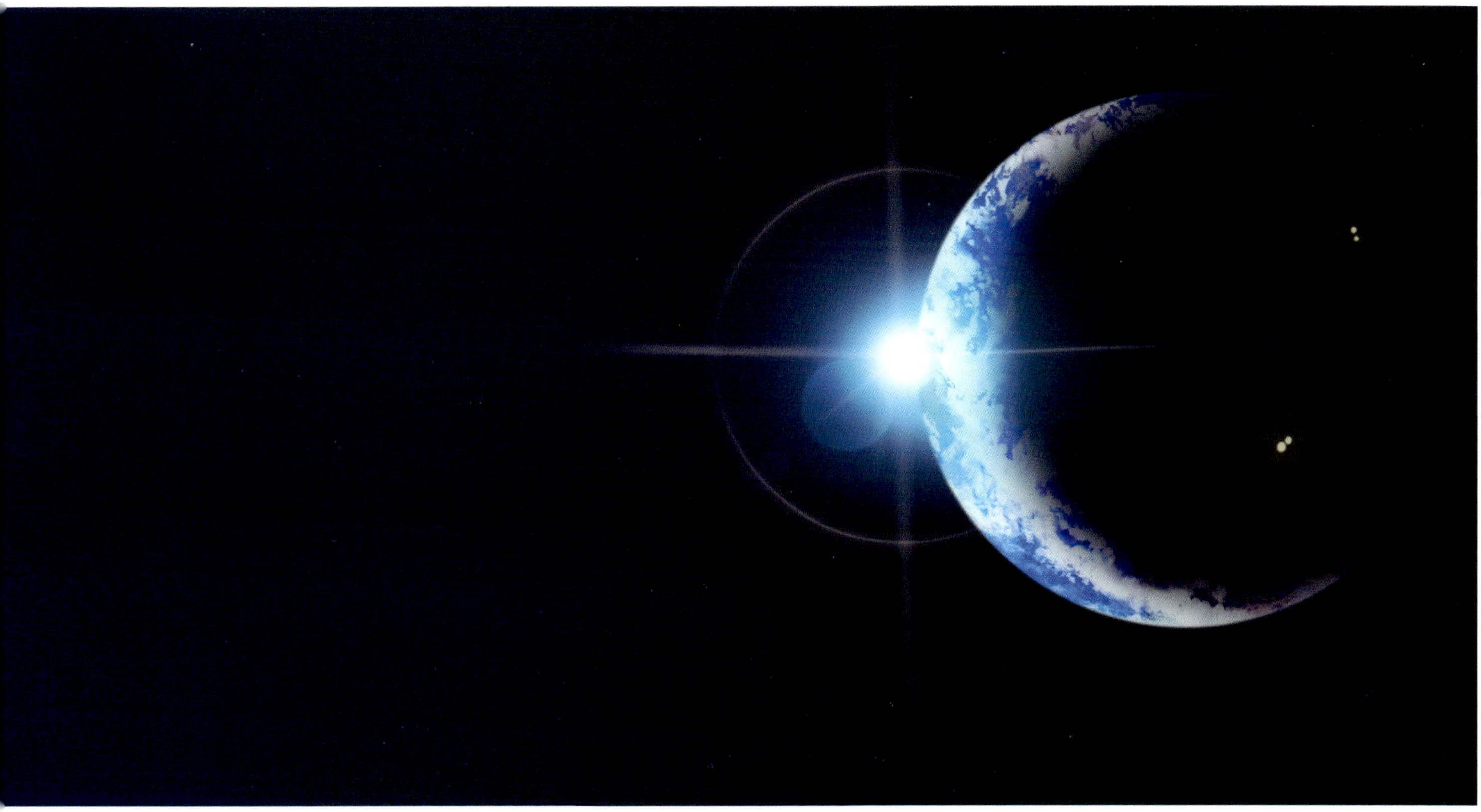

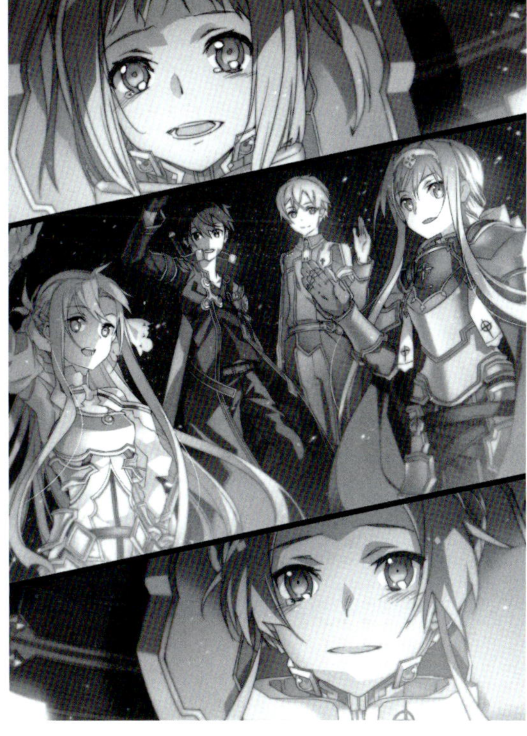

Dengeki Bunko
Sword Art Online 18: Alicization Lasting
Frontispiece: August 2016

This is based on an illustration from Kawahara-sensei's webpage when he was originally writing this story. That piece was very elongated and vertical. On the webpage, it starts with the planet, and then you scroll down to see the three kids. I thought the concept was brilliant, so I adapted it into a horizontal format for this version.

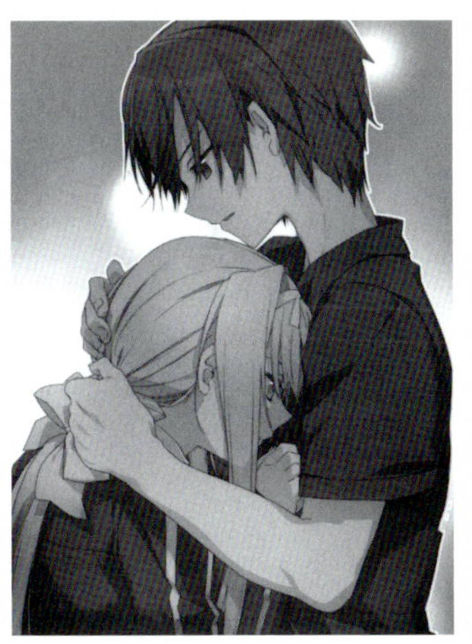
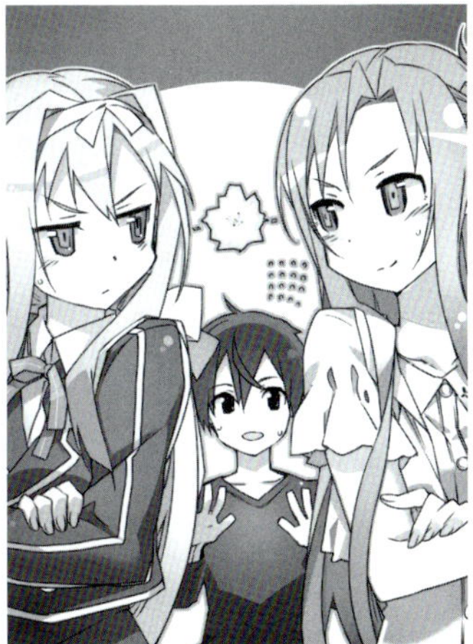

Dengeki Bunko
Sword Art Online 18: Alicization Lasting
Illustration: August 2016

At this point, we hadn't confirmed the story would be continuing, so the random clothes I drew for Stica and Laura ended up really hurting me down the line... If you don't spend the time to consider your character designs when doing light novel illustrations, you can really make headaches for yourself later.

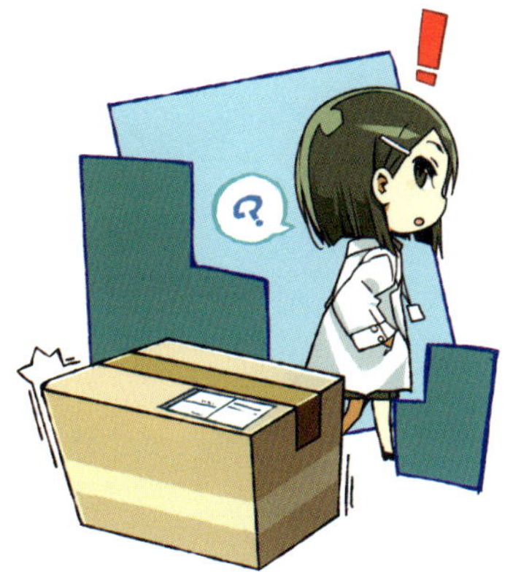

Dengeki Bunko
Sword Art Online 18: Alicization Lasting
Rear Cover: August 2016

Oh yeah, I didn't draw the box scene in the story illustrations.

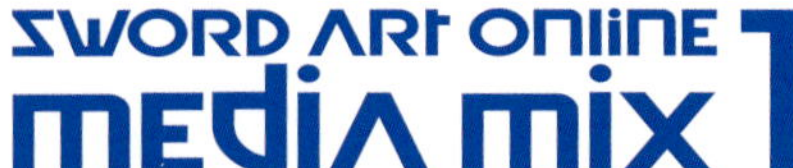

SWORD ART ONLINE media mix 1

This section is a collection of pieces I drew at the editor's request. Between Dengeki Bunko promotions and magazine covers, there's actually a substantial amount in here.

Dengeki Bunko Magazine, Jan. 2018 issue
Cover: December 2017

A pairing with Llenn from *SAO Alternative: Gun Gale Online*. Kuroboshi-san is so good, I could just die.

Llenn illustration:
Kouhaku Kuroboshi

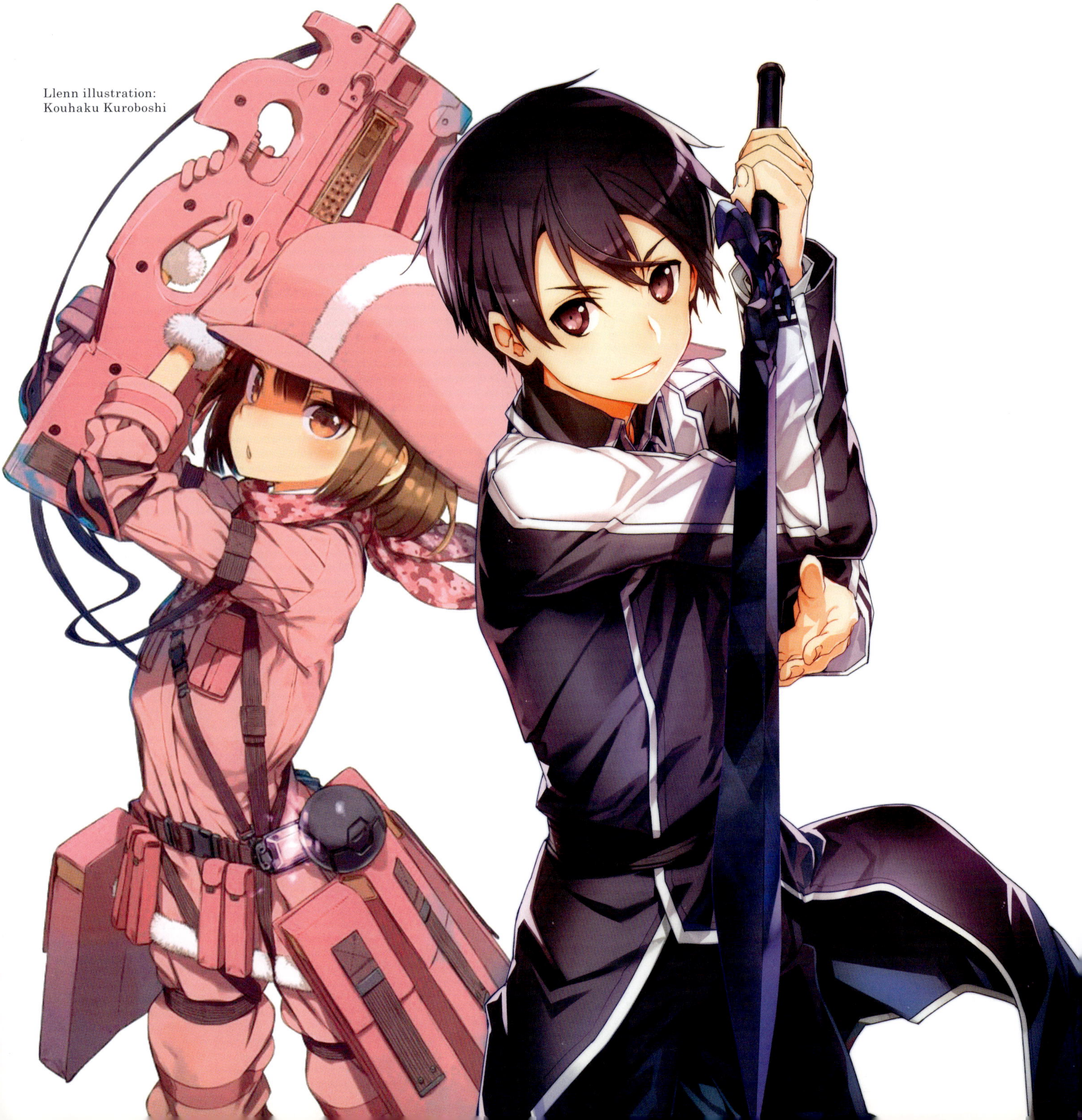

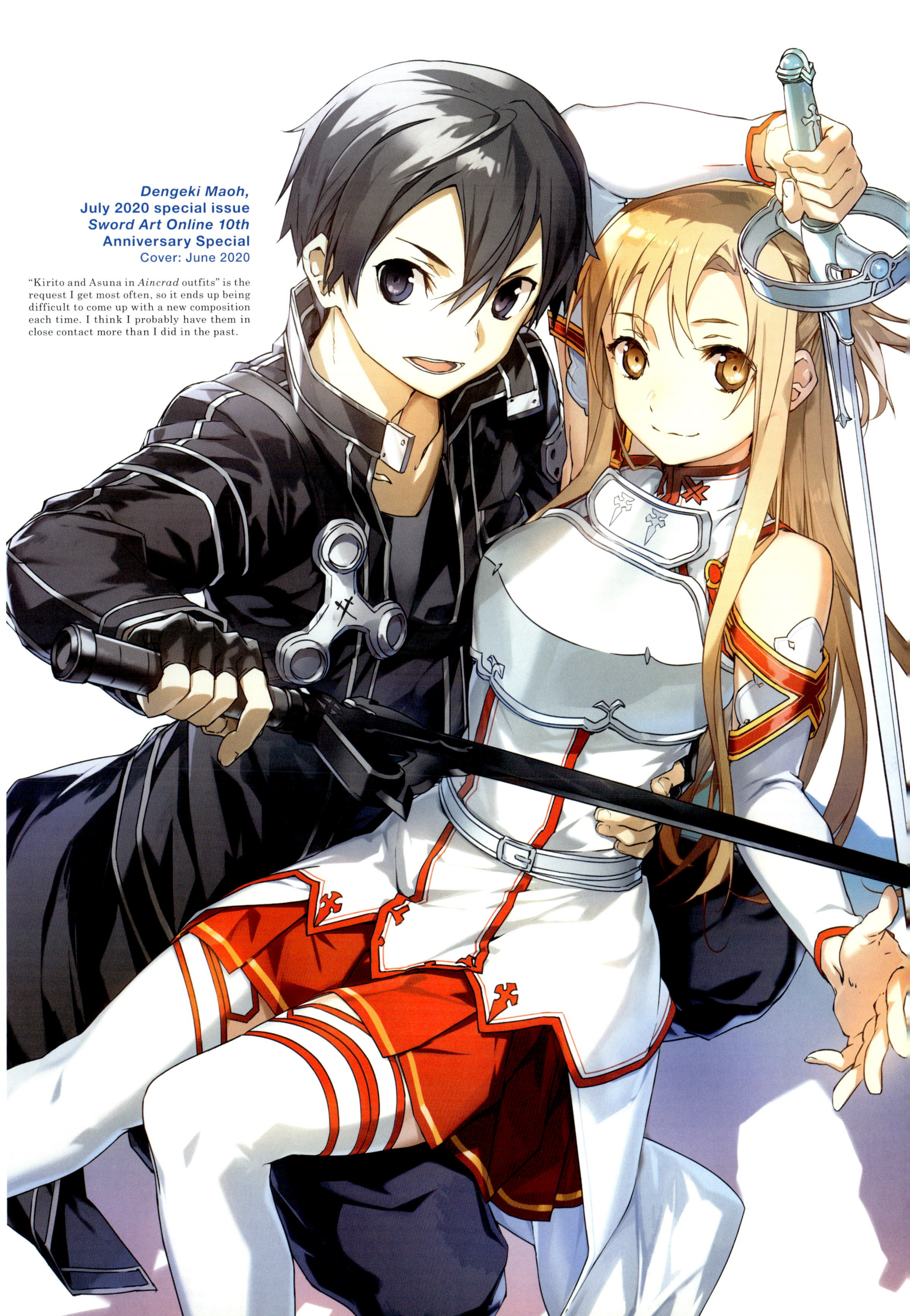

Dengeki Maoh,
July 2020 special issue
Sword Art Online 10th
Anniversary Special
Cover: June 2020

"Kirito and Asuna in Aincrad outfits" is the request I get most often, so it ends up being difficult to come up with a new composition each time. I think I probably have them in close contact more than I did in the past.

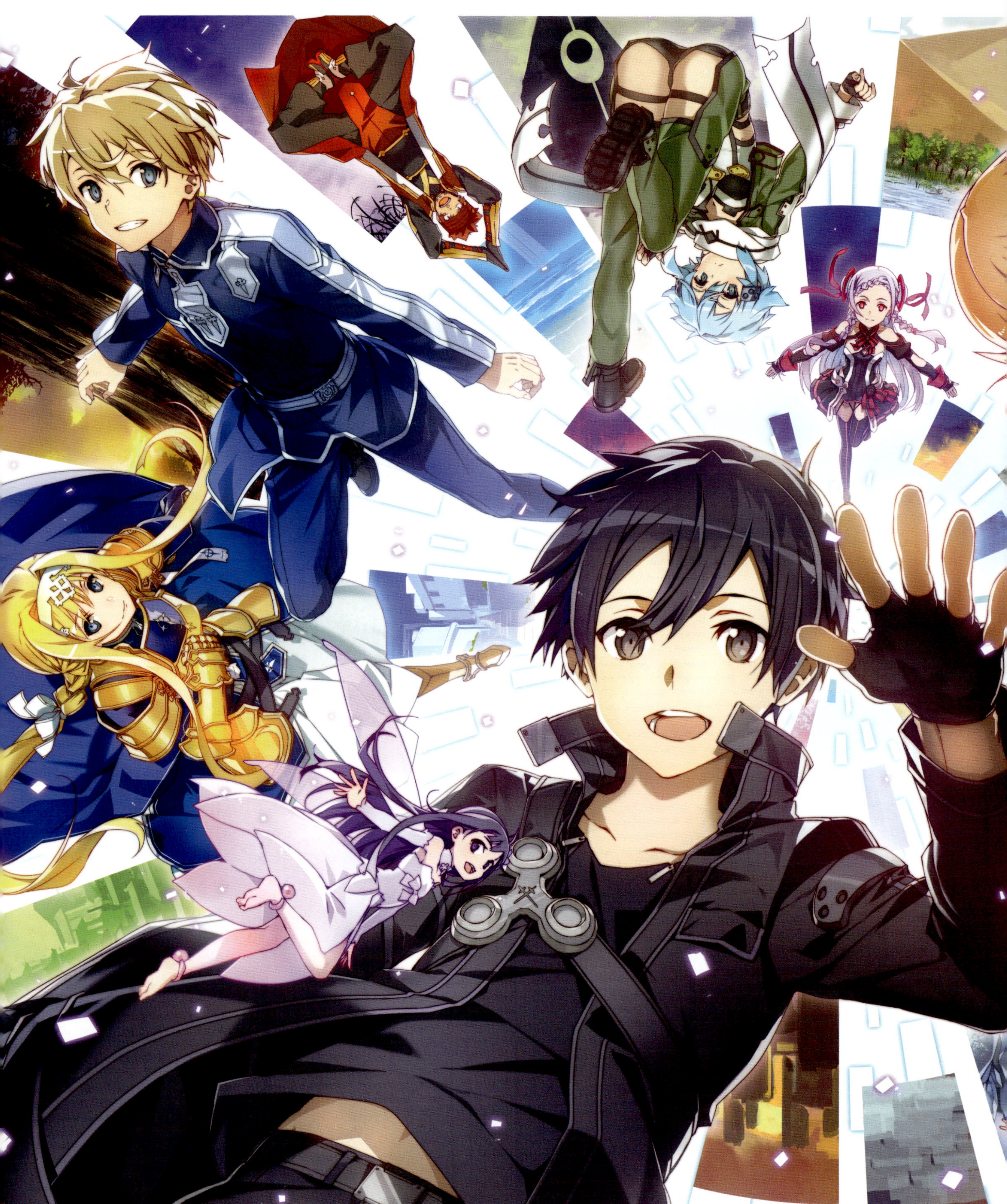

26th Dengeki Prize
Promo Illustration: May 2018

As a matter of fact, I was a judge for the Dengeki Illustration Prize, so I got to draw this for the occasion. The idea was to create the "Link Start" moment that shows everyone diving into the worlds of various stories.

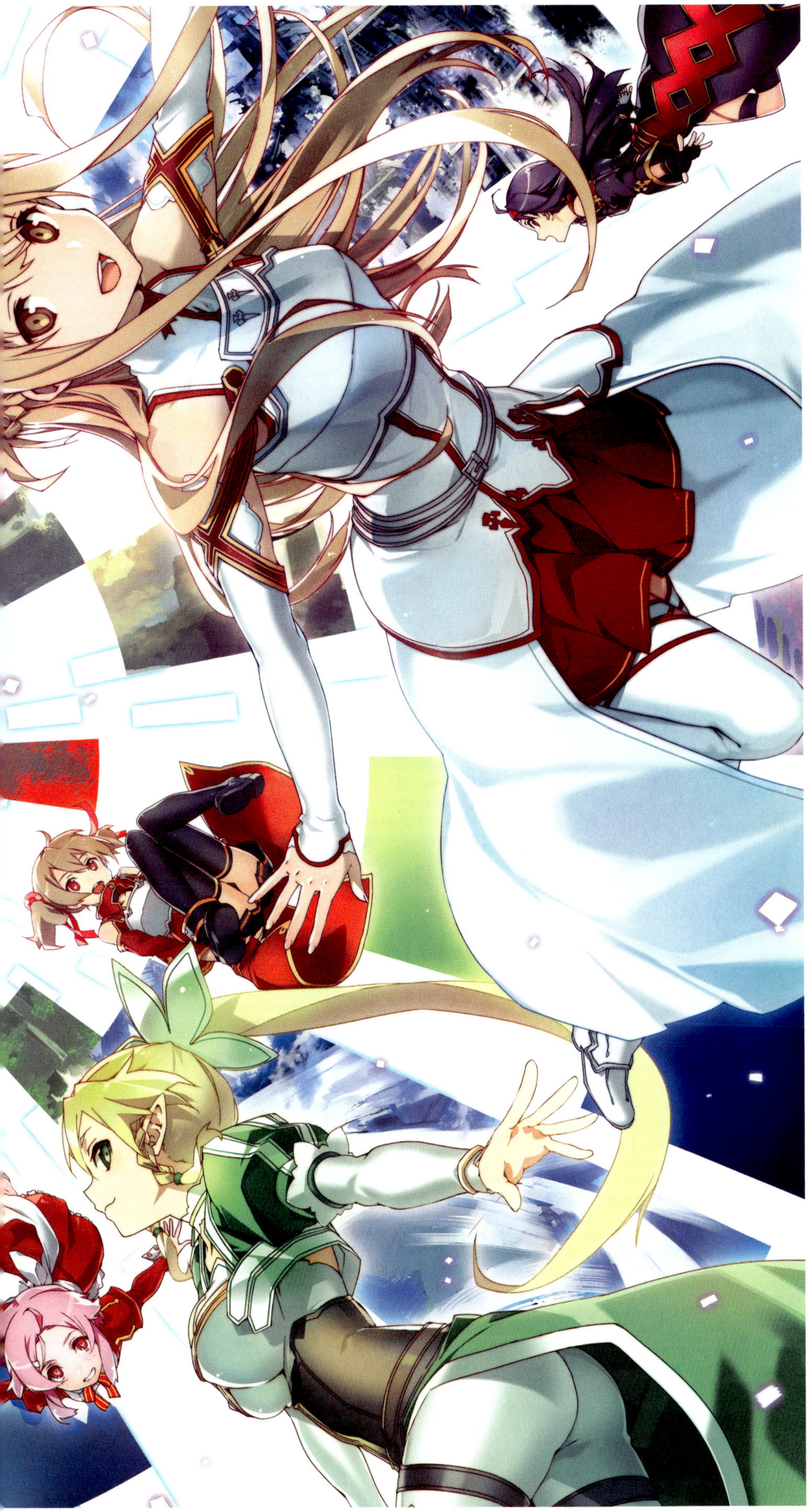

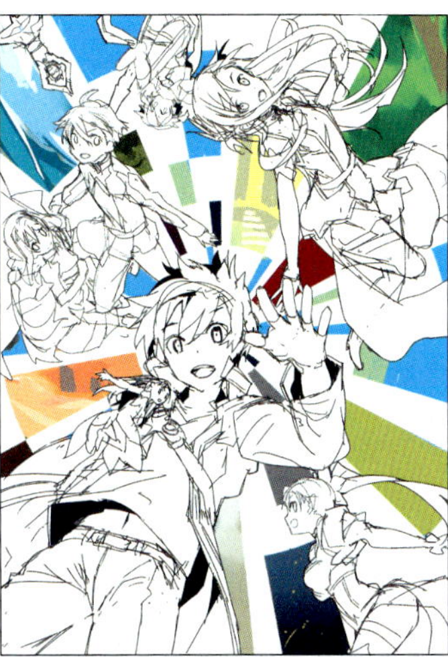

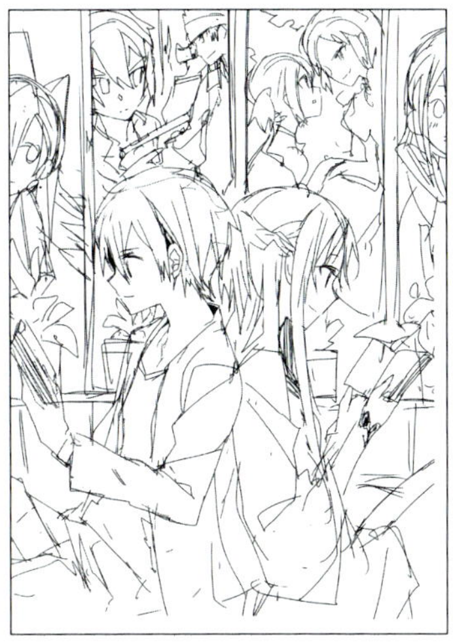

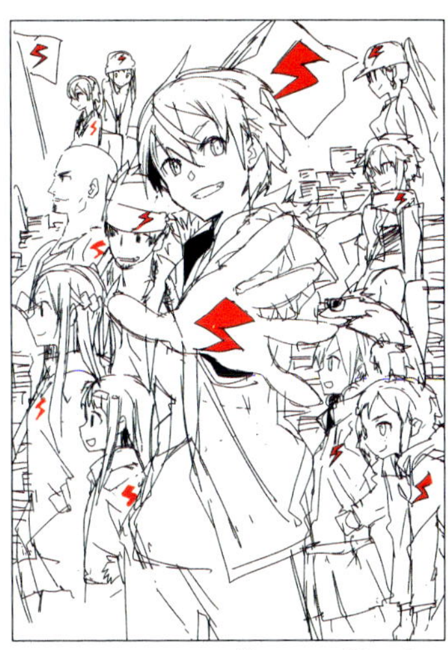

Alternate Sketches

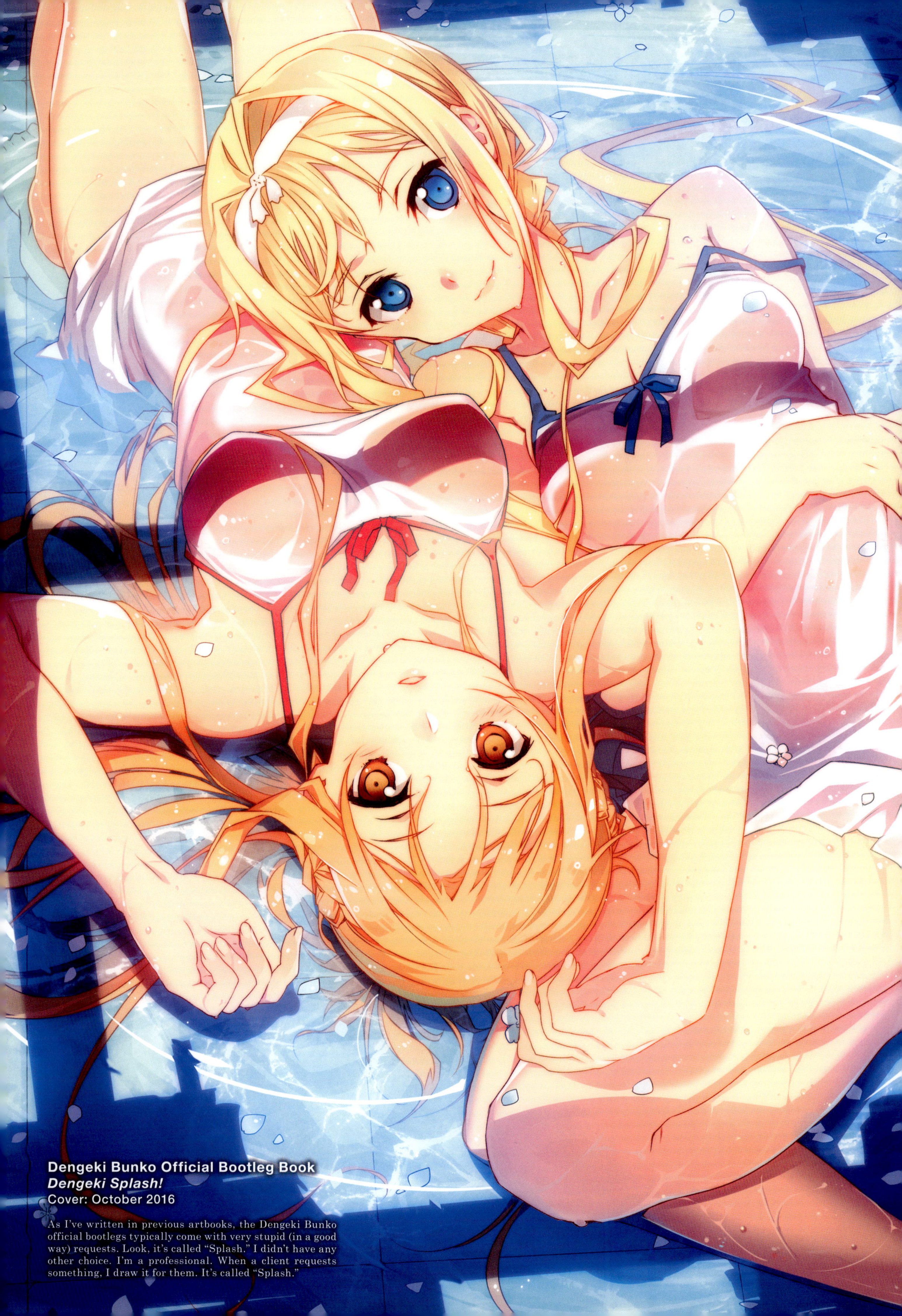

Dengeki Bunko Official Bootleg Book
Dengeki Splash!
Cover: October 2016

As I've written in previous artbooks, the Dengeki Bunko official bootlegs typically come with very stupid (in a good way) requests. Look, it's called "Splash." I didn't have any other choice. I'm a professional. When a client requests something, I draw it for them. It's called "Splash."

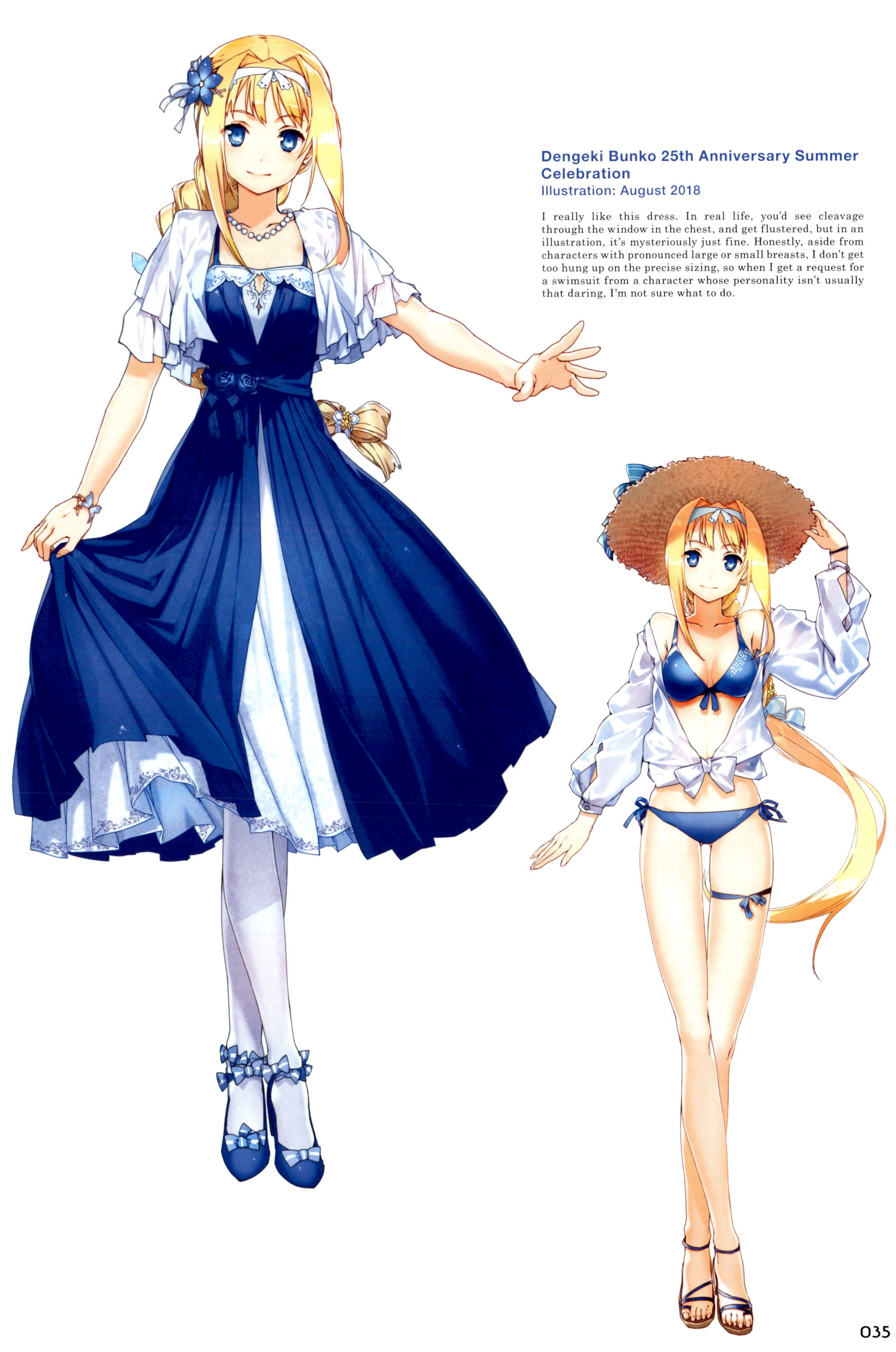

Dengeki Bunko 25th Anniversary Summer Celebration
Illustration: August 2018

I really like this dress. In real life, you'd see cleavage through the window in the chest, and get flustered, but in an illustration, it's mysteriously just fine. Honestly, aside from characters with pronounced large or small breasts, I don't get too hung up on the precise sizing, so when I get a request for a swimsuit from a character whose personality isn't usually that daring, I'm not sure what to do.

Dengeki Bunko Magazine, July 2018 issue
Cover: June 2018

Asuna and Alice are often treated as a set of two heroines in the Alicization arc, but to me, I've never seen them as especially linked. So if you'll notice, they're actually just barely not making contact here. Huh? "What about Splash?" No, you don't understand. That illustration had nothing to do with the characters' connections. All of my concentration was on the see-through coloring. (^q^)

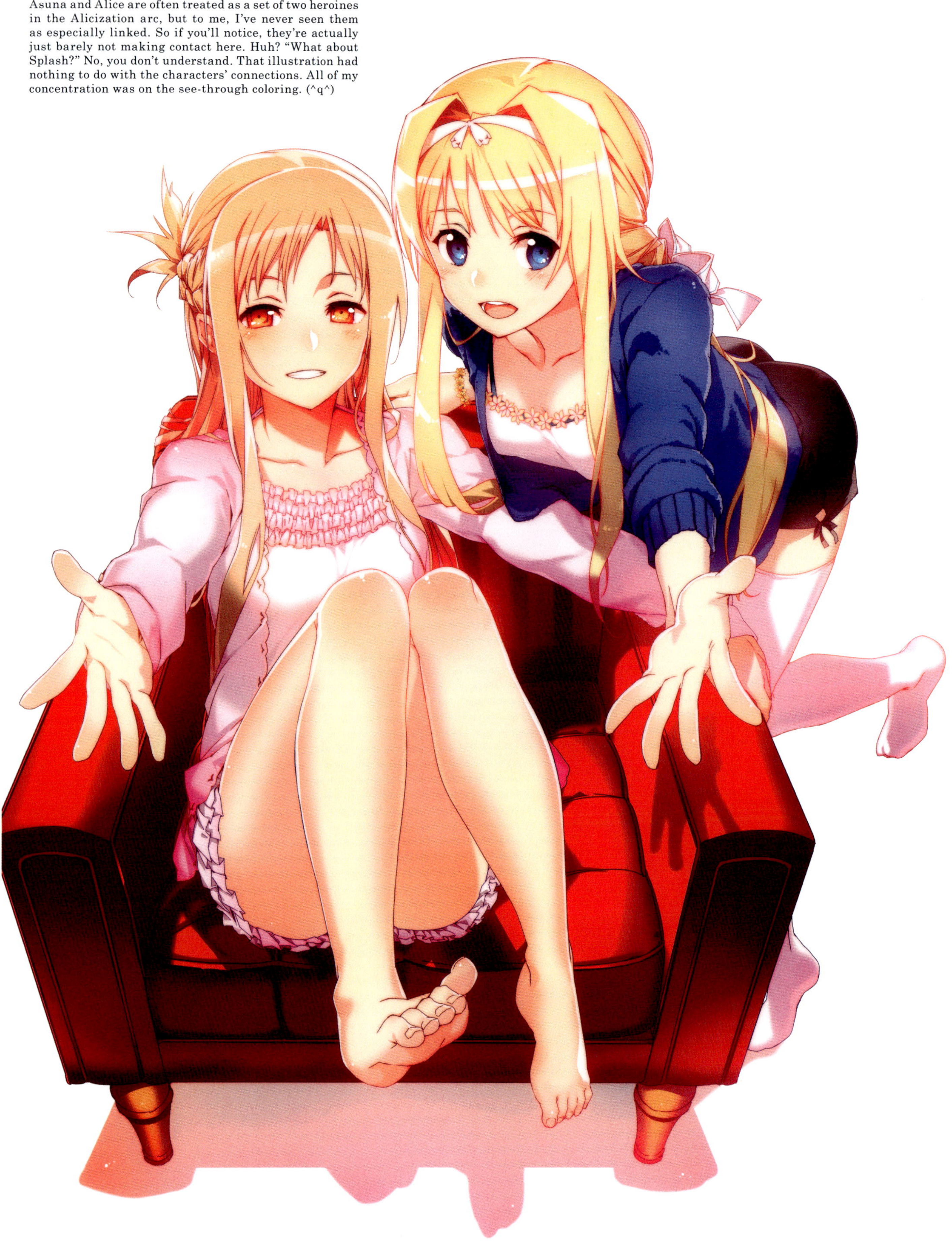

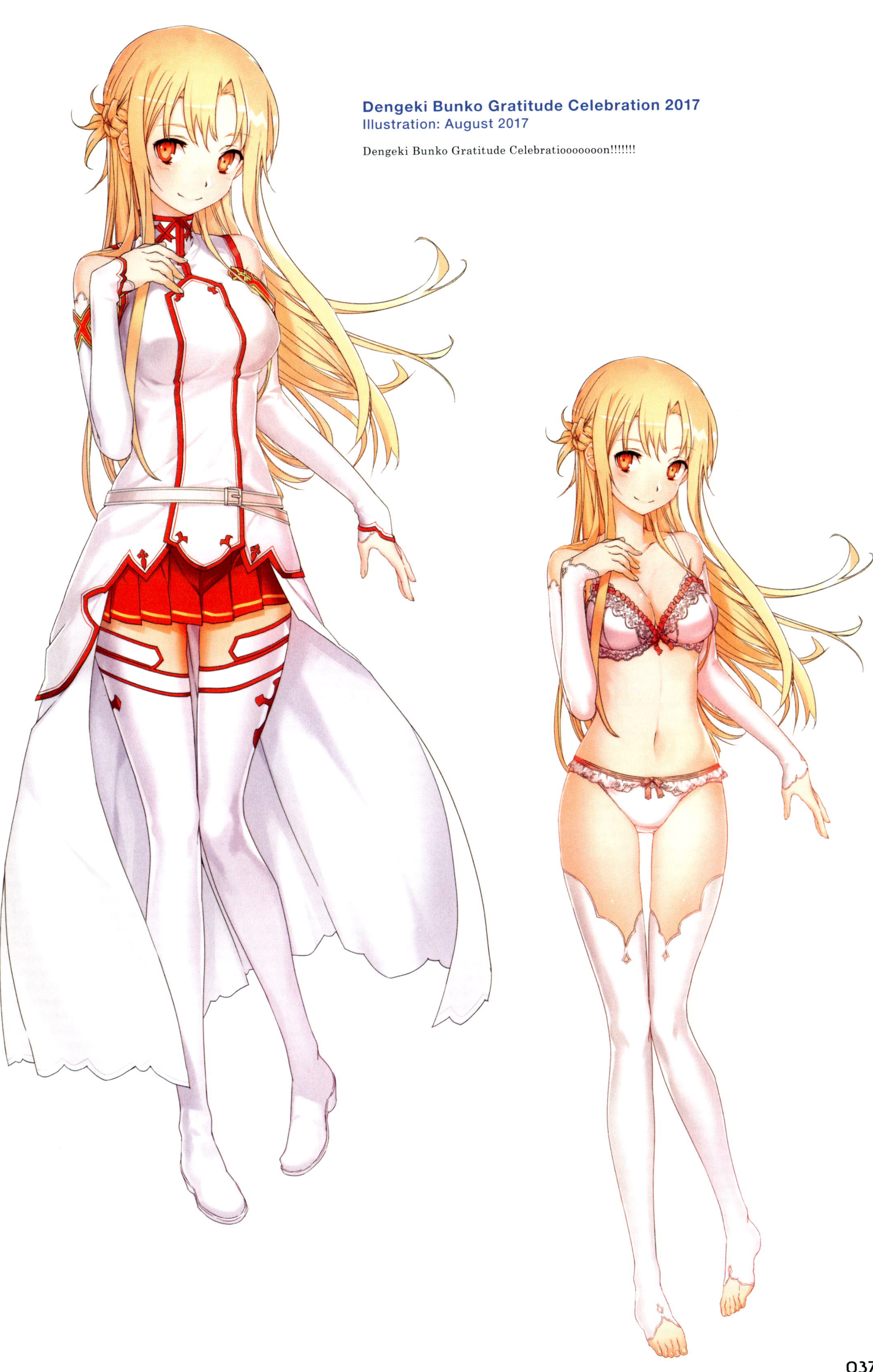

Dengeki Bunko Gratitude Celebration 2017
Illustration: August 2017

Dengeki Bunko Gratitude Celebratioooooooon!!!!!!!

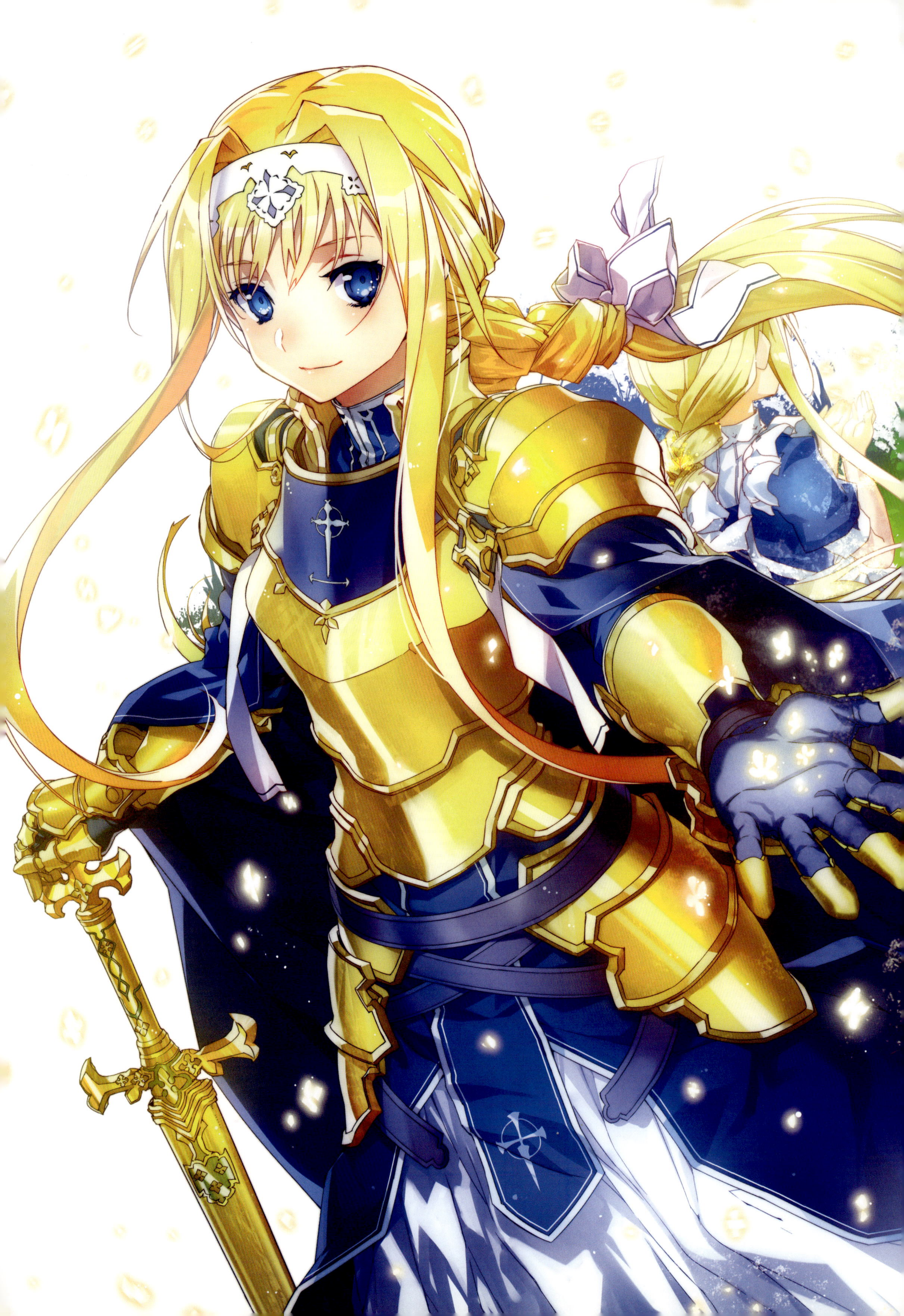

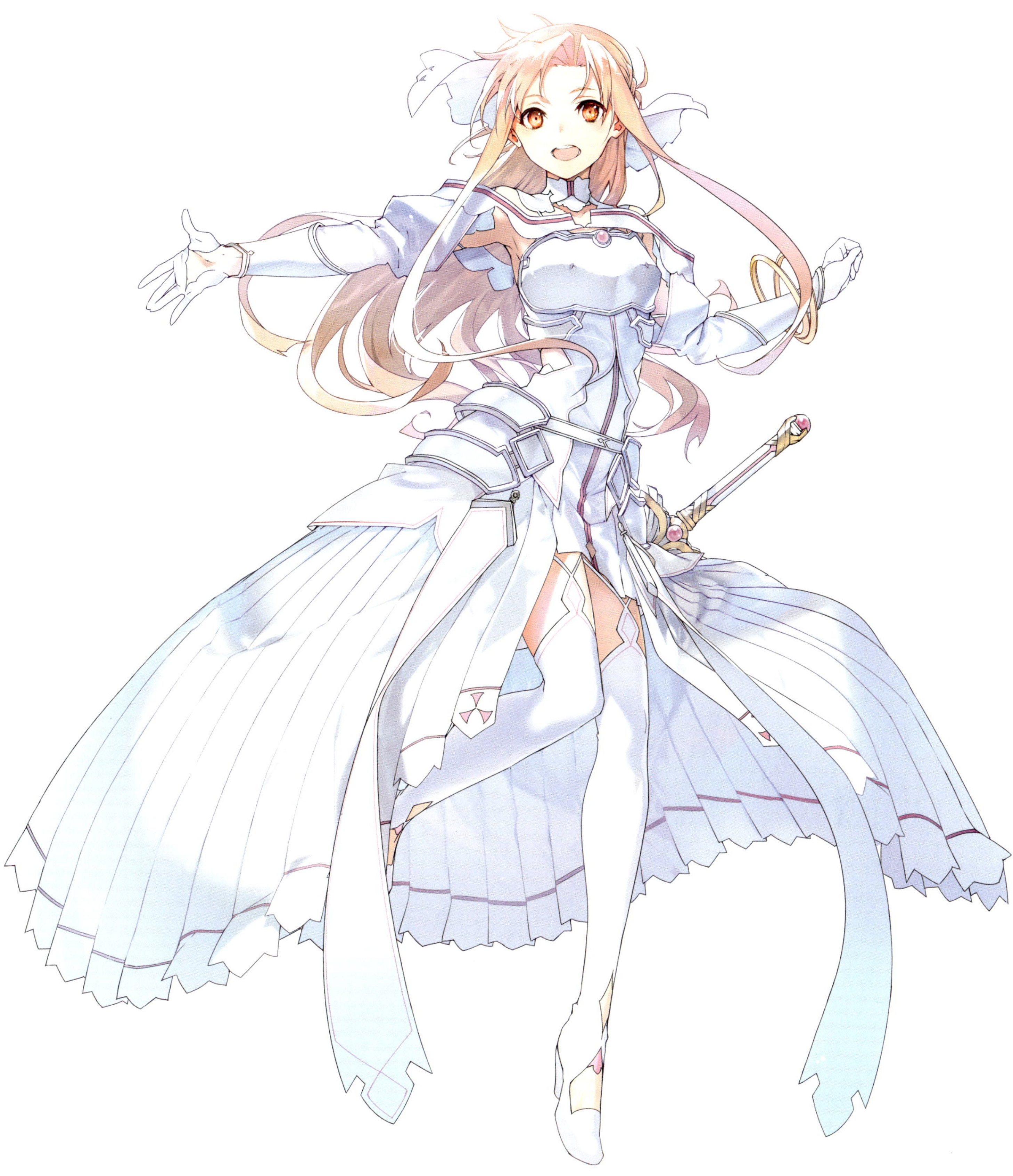

Kadokawa Light Novel Expo 2020, *Ranosupo!*
Illustration: March 2021

As I'll mention on the following page, this is after I settled down
on a coloring once I'd experimented a bit. I wanted her image to
look bright and clean.

Dengeki Bunko Magazine, November 2018 issue
Cover: October 2018

It's a bit hard to tell, but these are the two Alices.
Sometimes I wonder what the childhood Alice would've
been like if she had grown to adulthood.

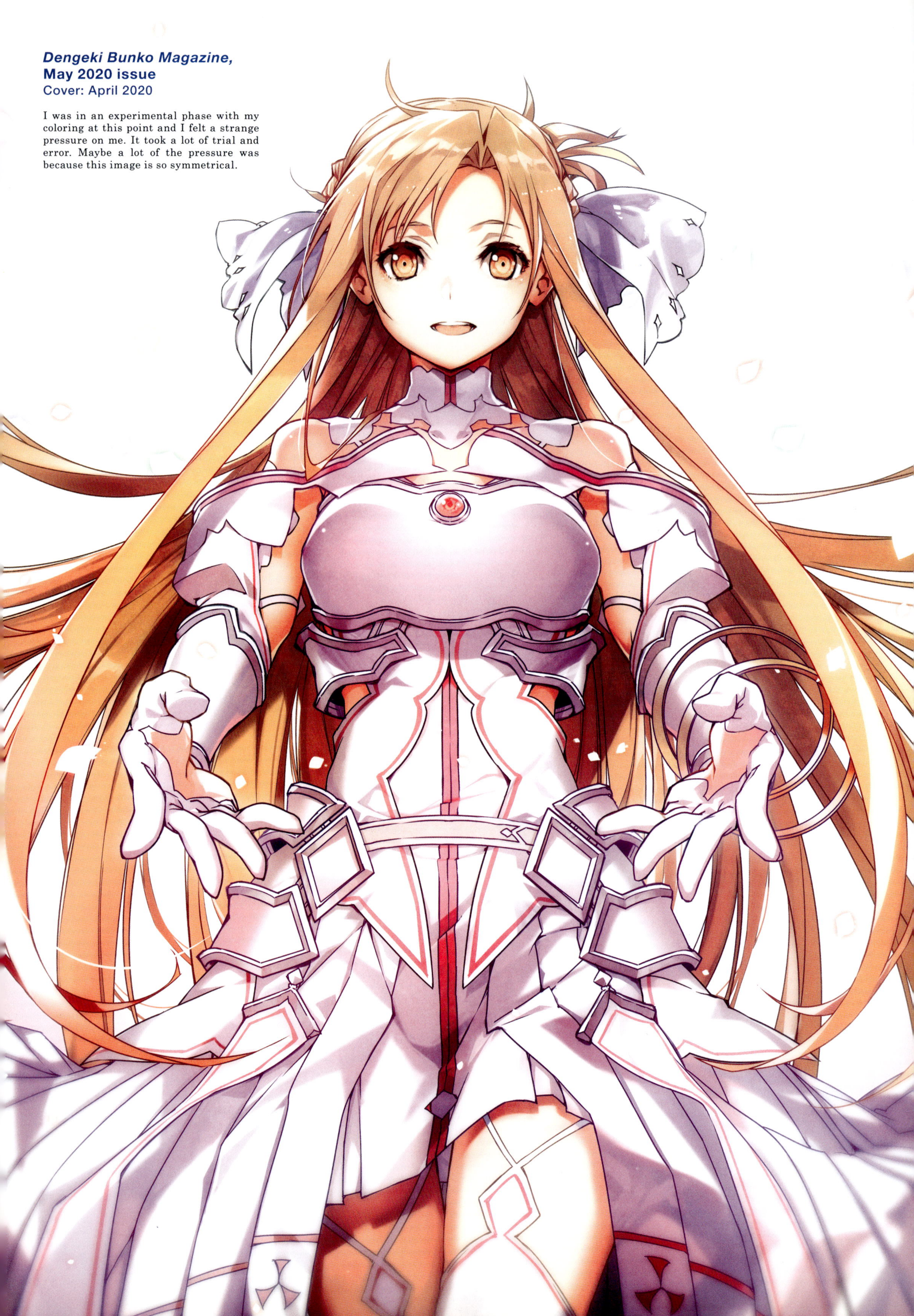

Dengeki Bunko Magazine,
May 2020 issue
Cover: April 2020

I was in an experimental phase with my coloring at this point and I felt a strange pressure on me. It took a lot of trial and error. Maybe a lot of the pressure was because this image is so symmetrical.

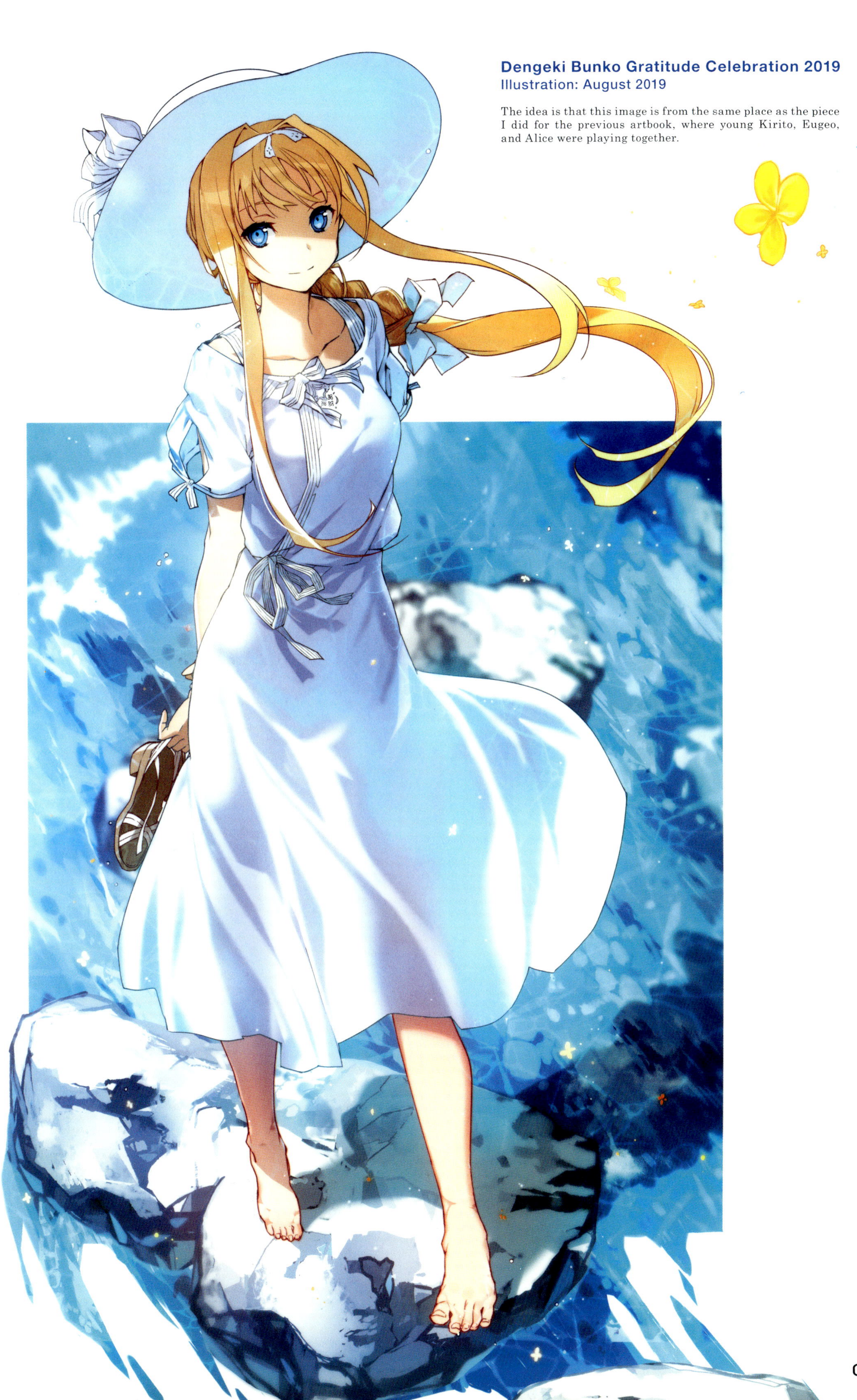

Dengeki Bunko Gratitude Celebration 2019
Illustration: August 2019

The idea is that this image is from the same place as the piece
I did for the previous artbook, where young Kirito, Eugeo,
and Alice were playing together.

SWORD ART ONLINE MOON CRADLE

The Moon Cradle arc is where the original web novel ends and all-new material begins. It's really fun to see where a story goes after it's reached an ending point.

Dengeki Bunko
Sword Art Online 19:
Moon Cradle
Cover: February 2017

Kirito and Ronie. I was hoping the change in Ronie's hair length would signal the passage of time to the reader.

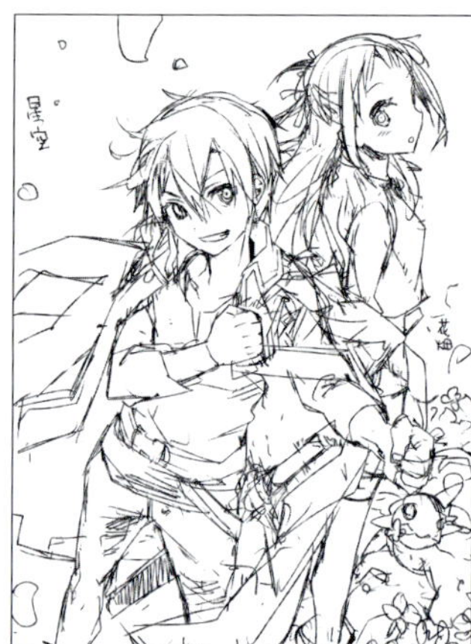

Rough Cover Sketch

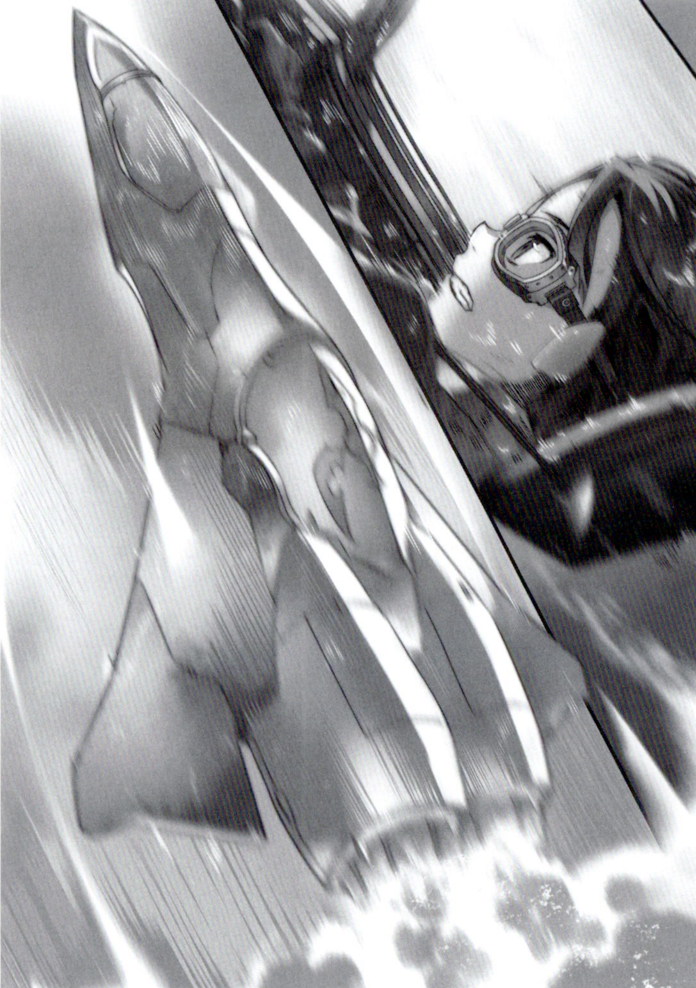

Dengeki Bunko
Sword Art Online 19: Moon Cradle
Illustration: February 2017

Kawahara-san sent me the specifications of Dragoncraft Prototype One. While reading the story text, I was imagining something more dragon-ish. But being more logical, given that Kirito knows what real fighter jets are like, as well as the evolution of airplane design, it would turn out more like this.

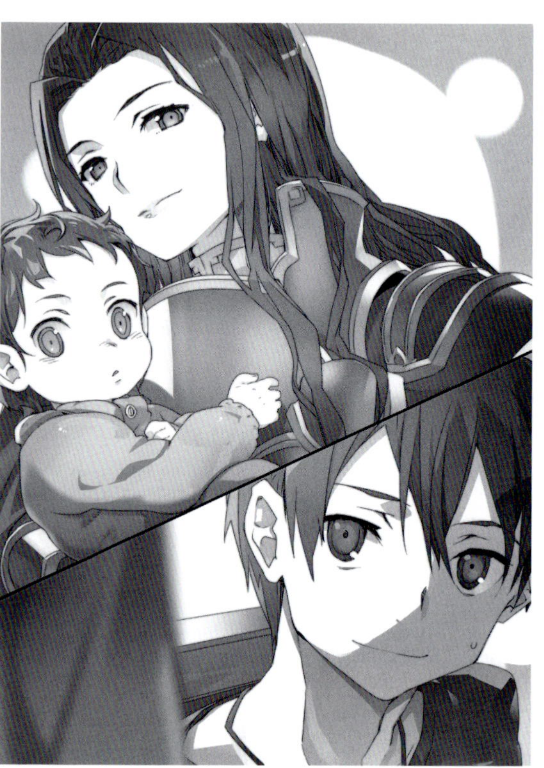

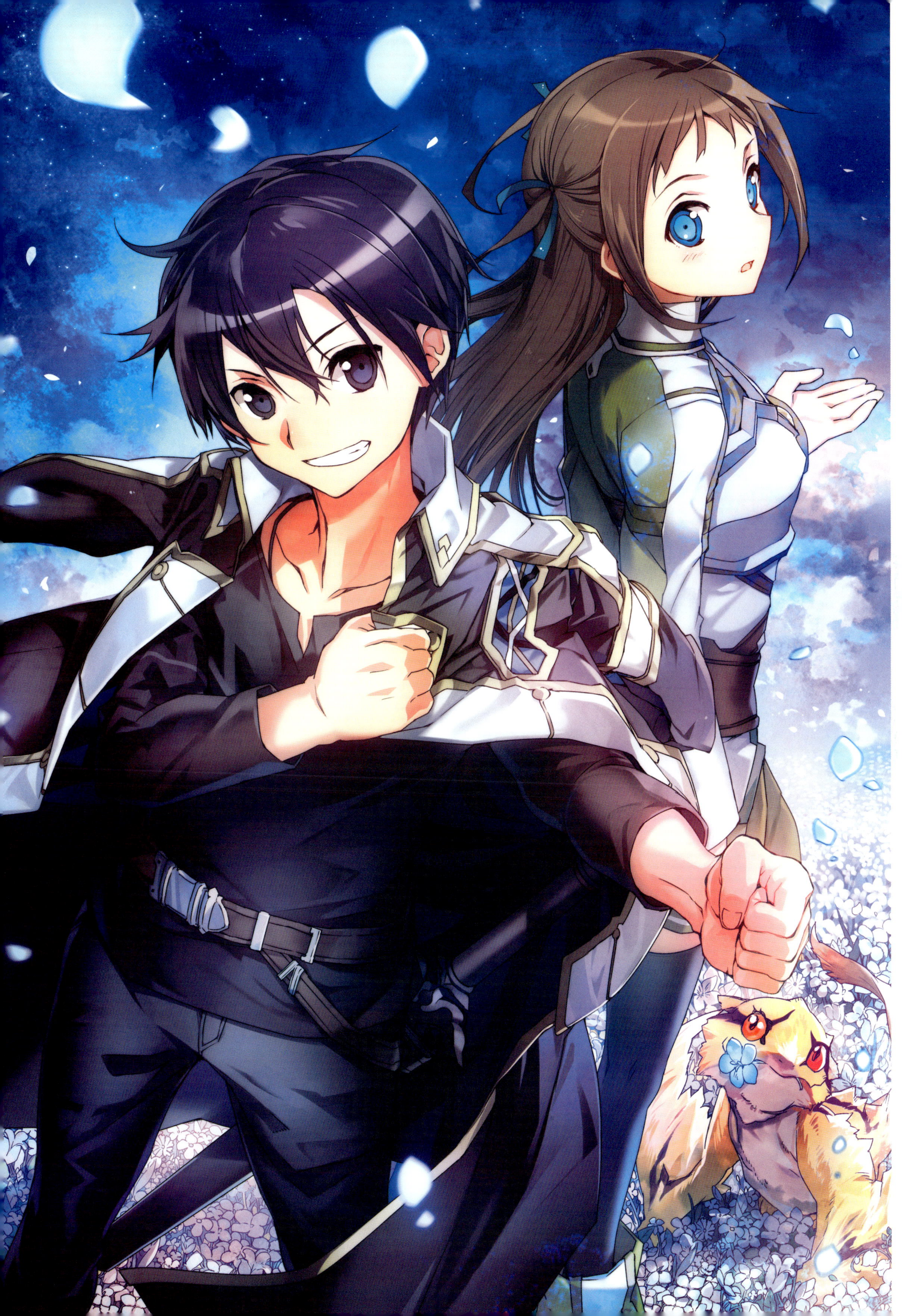

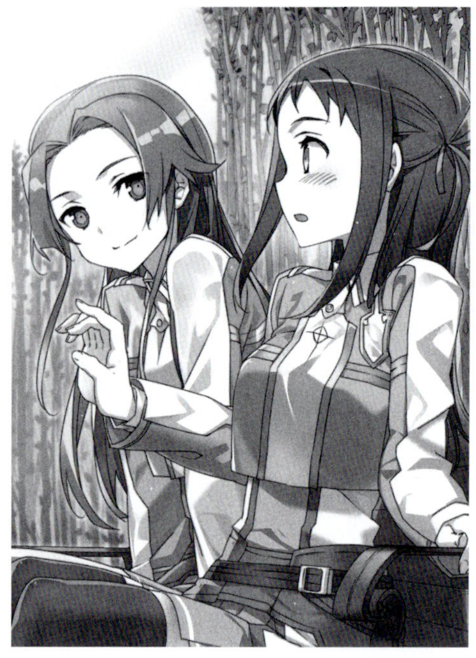

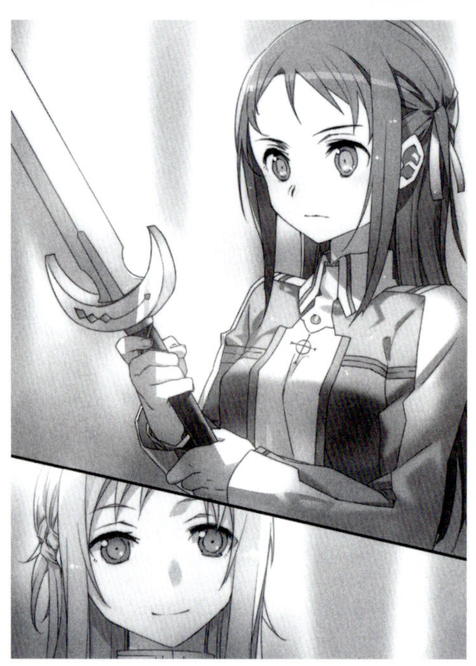

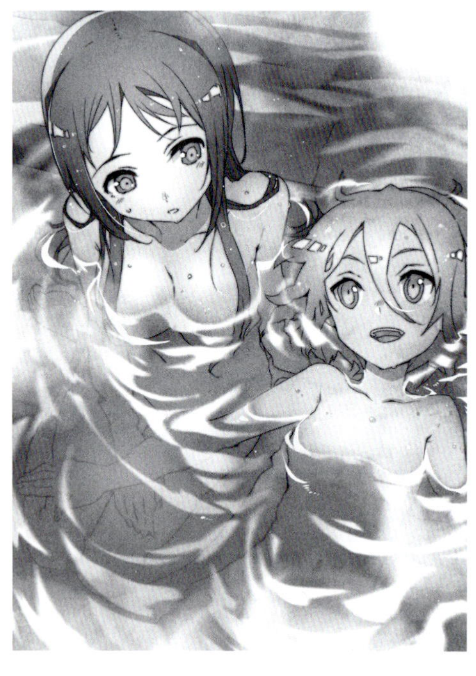

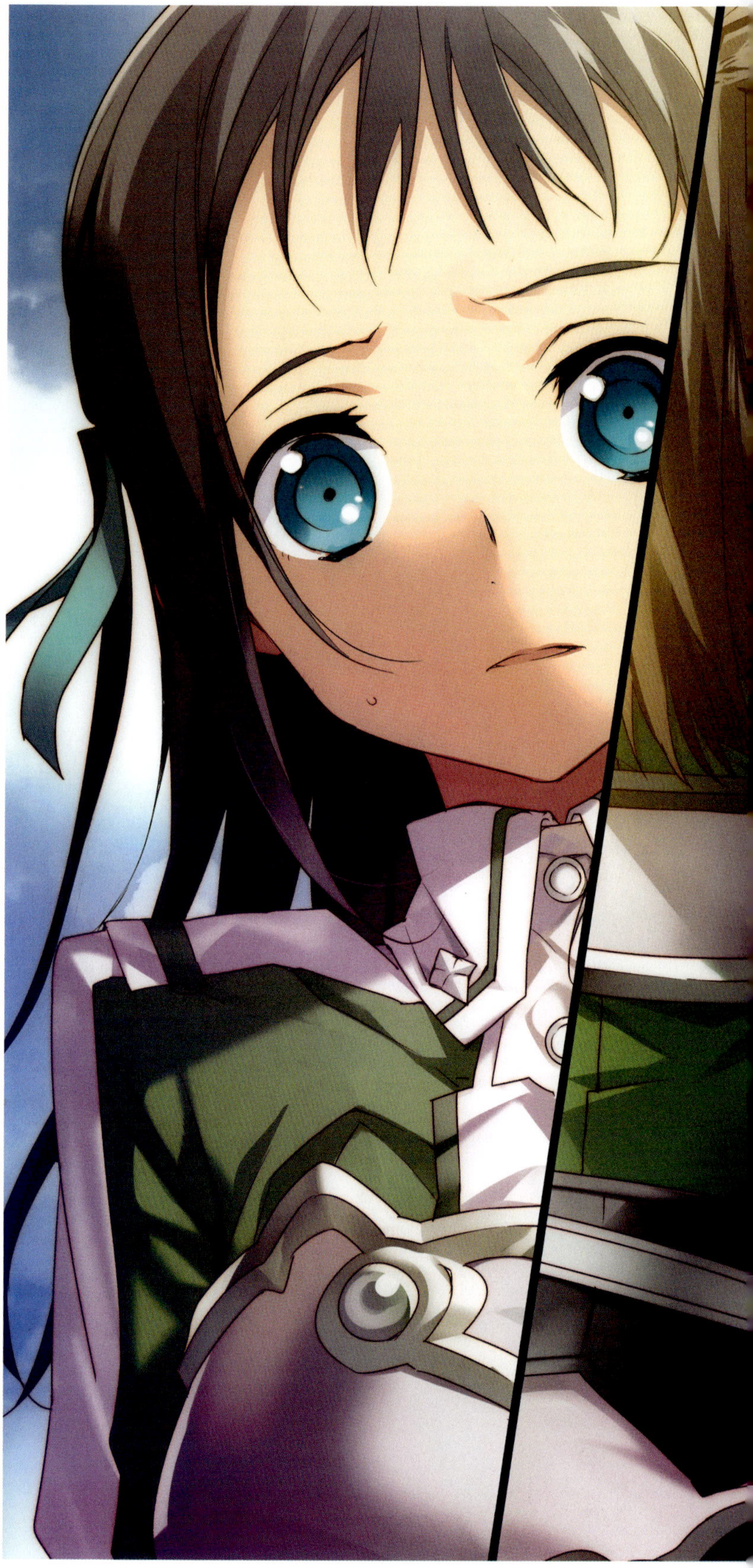

Dengeki Bunko
Sword Art Online 19: Moon Cradle
Illustration: February 2017

Somehow I end up drawing lots of bathing scenes.
Making an entire floor of Central Cathedral a bath-
house was a stroke of genius from Kawahara-san!

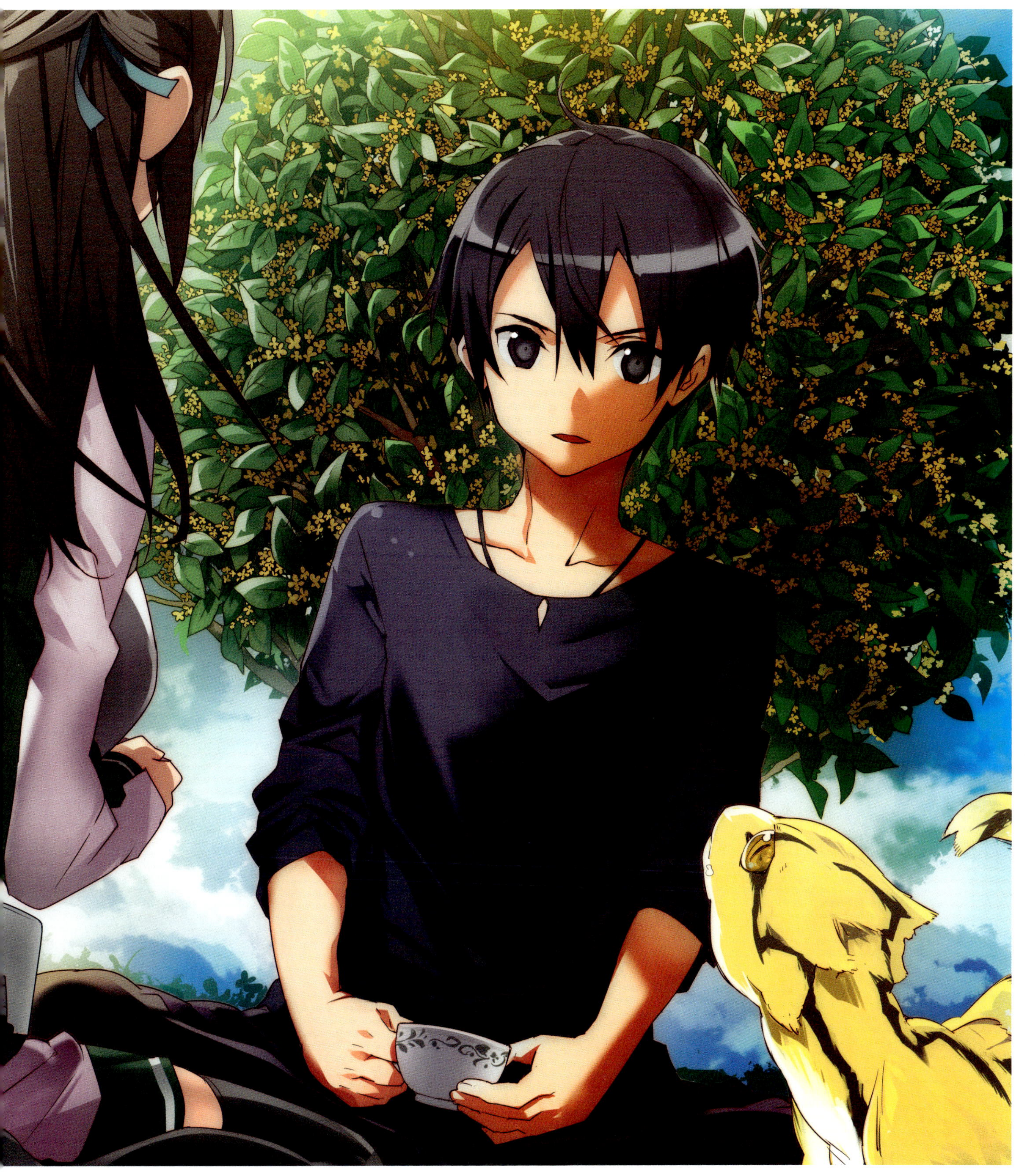

Dengeki Bunko
Sword Art Online 19: Moon Cradle
Frontispiece: February 2017

Placing a stronger shadow on a face makes it look more serious. It's strange how that works.

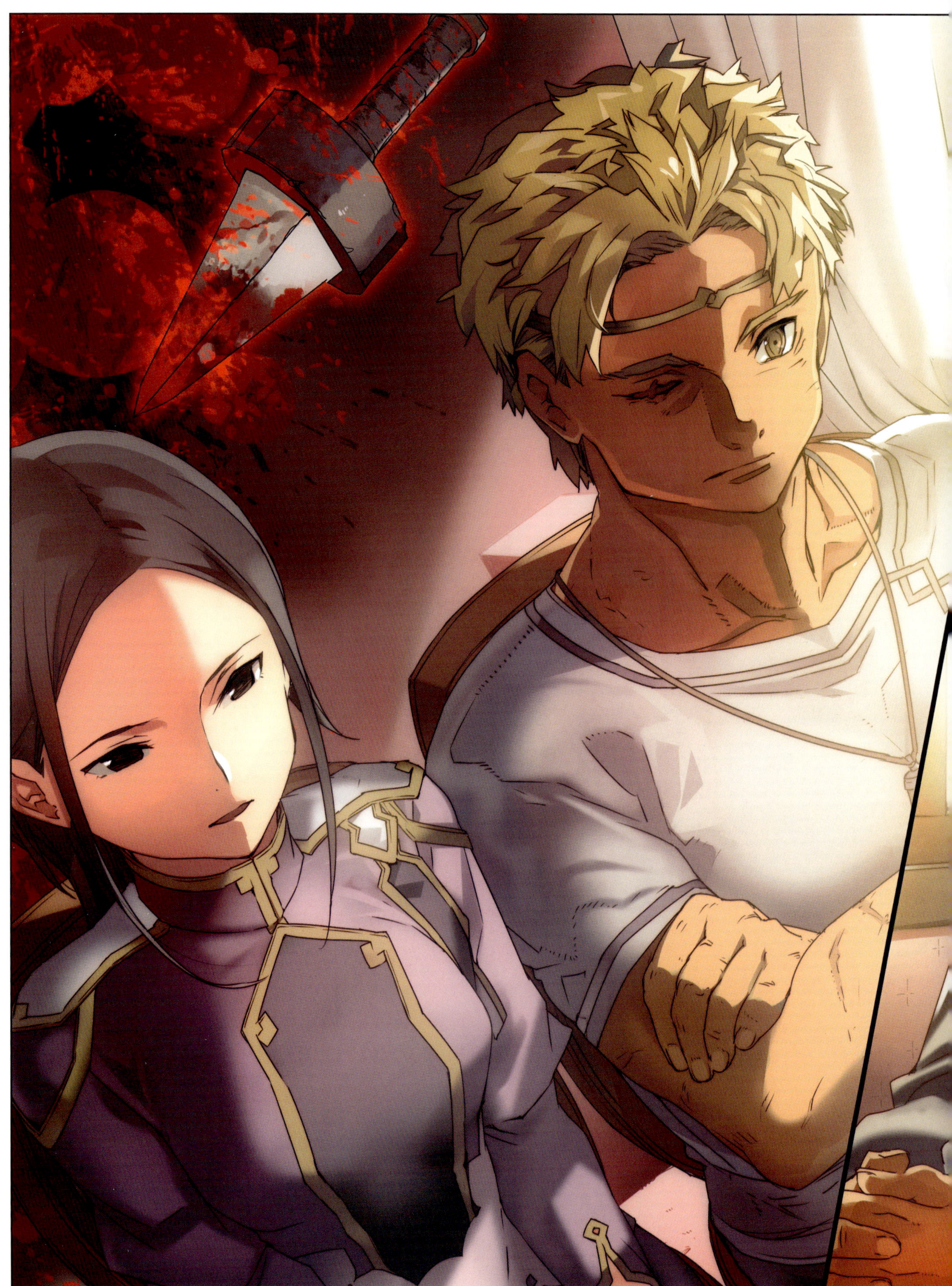

Dengeki Bunko
Sword Art Online 19: Moon Cradle
Frontispiece: February 2017

Iskahn and Sheyta make a great couple. I enjoyed drawing this one. Also, Kirito and Ronie are using a special oil to make their skin tanned. It's hard to tell because their shadows are heavy.

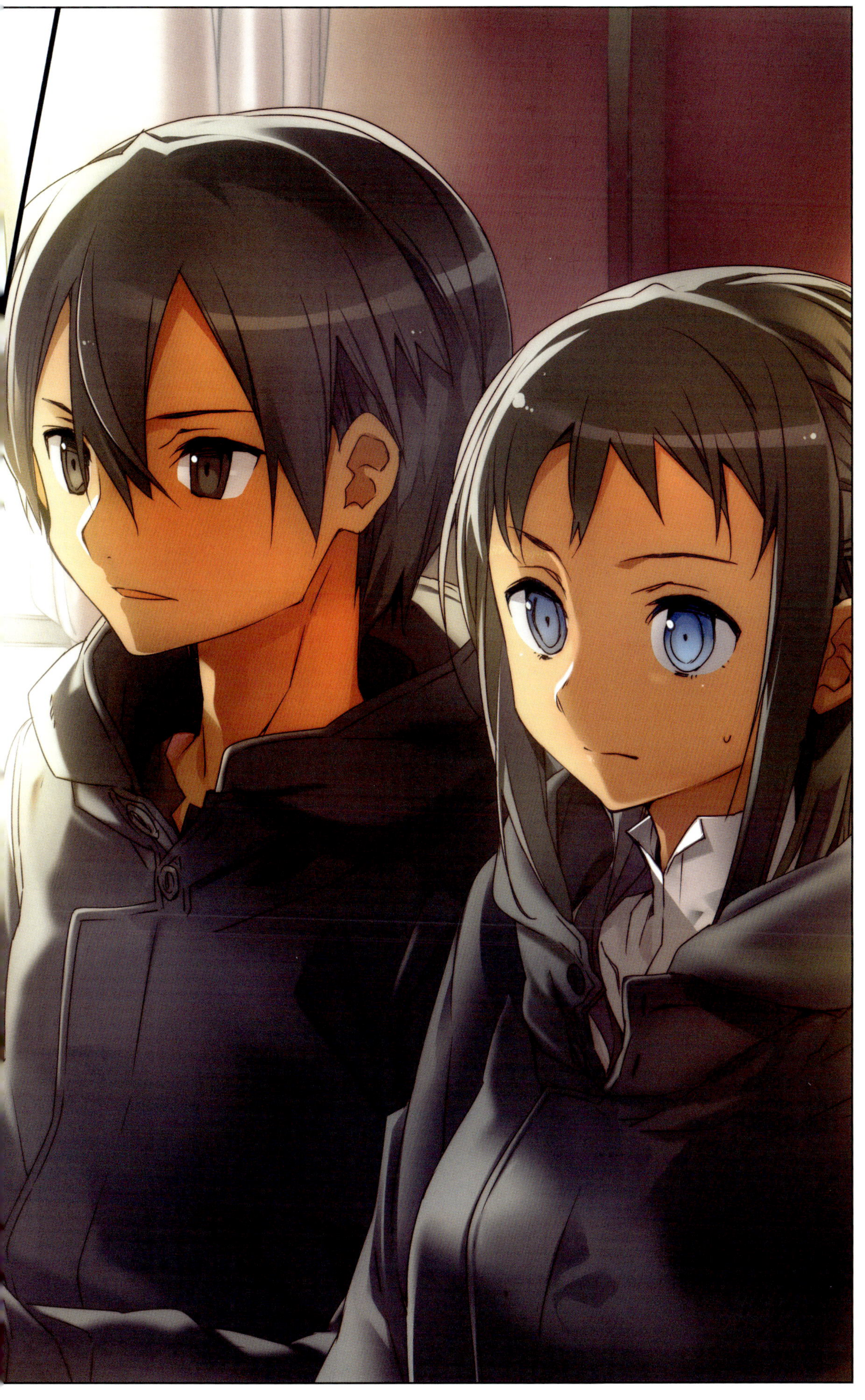

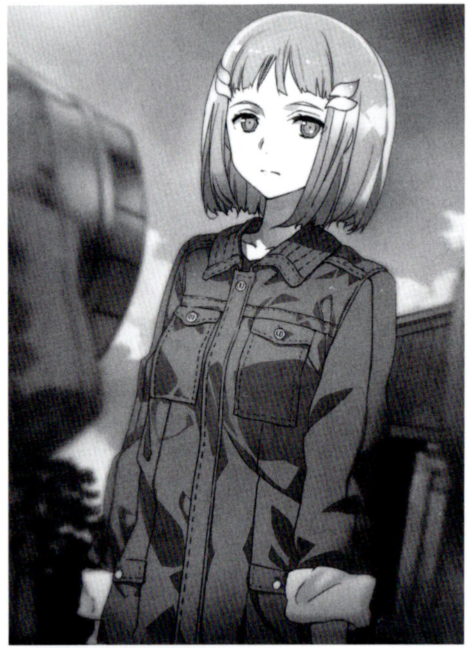

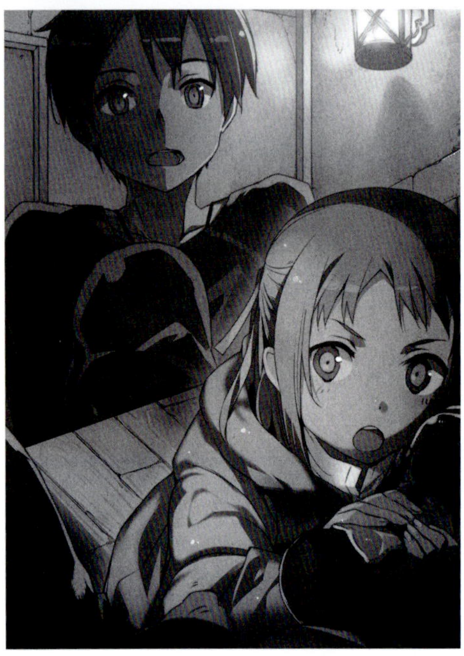

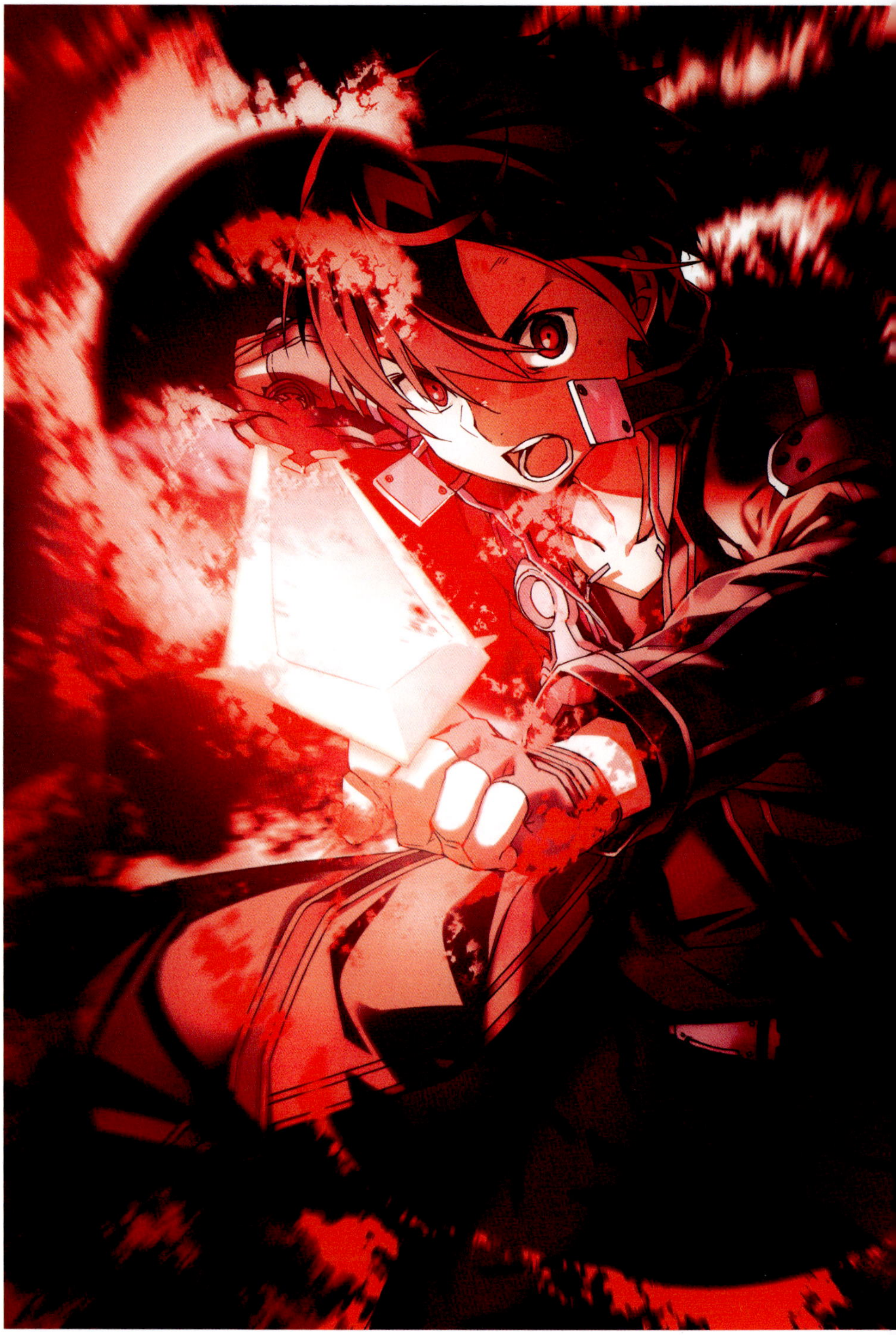

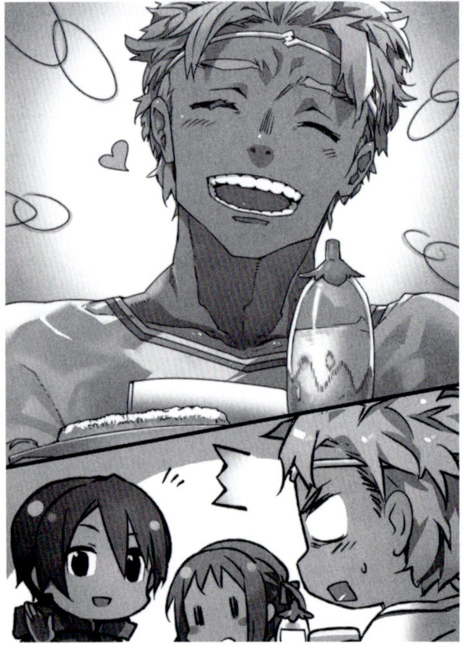

Dengeki Bunko
Sword Art Online 19: Moon Cradle
Frontispiece: February 2017

I made sure to have Kirito looking at the camera, and Iskahn
and Sheyta looking away, so it didn't feel like I was implying
that he was attacking them.

Dengeki Bunko
*Sword Art Online 19:
Moon Cradle*
Illustration: February 2017

I love proud papa Iskahn.
His gums are visible.

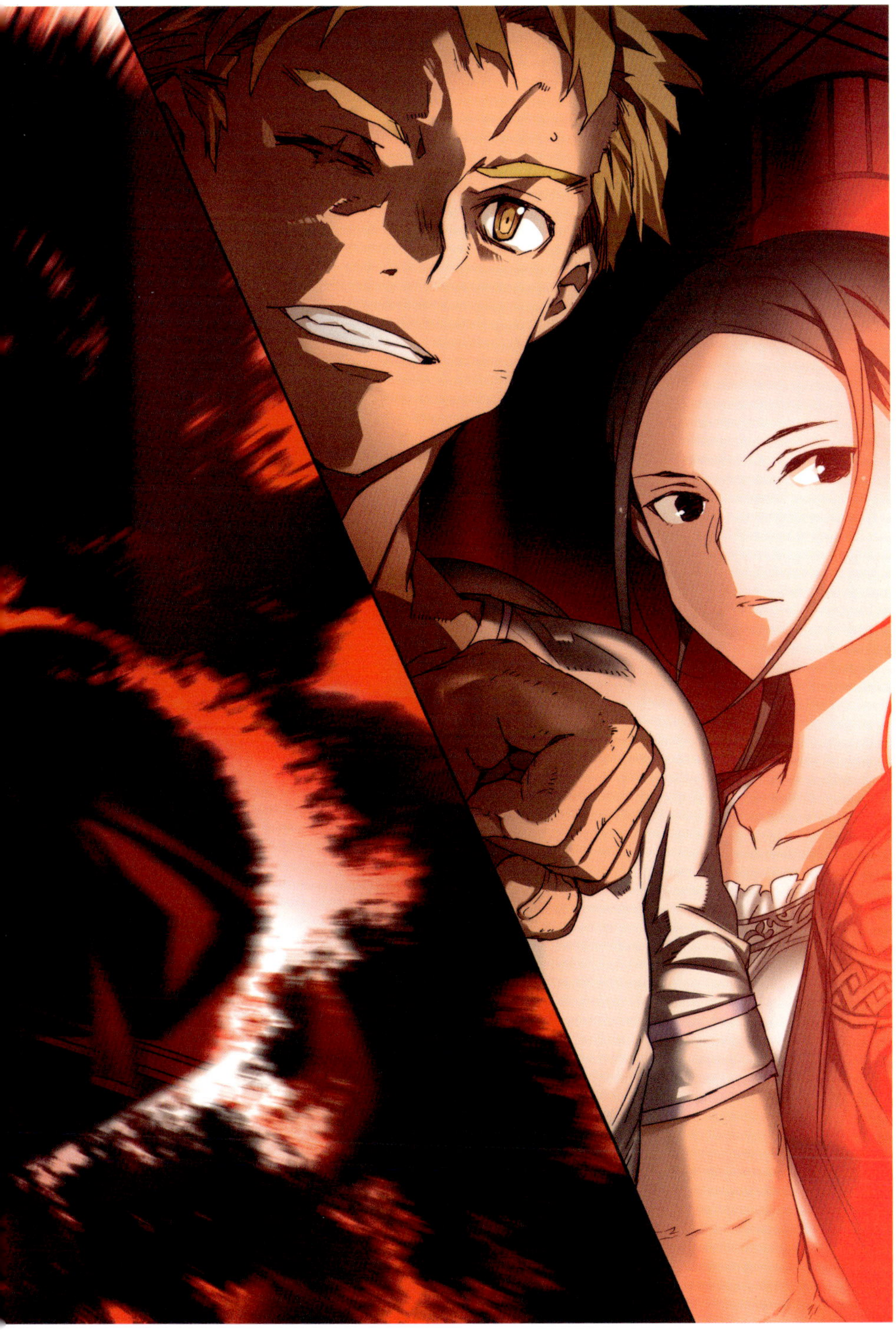

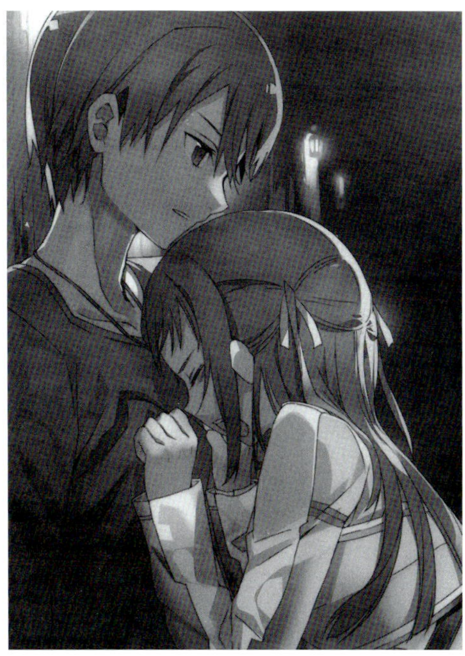

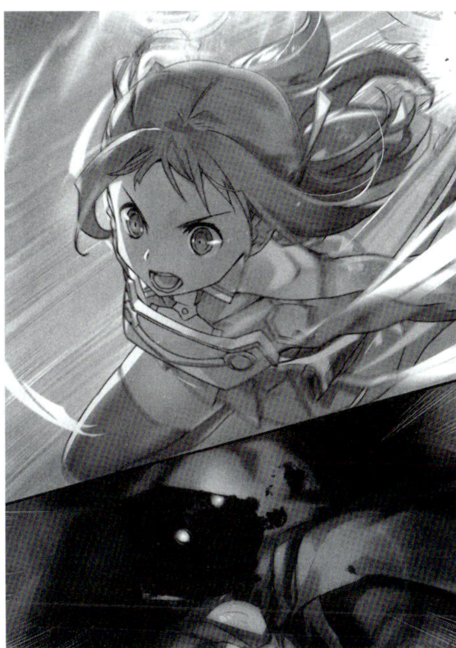

Dengeki Bunko
Sword Art Online 19: Moon Cradle
Illustration: February 2017

Ronie clinging to Kirito, and Ronie being heroic. The great thing about drawing the women in *SAO* is that they all fight.

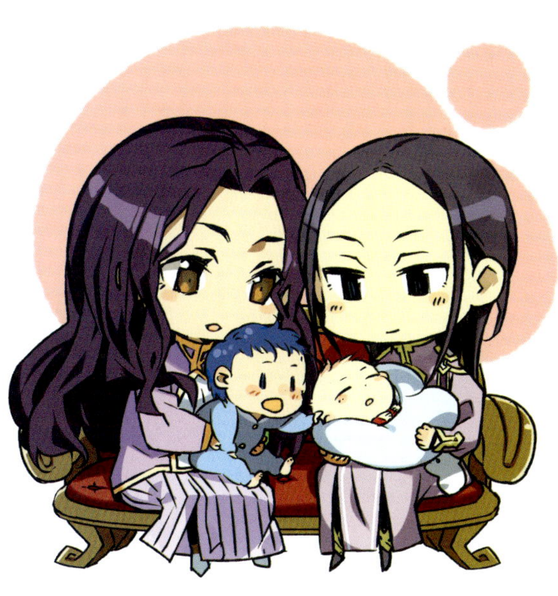

Dengeki Bunko
Sword Art Online 19: Moon Cradle
Rear Cover: February 2017

Mothers chatting. I want to see the world that these kids live in when they grow up.

SWORD ART ONLINE MOON CRADLE

Volume 20 is the end of the Moon Cradle arc.
The battle against the black emperors concludes here,
but it also sounds like it continues...?

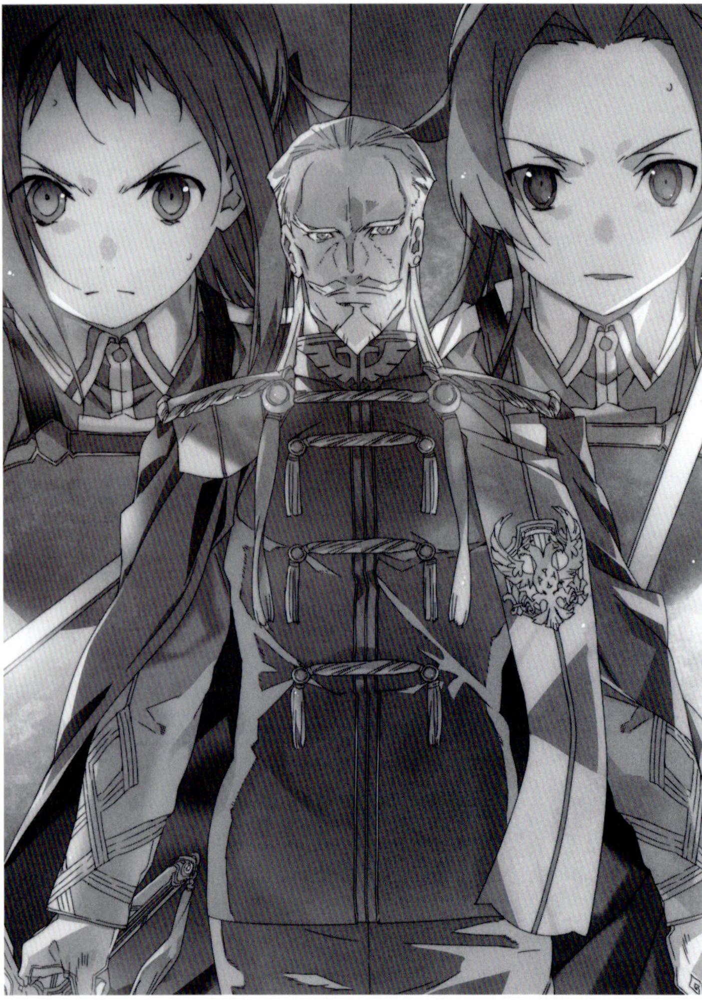

Dengeki Bunko
Sword Art Online 20: Moon Cradle
Cover: September 2017

The girls face off against Emperor Cruiga.
This one really shows Cruiga off.

Dengeki Bunko
Sword Art Online 20:
Moon Cradle
Illustration: September 2017

The Moon Cradle arc is from the
perspective of a grown Ronie and
Tiese, so they're on the cover. In
the Japanese version, the paper obi
strip that goes around the bottom
hides Asuna's face.

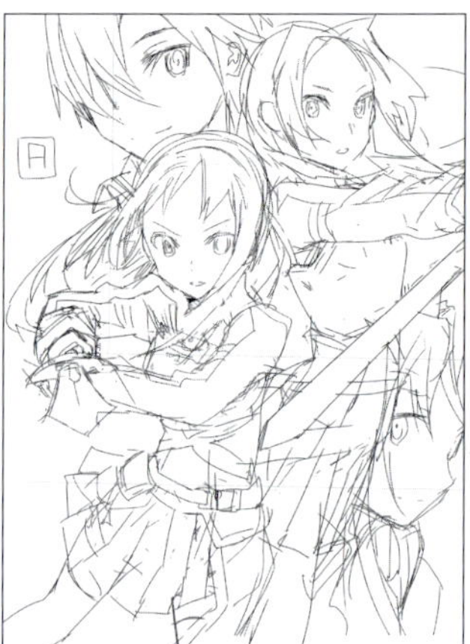

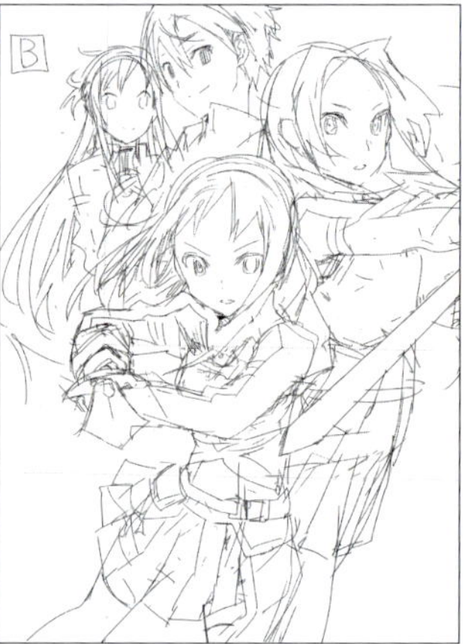

Alternate Sketches

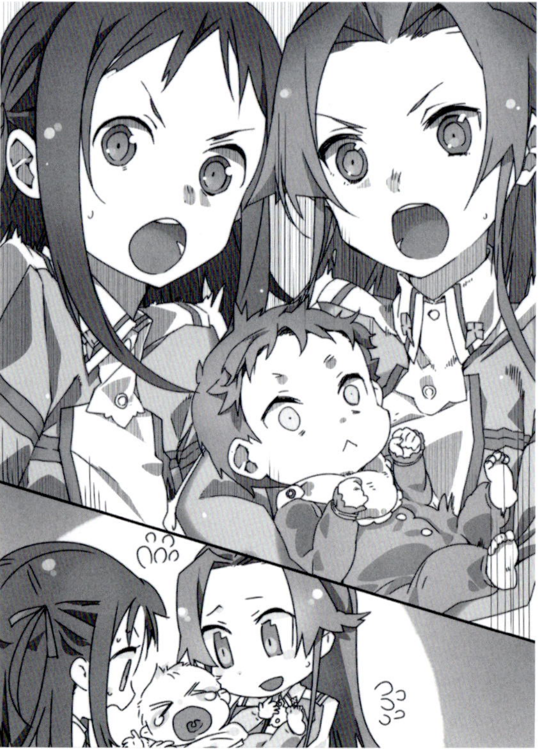

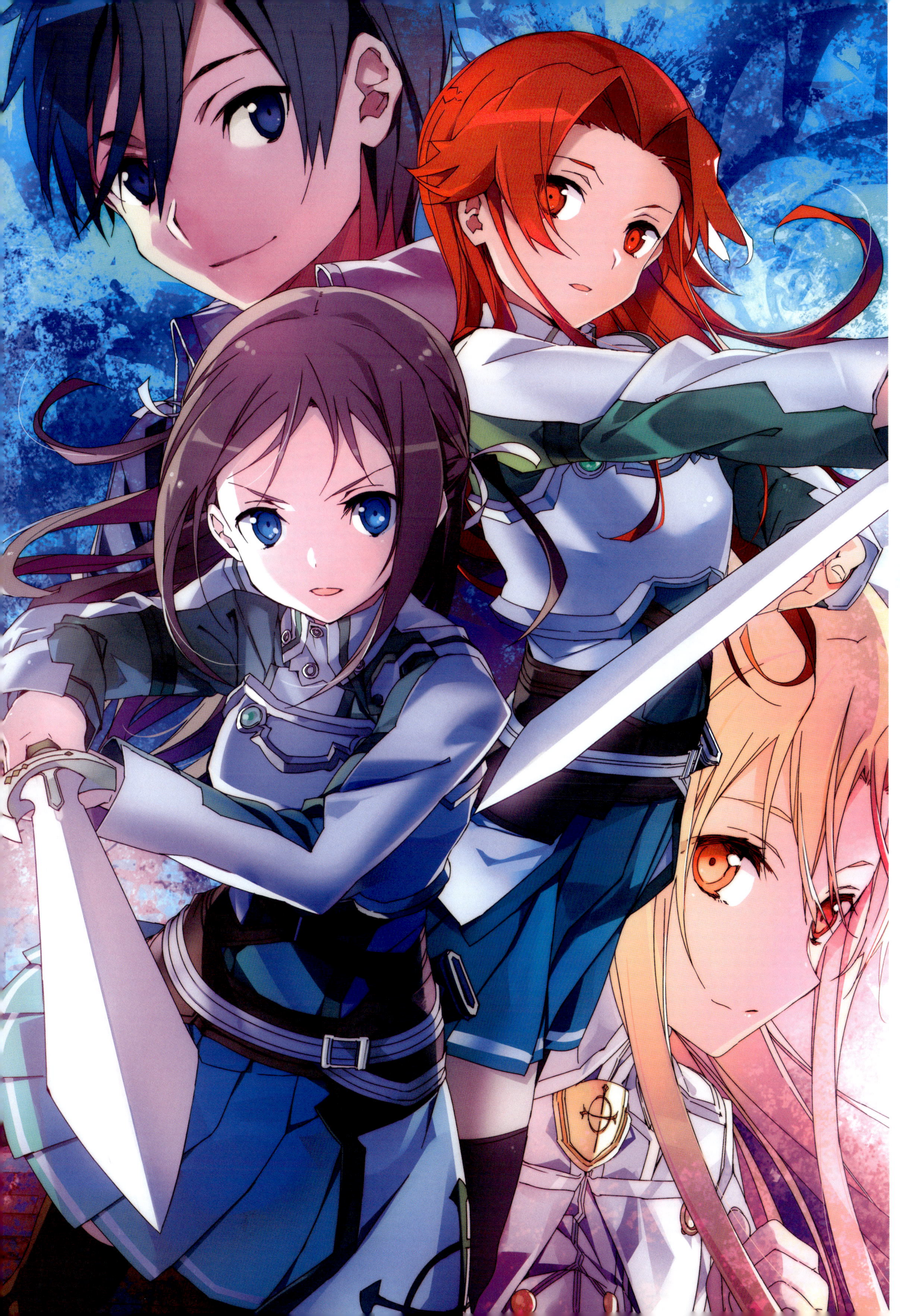

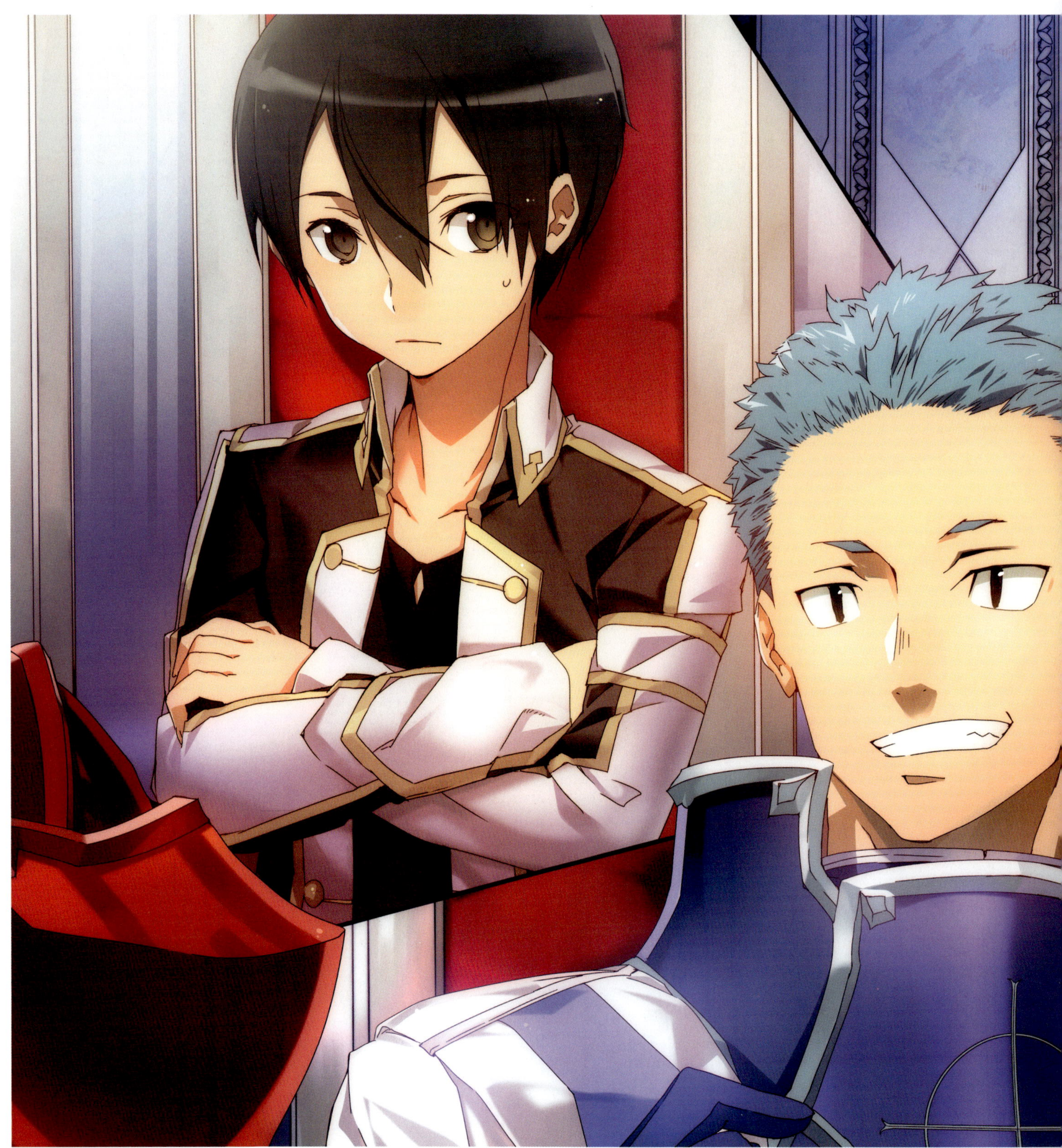

Dengeki Bunko
Sword Art Online 20: Moon Cradle
Frontispiece: September 2017

Our first look at the Integrity Knights, Nergius and Entokia.
Integrity Knights are easy to design because they have the same
armor motif. I wish we could see them in action.

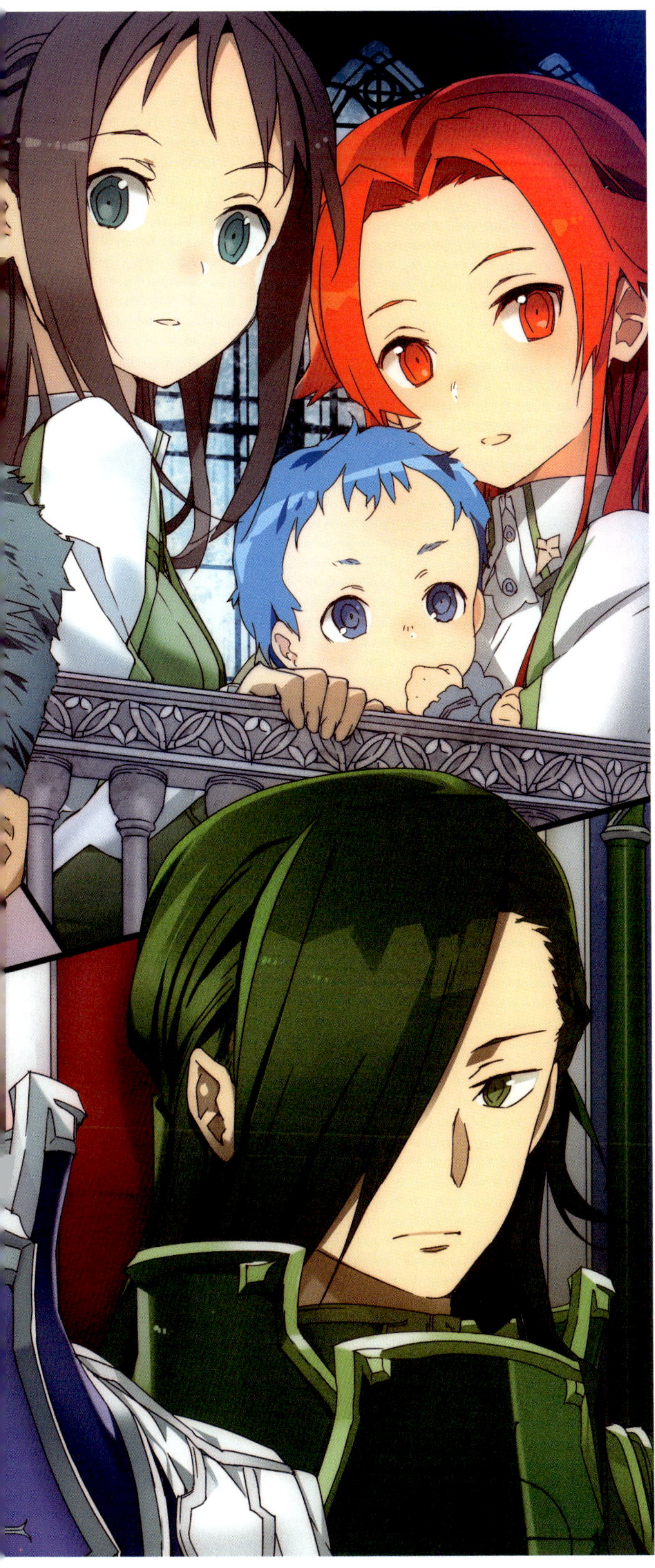

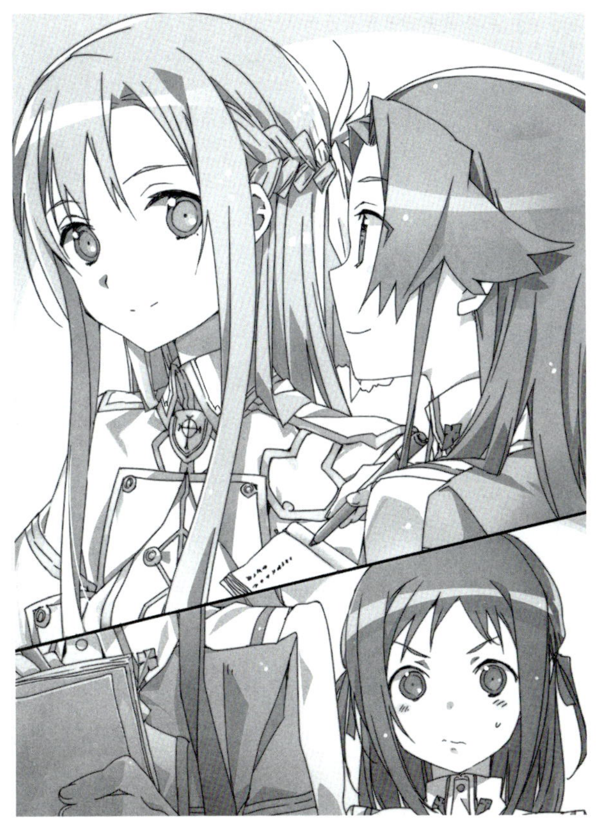

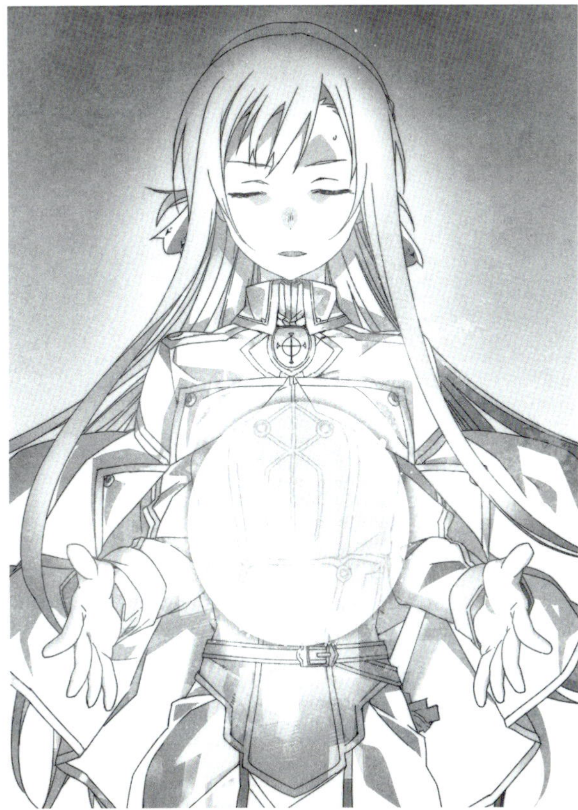

Dengeki Bunko
Sword Art Online 20:
Moon Cradle
Illustration: September 2017

Ronie's fun because her expression changes all the time. Hrrrg.

Dengeki Bunko
Sword Art Online 20: Moon Cradle
Frontispiece: September 2017

A pleasant group meal. Drawing a bunch of people eating at a table
is actually a fairly common illustration prompt, but it's rather hard.

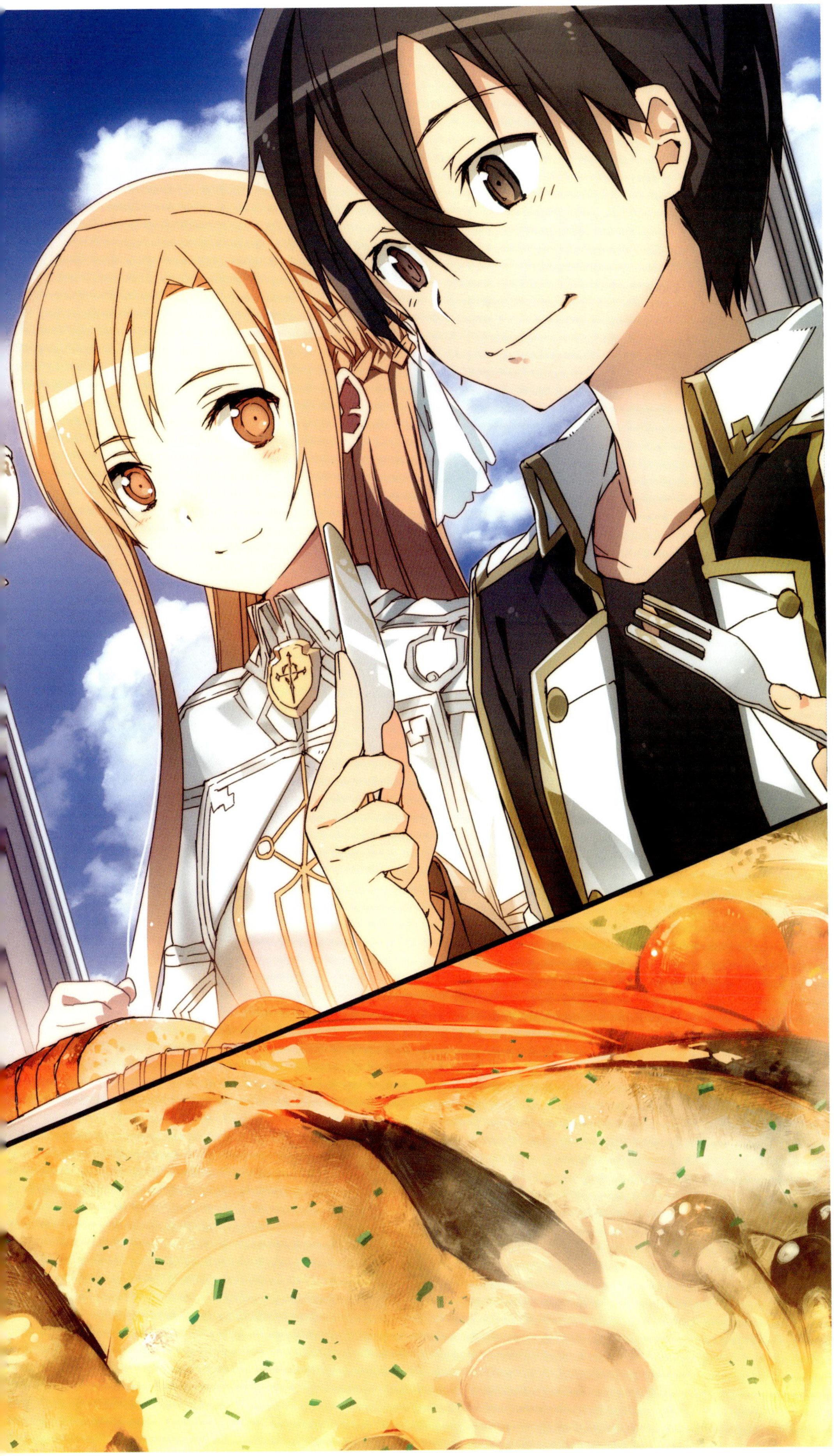

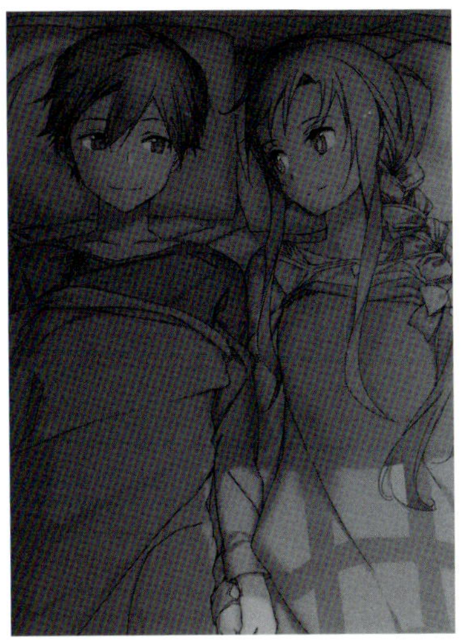

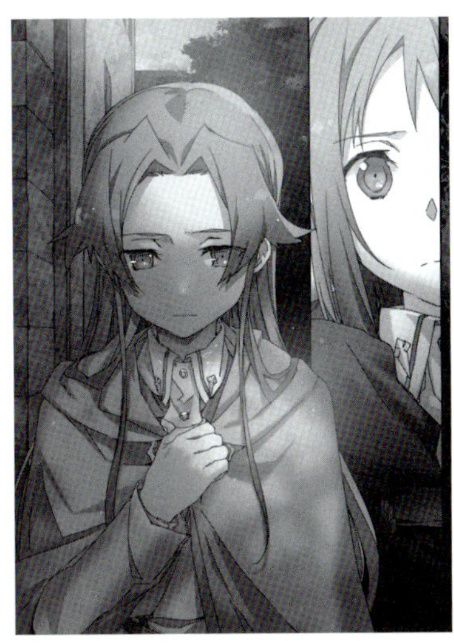

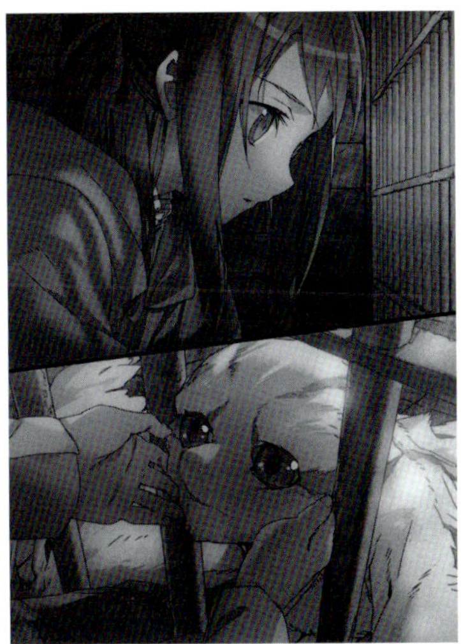

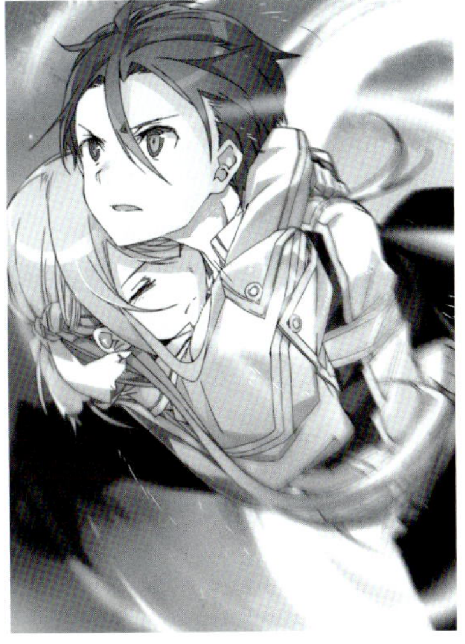

Dengeki Bunko
Sword Art Online 20: Moon Cradle
Illustration: September 2017

It's hard to depict flying through supernatural psychic powers, because in a still illustration, it just looks surreal. The pose they use when flying in *Dragon Ball*, with the fists extended, is really cool, but it doesn't fit here in *SAO*. It's easier when you can draw in a *whoosh!* sound effect, too.

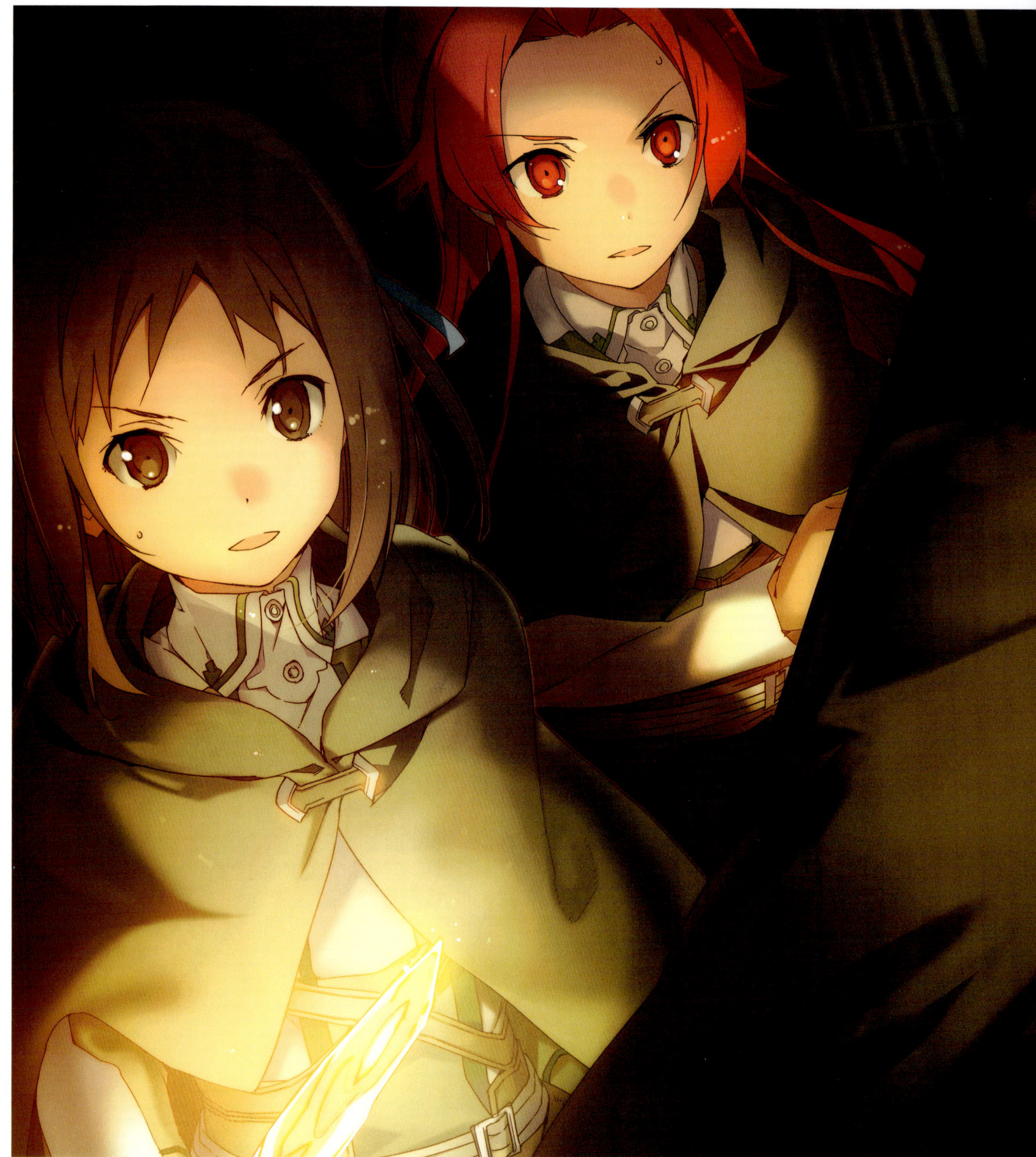

Dengeki Bunko
Sword Art Online 20: Moon Cradle
Frontispiece: September 2017

Ronie and Tiese face off against the mysterious black-robed figure.
It's tricky, because having a mystery black robe in darkness gives you
almost nothing to go off of. And in the Japanese *bunko* format, it's
pretty small. Thankfully, there's text that goes over this to draw your
attention.

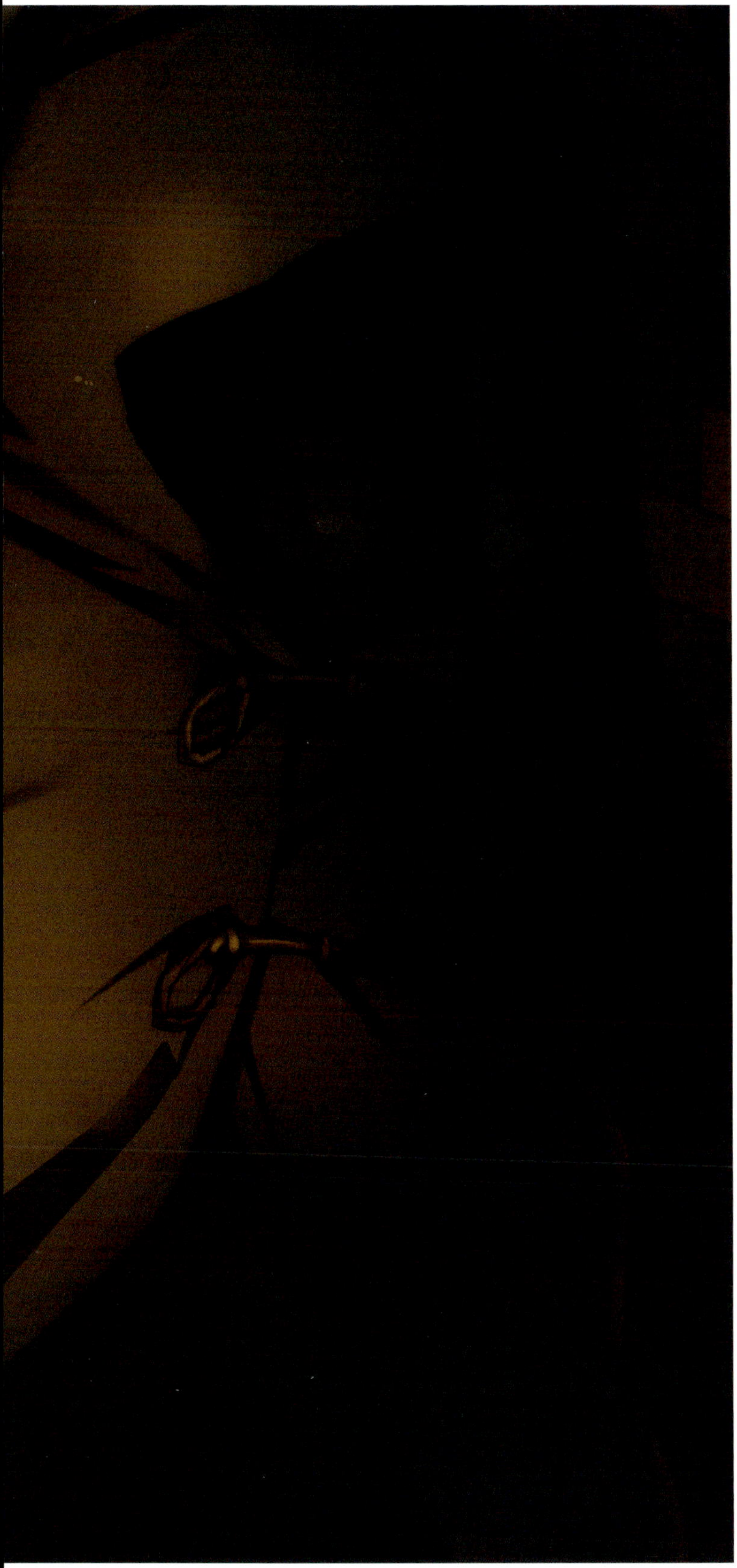

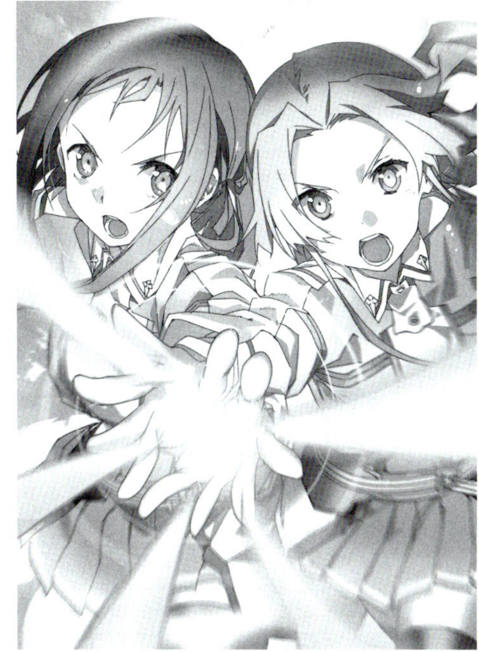

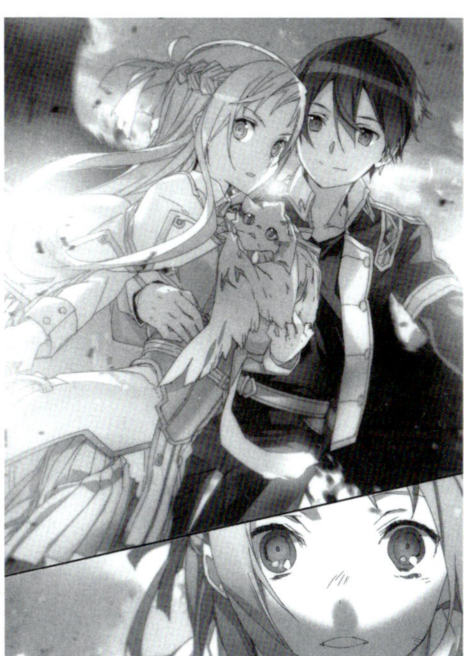

Dengeki Bunko
Sword Art Online 20: Moon Cradle
Illustration: September 2017

It's them! In the bottom illustration, it might look like Ronie is feeling inferior to the perfect couple, but that's not the point of the scene.

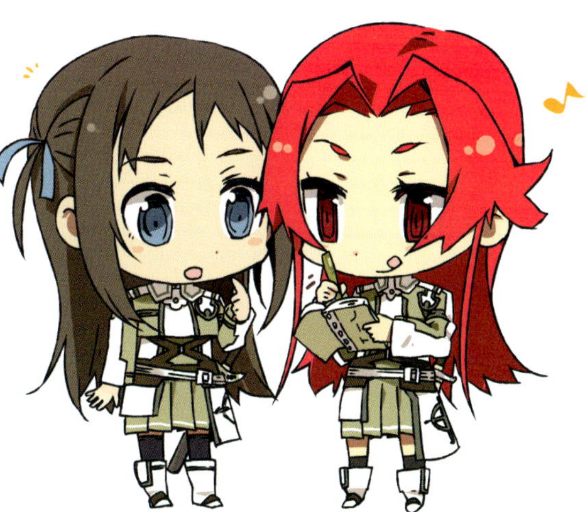

Dengeki Bunko
Sword Art Online 20: Moon Cradle
Rear Cover: September 2017

Tiese jotting down notes.

SWORD ART ONLINE media mix 2

Here's a collection of pieces I did in relation to the anime.

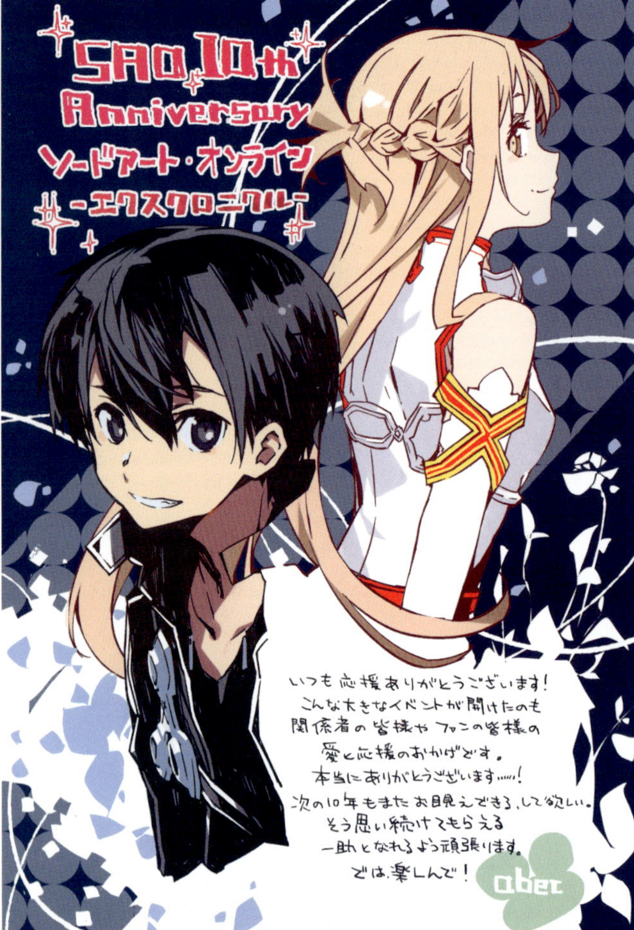

*Text: SAO 10th Anniversary / Sword Art Online / -EX-CHRONICLE-
"Thanks for all of your support! It's because of the love and
enthusiasm from the fans and the people involved that a big event
like this is possible. Thank you so much for making it happen! I
hope that we're able to see another big anniversary in 10 more
years. And I'll do my best to make that happen. Have fun!"*

Sword Art Online -EX-CHRONICLE- Event
Submitted Illustration: August 2019

This was a submission to an in-person *SAO* event. It's fun to do offline
events because they put so much effort into them.

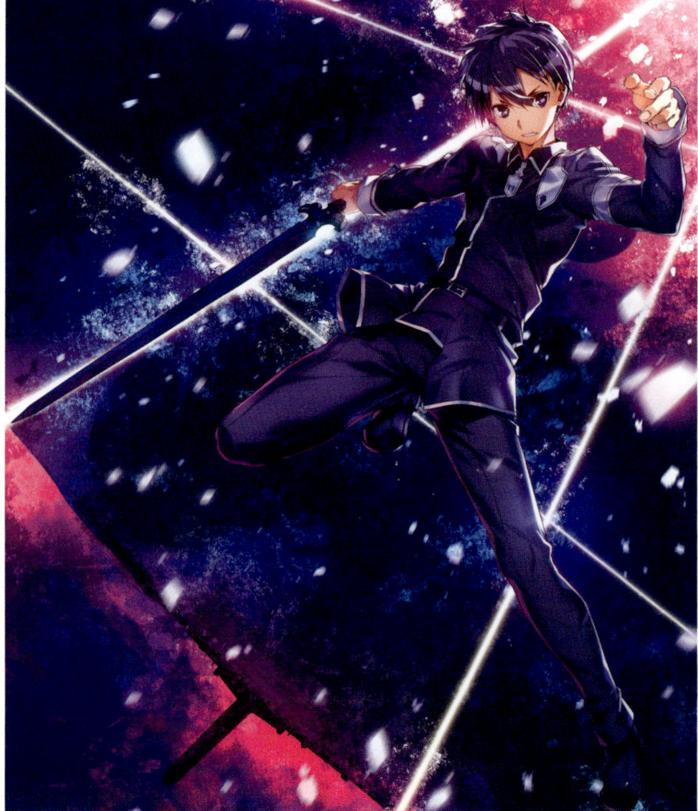

TV Animation *Sword Art Online Alicization*
1st Cour Opening Song
LiSA - ADAMAS
Limited Edition Jacket Illustration: December 2018

This was a CD jacket with only Kirito on the cover, but
they wanted it to be a fold-out poster, so that the top
right corner with Kirito's face would be the part that
faces outward. I remember struggling to come up with a
composition that made use of all that space.

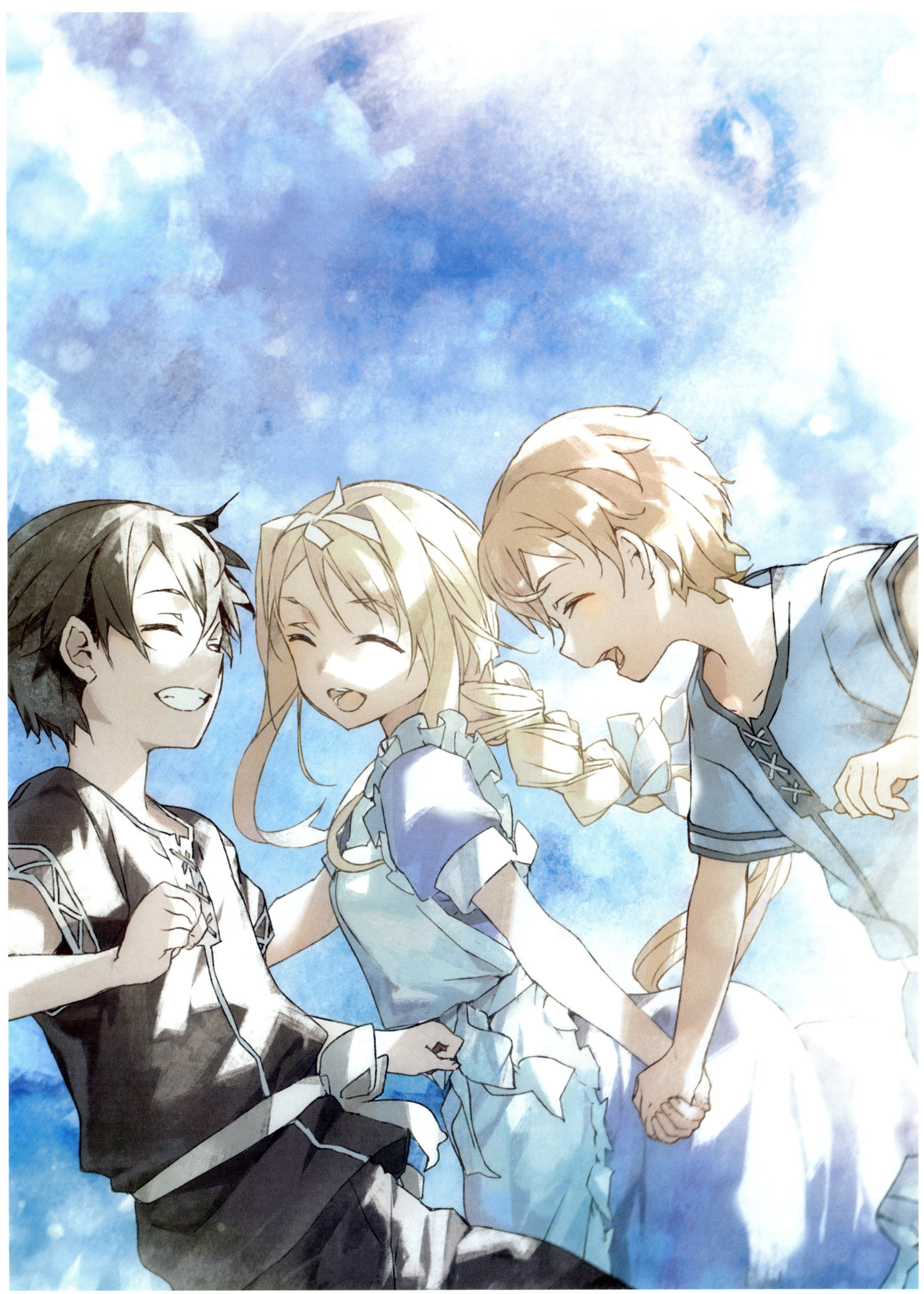

TV Animation, *Sword Art Online Alicization: War of the Underworld*
Episode 23 Special Promotion Illustration: September 2020

If you visit the IP address that appears in the episode,
it brings up a page with this illustration.

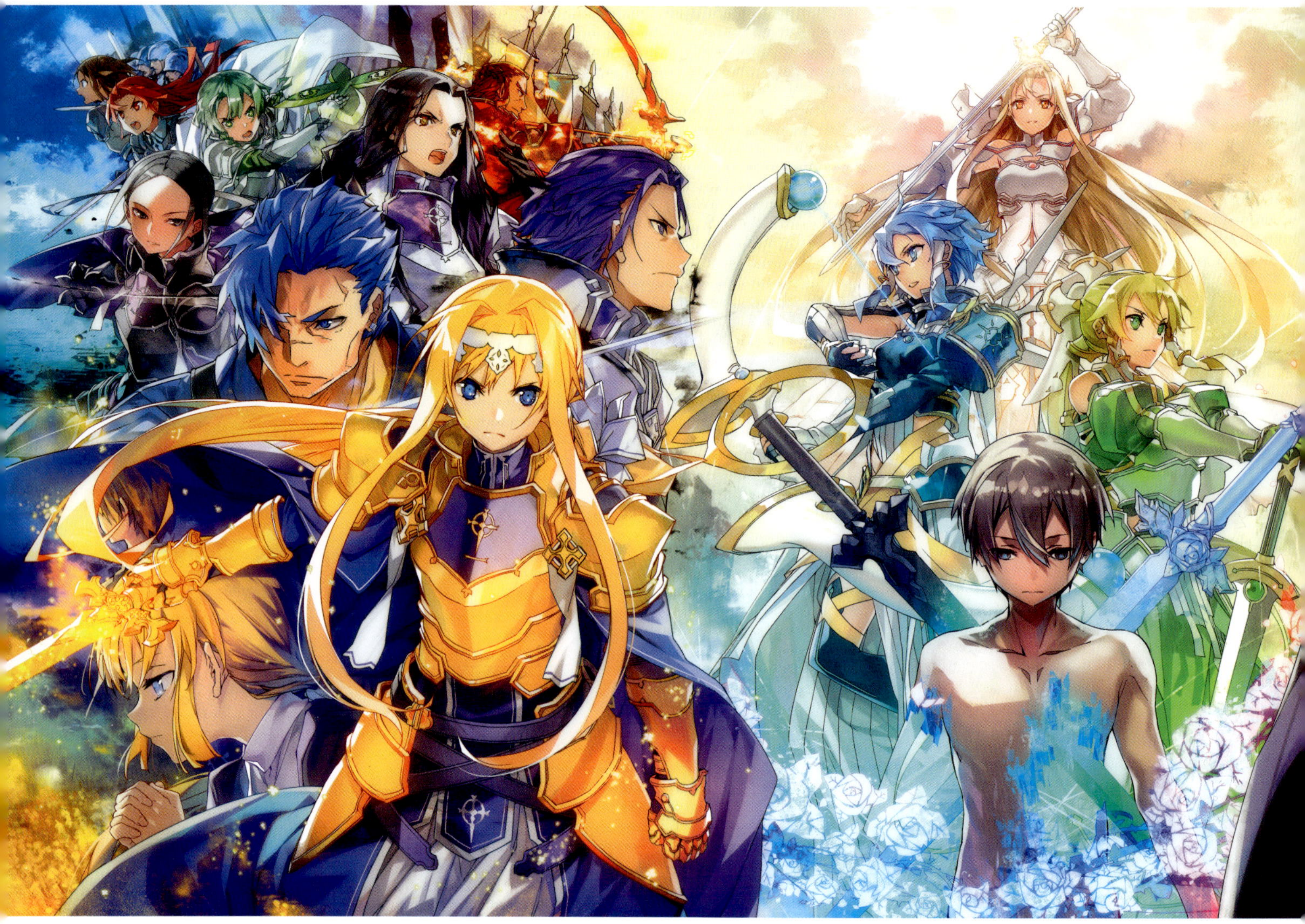

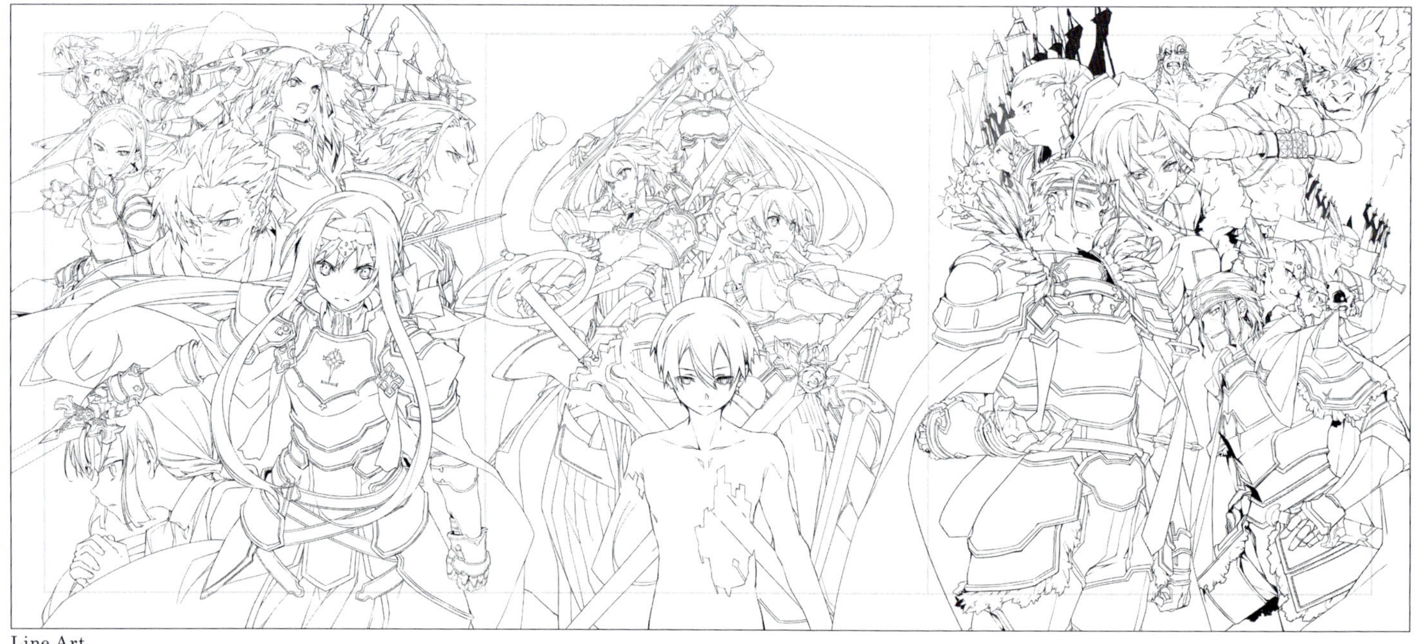

TV Animation, *Sword Art Online Alicization: War of the Underworld* BD/DVD, Vol. 1
Limited Edition *War of the Underworld* Box Illustration: December 2019

I was absolutely determined to draw this illustration. I've been doing lots of disc box art along these lines, but in this case, I really crushed it. It was really, really hard, but I'm glad I did it.

Line Art

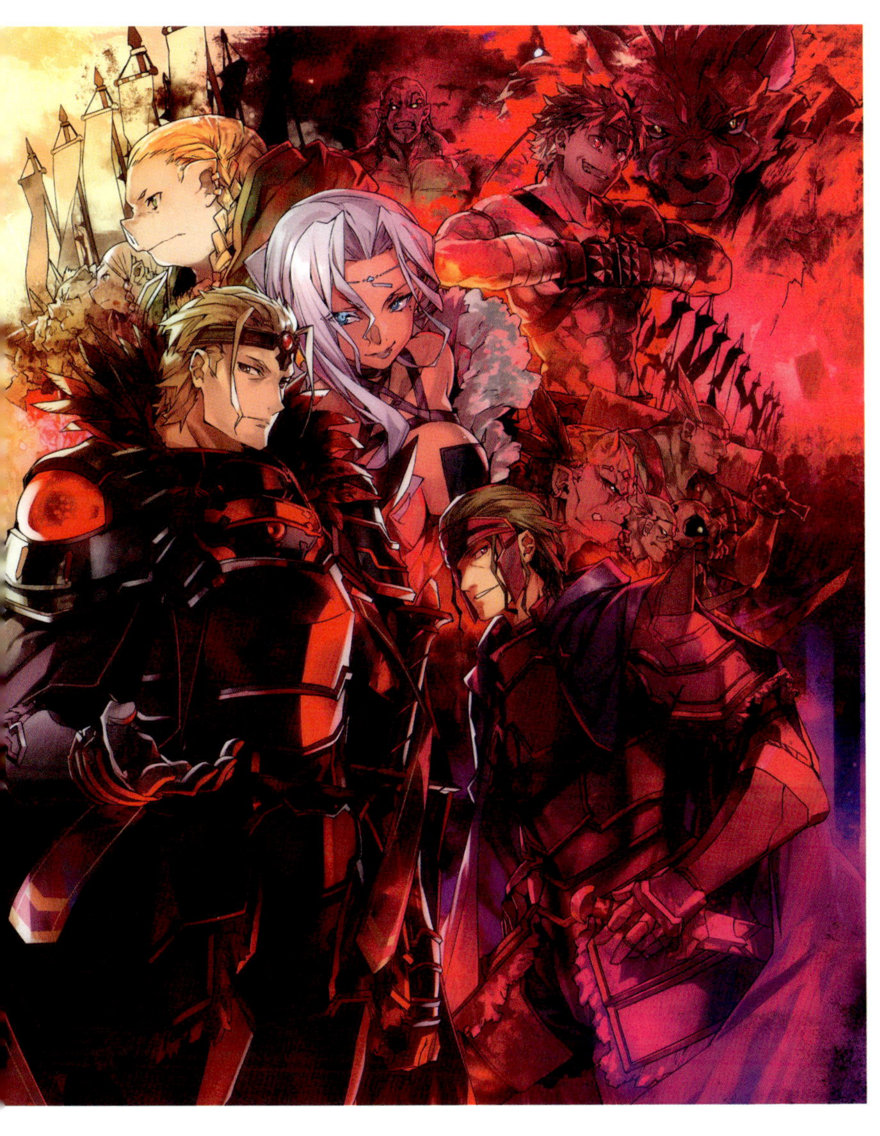

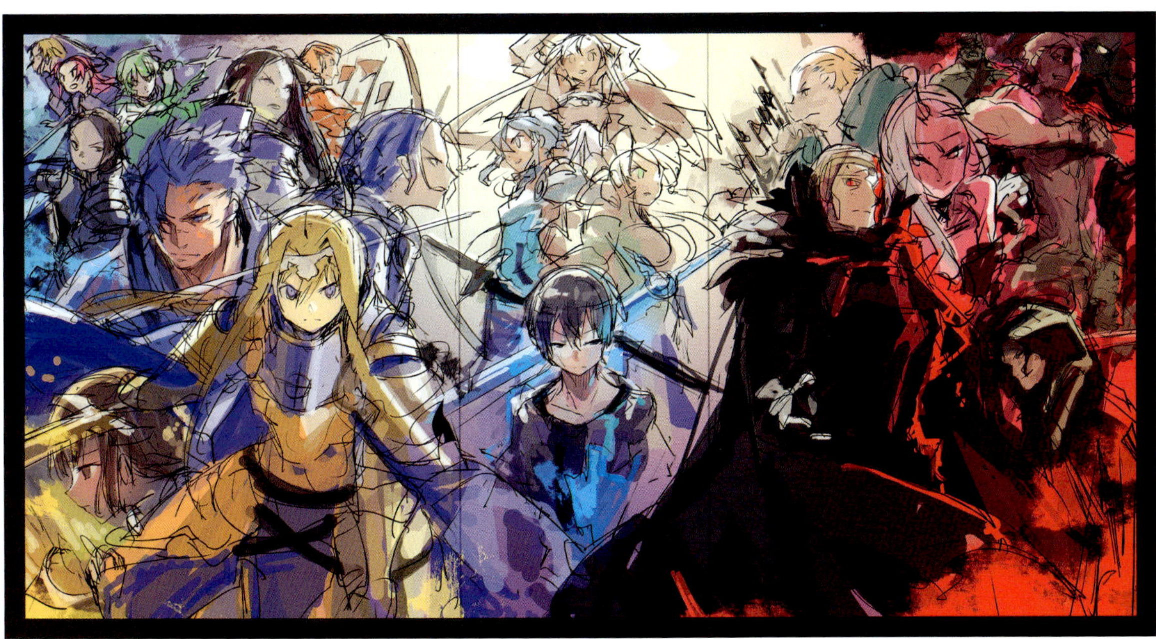

Rough Sketch

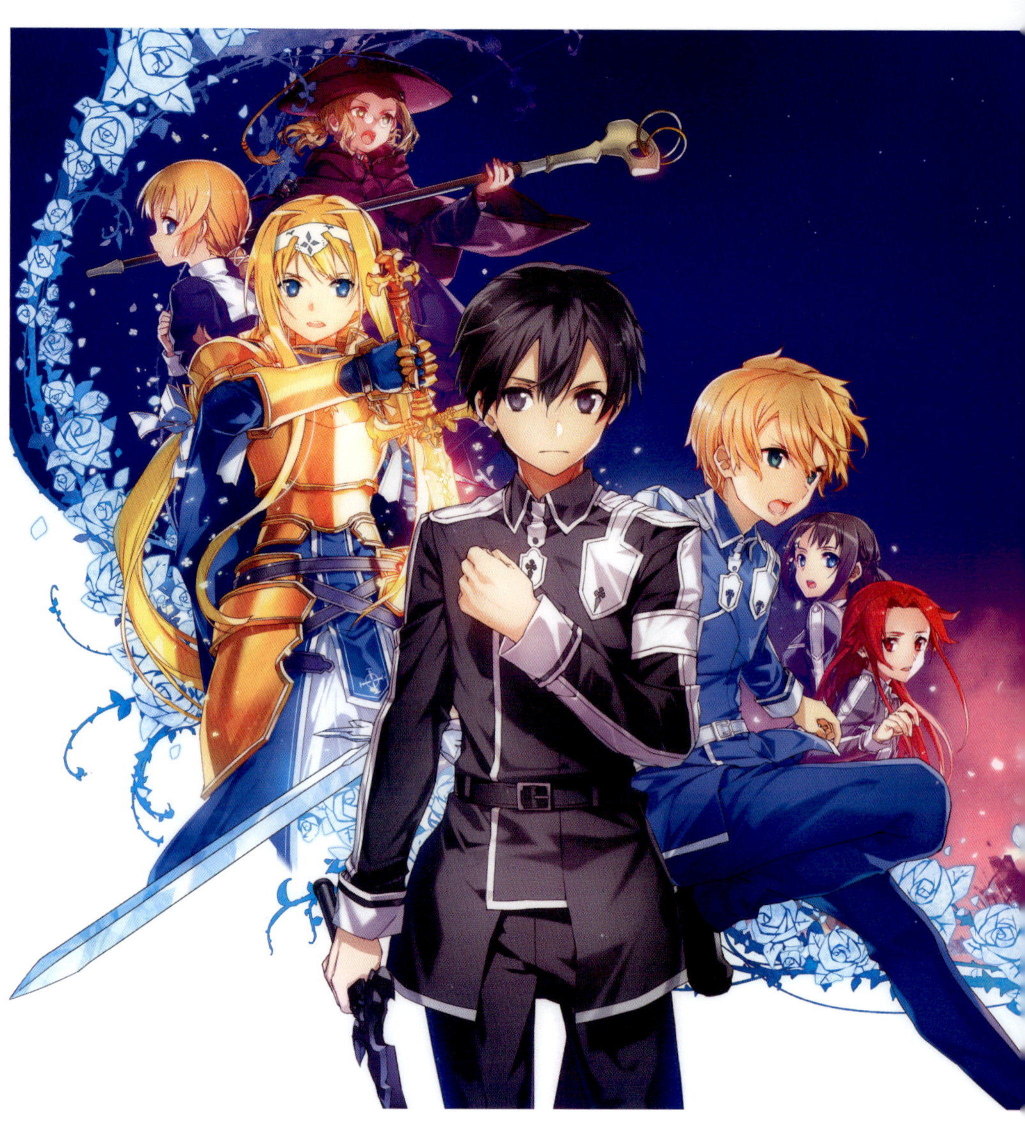

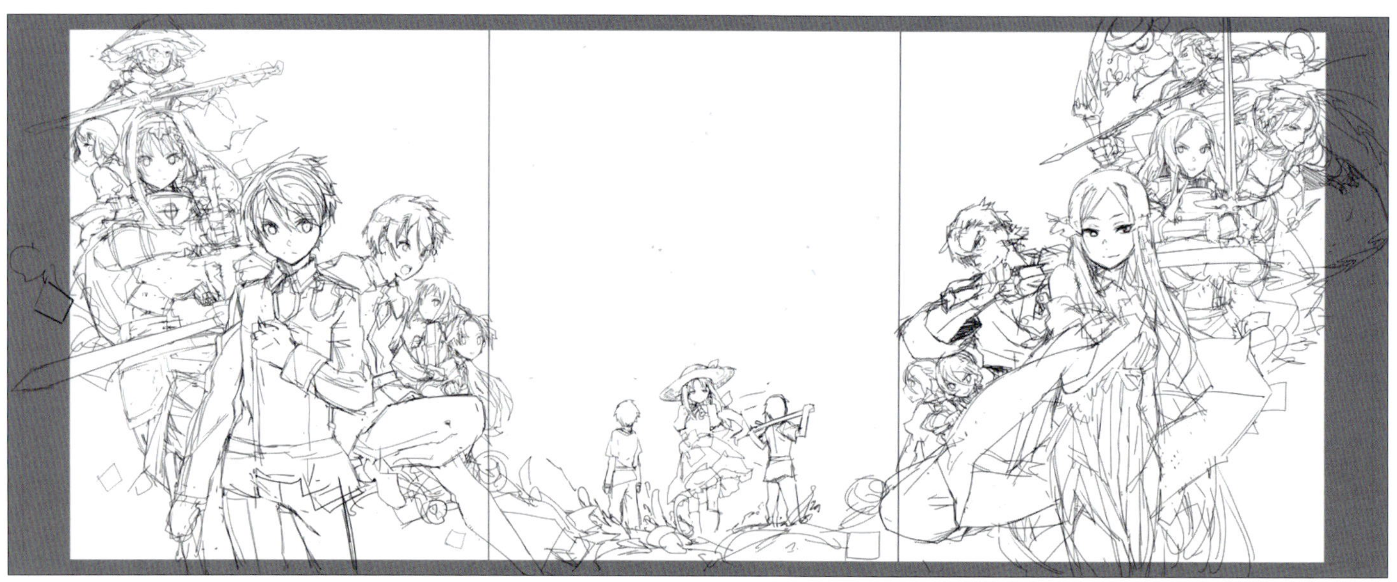

Rough Sketch

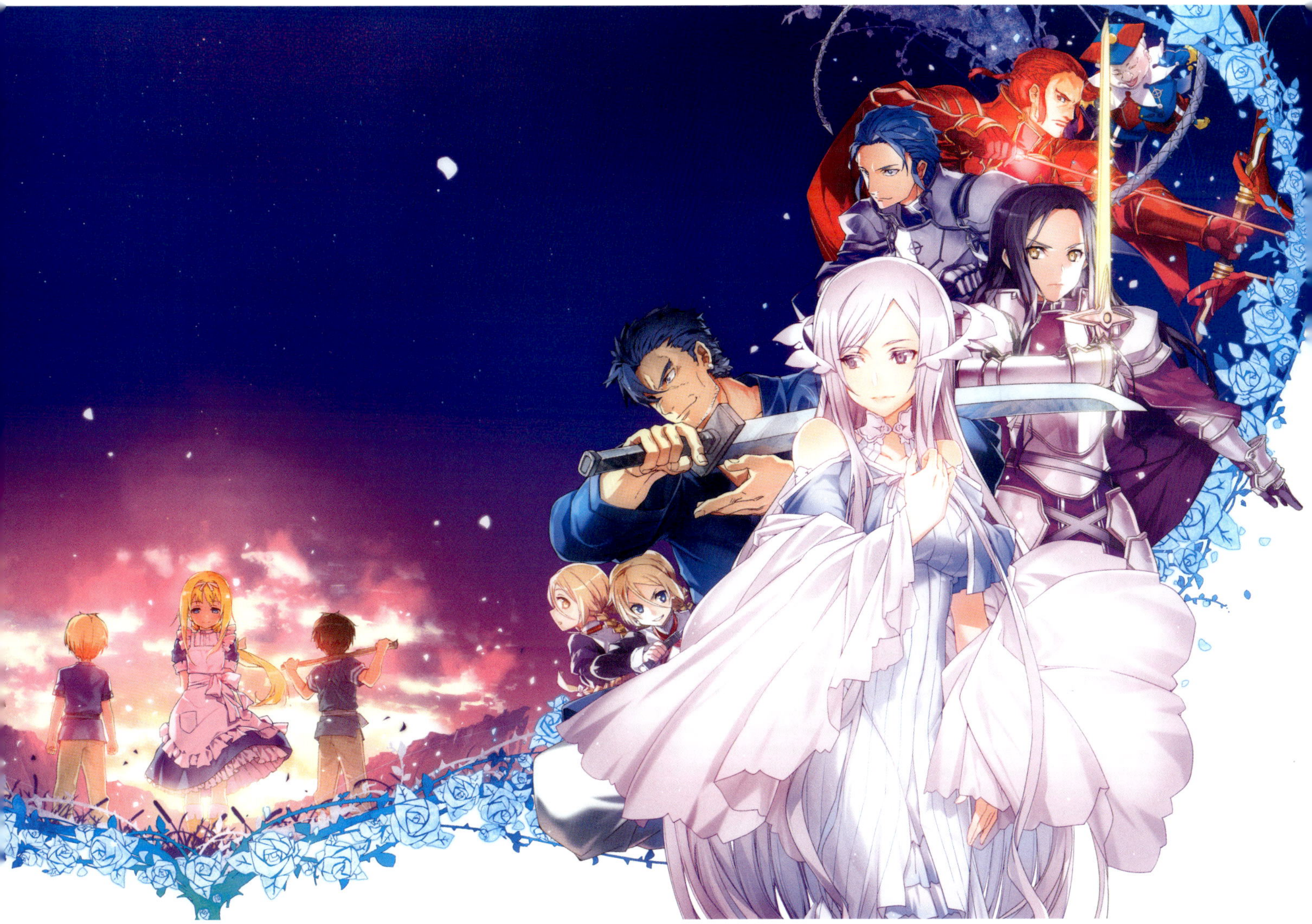

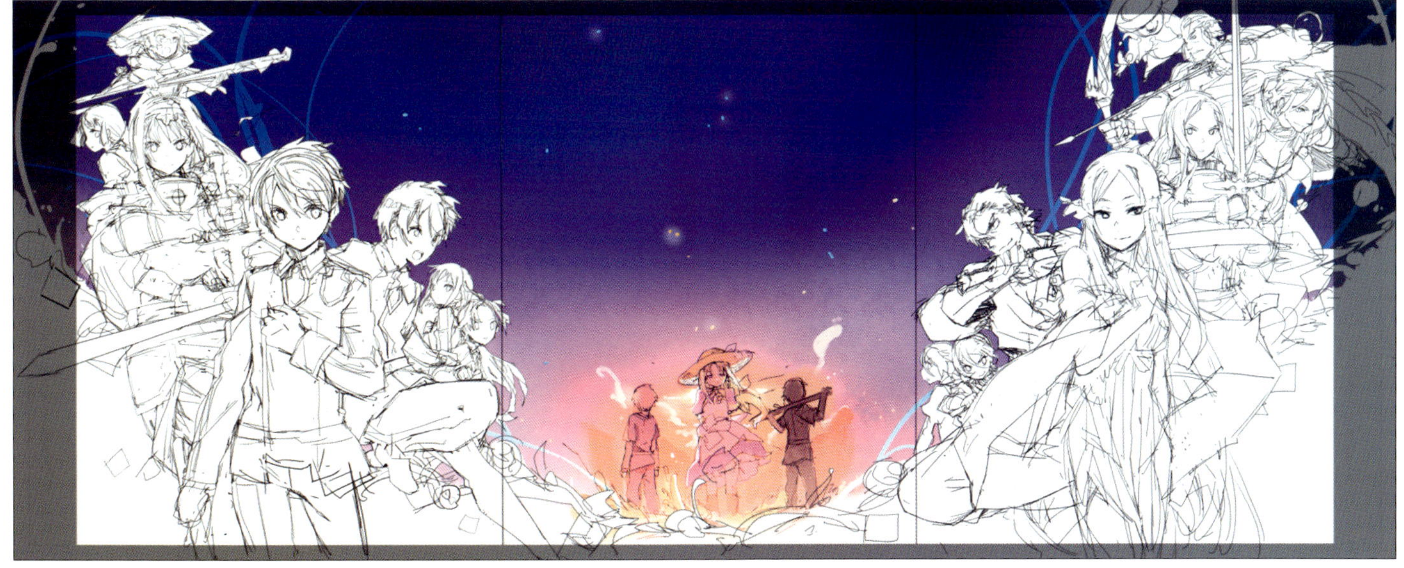

**TV Animation, *Sword Art Online Alicization*
BD/DVD, Vol. 2**
Limited Edition Human Realm Box Illustration: February 2019

If you look at the *Underworld* box set first, the empty space here seems very noticeable. See, I thought they would put some text in the upper right corner above Kirito's head, like the books do, but instead, they only put the text over young Alice instead. The space! All that space! This is why you make sure you indicate your intentions to other designers.

Rough Sketch

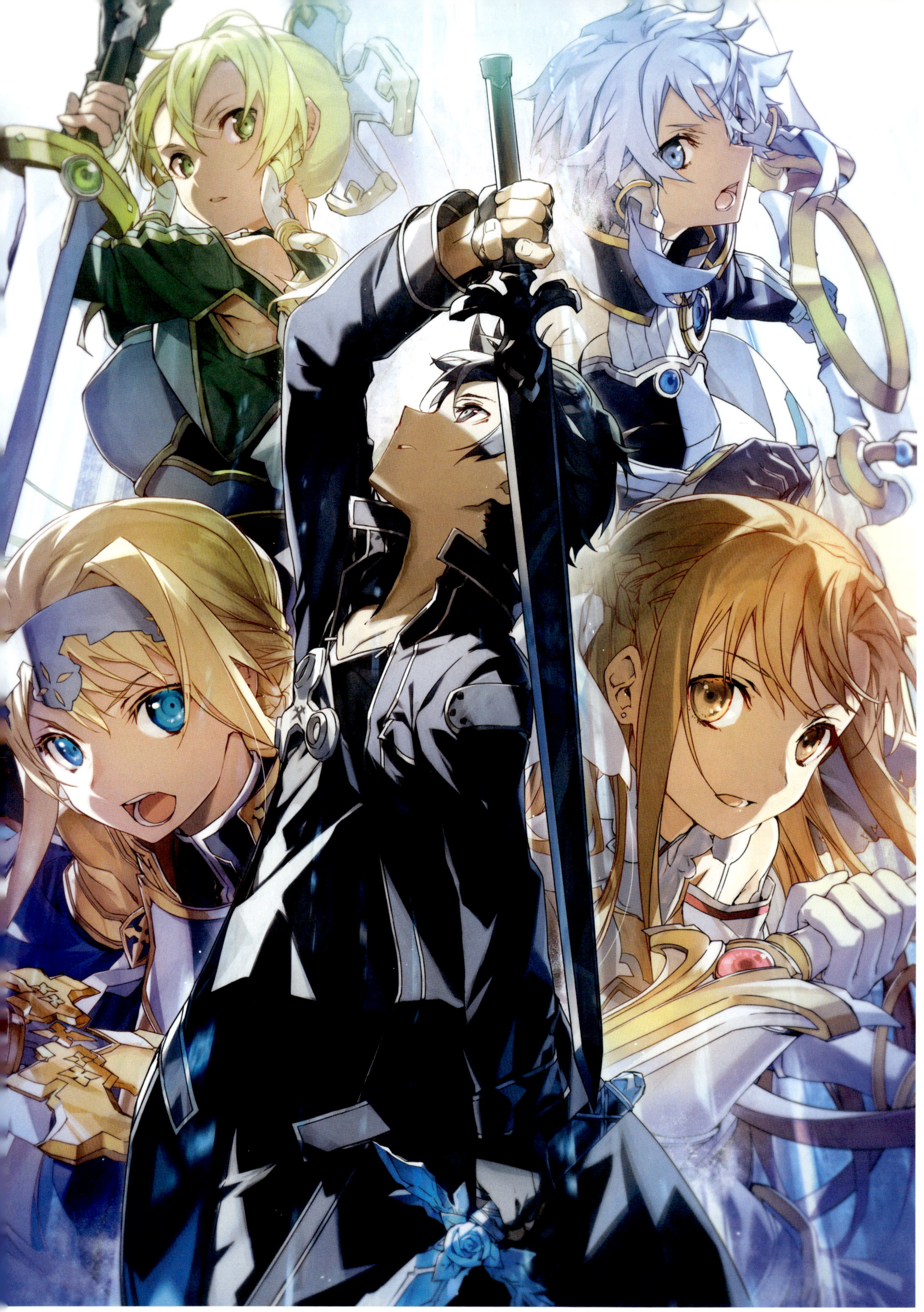

TV Animation, *Sword Art Online Alicization: War of the Underworld*
BD/DVD Series Purchase Bonus B2 Tapestry: December 2019

This is definitely one of my favorite pieces. I've realized that I really like being
able to set my own light sources and draw the shadows where I want them.

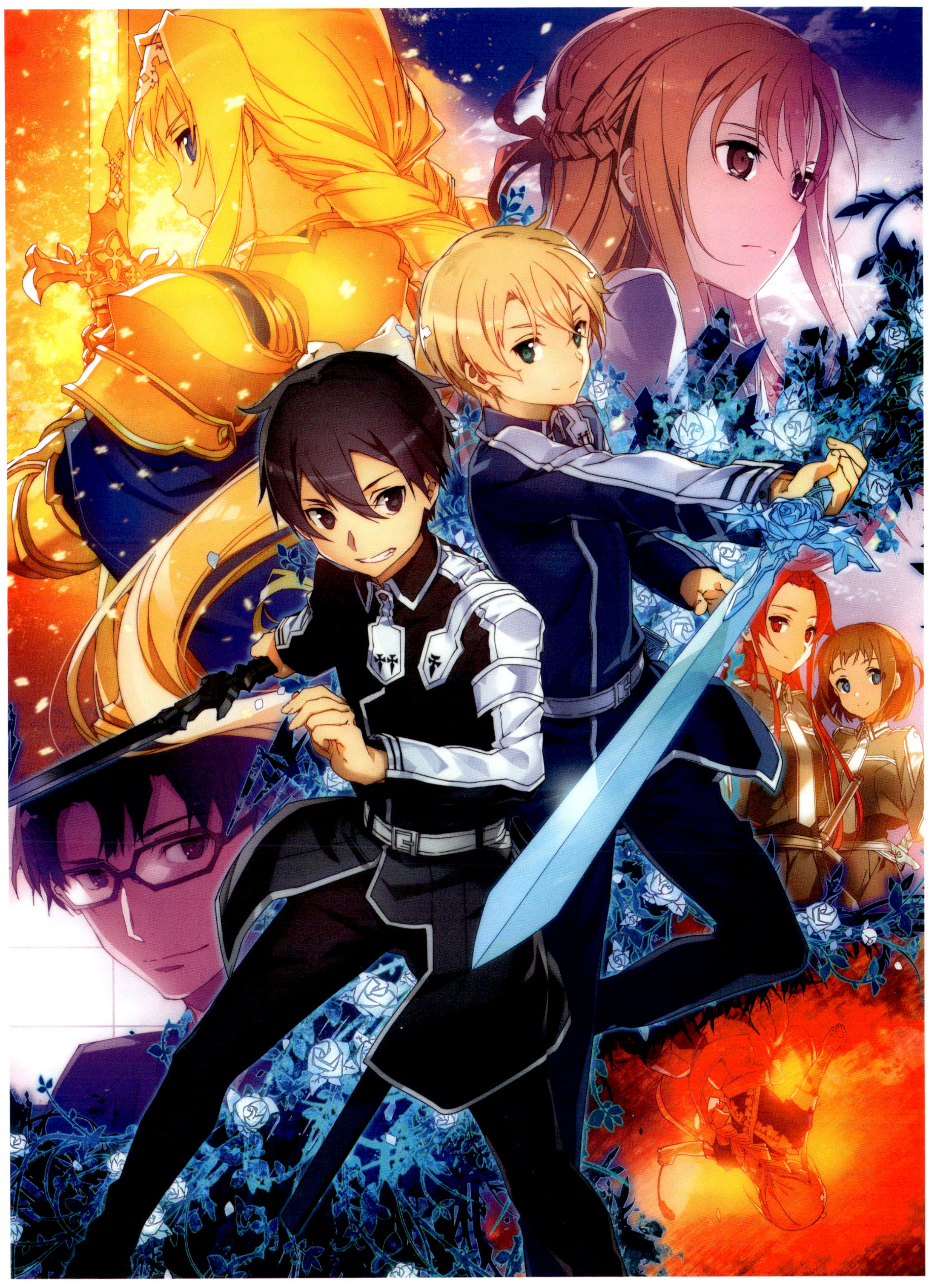

TV Animation, *Sword Art Online Alicization*
Initial Key Visual: October 2017

This is a key visual, meaning it's supposed to represent the characters and the general aesthetic of the show. I like the way I used the roses here.

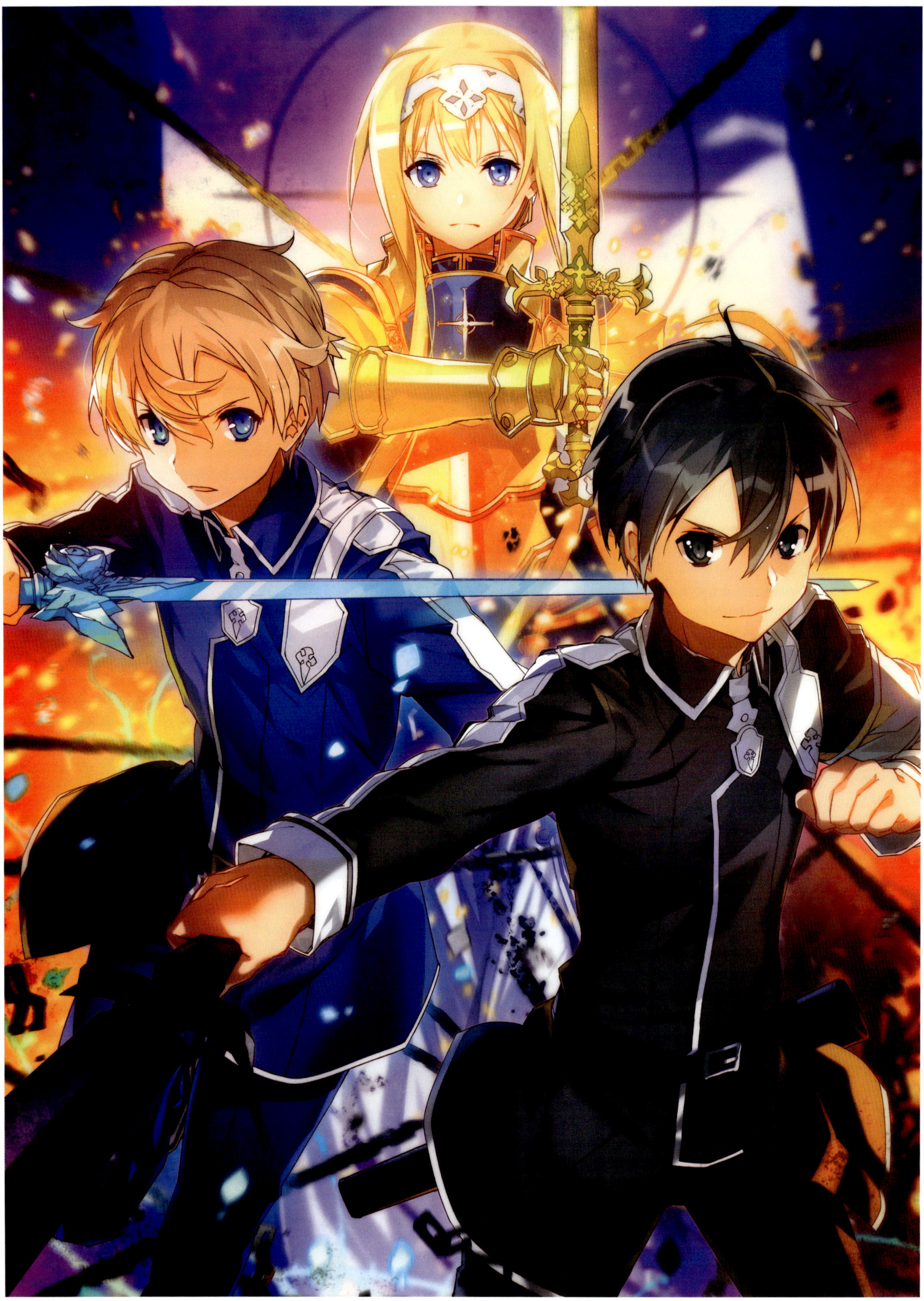

This bonus illustration needed to be these three, so it's more on the serious side. I don't remember all the details, but I think the chains were an important theme here.

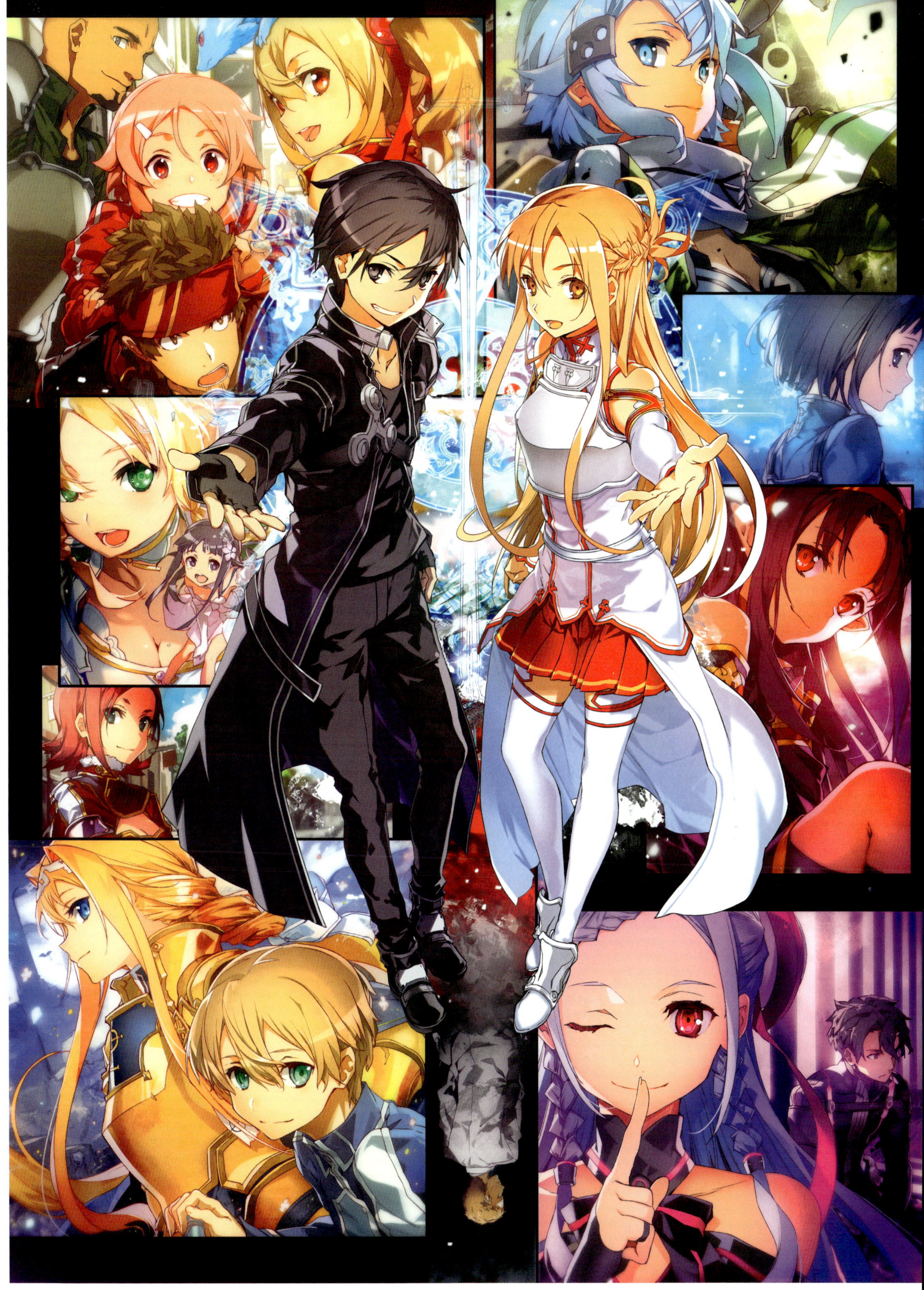

Sword Art Online -EX-CHRONICLE- Event
Key Visual: March 2019

An illustration for the -EX-CHRONICLE- in-person event. Since it's called "chronicle," I wanted to put characters from all the story arcs in it. Might be a bit overstuffed, but I pulled it off.

SWORD ART ONLINE
Unital Ring

The first volume of a new story arc, tackling a new VRMMO survival game. In terms of illustration work, everyone gets an equipment redesign. Also, Alice gets big fluffy ears. It's cute.

Dengeki Bunko
Sword Art Online 21:
Unital Ring I
Cover: December 2018

Is it just me, or does Kirito look way off in armor, since he's usually in light gear? I was thinking, based on the type of game they're in this time, that maybe it would be better not to design them like a Japanese game, but more in the Western game style. I just remember that the notes were "Make sure they're not too boring."

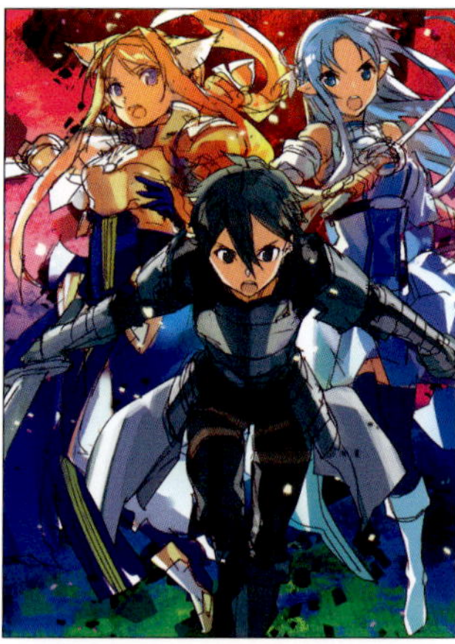

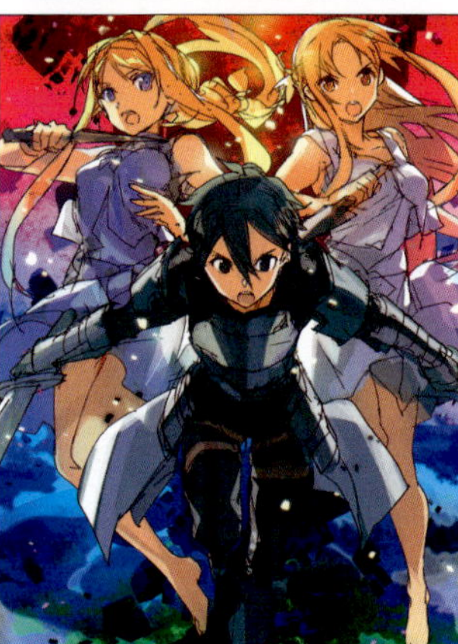

Alternate Cover Sketches

Dengeki Bunko
Sword Art Online 21: Unital Ring I
Illustration: December 2018

The moment he materializes his sword on his back, Kirito falls over from the weight and clings to their belts. It's one of those "Why are you grabbing that?" "Nice job, dude!" scenes. This is the kind of crime the veteran hero in the 21st volume can get away with.

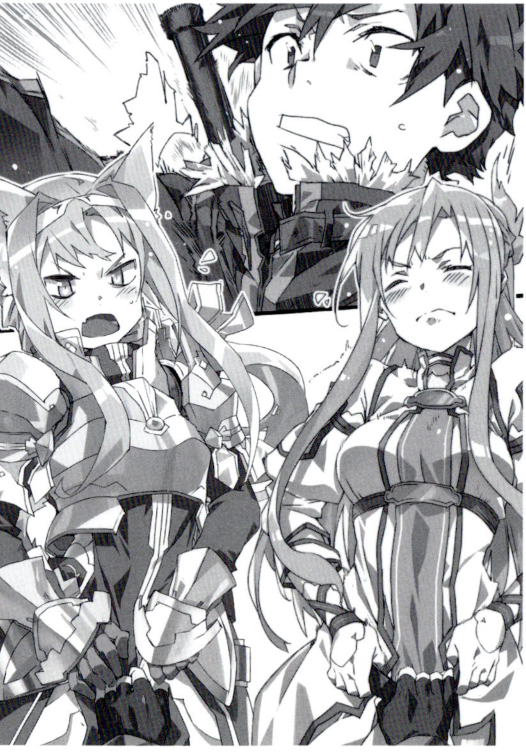

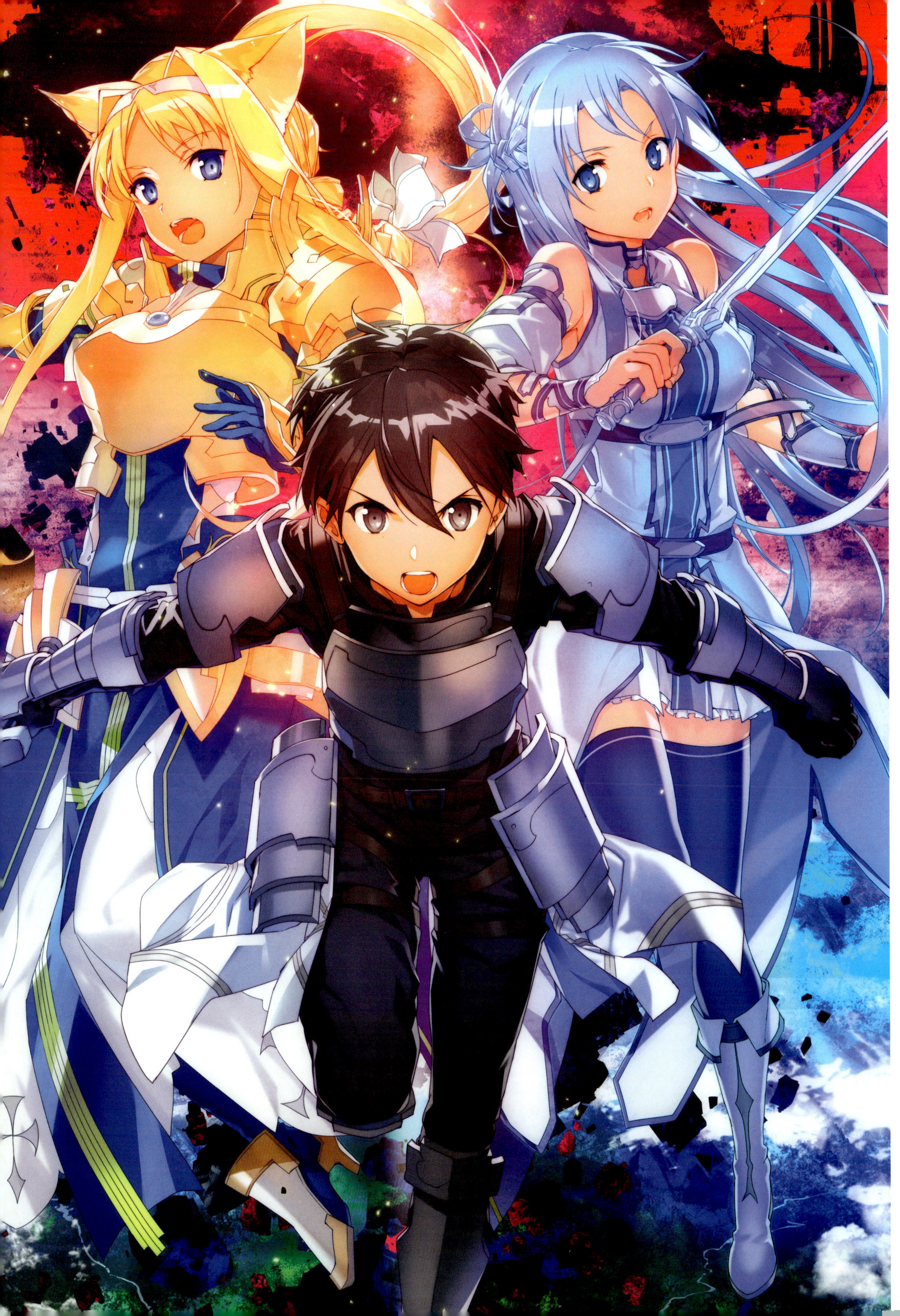

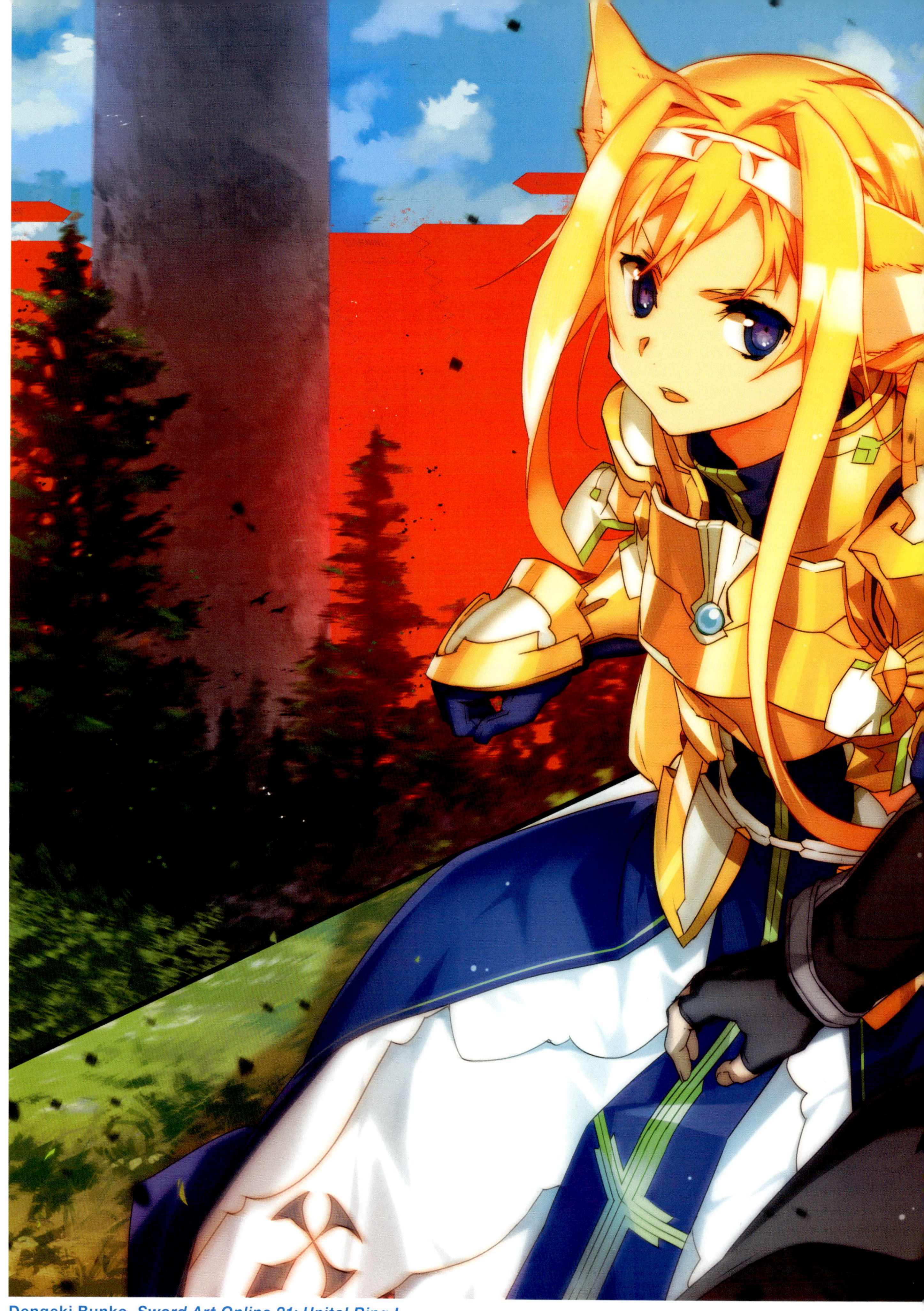

Dengeki Bunko, *Sword Art Online 21: Unital Ring I*
Frontispiece: December 2018

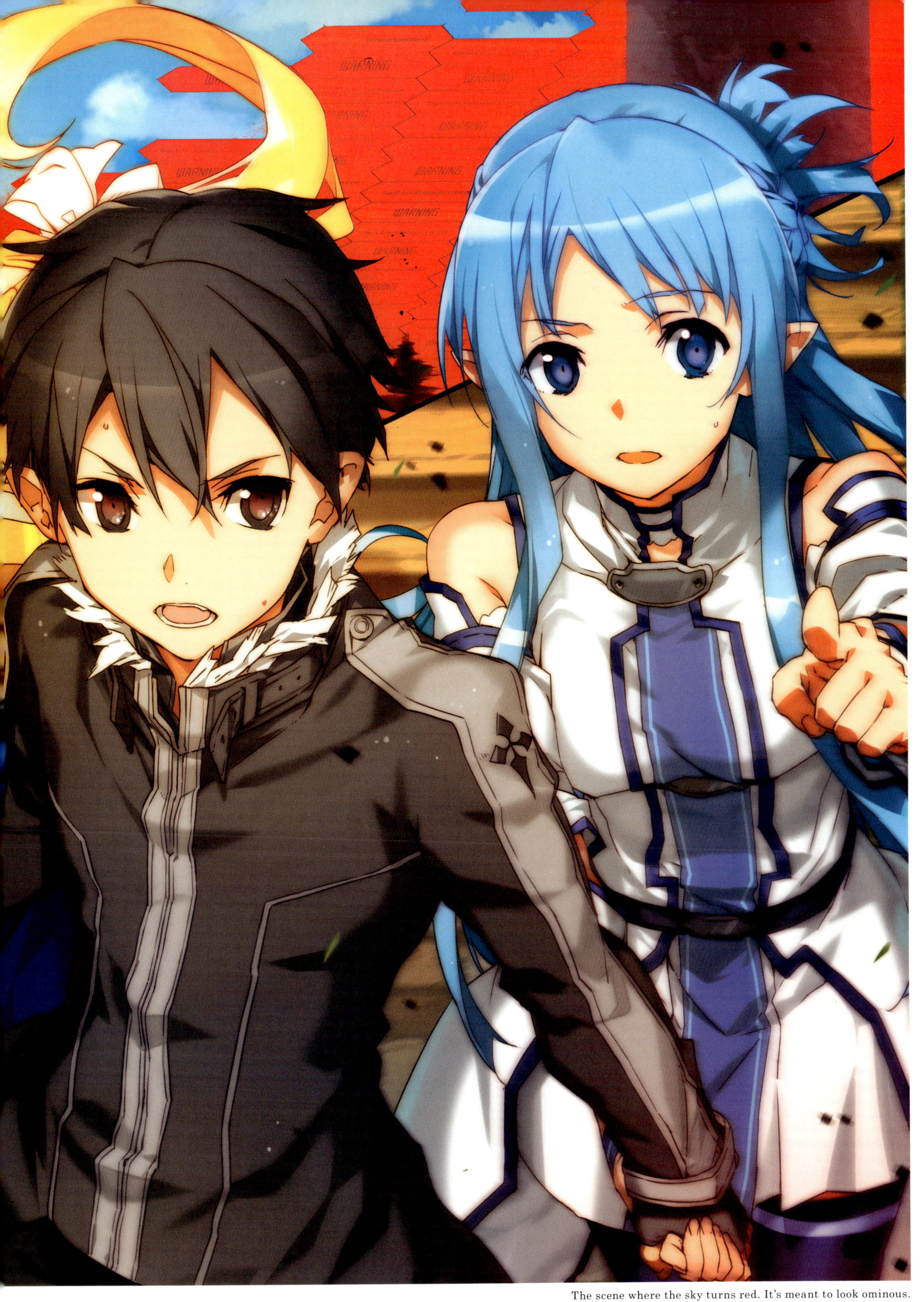

The scene where the sky turns red. It's meant to look ominous.

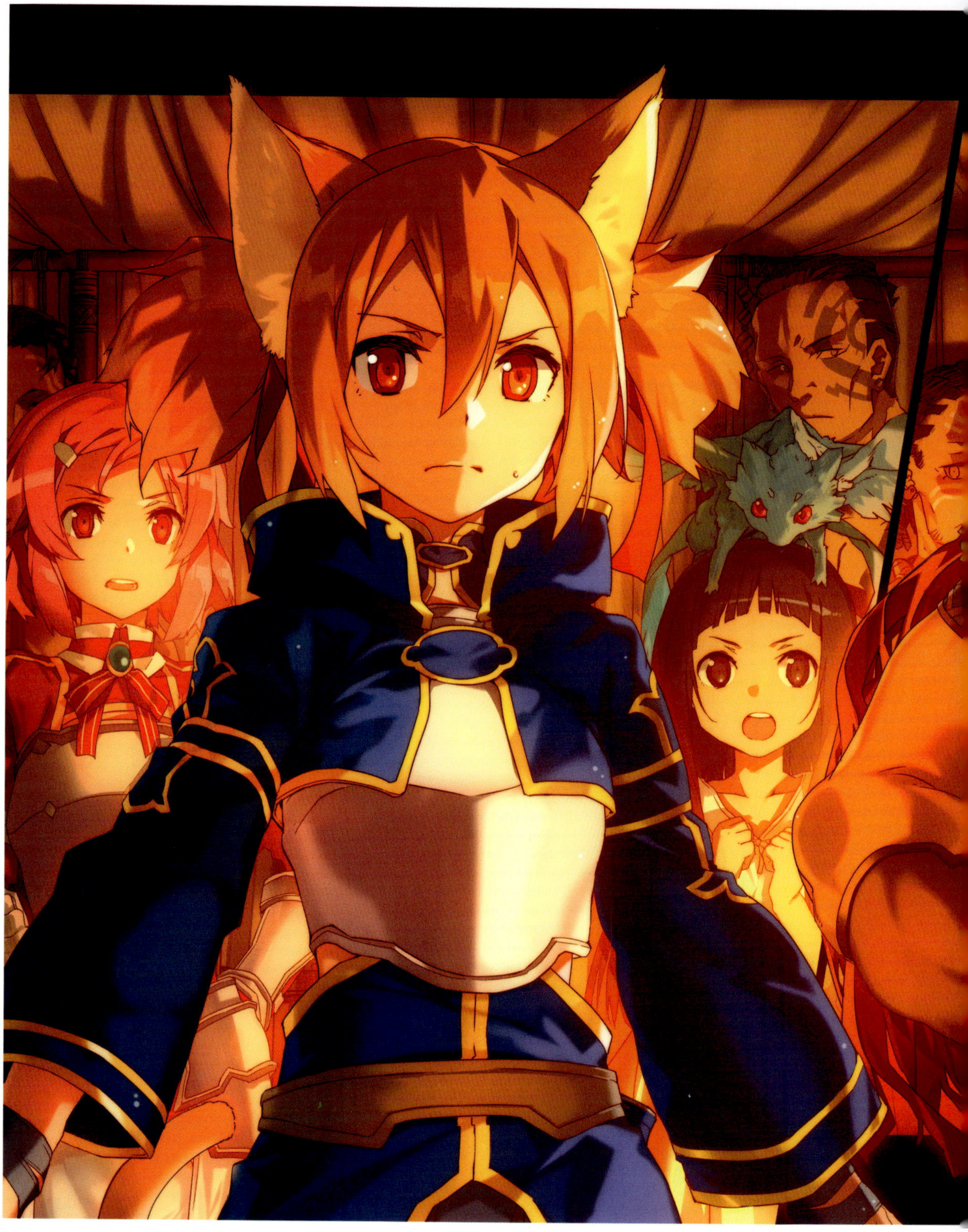

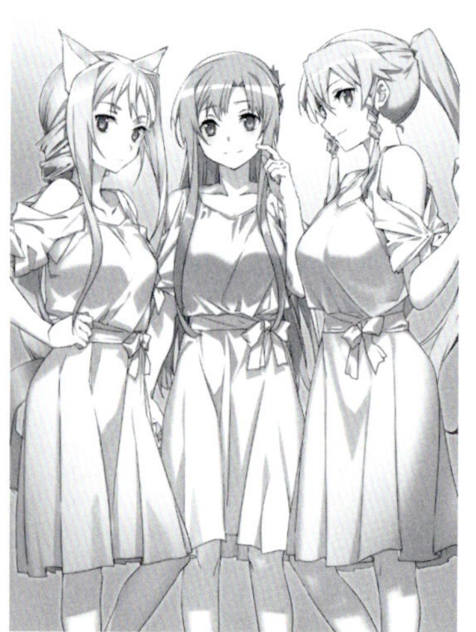

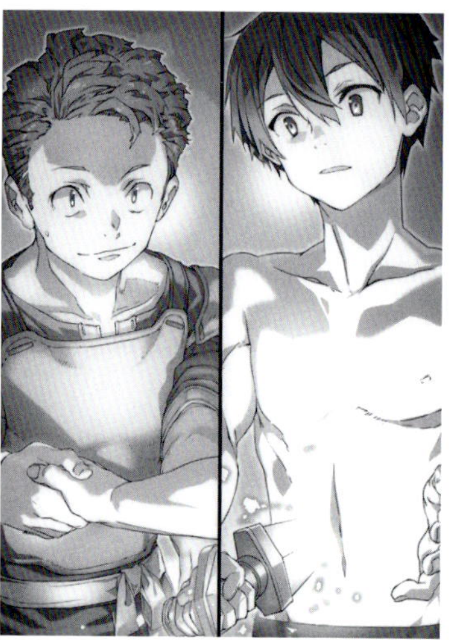

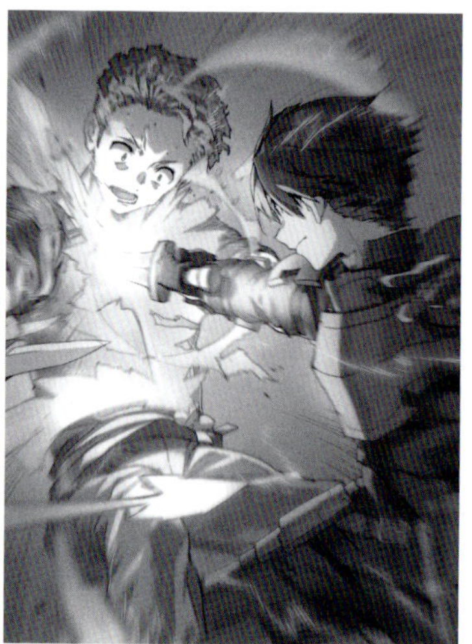

**Dengeki Bunko,
*Sword Art Online 21:
Unital Ring I***
Illustration: December 2018

In this new arc, there's not even any civilization, much less gear, but you don't want to be too plain, or it'll be boring... It's tricky. When illustrating a story about a game, it's truly a difficult task to design the game's starter equipment when you don't know where the story is going and what the overall design of the game will be when it's finished.

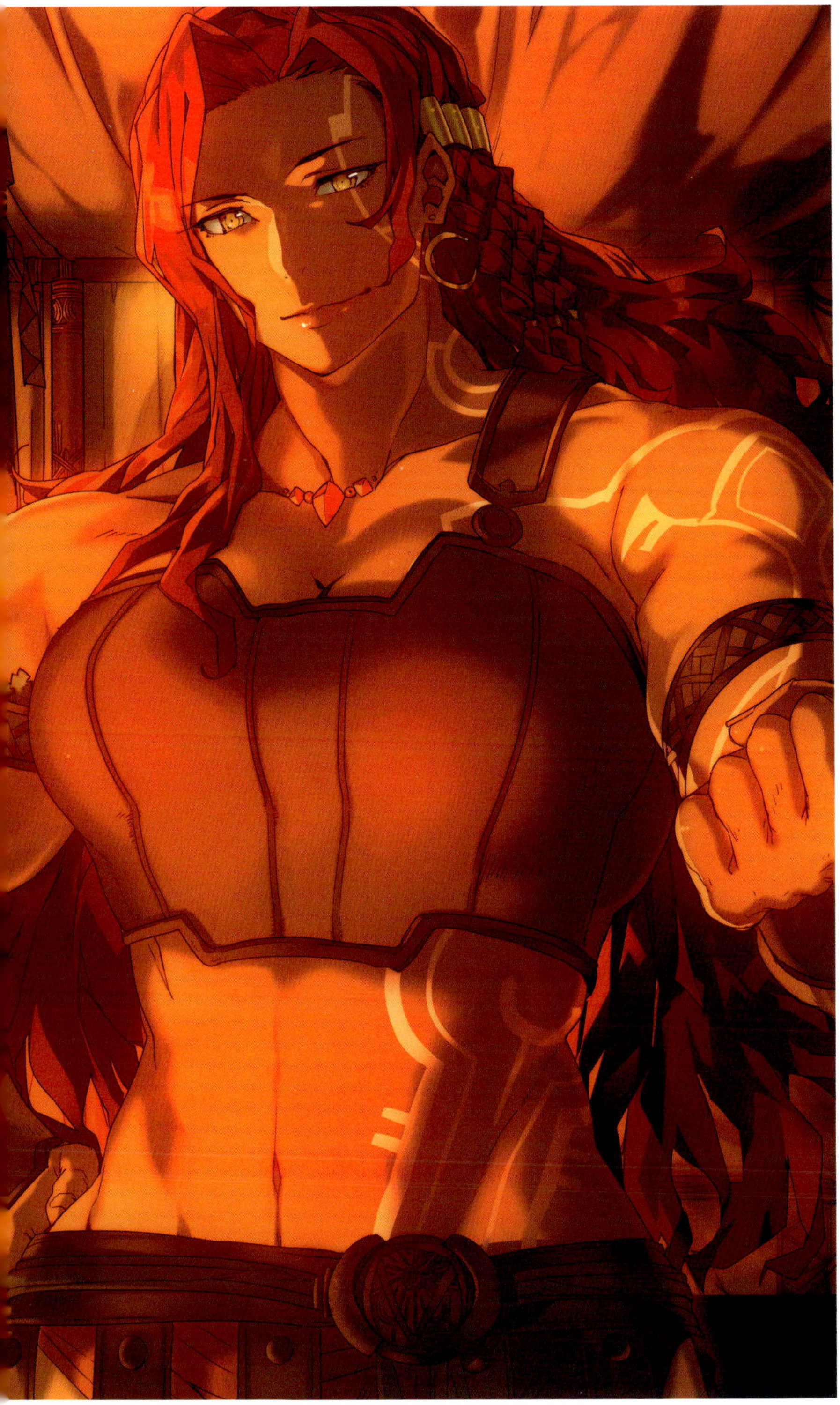

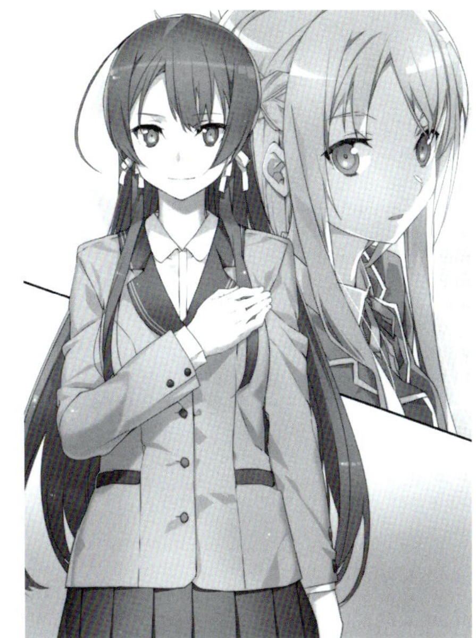

Dengeki Bunko,
Sword Art Online 21: Unital Ring I
Illustration: December 2018

Two pics from the real world. I remember that fans were more excited about seeing Argo than the new character, Shikimi Kamura.

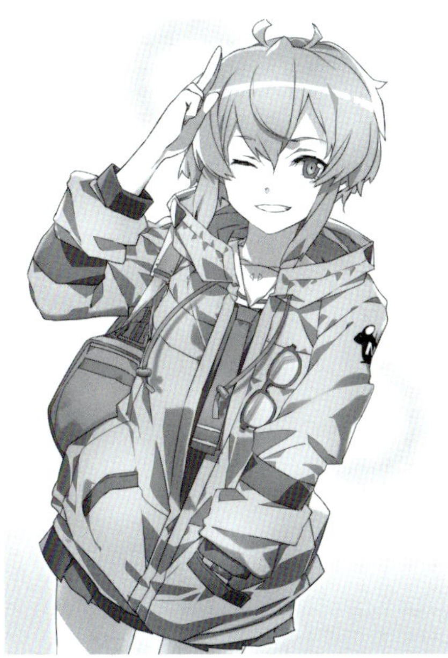

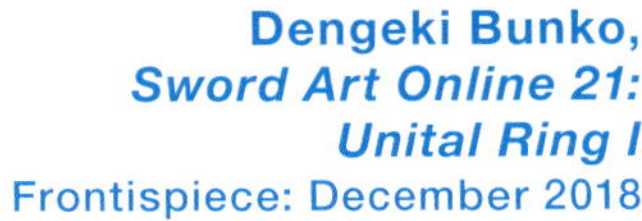

Dengeki Bunko,
Sword Art Online 21:
Unital Ring I
Frontispiece: December 2018

Silica faces off against Yzelma and the Bashin. Their ranks would be so different in real life. Is this the first muscle babe we've had in *SAO*?

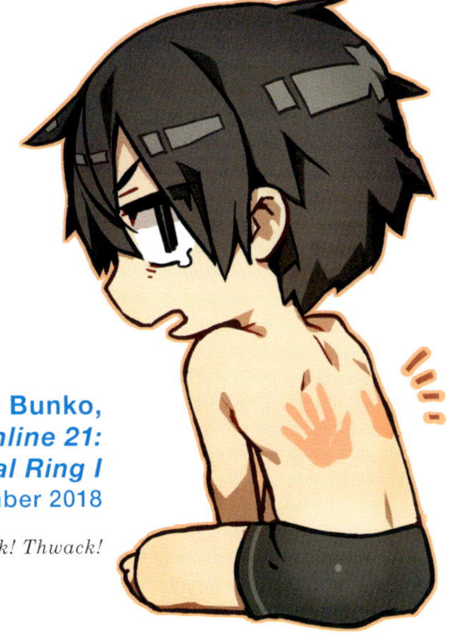

Dengeki Bunko,
Sword Art Online 21:
Unital Ring I
Rear Cover: December 2018

Thwack! Thwack!

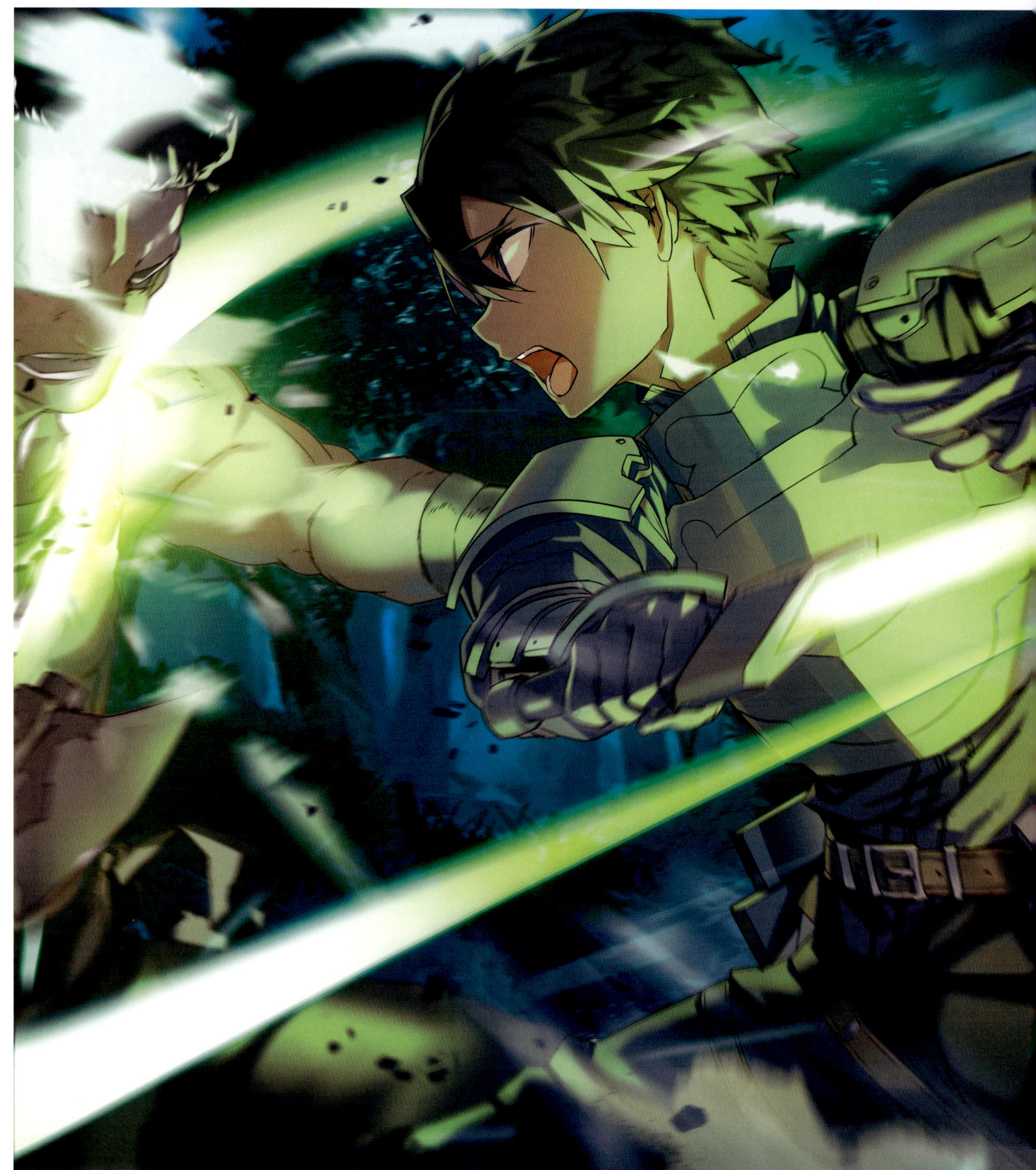

Dengeki Bunko,
Sword Art Online 21: Unital Ring I
Frontispiece: December 2018

Zwabamm!

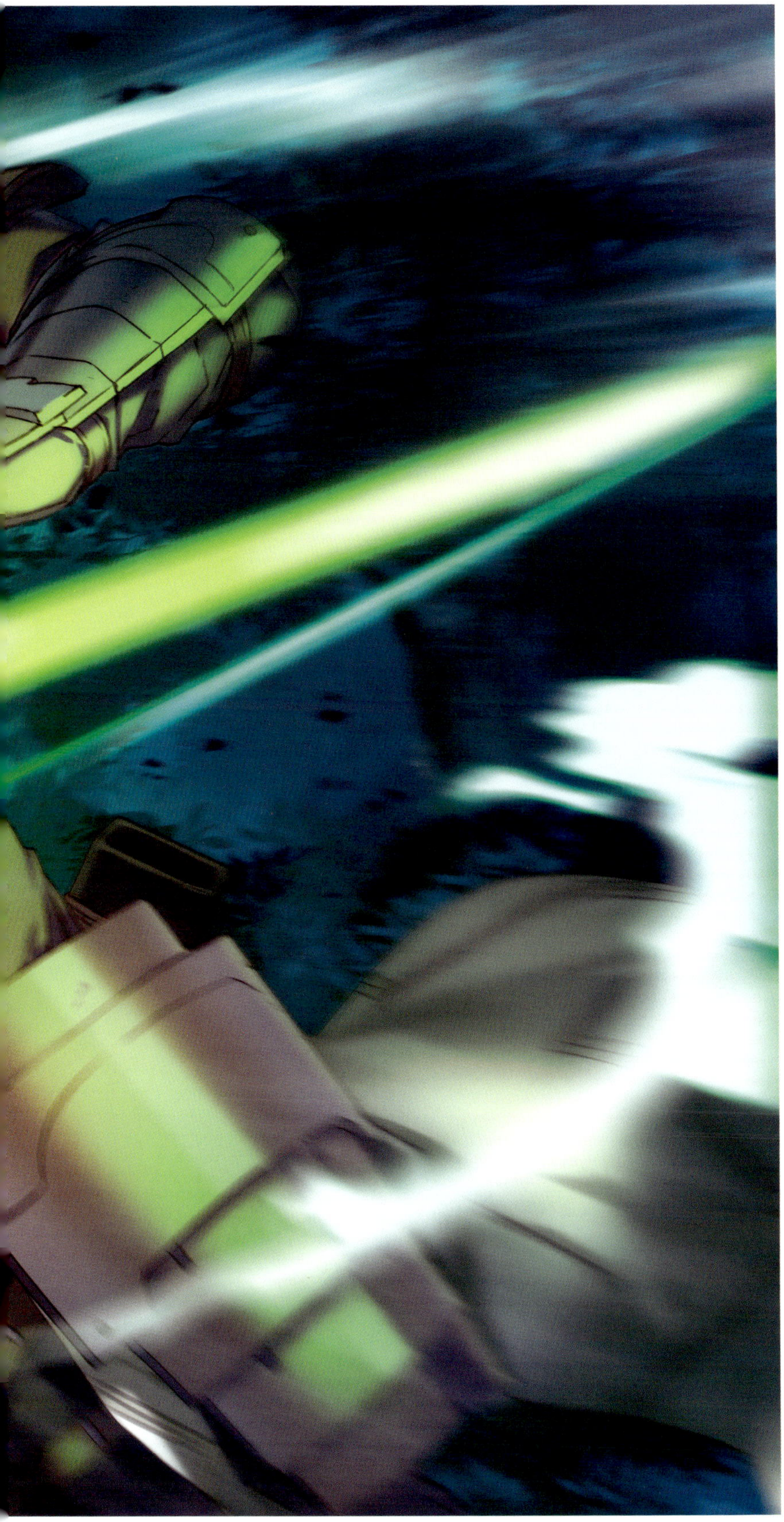

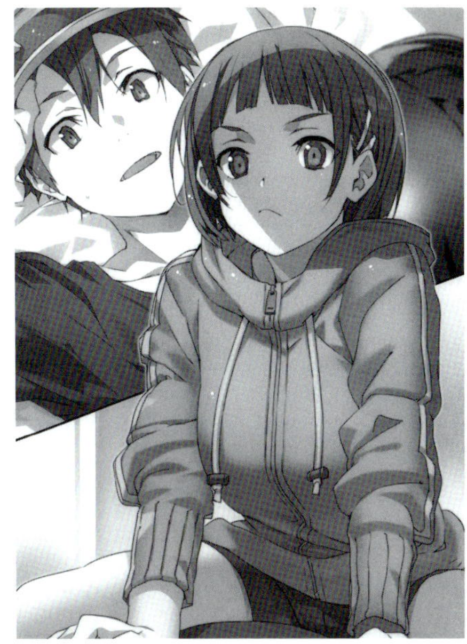

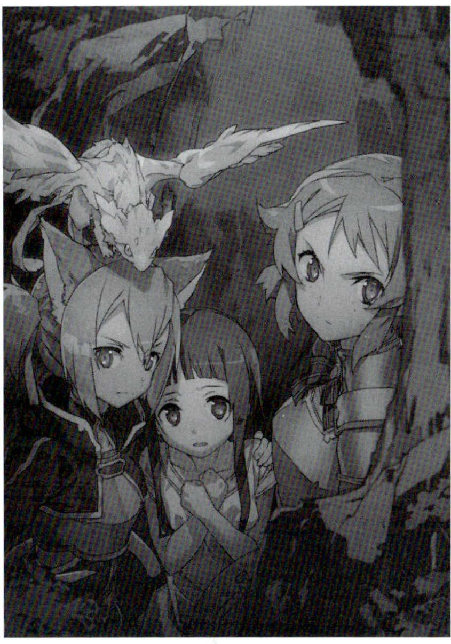

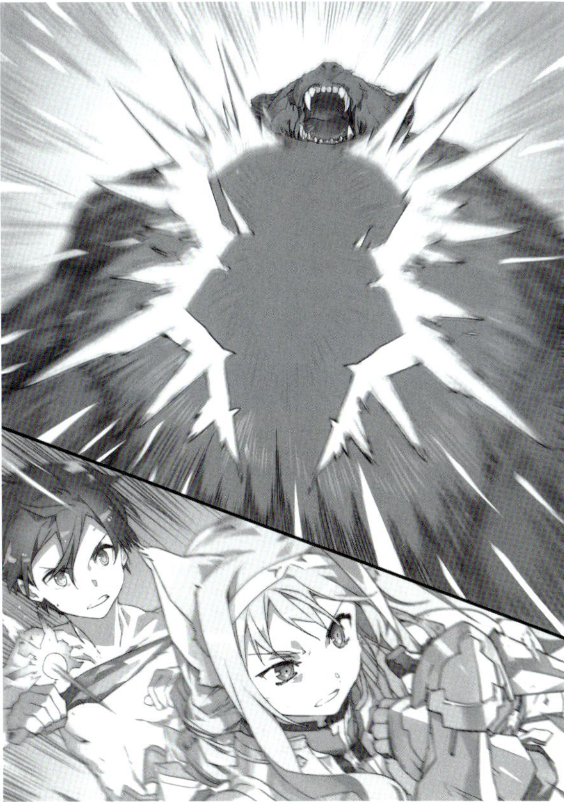

**Dengeki Bunko,
*Sword Art Online 21:
Unital Ring I***
Illustration: December 2018

A hiding scene with Silica, Yui, and Liz. Looking at it now, I'm sure I wanted to include Pina being alert and guarded, but with your wings outstretched, they're going to spot you!

SWORD ART ONLINE
kiss and fly

A short story collection populated by pieces that were written as extras for Blu-ray and DVD releases.

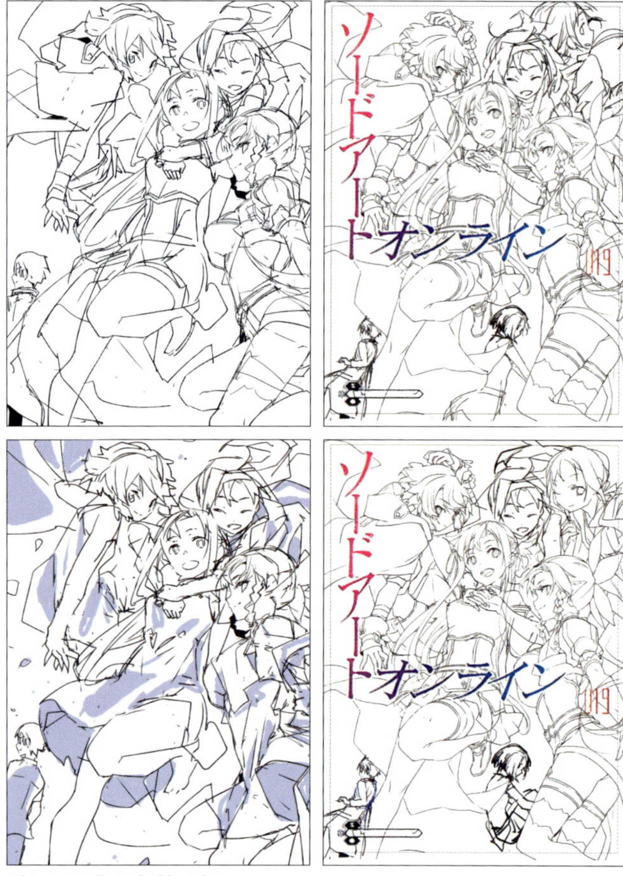

Alternate Rough Sketches

Dengeki Bunko,
Sword Art Online 22: Kiss and Fly
Cover: October 2019

The central characters for these stories went front and center on this one. In my rough sketches, I had Ran and Sachi in some and left them out in others. I'm always trying to figure out how much I should pack into the cover. Ultimately, just the four of them makes for the cleanest art.

Dengeki Bunko,
Sword Art Online 22: Kiss and Fly
Illustration: October 2019

Surprisingly, I've never really had Asuna do any uncharacteristically over-the-top poses, so it's fun when I get to put her into one of those situations. Doggy looks unbothered.

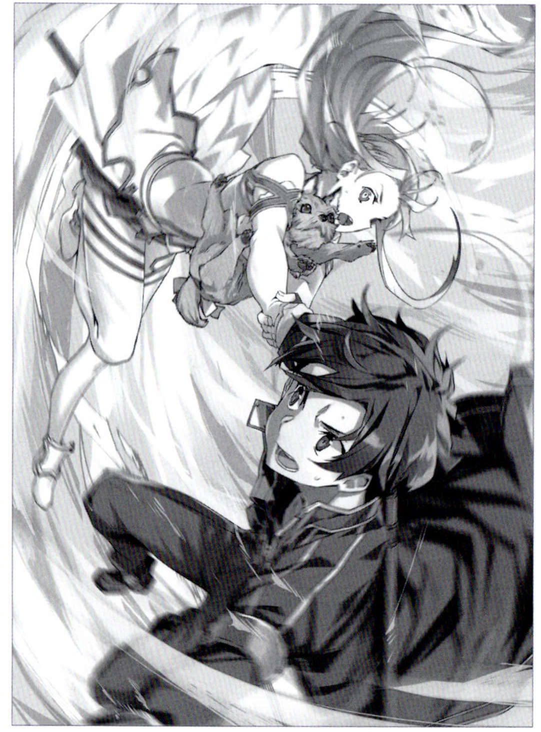

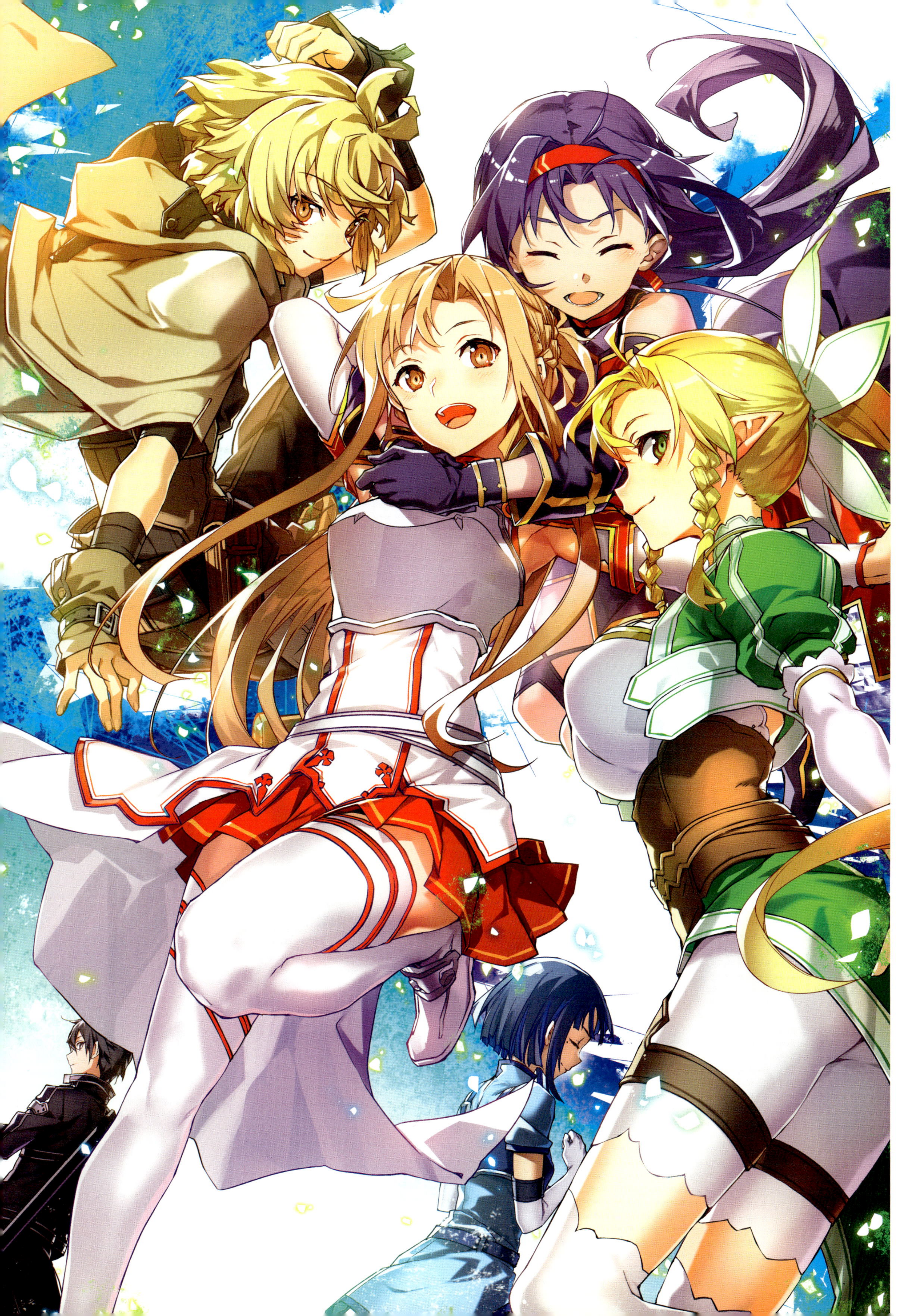

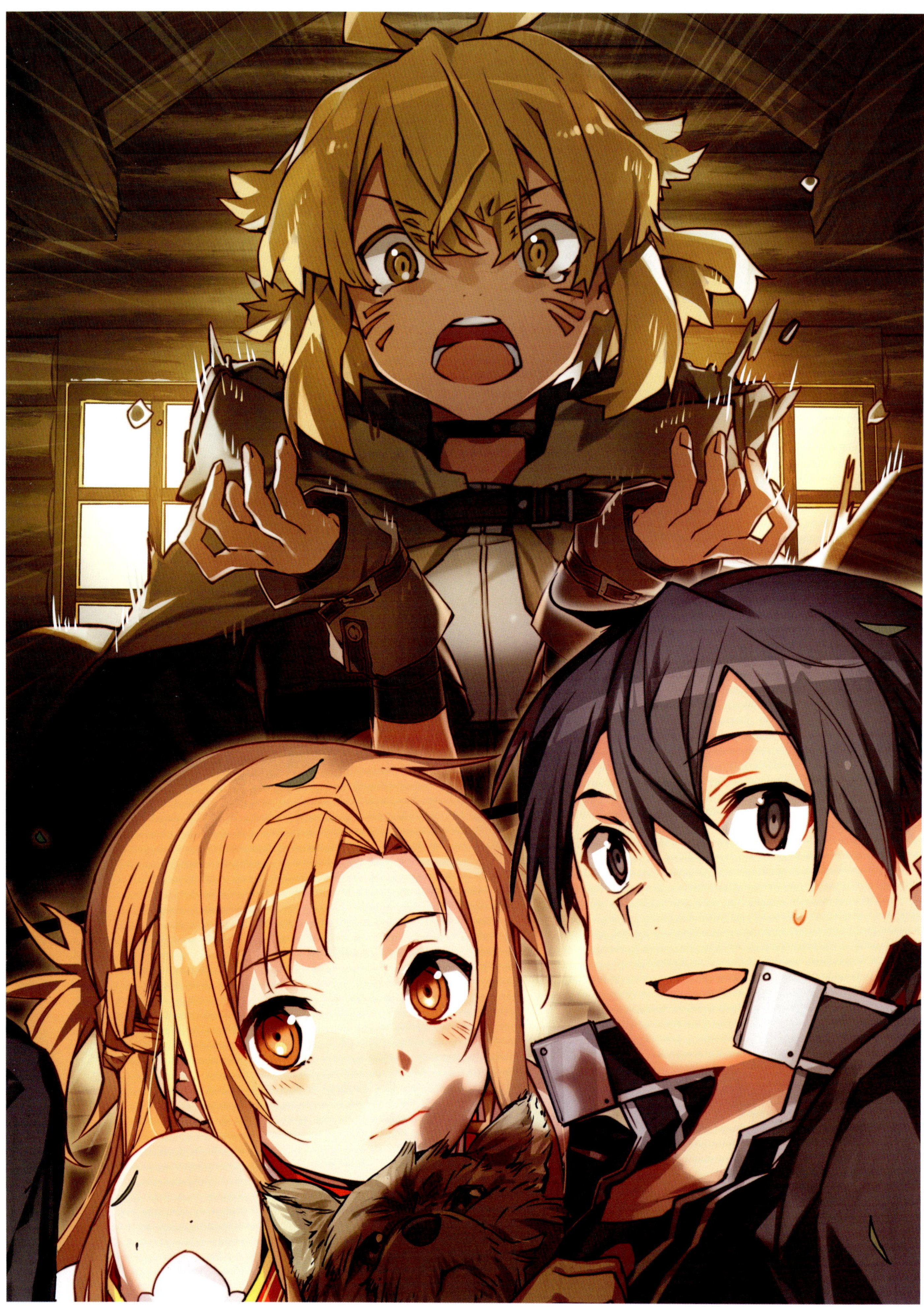

Dengeki Bunko,
Sword Art Online 22: Kiss and Fly
Frontispiece: October 2019

Here's Argo, shocked that after she called for help, the other two got stuck in the trap with her. I like these expressions. Also, that gear's unique to this volume. It's hard to tell because the designs are very similar.

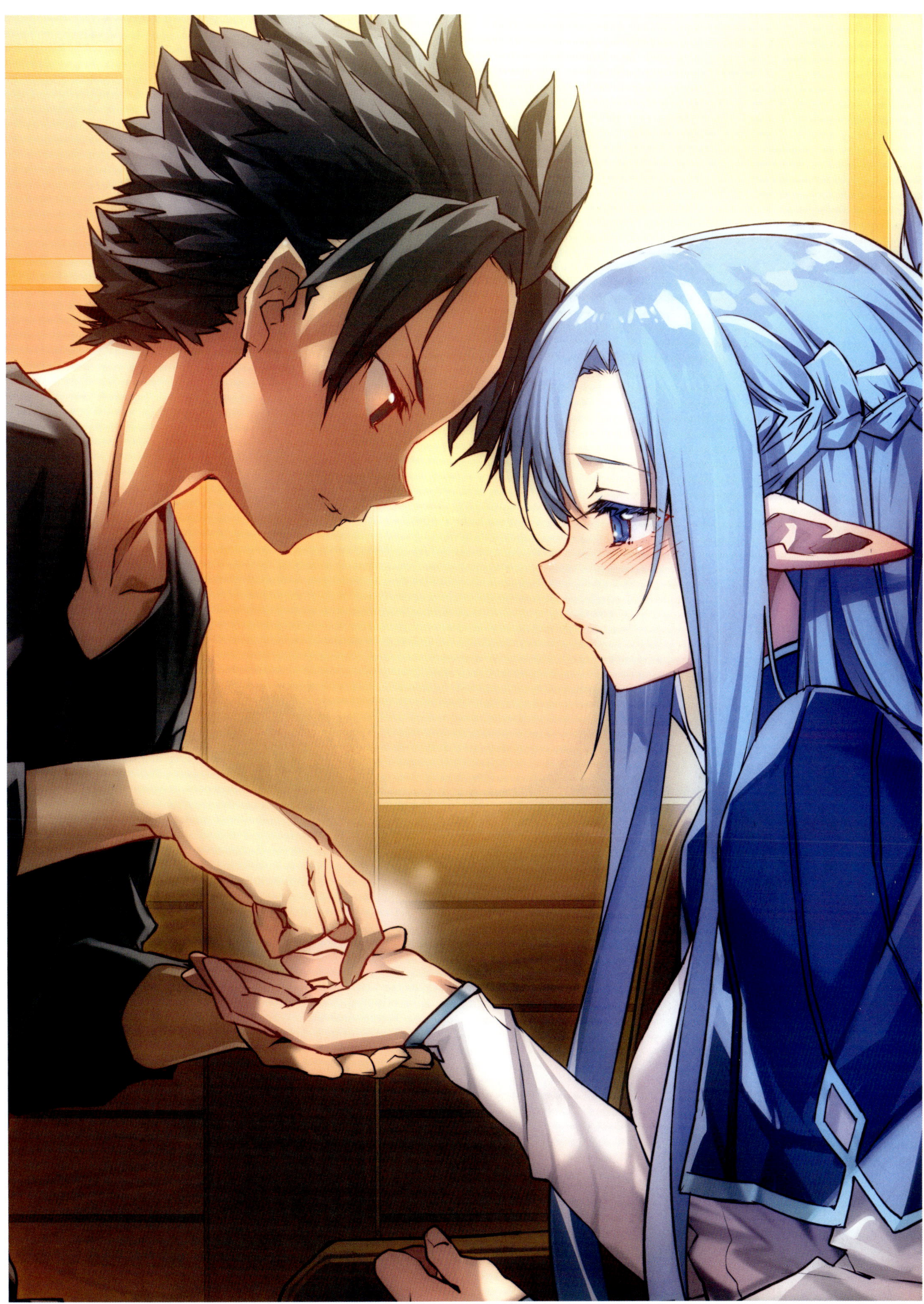

Dengeki Bunko,
Sword Art Online 22: Kiss and Fly
Frontispiece: October 2019

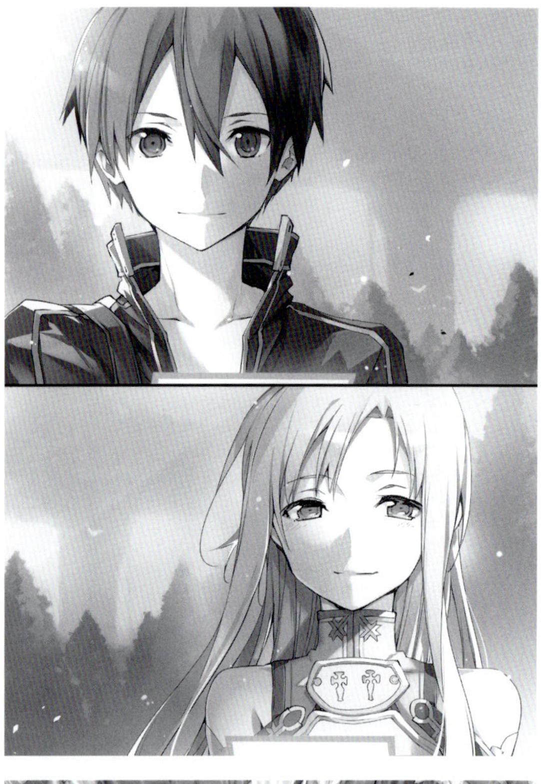

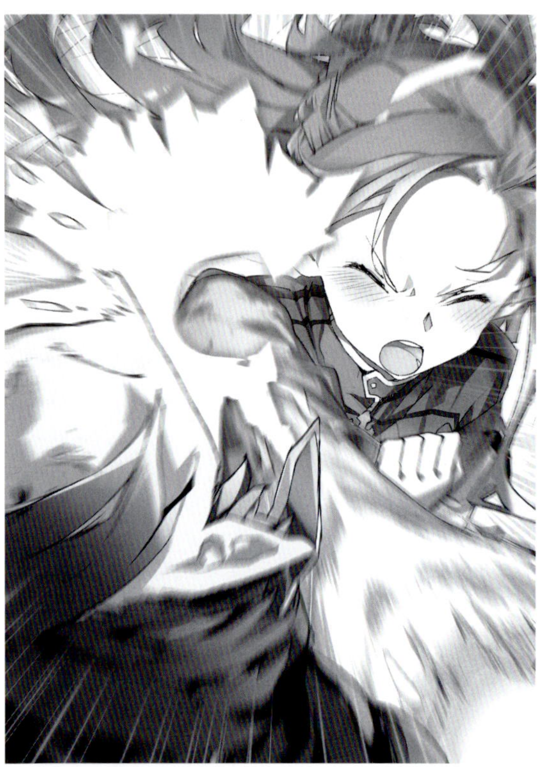

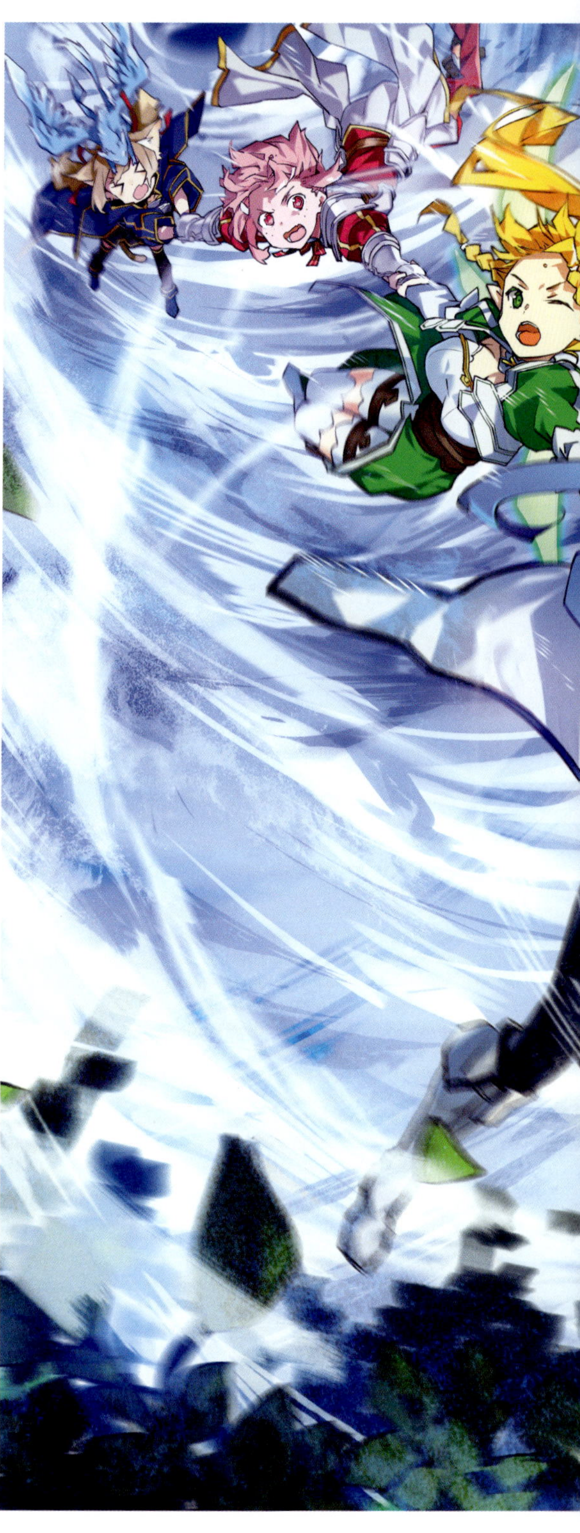

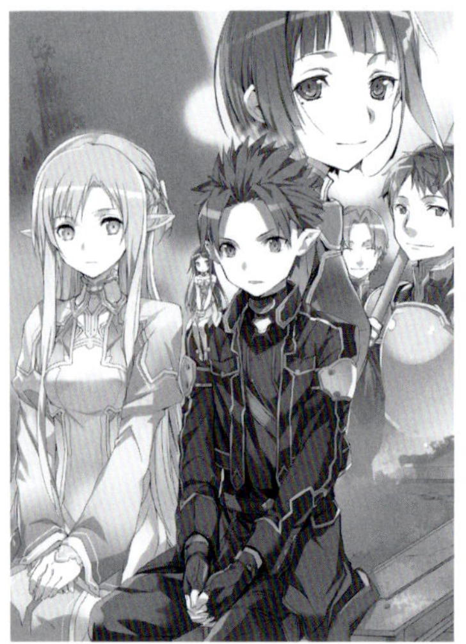

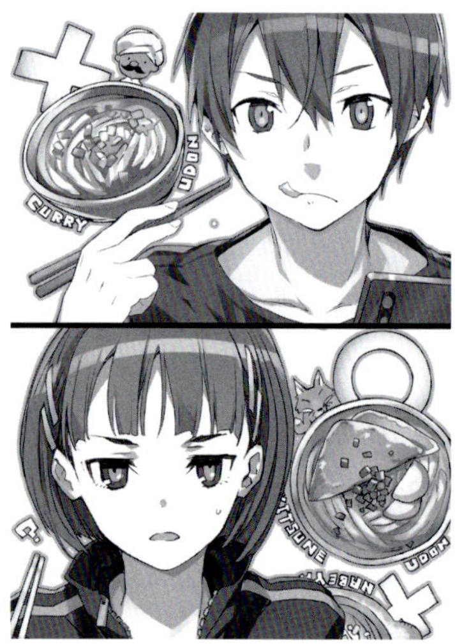

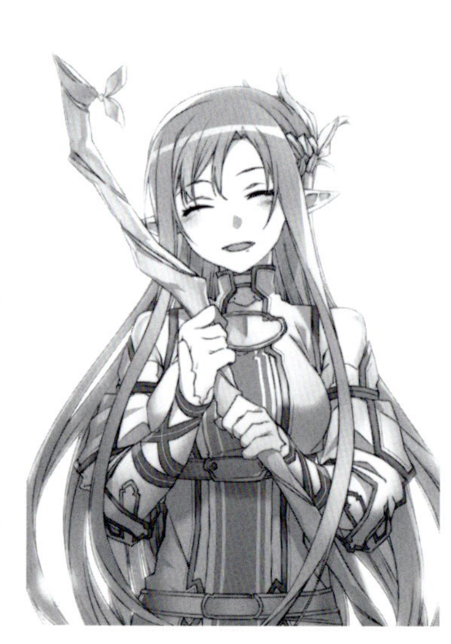

**Dengeki Bunko,
Sword Art Online 22:
Kiss and Fly**
Illustration: October 2019

Some of these illustrations were from the original anime DVD bonus, so I retouched the older ones a bit.

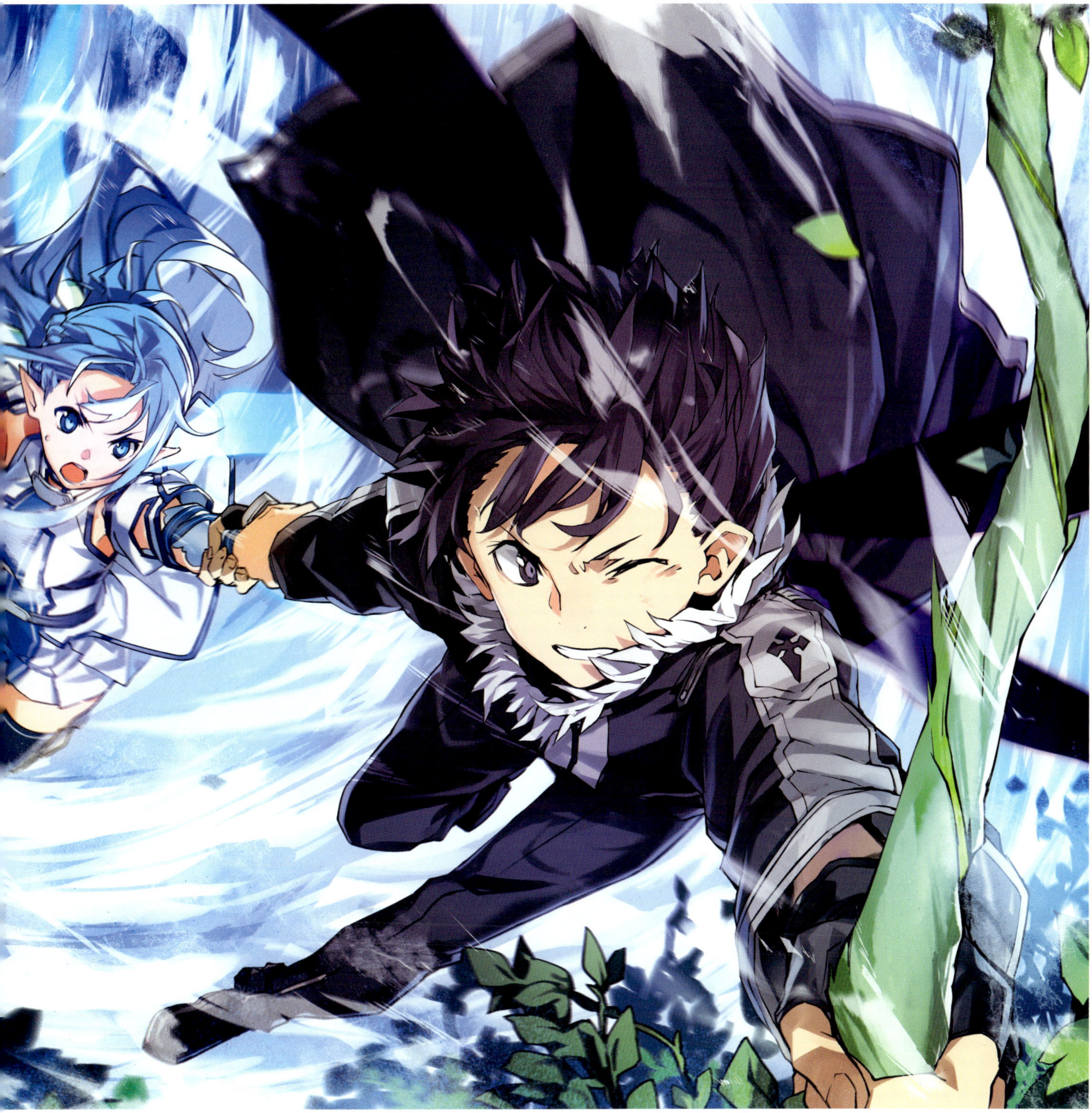

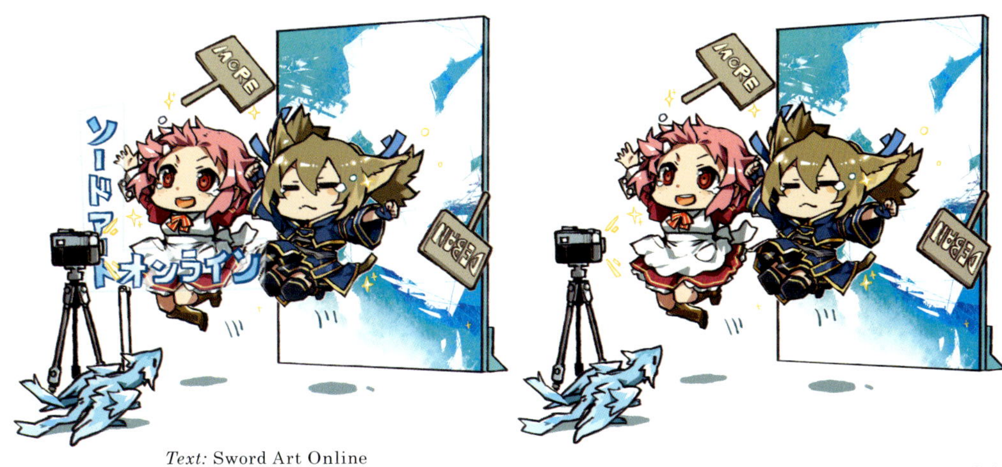

Dengeki Bunko,
Sword Art Online 22: Kiss and Fly
Frontispiece: October 2019

In scenes like this, it's Silica and Liz who really stand out. Especially Silica. I just love working with characters who will give you oversized reactions. Also, when drawing scenes of flying and being blown around, it makes you think that wearing a skirt in *ALO* has to be simply insane.

Dengeki Bunko,
Sword Art Online 22:
Kiss and Fly
Rear Cover: October 2019

Leafa, you traitor!

Text: Sword Art Online

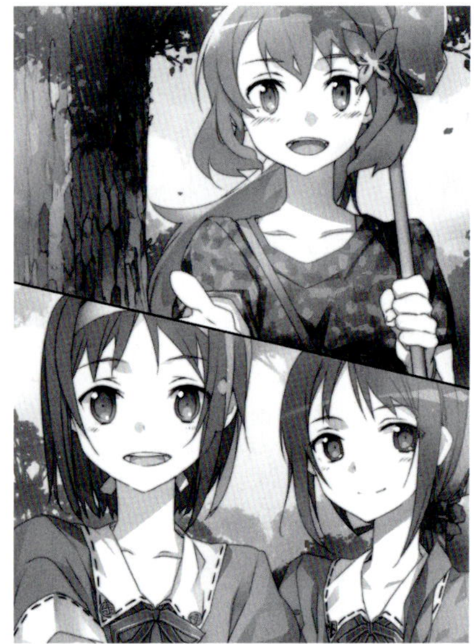

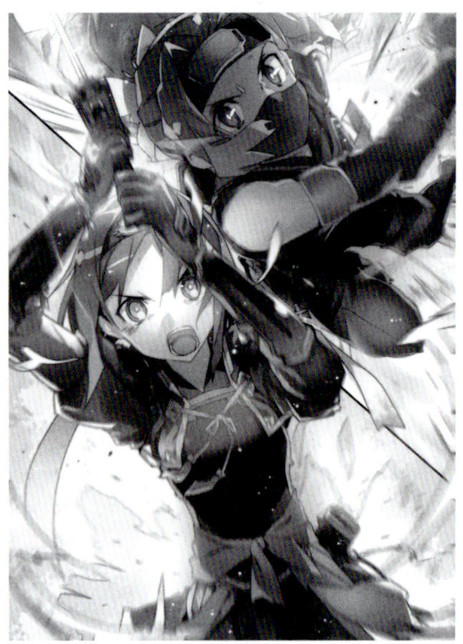

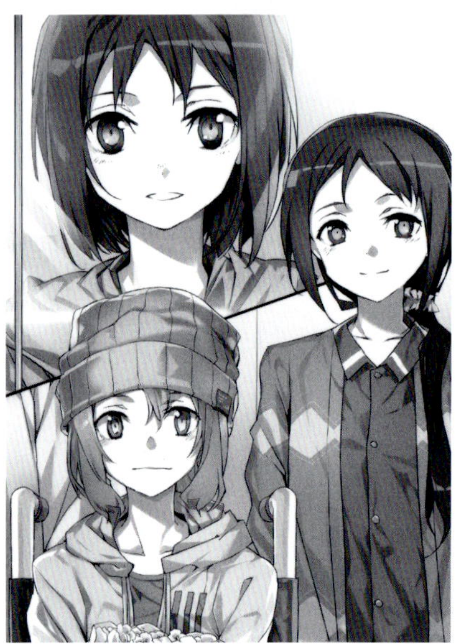

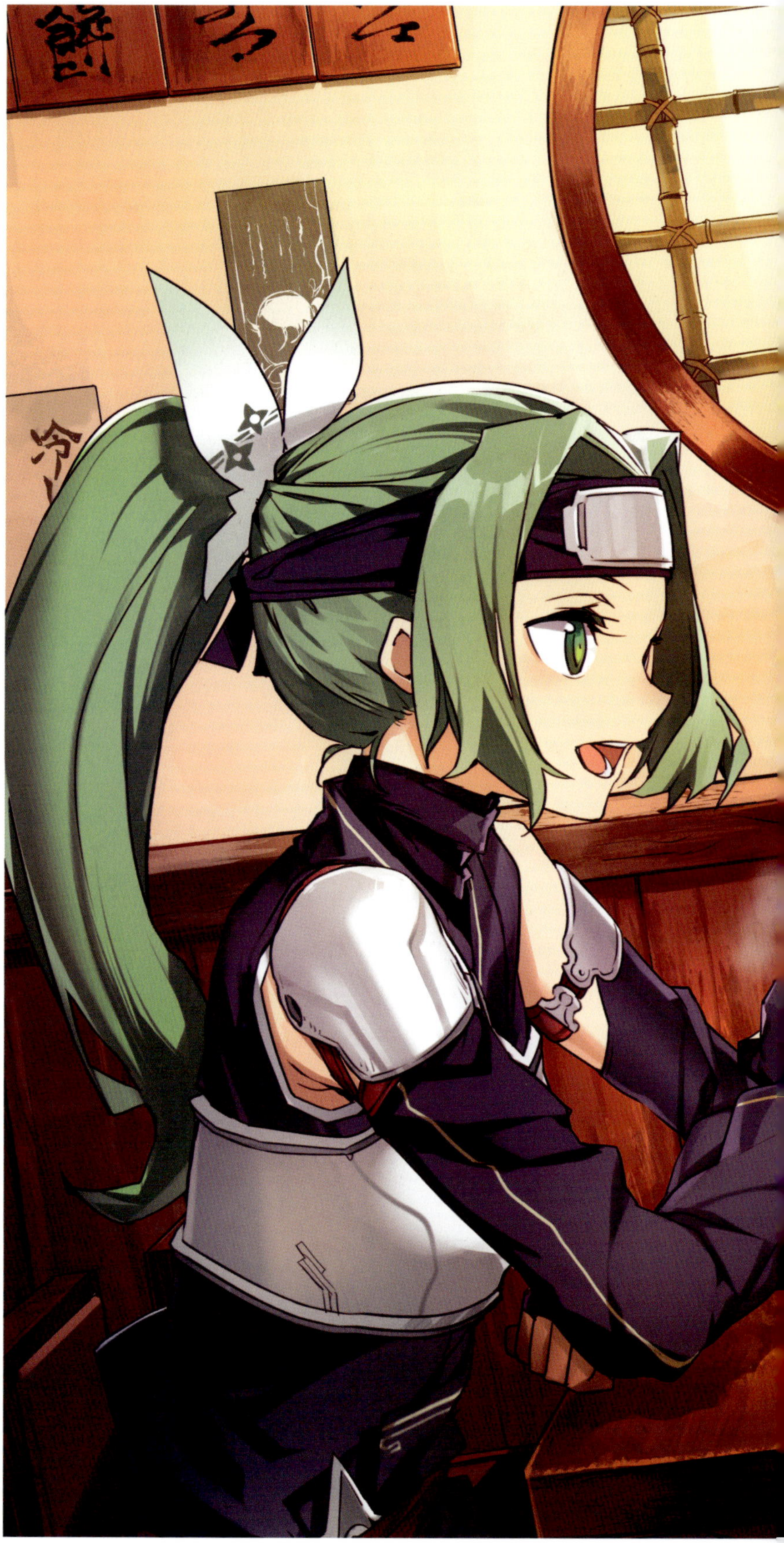

Dengeki Bunko,
Sword Art Online 22: Kiss and Fly
Illustration: October 2019

This is Yuuki's past. Her face wouldn't have been exactly the same in each different game she played, but I chose to make them match. Compared to manga, you have fewer opportunities to depict stuff like that in novel illustrations, so it's tricky to pull off.

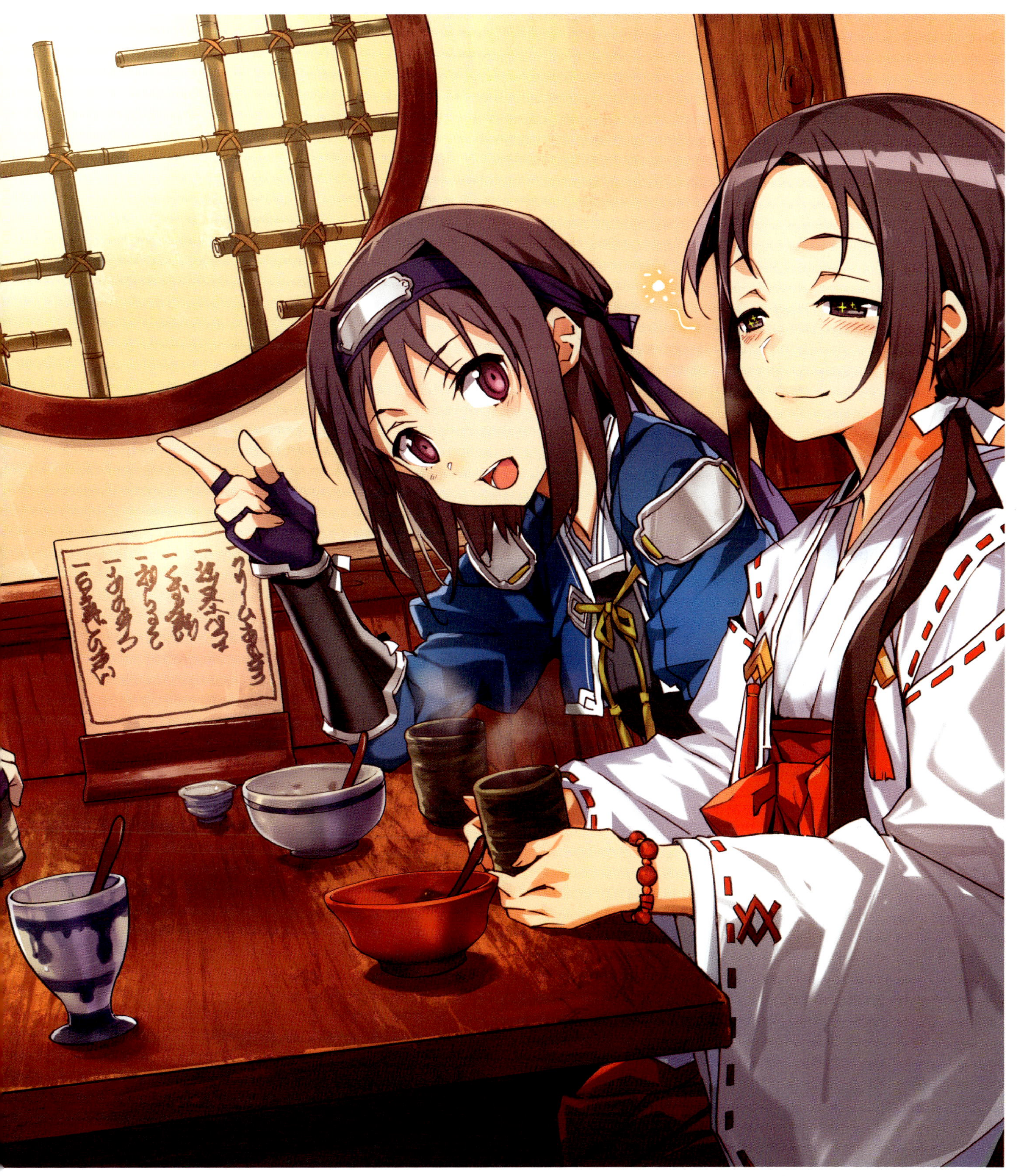

Dengeki Bunko,
Sword Art Online 22: Kiss and Fly
Frontispiece: October 2019

The trio enjoys some sweets. It's nice that this is Japanese-themed, so I can just write Japanese on the sign and not come up with some made-up script.

This section is for some illustrations I drew for various video games.

Take 1

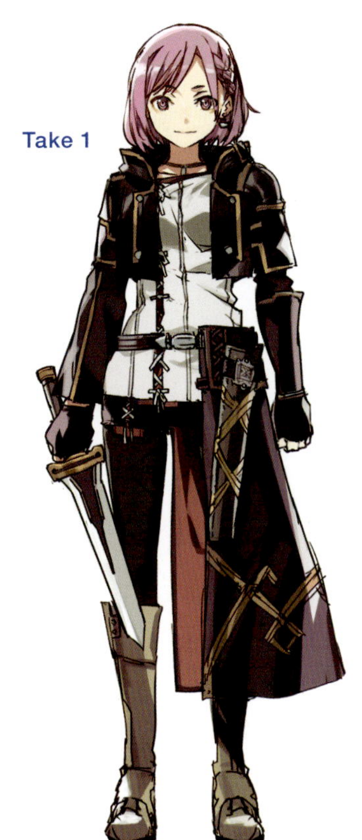

Take 2

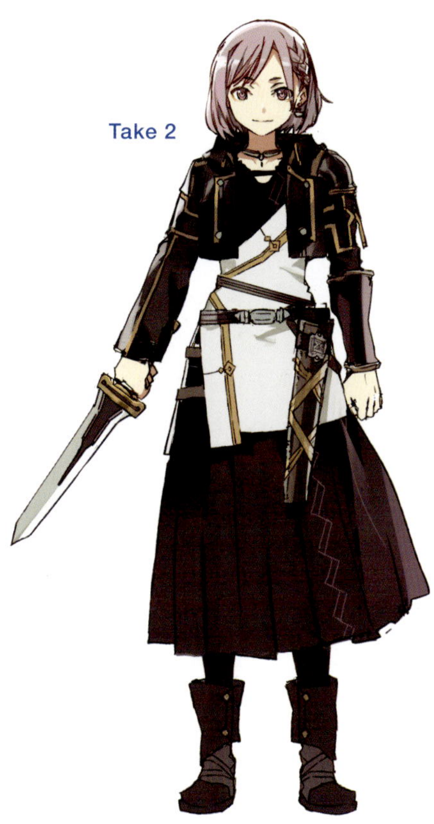

Take 3

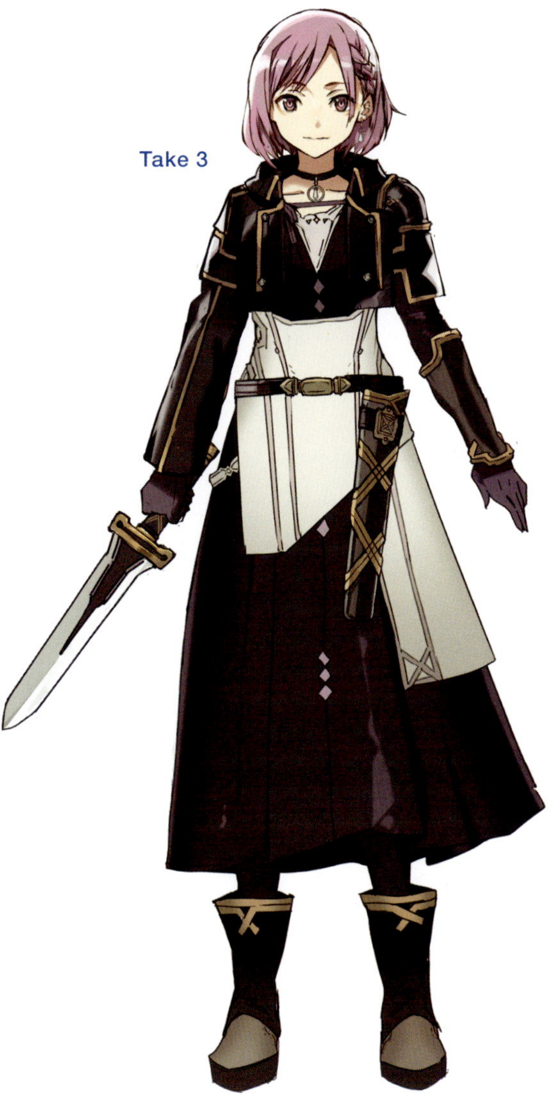

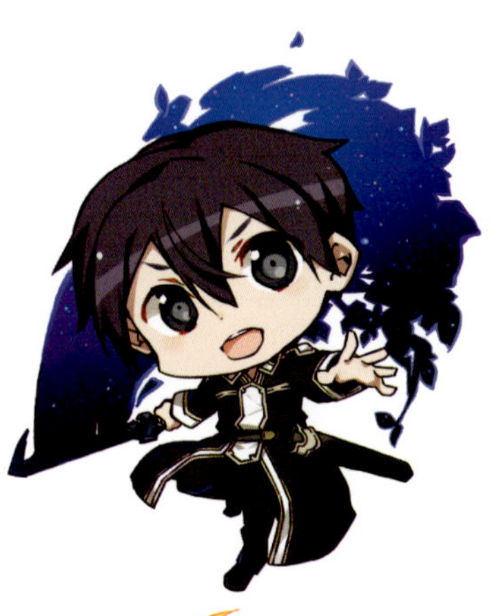

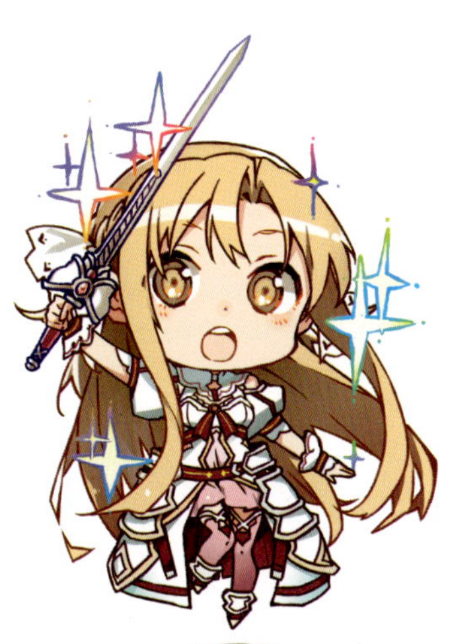

Game
Sword Art Online Alicization Lycoris
ReoNa the Adventurer Character Design: July 2020

This is an avatar design for ReoNa's character in the game. When it comes to games, I'm usually considered part of the original creative team, so it's rare that they ask for multiple takes. This one, they went for Take 3. But I'm glad they did.

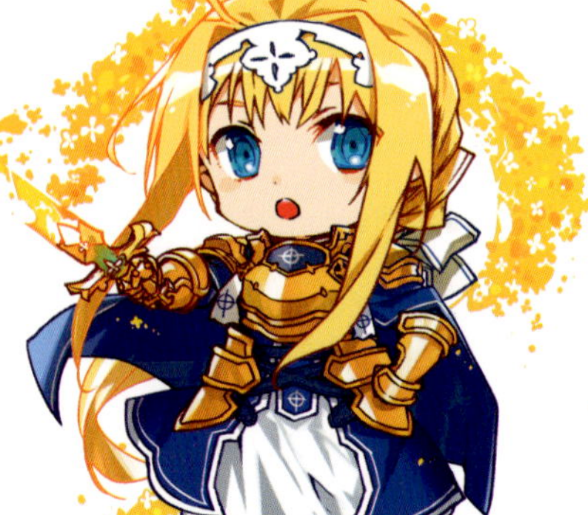

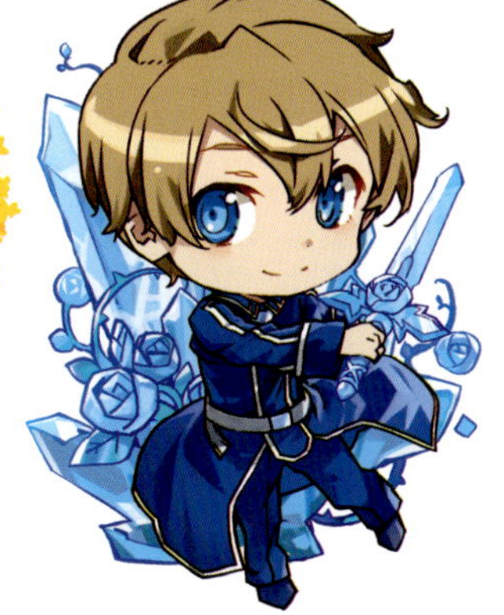

Game
Sword Art Online Alicization Lycoris
Dengeki Special Pack Bonus Acrylic Keyholders: July 2020

I like drawing chibi versions of characters, and I've always thought I was good at it. Nowadays there's such a high demand that some artists exclusively work on these kinds of designs. When I see the sample merchandise come in, I always think, "Dammit, that's so cute!"

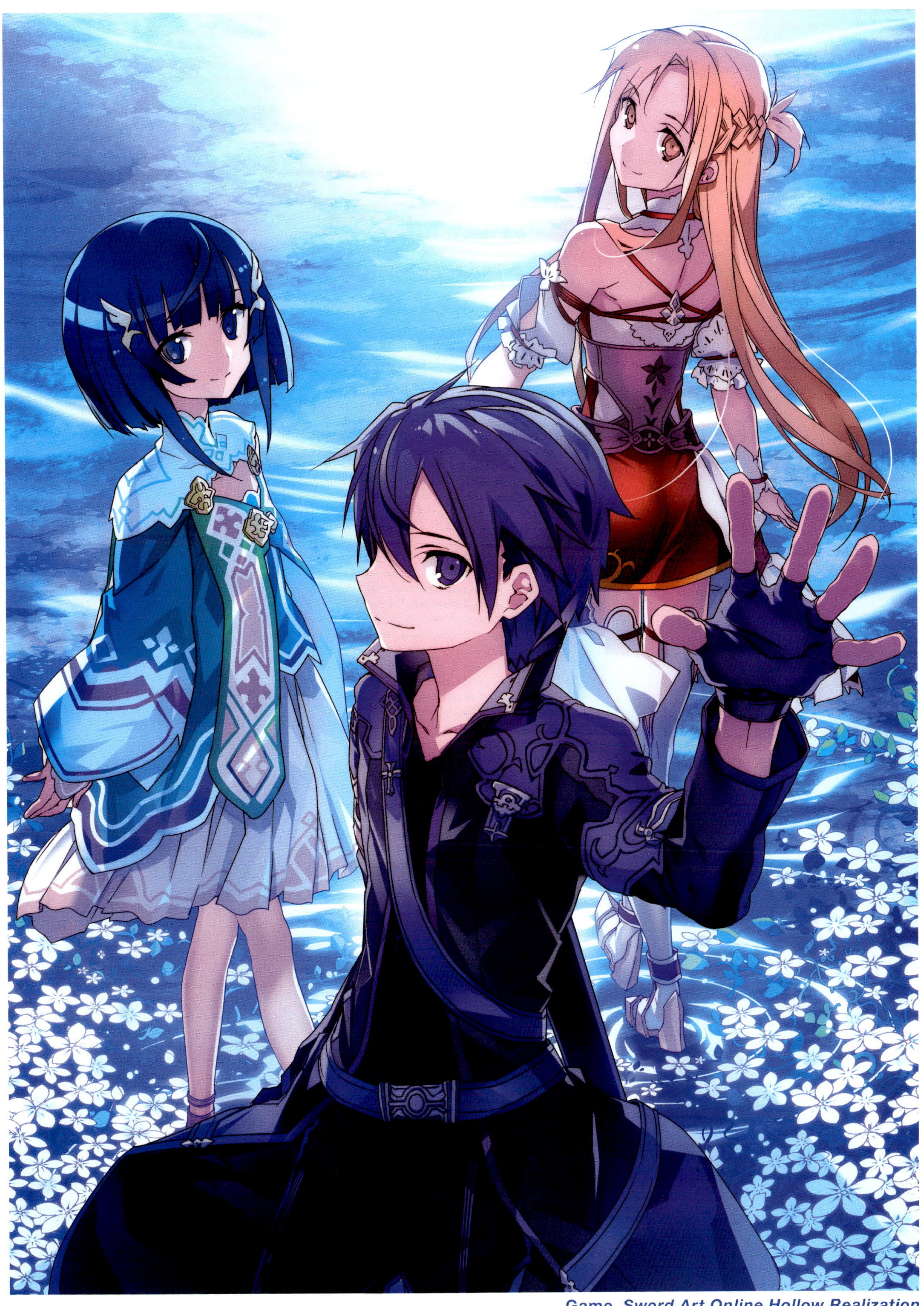

In games, even the existing characters get new outfits. I consider my outfit designs to have lots of moving parts, but when designing for a 3D game there are even more bits and pieces to worry about. It makes me realize that working on light novels, I don't often worry about the design of the character's back, but in a game, it's probably the thing you'll be looking at the most.

I designed this illustration in three parts. For video game covers, they'll give you very specific instructions about layout, and I usually draw it based on those specifications. It's hard because there are lots of characters to do.

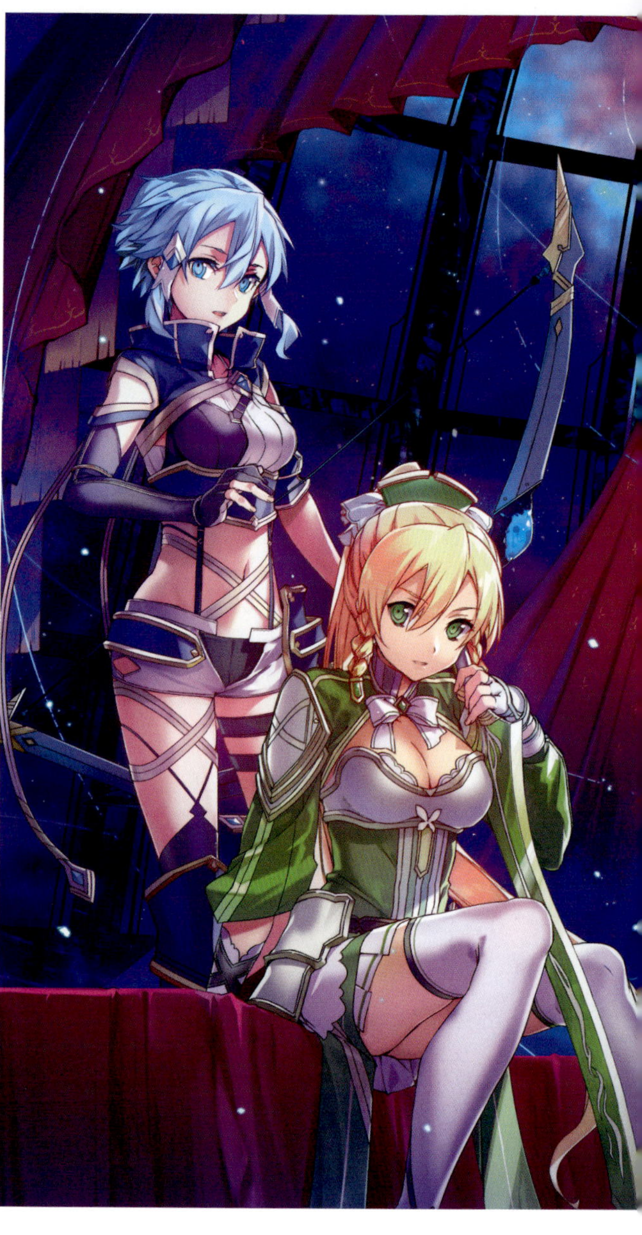

Sword Art Online Game Series 5th Anniversary
Original Avatar Contest Project: October 2018

These were designed based on the winners of the avatar contest. It was a lot of fun. I would have liked to see them next to the original designs, though.

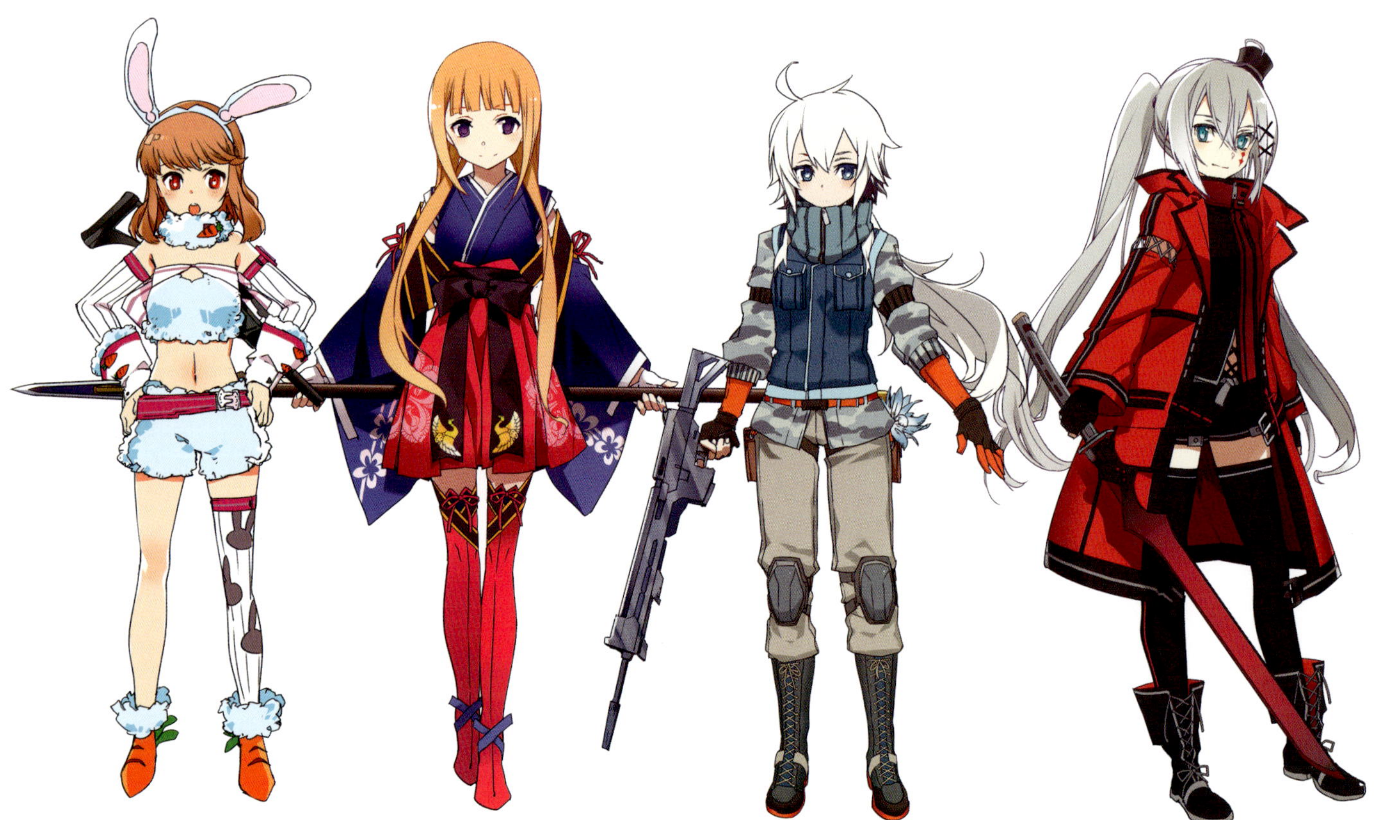

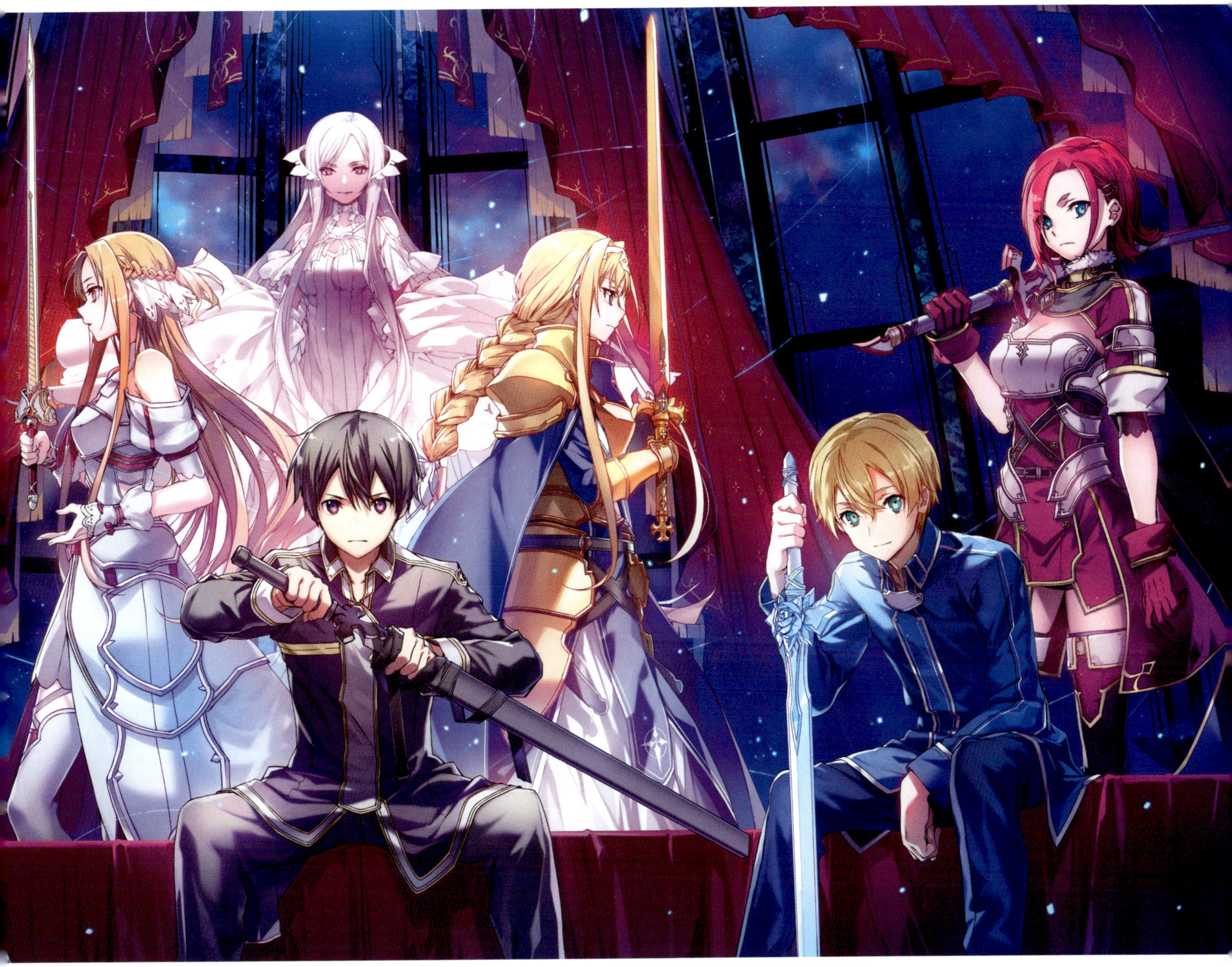

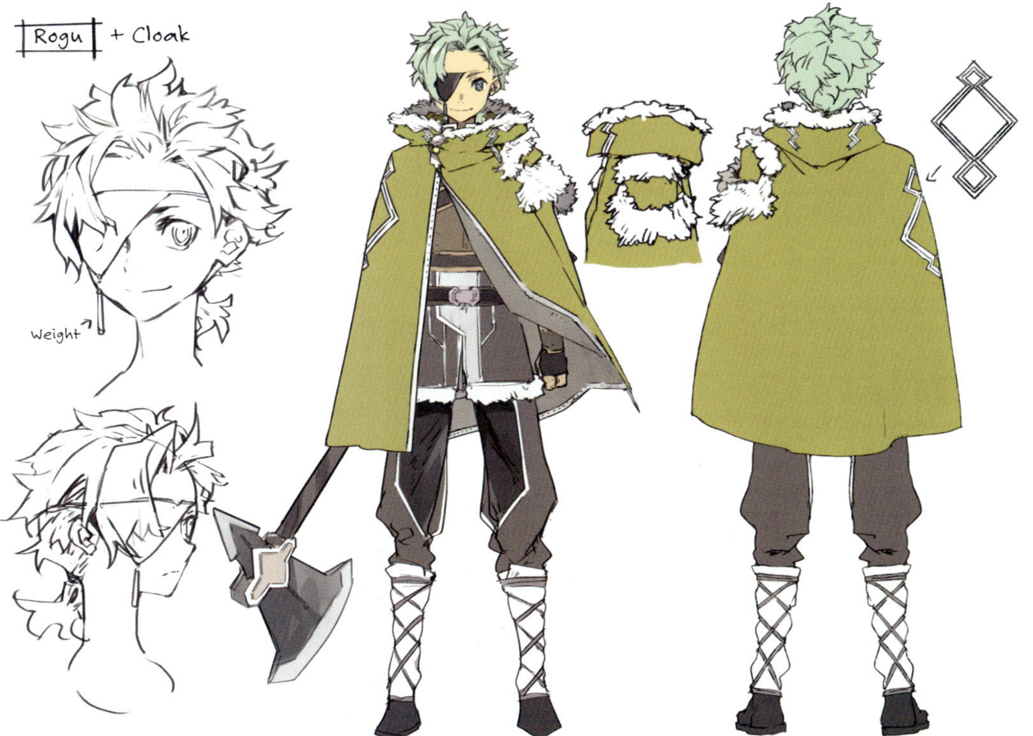

Game
Sword Art Online Alicization Lycoris Expansion DLC "Matricaria"
Rogu Character Design: July 2022

Lots of character designs for game-original characters have a rough sketch according to the team's specs already, and my job is just to polish them up, but Rogu was a rare case of getting to design it entirely on my own. For that reason, he's a little understated.

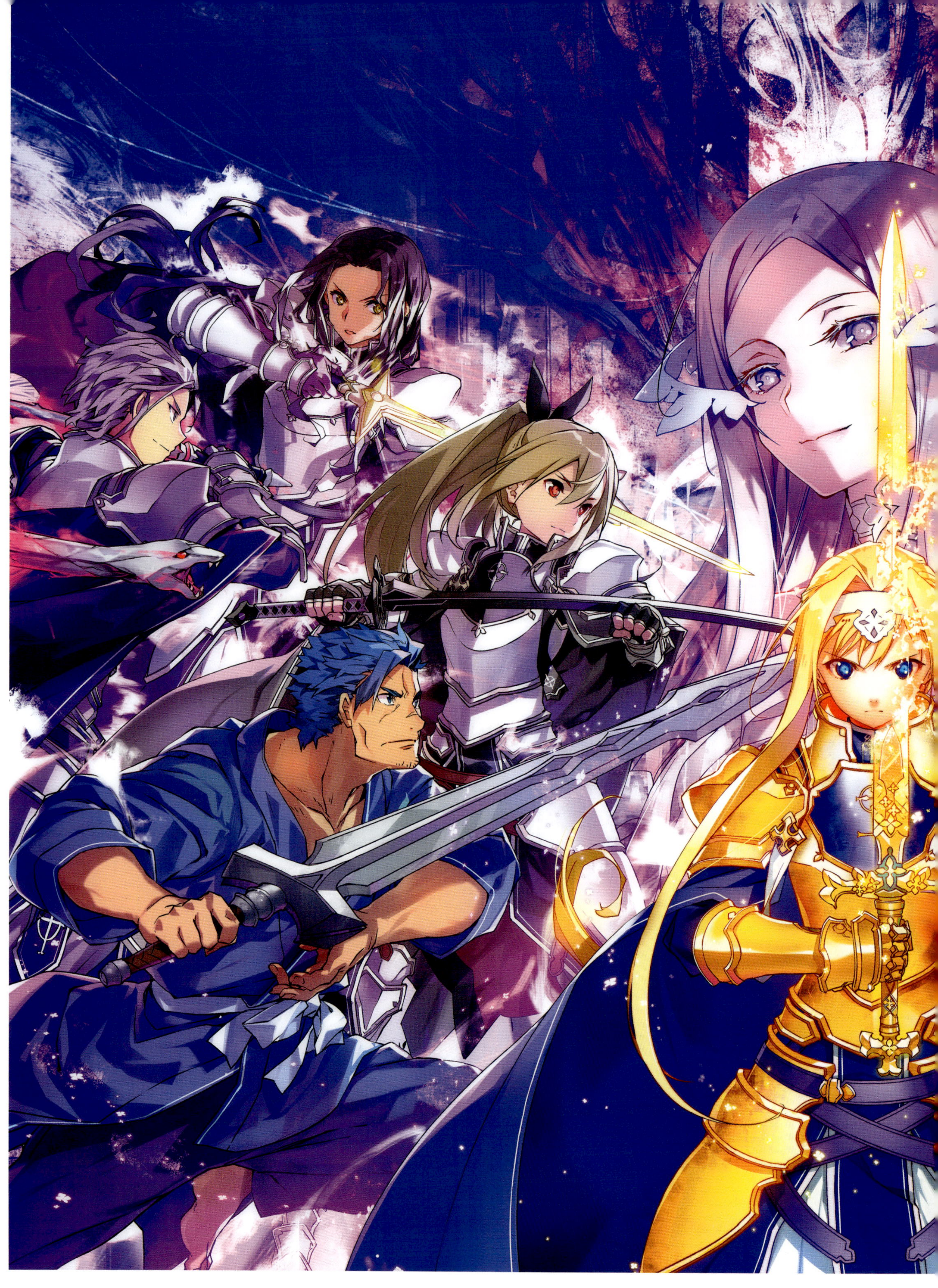

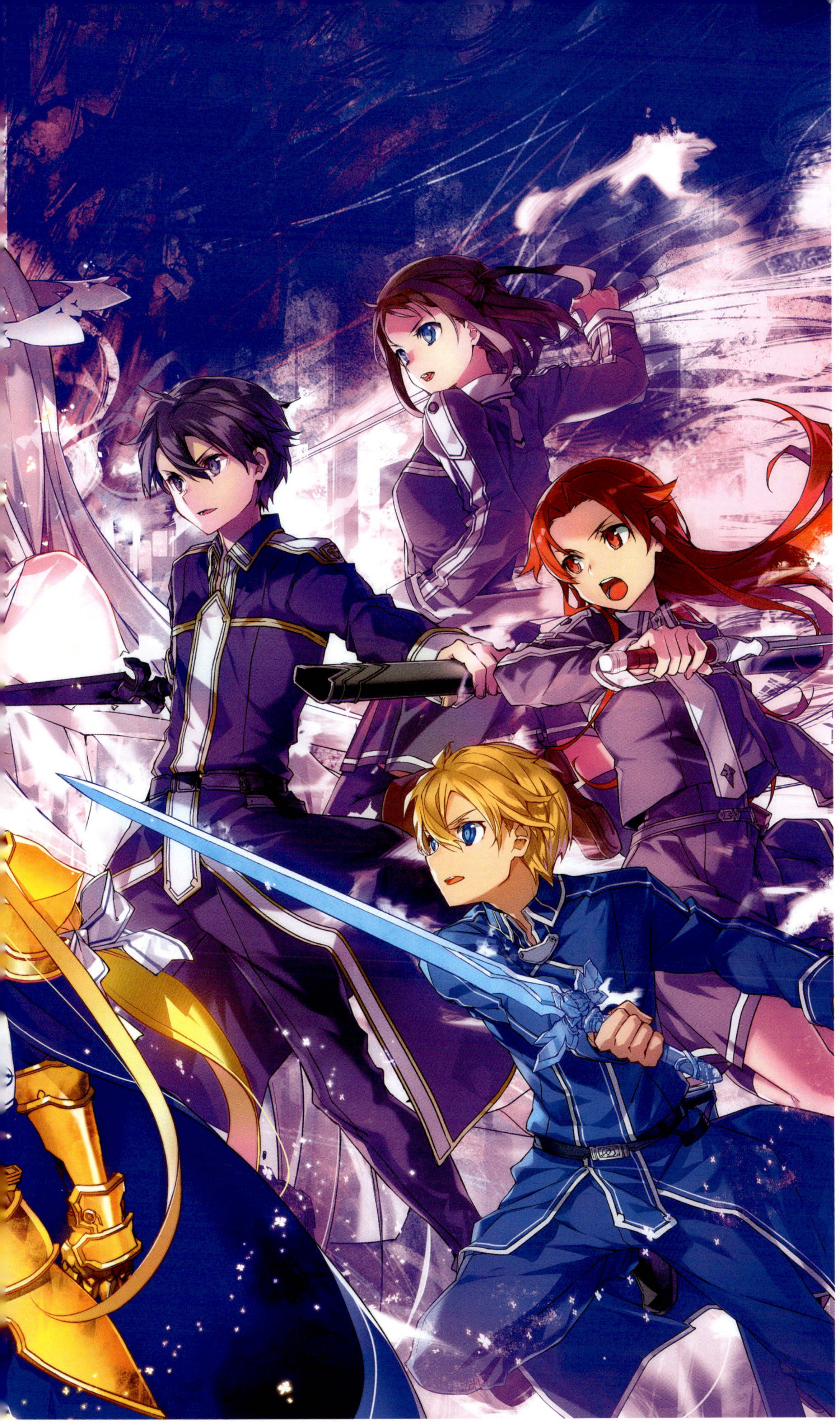

This is obvious stuff, but swords are straight, and straight lines are easy to recognize. What this illustration shows is that it's neat when all those straight swords are pointing at the center of the canvas. Also, even looking at it myself, I cannot figure out how I drew the pattern in the background. How fascinating.

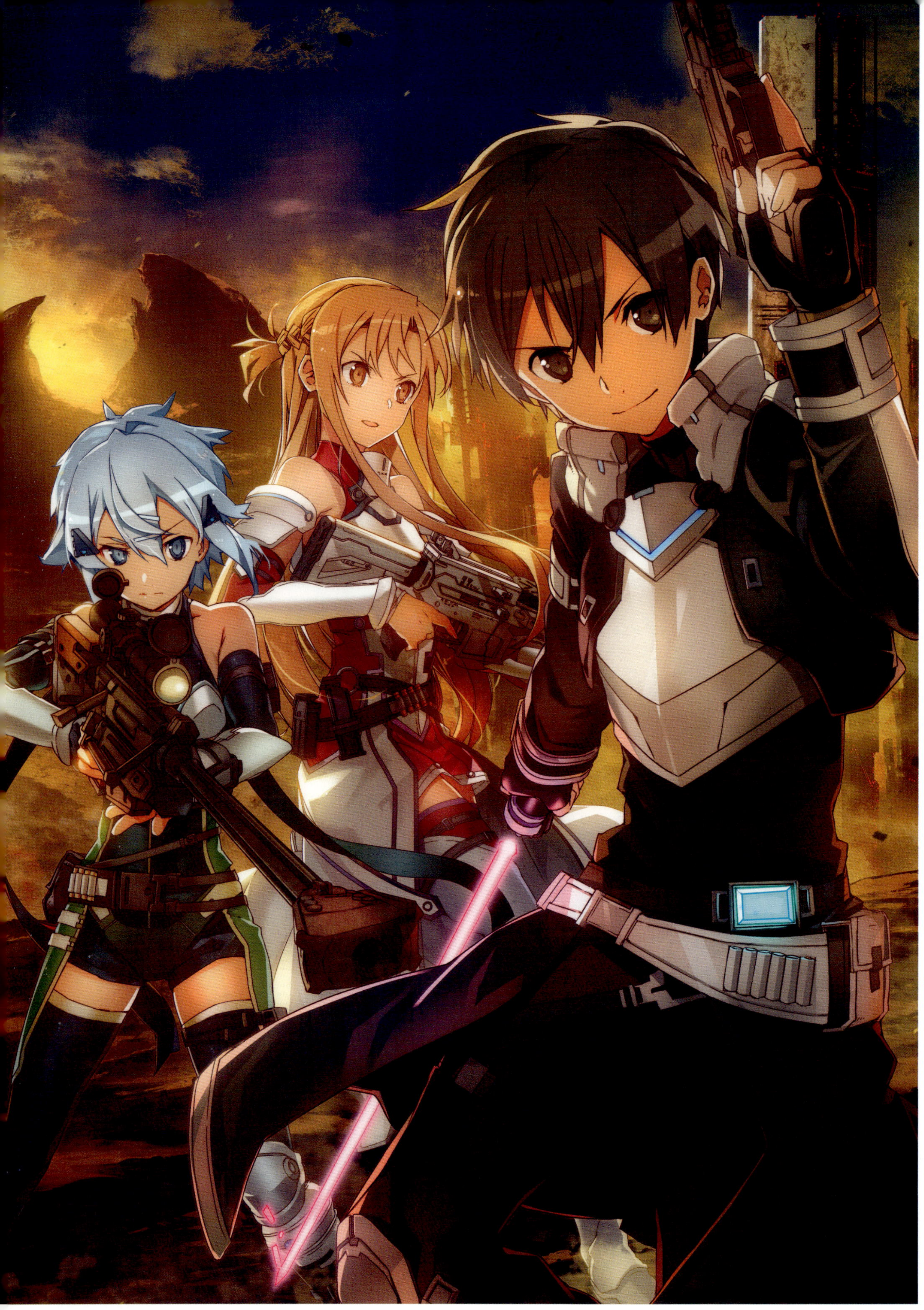

Game, *Sword Art Online: Fatal Bullet*
Limited Edition First Pressing Special Edition Box Packaging: February 2018

I always get hired to work on the package design for the games, but it's hard
work because the visuals of the games are always evolving and developing.
Also, I really want some 3D models of the guns in the game.

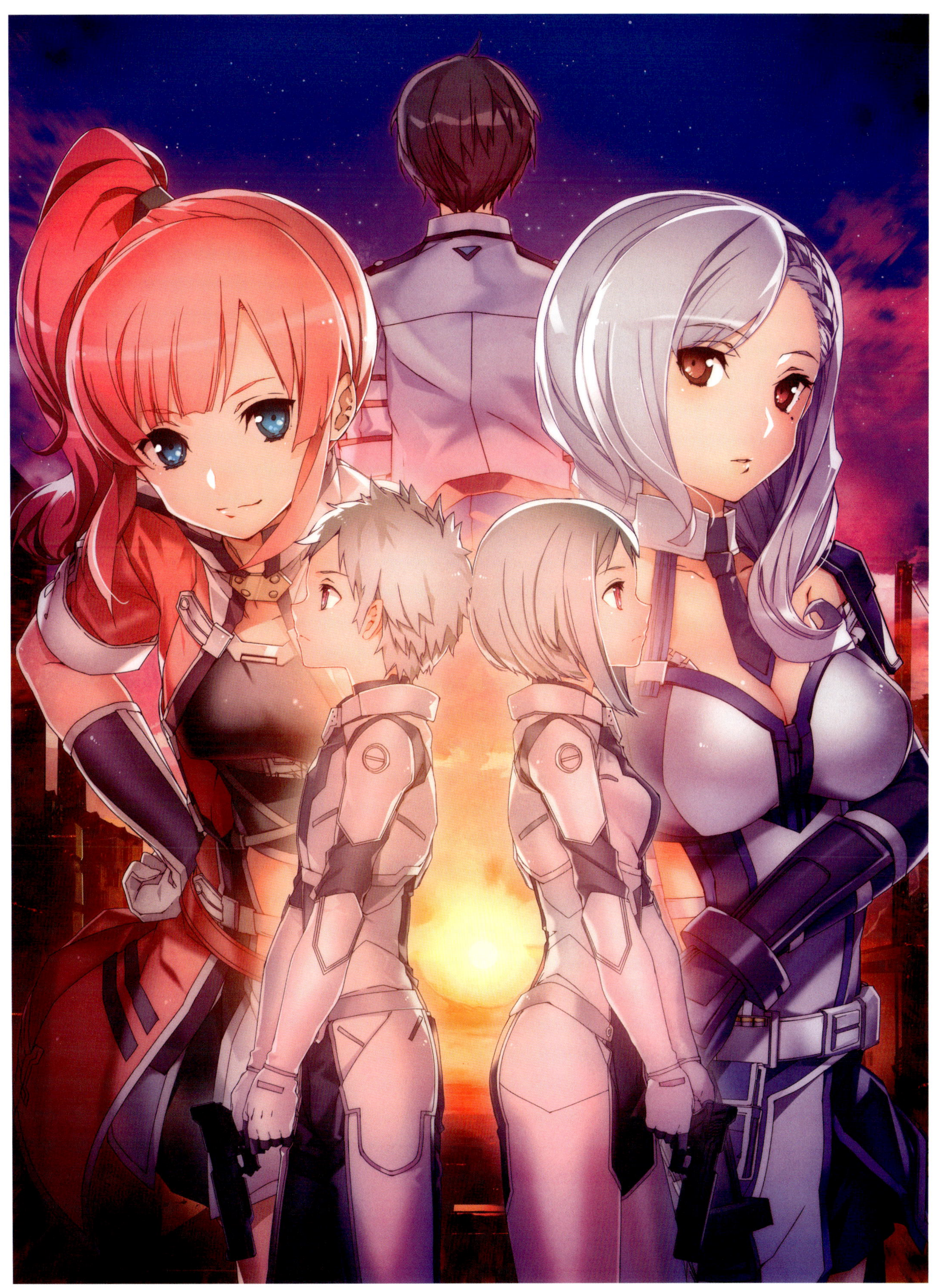

Game, *Sword Art Online: Fatal Bullet*
Dengeki Special Pack Bonus B2 Tapestry: February 2018

Obviously, I'm doing these before the games are out, so I don't have a chance to play them. That means whenever I get requests that only include new characters unique to the game, I don't have the luxury of knowing how they normally move and behave, so I end up sticking even closer to the details of the request than usual.

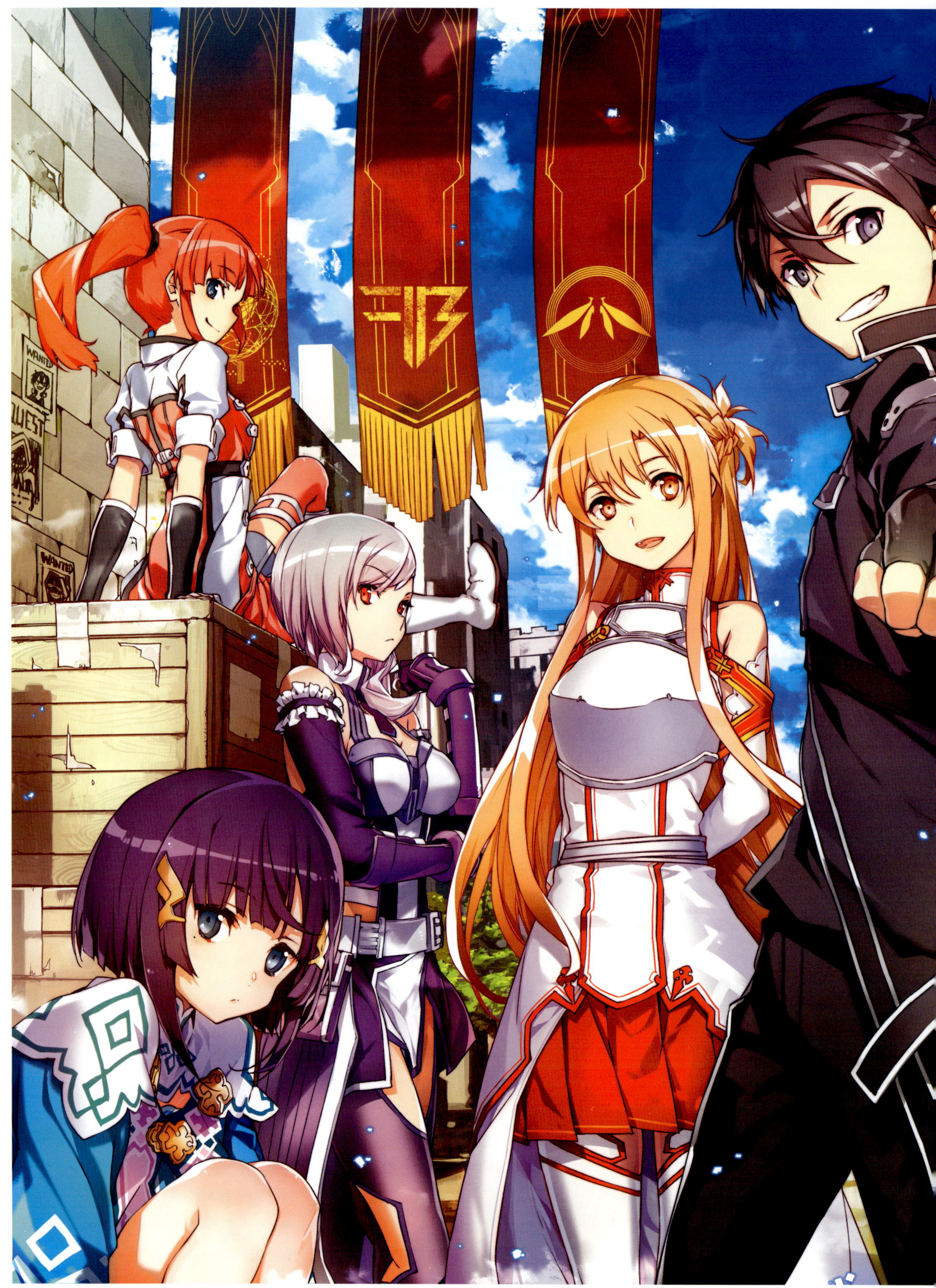

SAO Game Strategy Meeting 2019 Event
Key Visual: August 2019

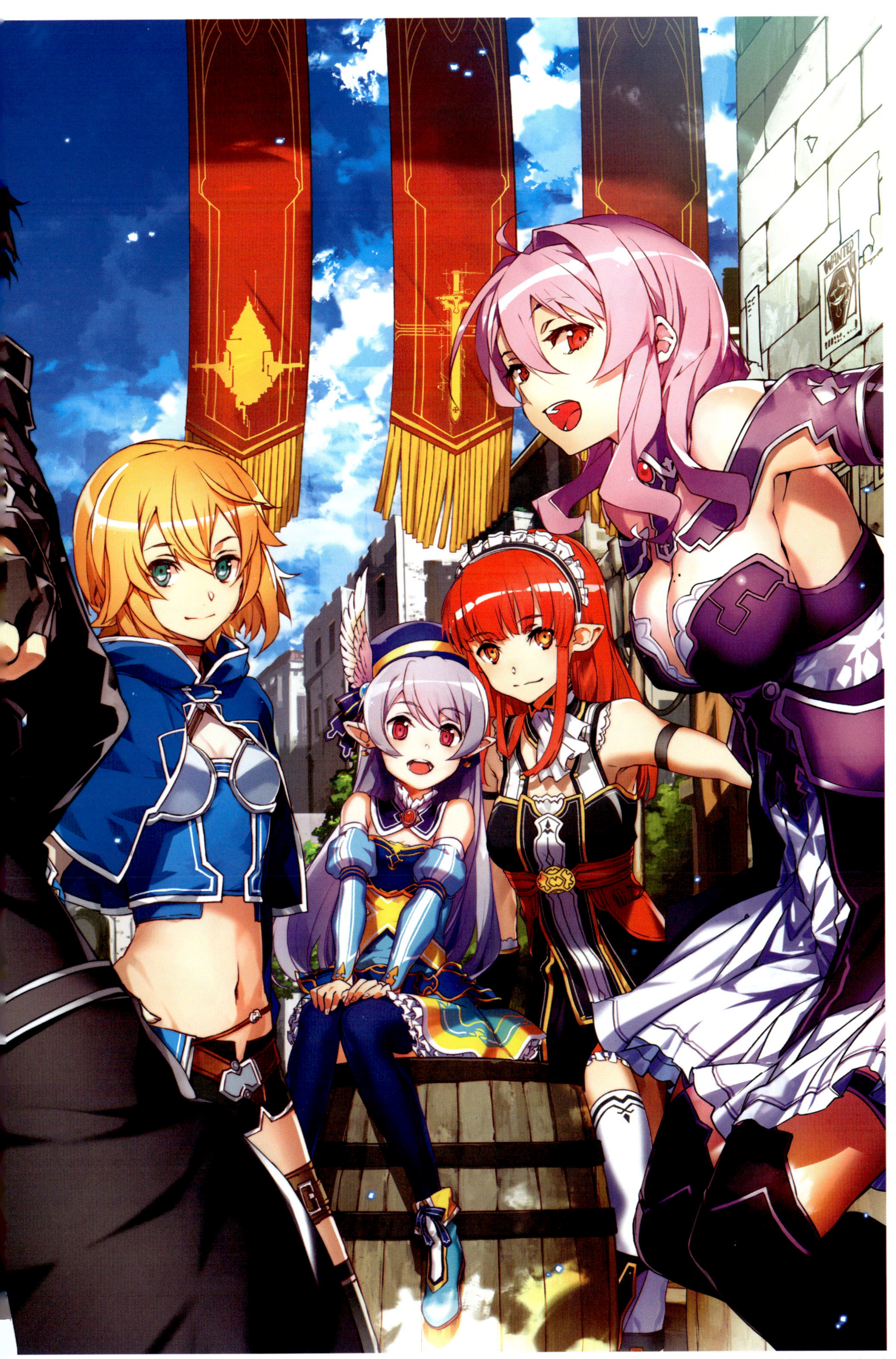

Here's all the game-original heroines meeting up in town. Beyond the concept, I was free to do what I wanted with this. Looking at the specs now, it says "cool and crisp," but I think my conception of a video game strategy meeting was more of a fun festival atmosphere, so it ended up being more bright and lively.

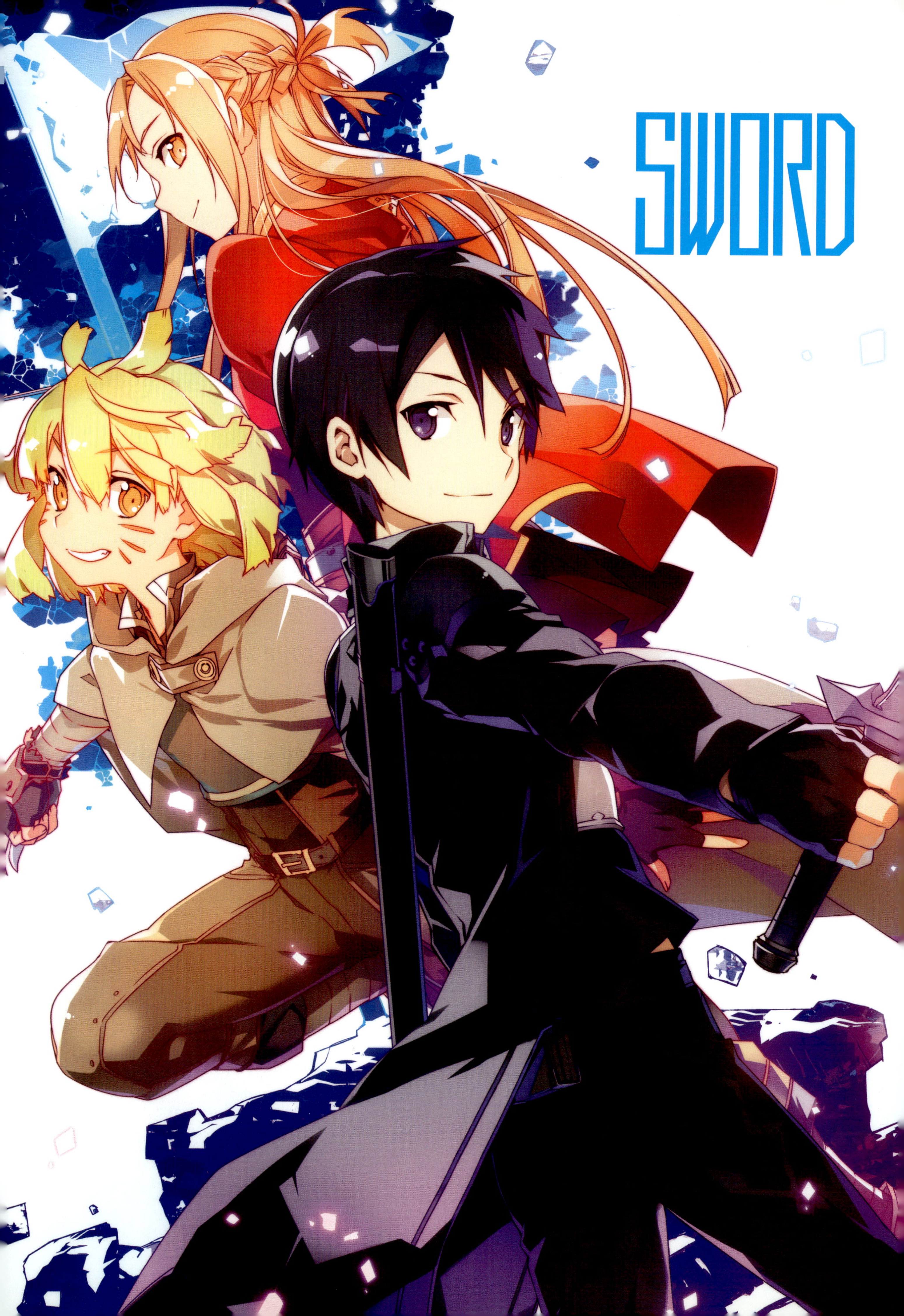

SWORD

ART ONLINE PROGRESSIVE 004

The fourth volume of the *Progressive* series, which retells the story in chronological order, starting from the first floor. This is the story that was adapted into the *Scherzo of Deep Night* movie.

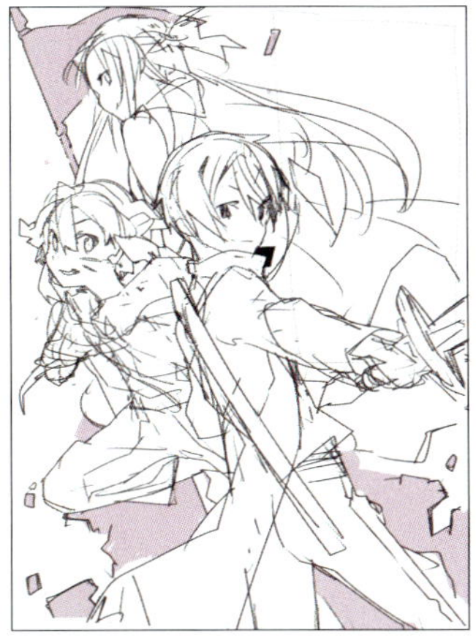

Rough Sketch

Dengeki Bunko
Sword Art Online Progressive 4
Cover: December 2015

Argo's totally a main character now, so this is her first cover. Looking back at this book, it's surprising how little she actually showed up, though.

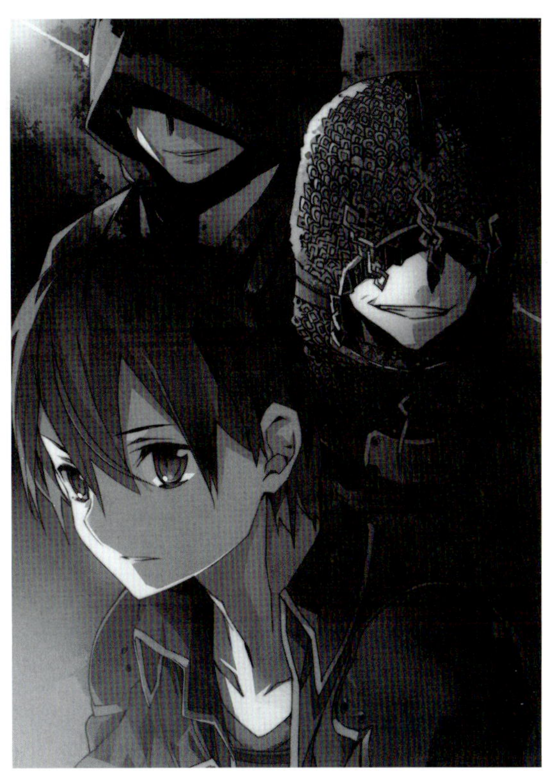

Dengeki Bunko
Sword Art Online
Progressive 4
Illustration: December 2015

Timeline-wise, this is before the first light novel, but I find it interesting that Asuna's expressions are so rich already. Of course, most of that change is due to me, as the person responsible for the output, but maybe some of that discrepancy is due to the first novel focusing more on the death game angle, while this series and its several volumes are more focused on the characters.

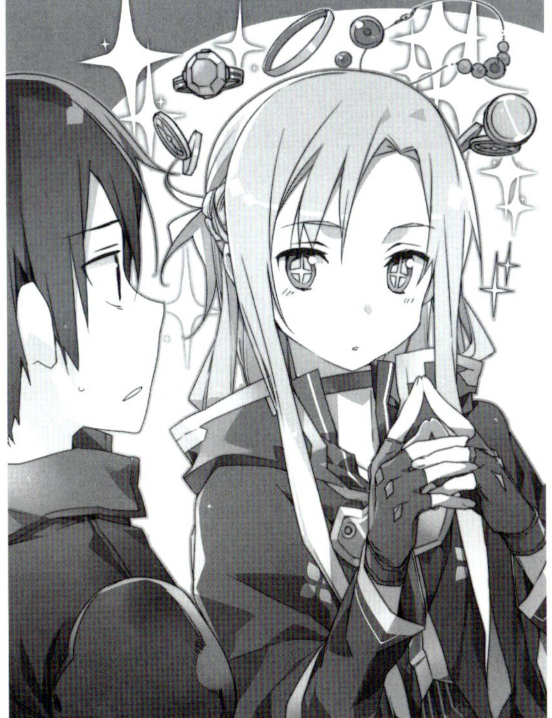

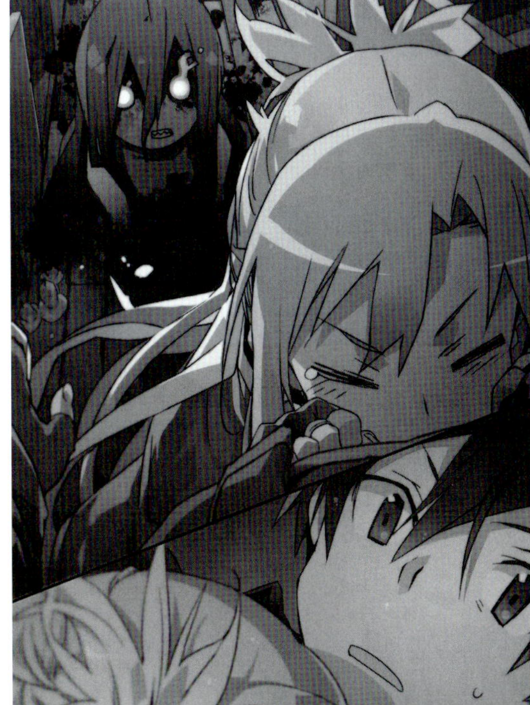

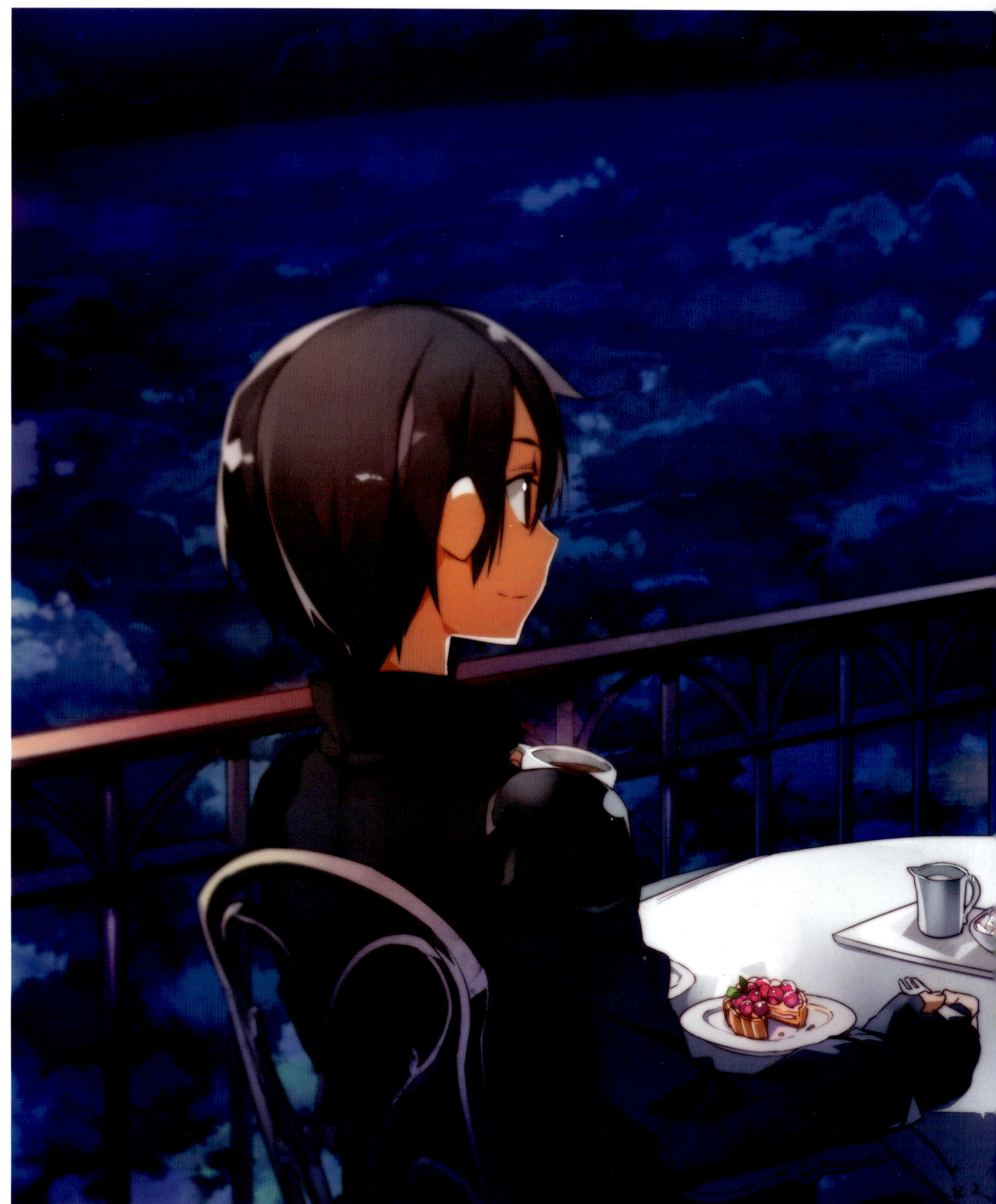

Dengeki Bunko
Sword Art Online Progressive 4
Frontispiece: December 2015

Eating pie on the terrace. Honestly, this restaurant would have anyone with a fear of heights absolutely jelly-legging it out there.

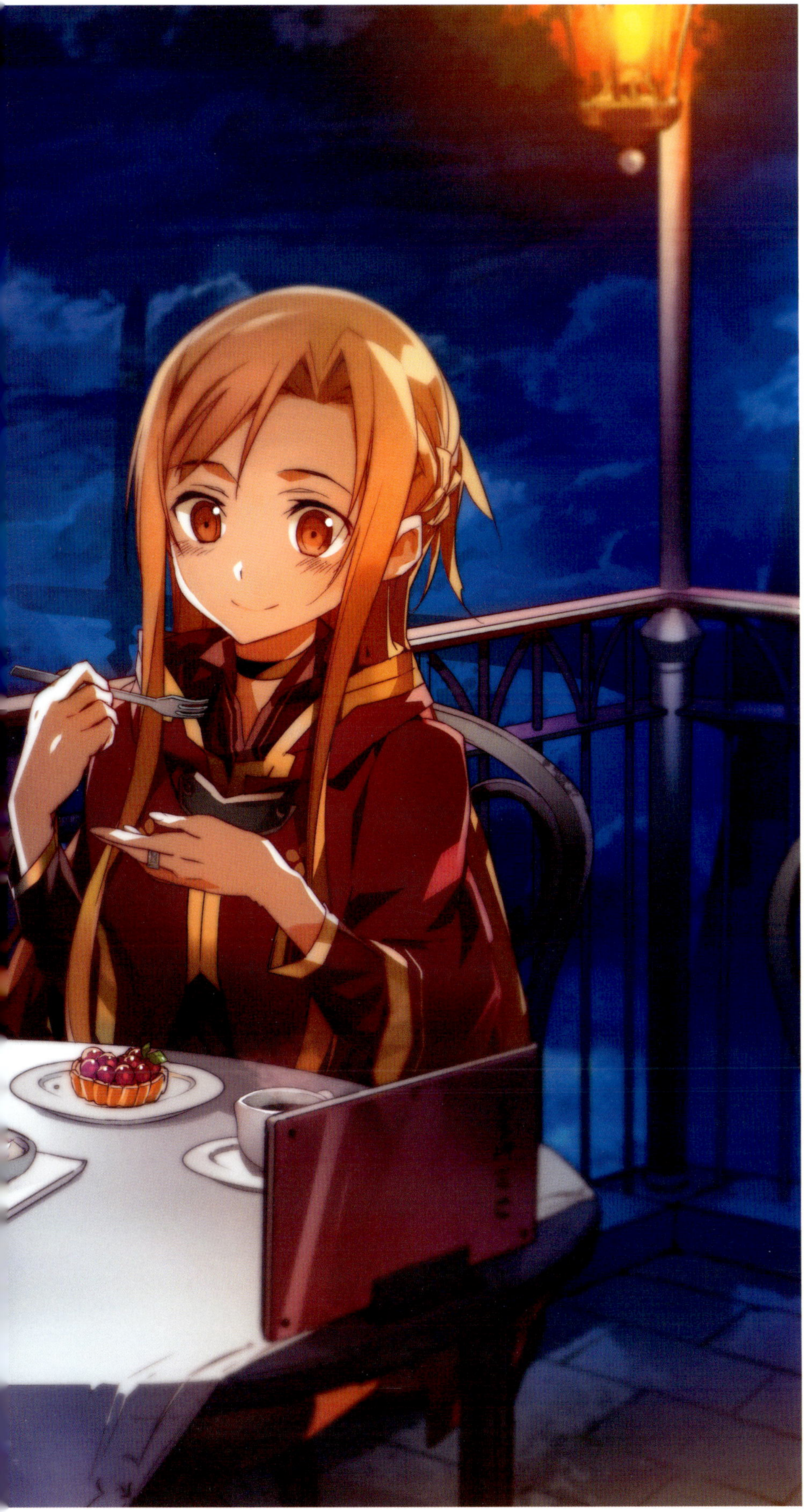

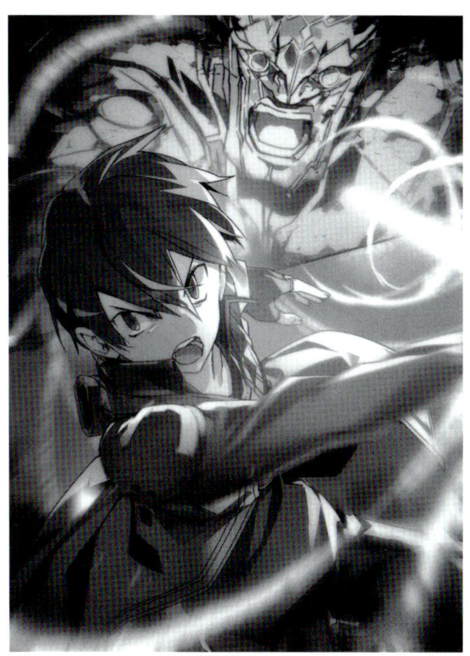

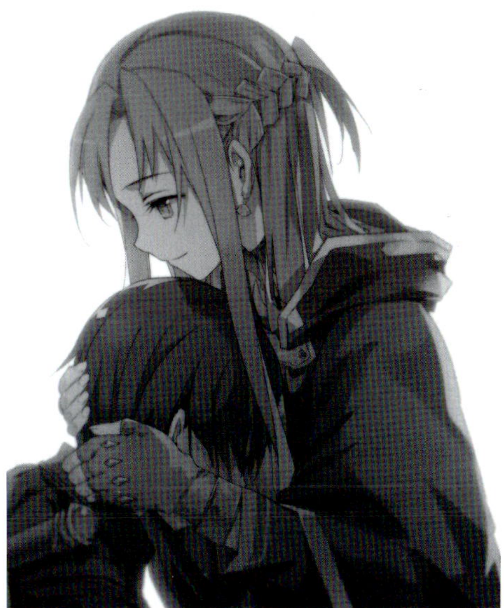

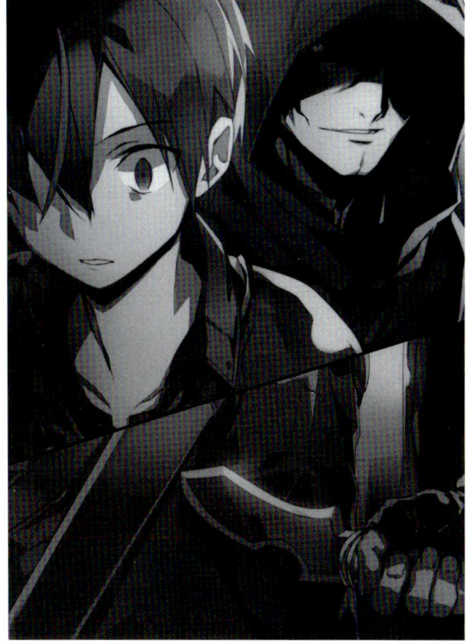

Dengeki Bunko
Sword Art Online Progressive 4
Illustration: December 2015

As usual, PoH hides his face. Given that this is a game, I imagine that putting on a hood is basically completely shading out your face, like the black mages in the *Final Fantasy* series.

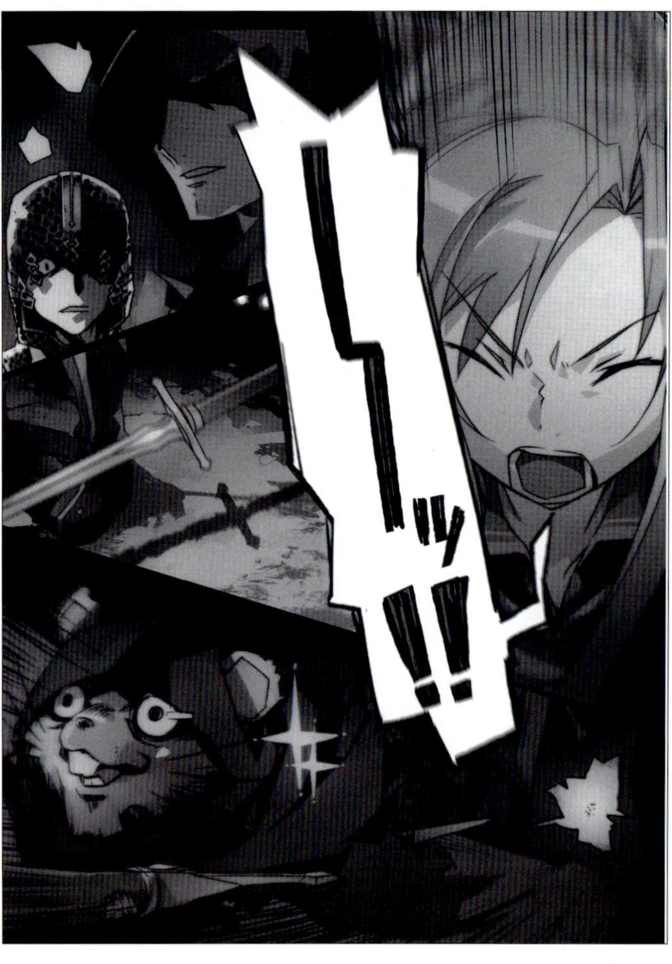

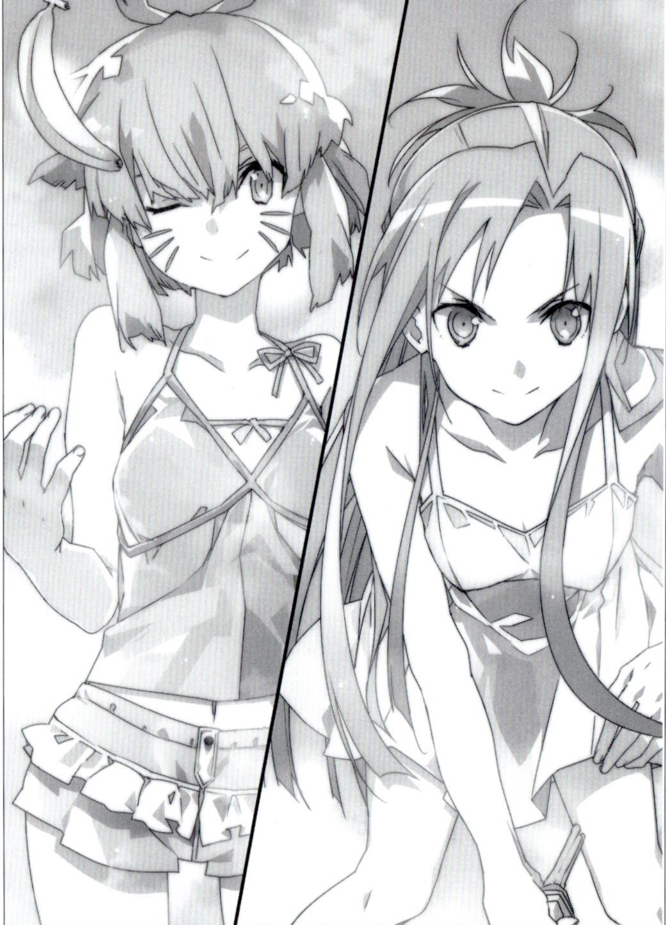

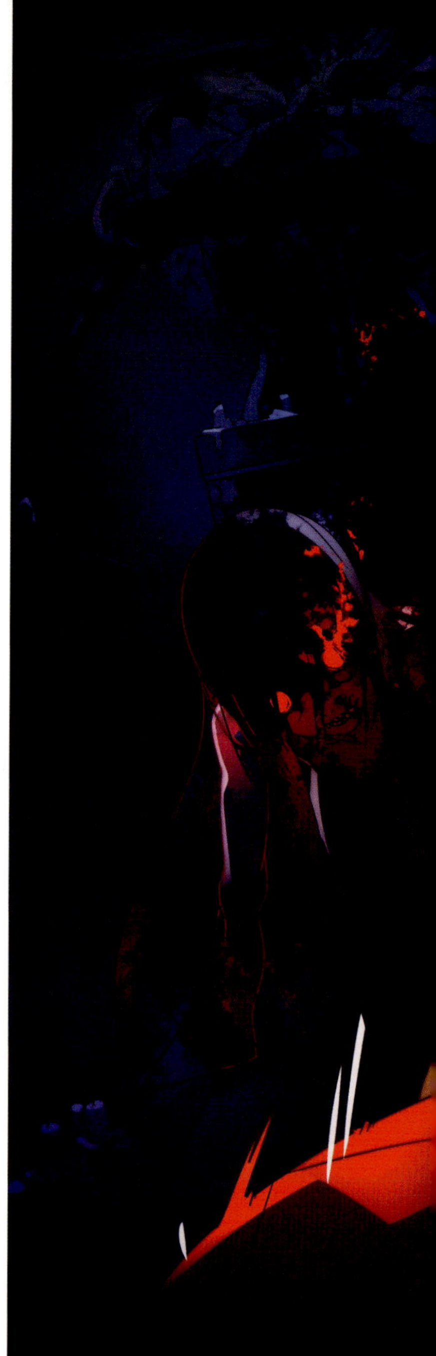

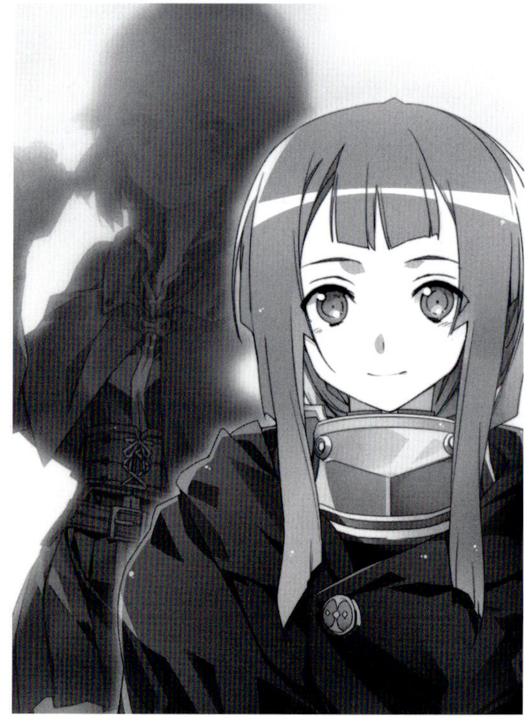

Dengeki Bunko
Sword Art Online Progressive 4
Illustration: December 2015

It's so much easier to give some momentum to your illustration when you use manga effects or speech bubbles like this. Also, I forgot that I was the one who designed the shrewman stealing the fallen items, so I was in some interview and accidentally praised my own work by saying, "Whoever did that designed it really well!" That's so embarrassing...

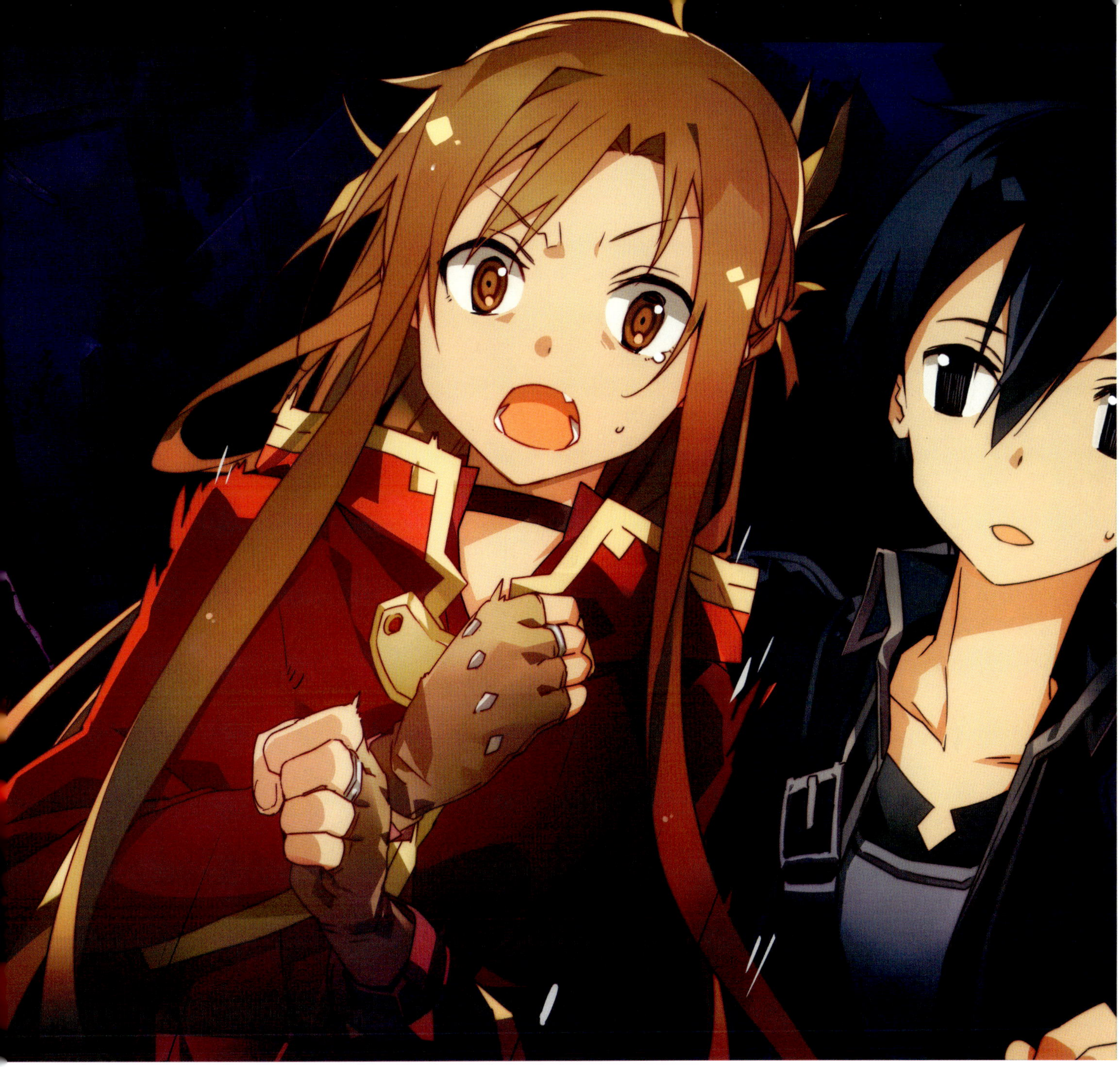

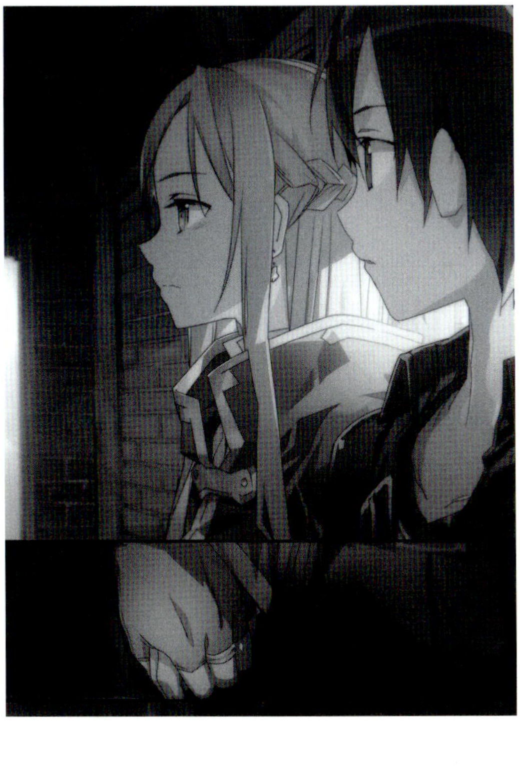

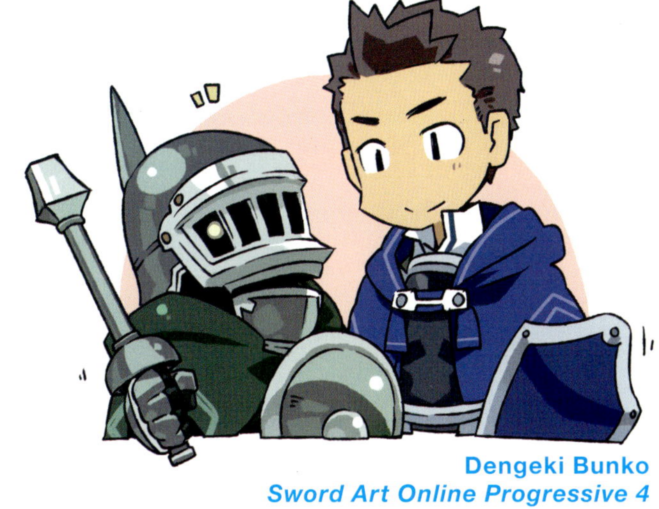

Dengeki Bunko
Sword Art Online Progressive 4
Frontispiece: December 2015

Asuna terrified of ghosts. It's comedic, yes, but when you're in VR with all your senses engaged, I have to imagine that horror stuff is absolutely heart-stopping.

Dengeki Bunko
Sword Art Online Progressive 4
Rear Cover: December 2015

Do you like your heavily armored, mace-wielding girlfriend? I do.

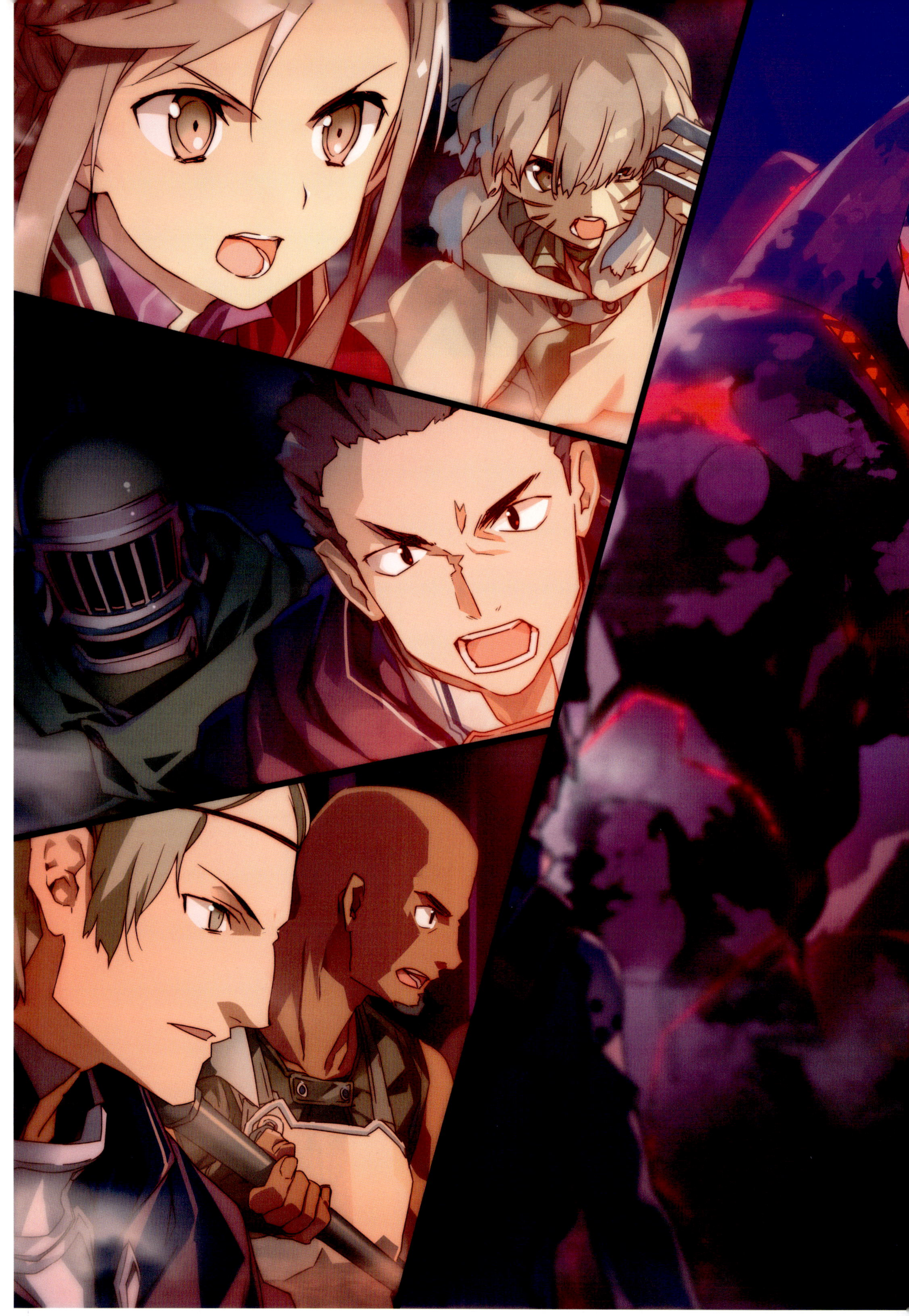

Dengeki Bunko
Sword Art Online Progressive 4
Frontispiece: December 2015

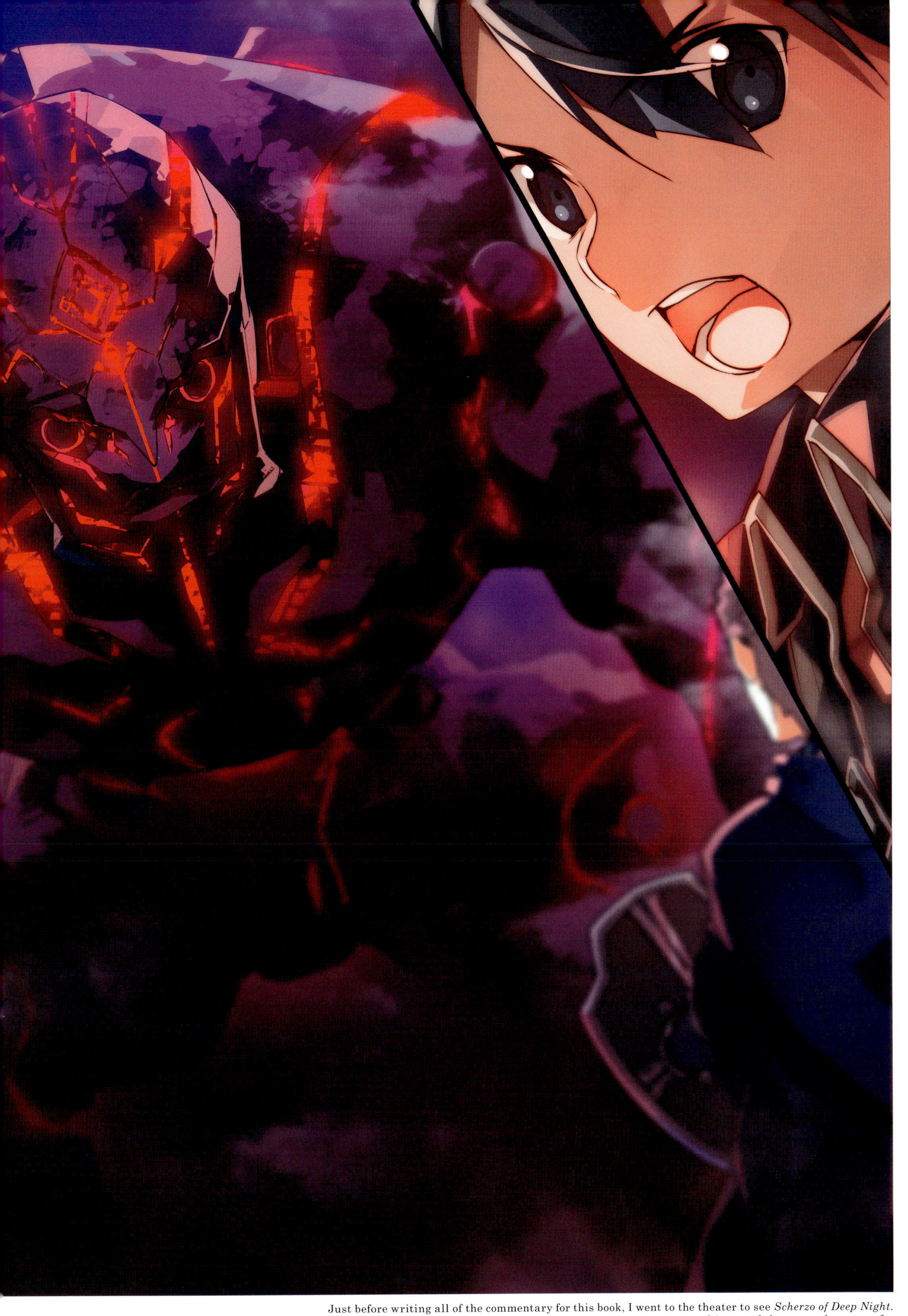

Just before writing all of the commentary for this book, I went to the theater to see *Scherzo of Deep Night*. My version of this pales in comparison, but getting to see it recreated is one of the great pleasures of a multi-media series like this one. Also, look at how surreal Liten is there, among the close-ups designed to show the characters' emotions.

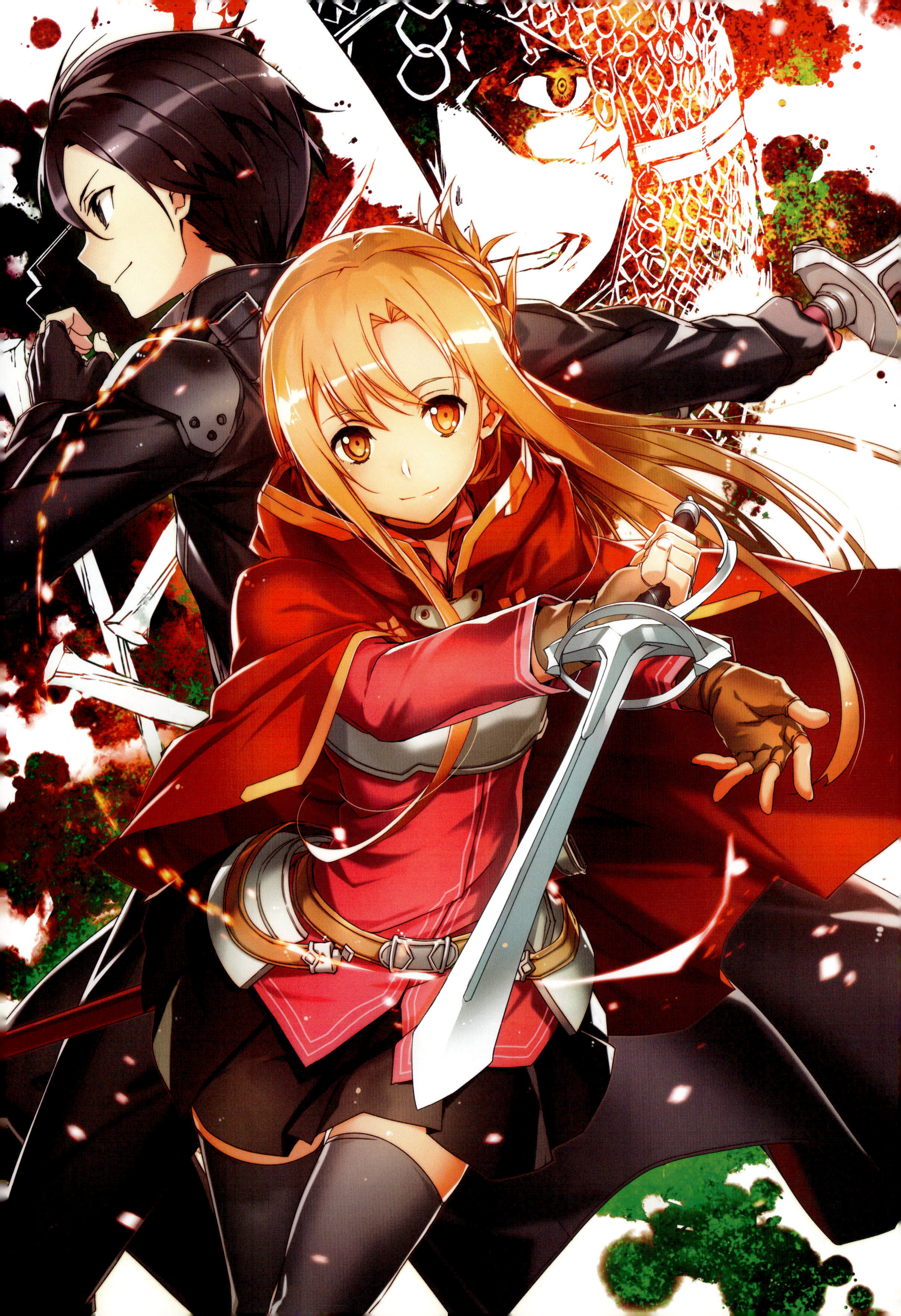

SWORD ART ONLINE PROGRESSIVE 005

This is the start of a two-volume story. If they all take two volumes to tell, what volume will it be when we reach the seventy-fifth floor?!

Dengeki Bunko
Sword Art Online Progressive 5
Cover: February 2018

I normally try to put the outline of an item or keyword that's central to the plot as the background element, but in this case I just slapped Morte's face in there. Also, the green touches are meant to symbolize poison, which I think is a common visual cue in games. It's also depicted as purple quite often.

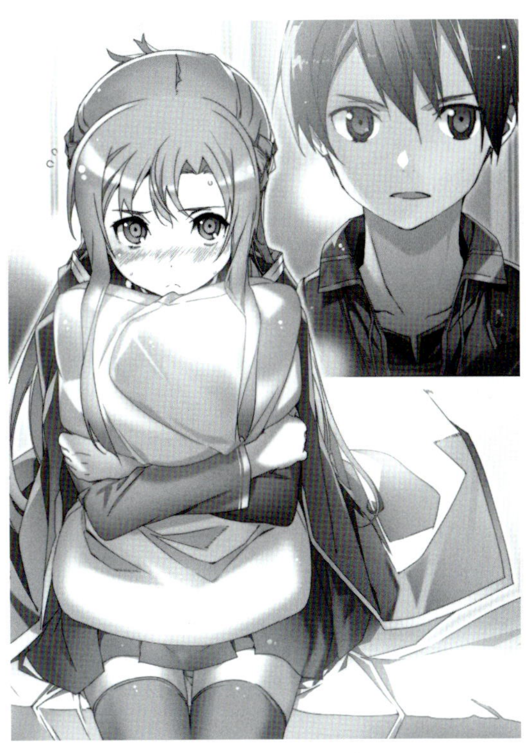

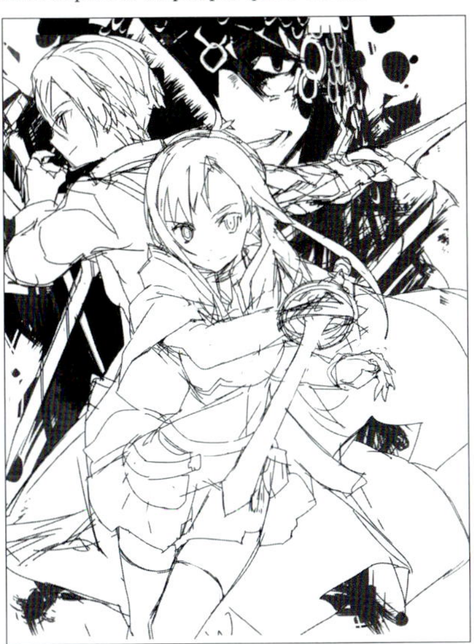

Rough Sketch

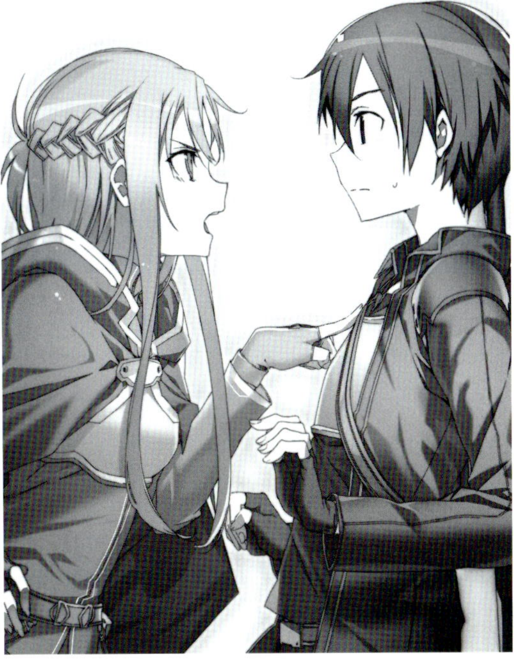

Dengeki Bunko
Sword Art Online Progressive 5
Illustration: February 2018

If you only look at the story illustrations, you might assume that the *Progressive* series is nothing but Kirito and Asuna flirting with each other. What? You mean that's what the main series is like, too...?

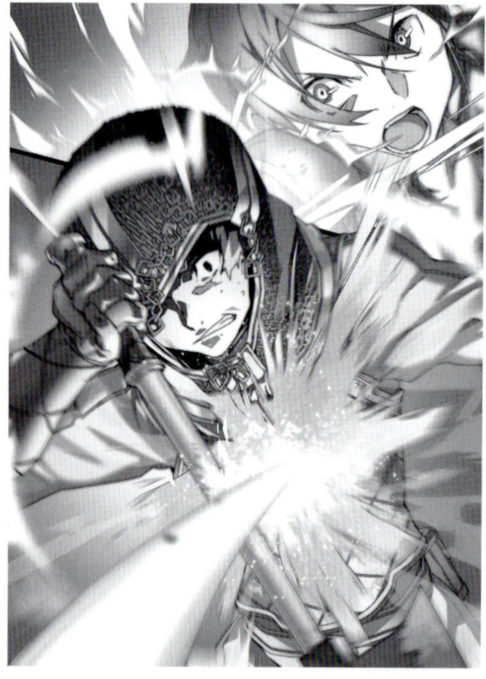

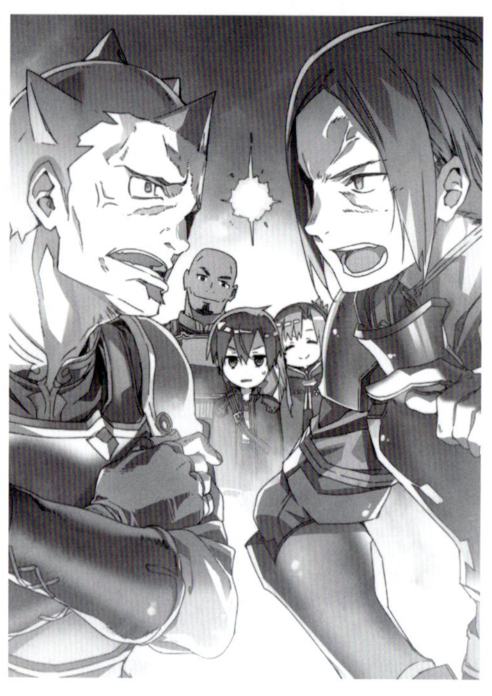

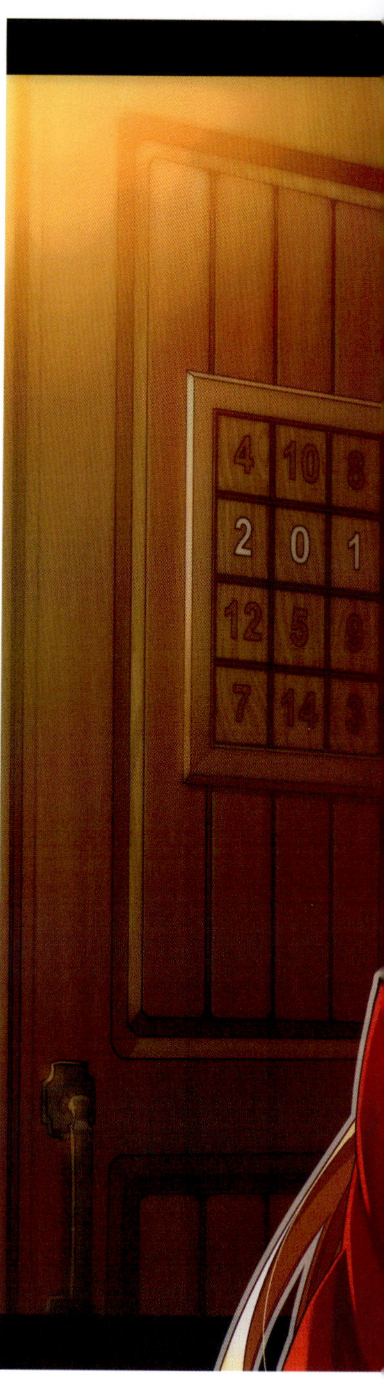

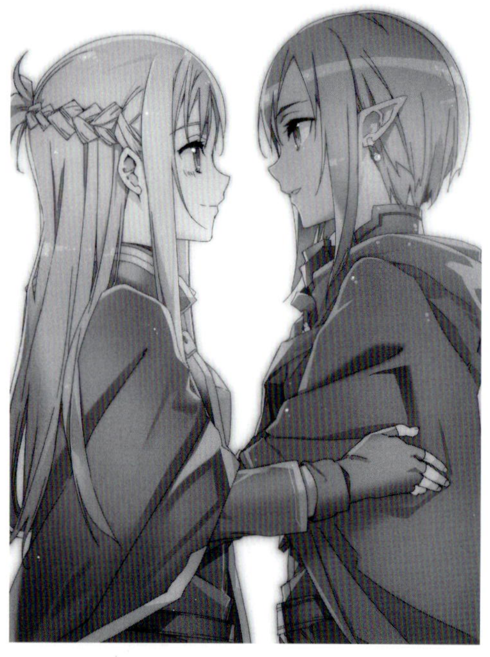

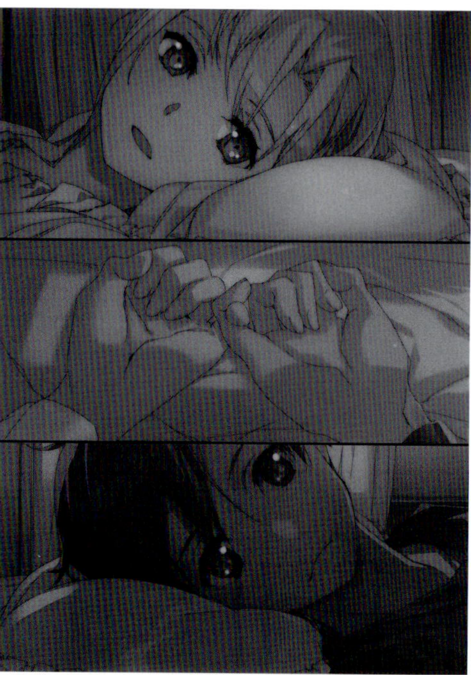

Dengeki Bunko
Sword Art Online Progressive 5
Illustration: February 2018

It's so much fun to draw Kibaou. I wonder—
If Diavel were still alive, would these two
have gotten along fine?

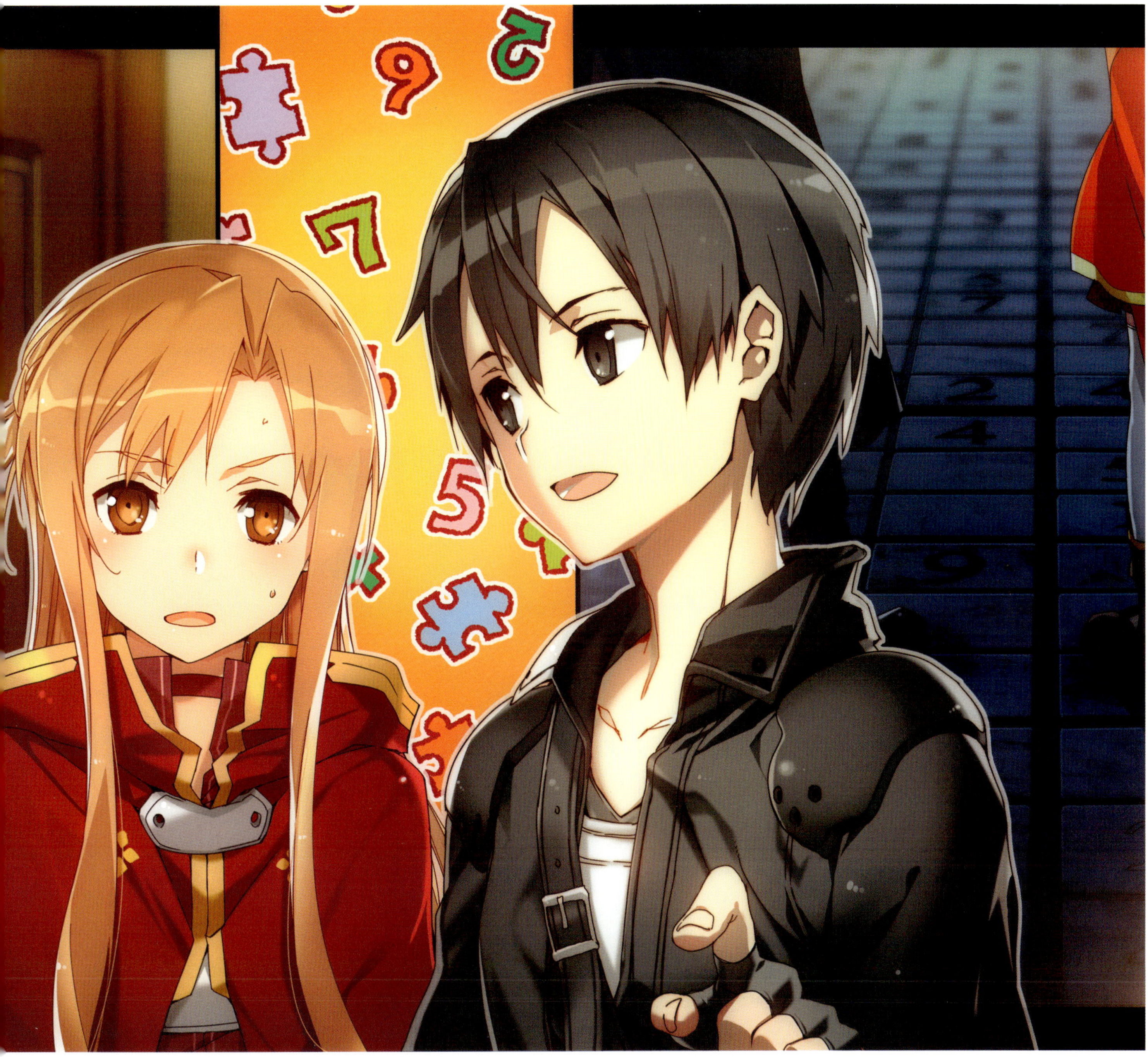

Dengeki Bunko, *Sword Art Online Progressive 5*
Frontispiece: February 2018

Sometimes I do sudoku as a little mental exercise. I feel like a town full of puzzles would be really fun to solve, but if you lived there, it would probably be a drag.

Dengeki Bunko
Sword Art Online Progressive 5
Rear Cover: February 2018

I've never solved a Rubik's Cube.

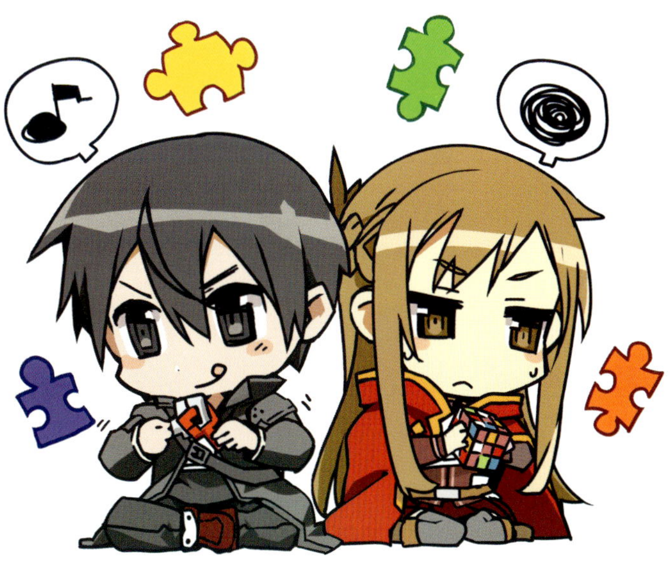

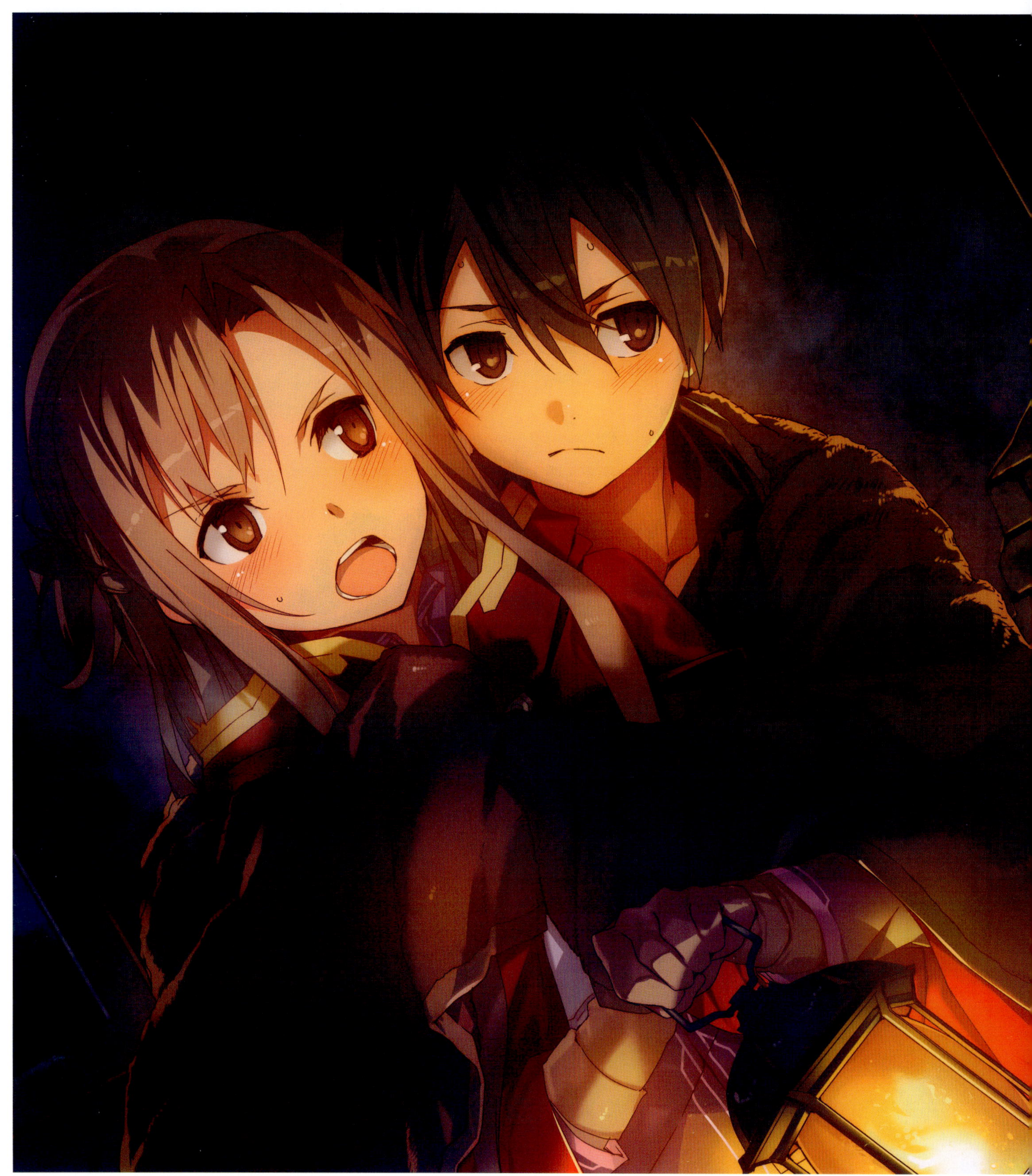

Dengeki Bunko
Sword Art Online Progressive 5
Frontispiece: February 2018

They are totally an item, right?

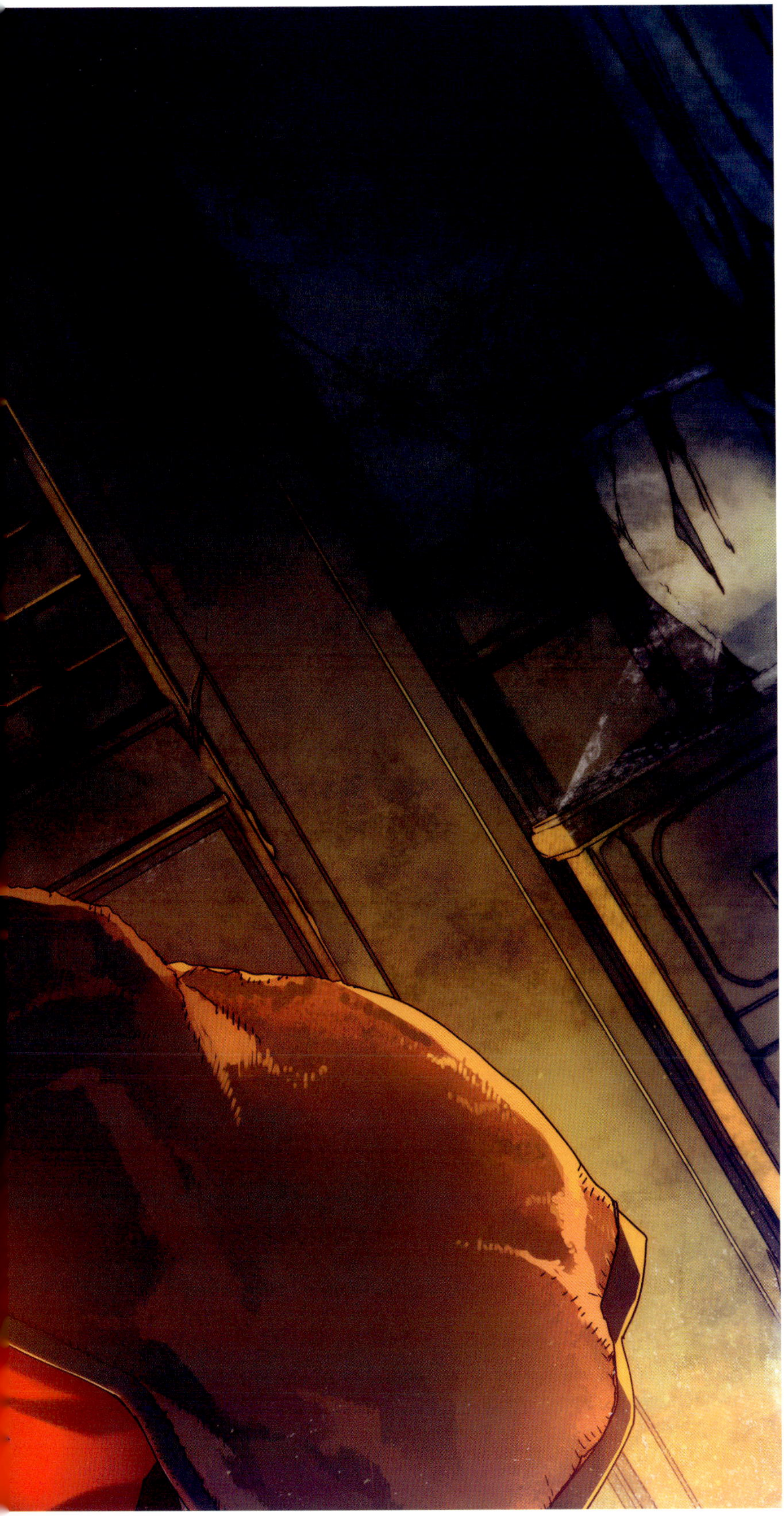

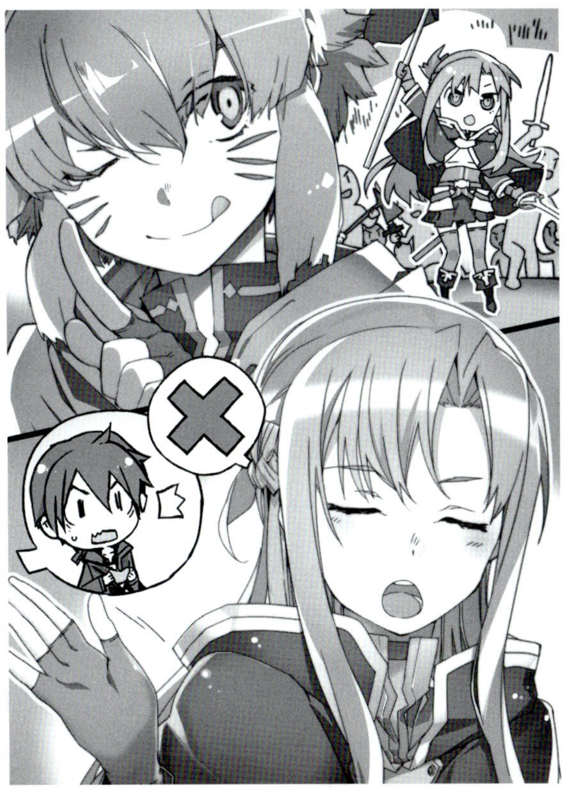
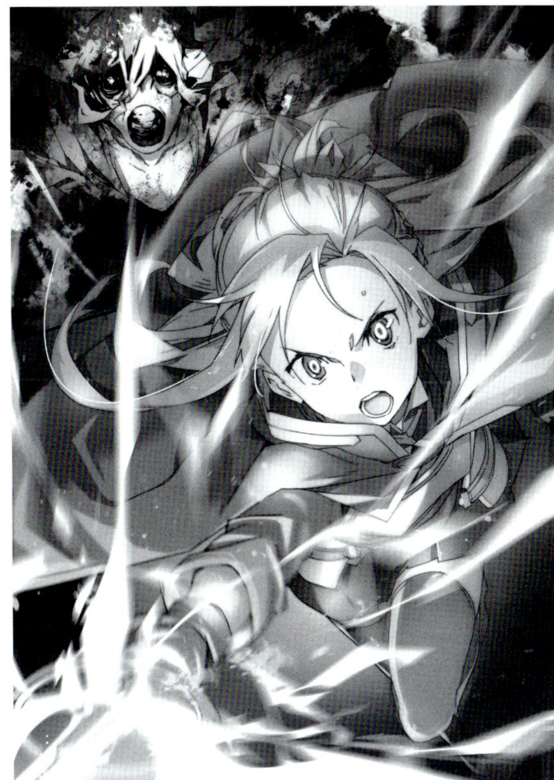

Dengeki Bunko
Sword Art Online Progressive 5
Illustration: February 2018

The top one is Argo saying that if Asuna started a guild, people would flock to her. I think it's funny to imagine Asuna in her pre-Kirito desperation state, eyes spinning, shouting, "Everyone, follow me!" Setting aside whether it's in her personality or not.

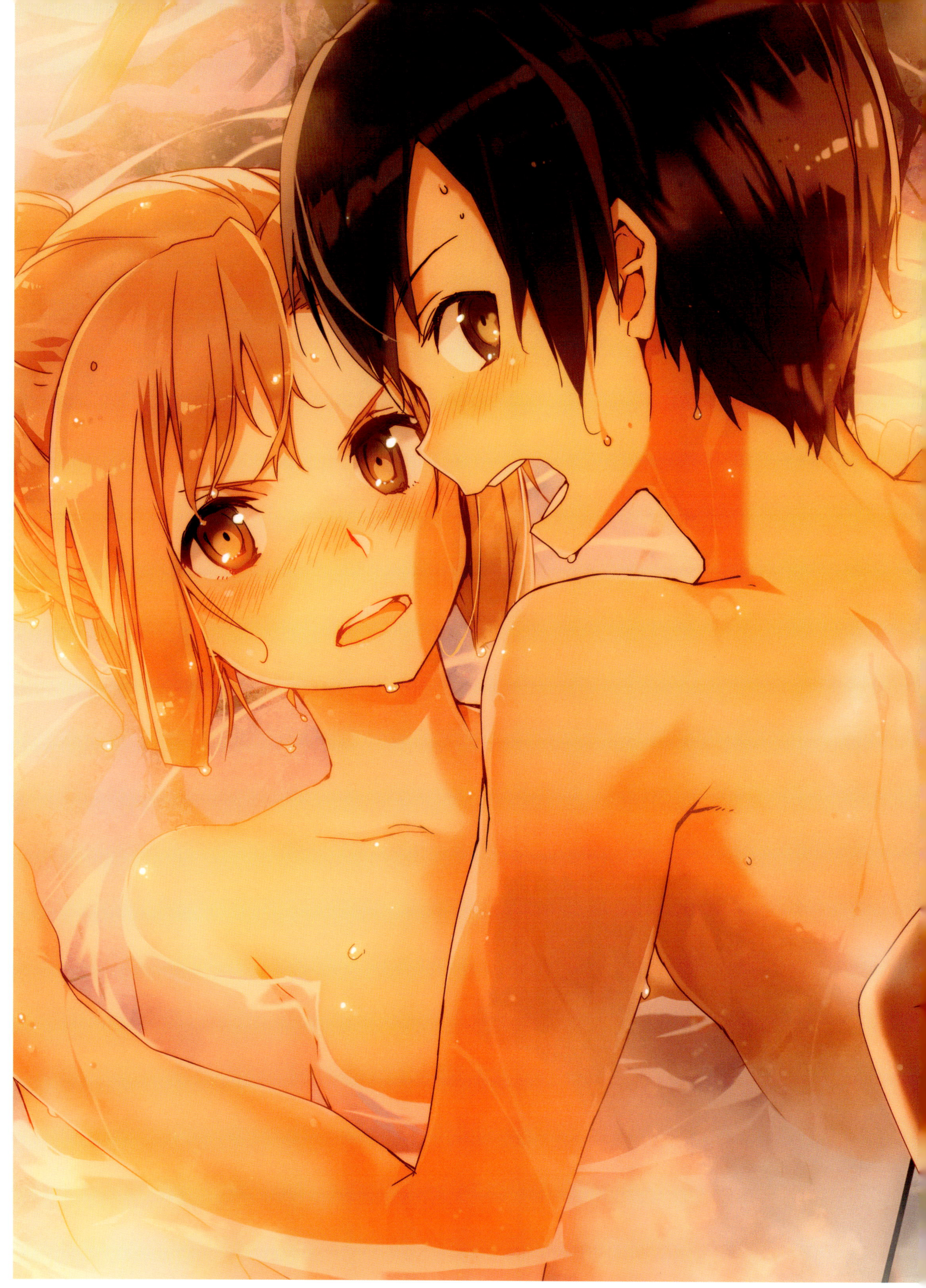

Dengeki Bunko, *Sword Art Online Progressive 5*
Frontispiece: February 2018

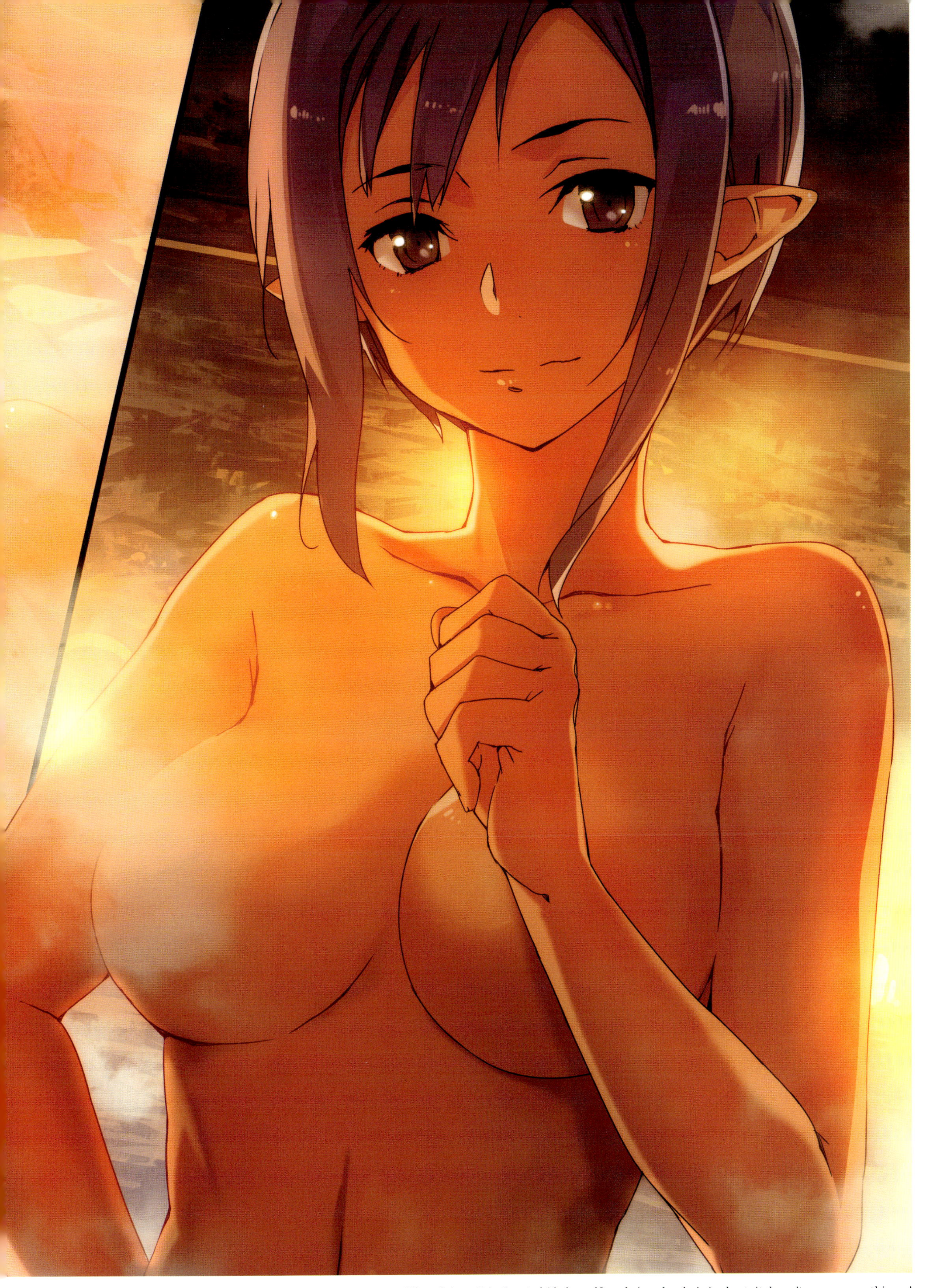

Kizmel doesn't bother to hide herself, and since her hair is short, it doesn't...cover...anything...!

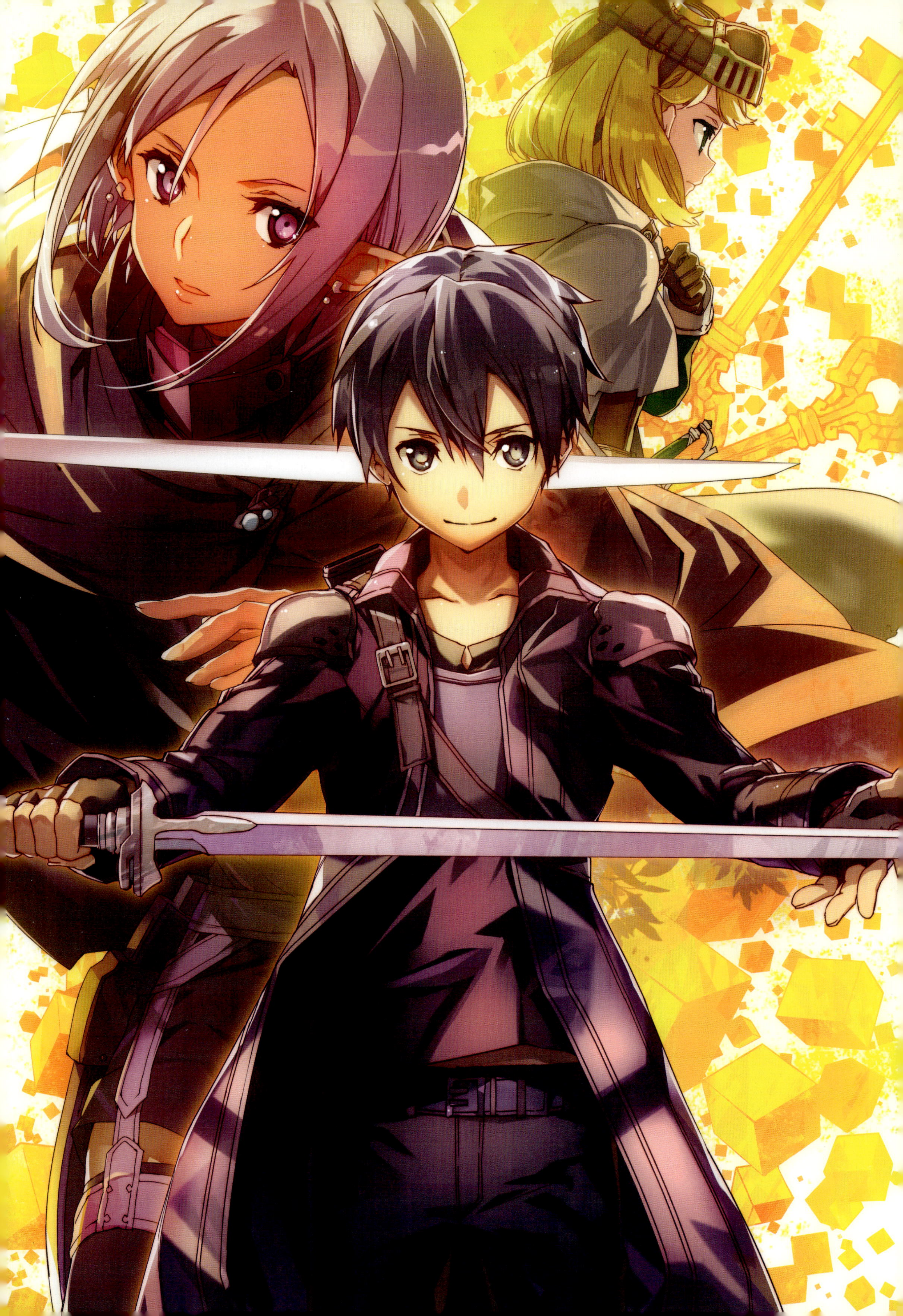

SWORD ART ONLINE PROGRESSIVE 006

The second half of this two-volume story. Of course, in addition to the ongoing floor-by-floor gameplay, the *Progressive* series features lots of fun bonuses like foodie tours and quests to solve.

Dengeki Bunko
Sword Art Online Progressive 6
Cover: May 2018

The new character in this volume, Myia, wears a leather mask, but it's kind of hard to tell from how I did this cover. I regret that one. The motif in the background is cubes and keys.

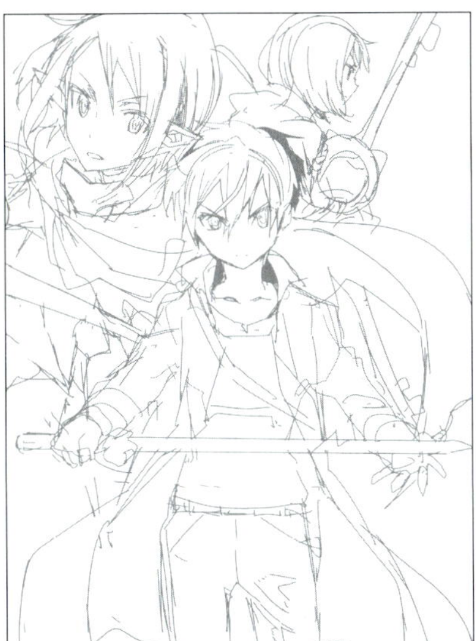

Rough Sketch

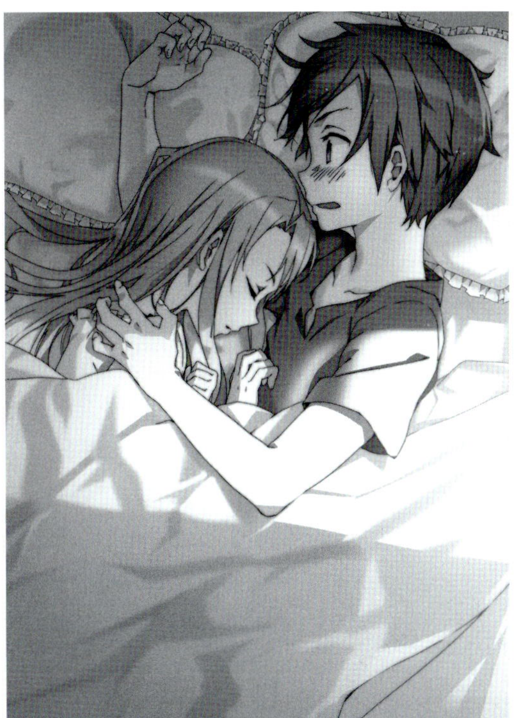

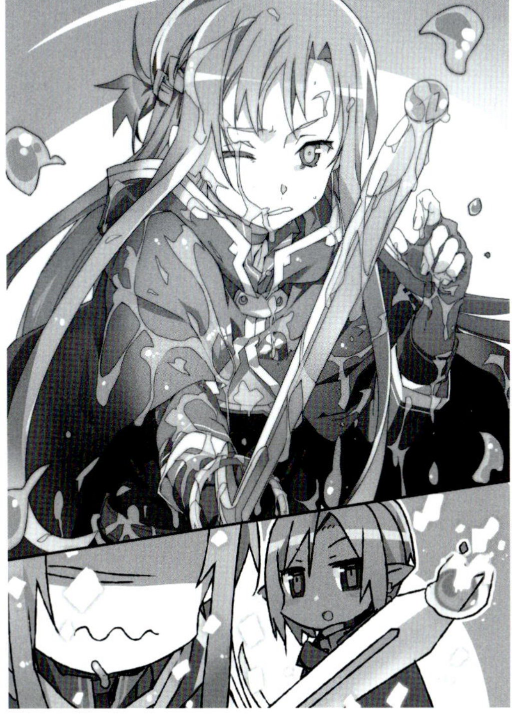

Dengeki Bunko
Sword Art Online Progressive 6
Illustration: May 2018

More romcom moments!

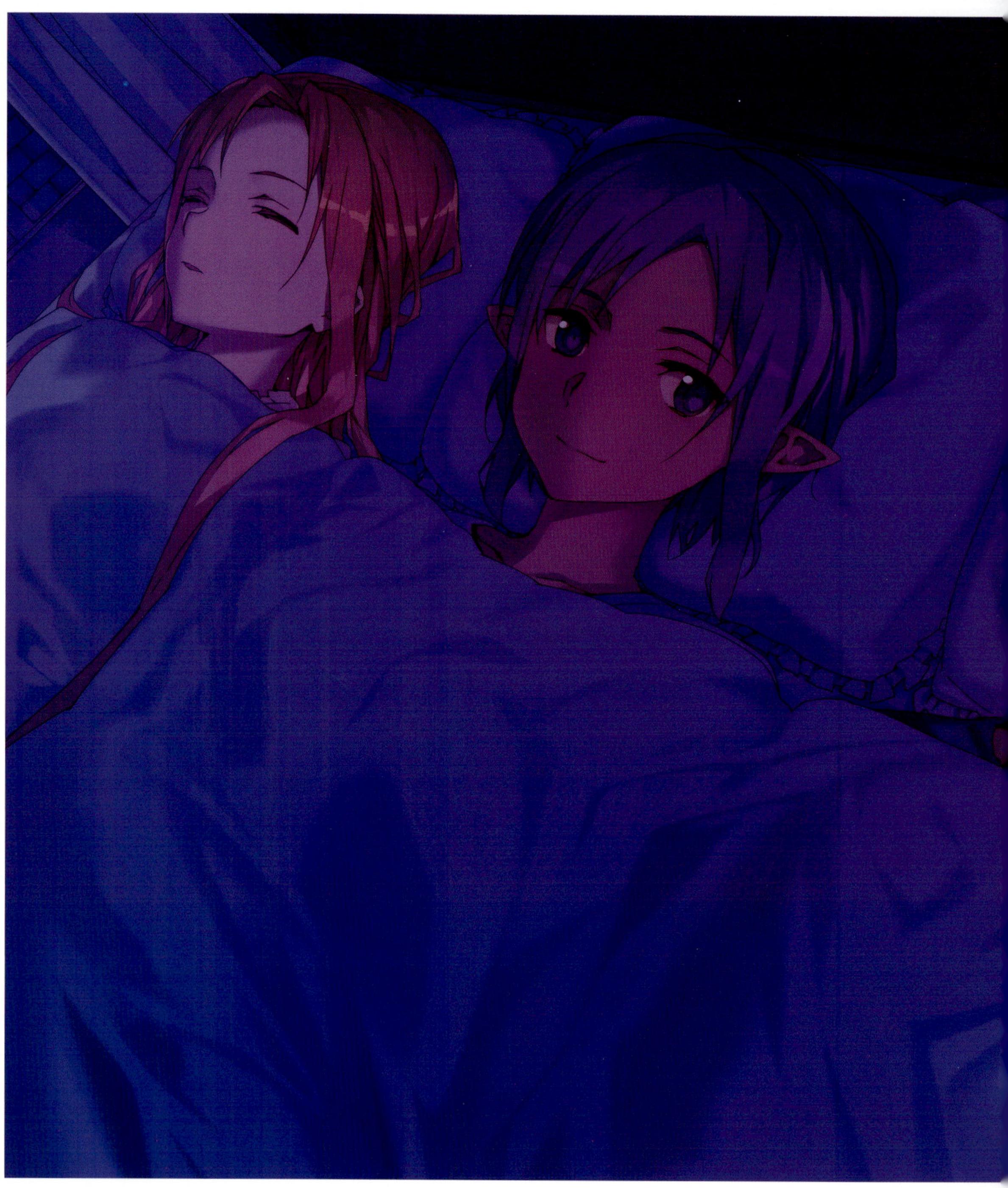

Dengeki Bunko
Sword Art Online Progressive 6
Frontispiece: May 2018

Longhaired characters sleeping or in the bath gives me lots
to think about, but I usually choose not to bundle up the hair,
because if it rests on the body or blanket, it helps create a
visual sense of volume. I figure it's okay, because it's a game.

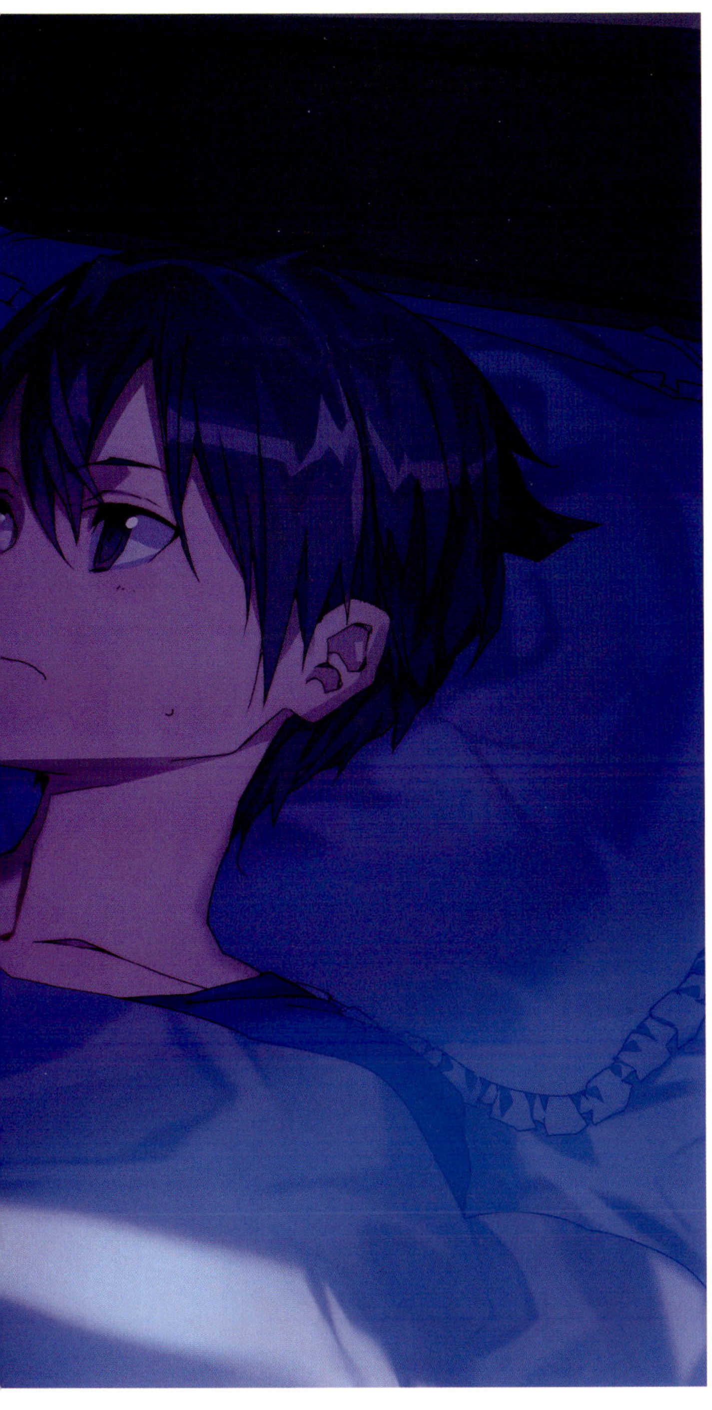

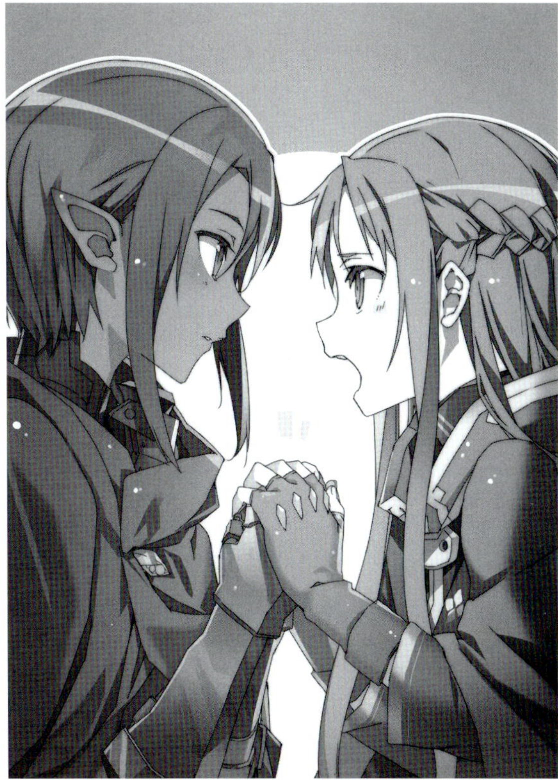

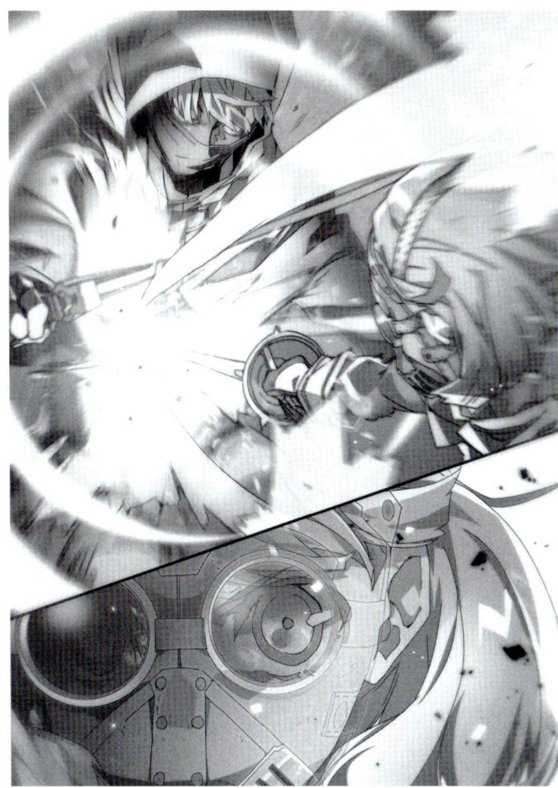

Dengeki Bunko
Sword Art Online Progressive 6
Illustration: May 2018

I love scenes where they're like,
"Whoa, that girl's strong!"

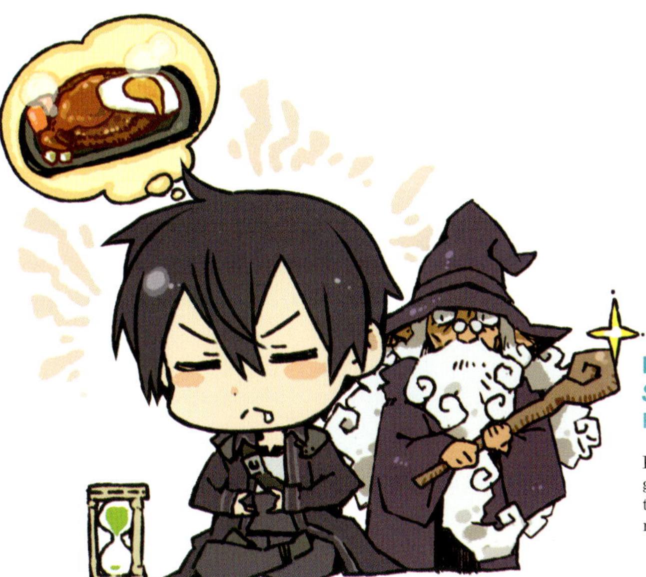

Dengeki Bunko
Sword Art Online Progressive 6
Rear Cover: May 2018

Kirito does zen meditation and still can't get over his attachment to meat. It occurred to me that *SAO* has a surprising lack of old man characters.

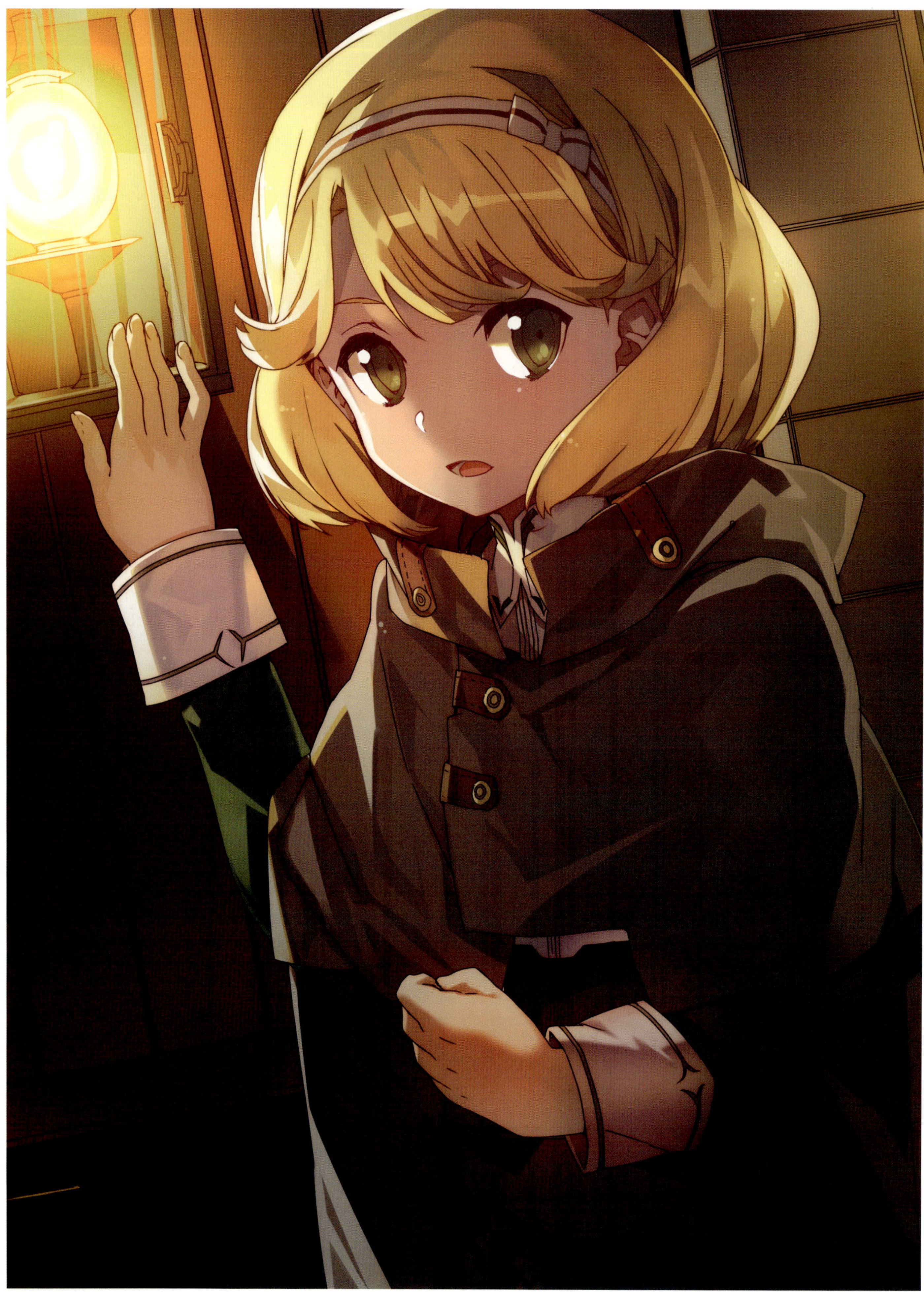

Dengeki Bunko
Sword Art Online Progressive 6
Frontispiece: May 2018

Dengeki Bunko
Sword Art Online Progressive 6
Frontispiece: May 2018

An introduction of Guild Qusack: Gindo, Lazuli, and Temuo. I feel it's important to pack all these secondary characters together to show them off, but sometimes when they get animated, the anime staff will put together designs and those end up becoming general references

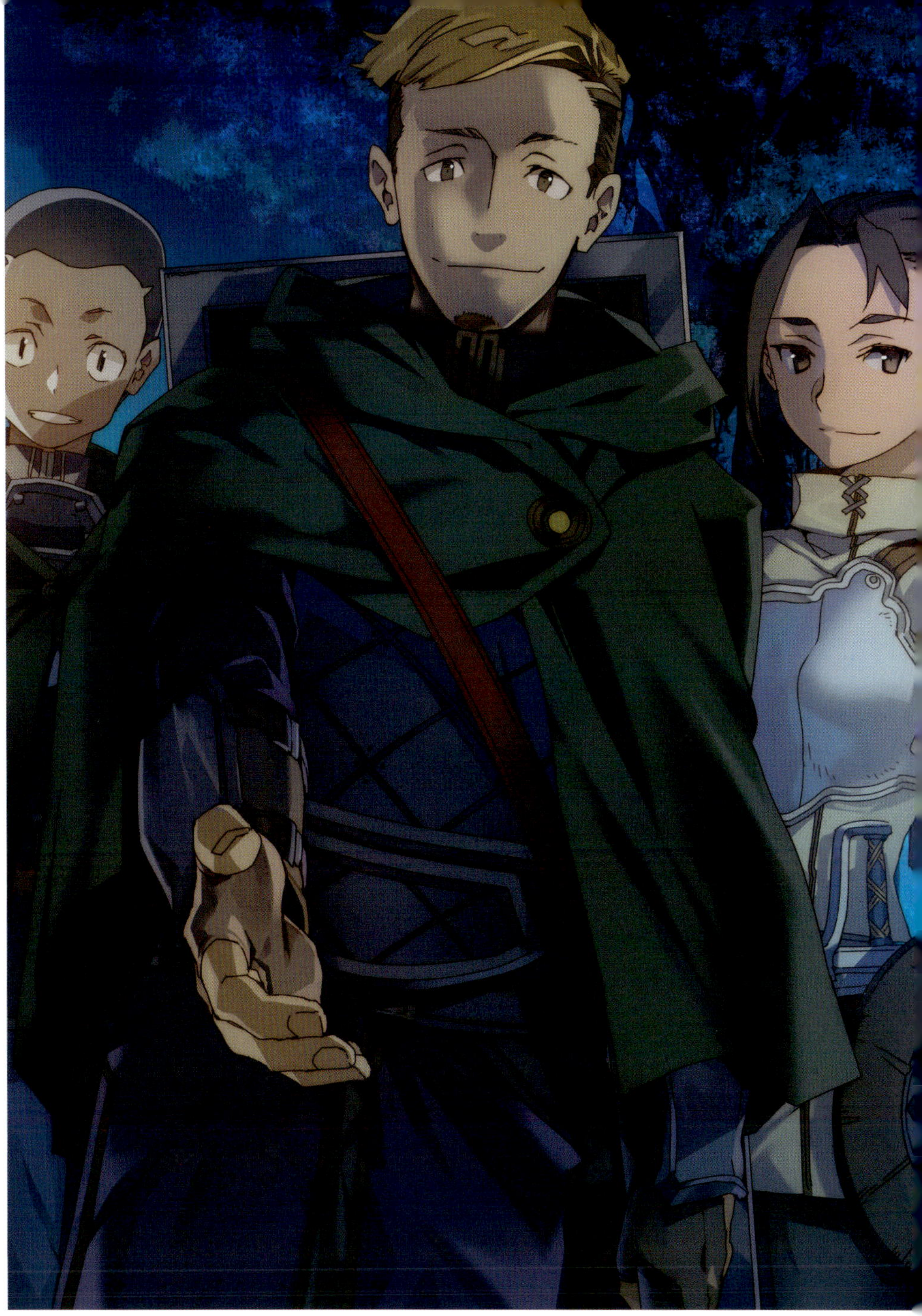

Dengeki Bunko
Sword Art Online Progressive 6
Illustration: May 2018

Boy, the elves sure are strong characters, huh? And when there's a bath scene, it always gets drawn. By the way, there are lots of foreign translations of these books, and depending on the country, some of them add way, way more steam.

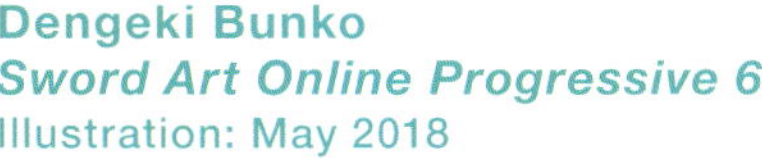

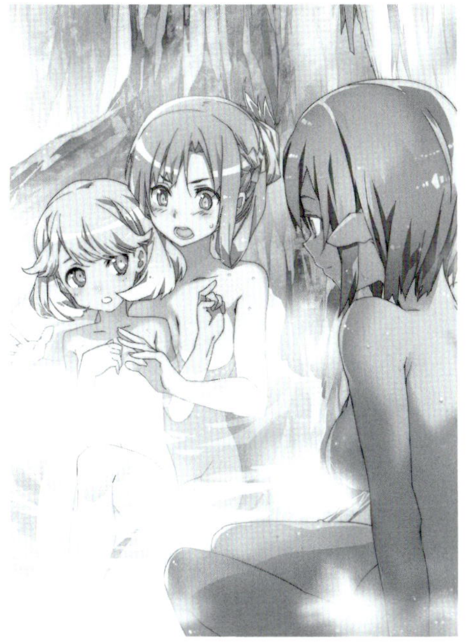

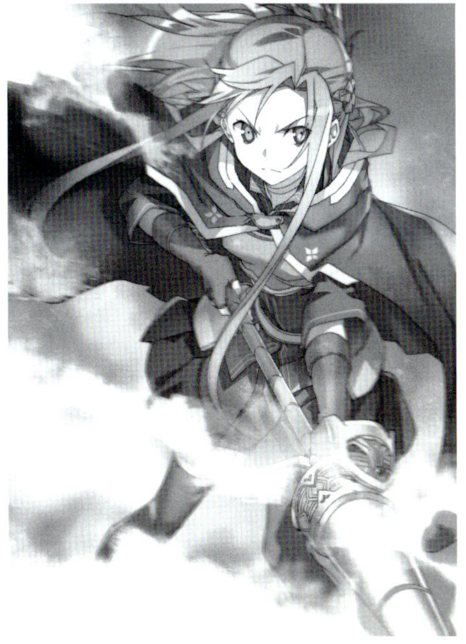

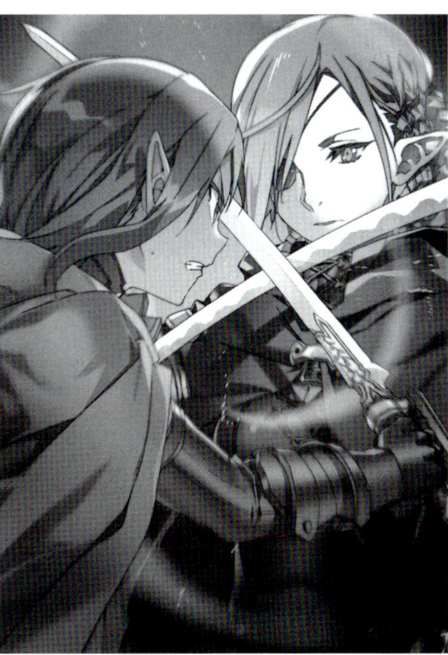

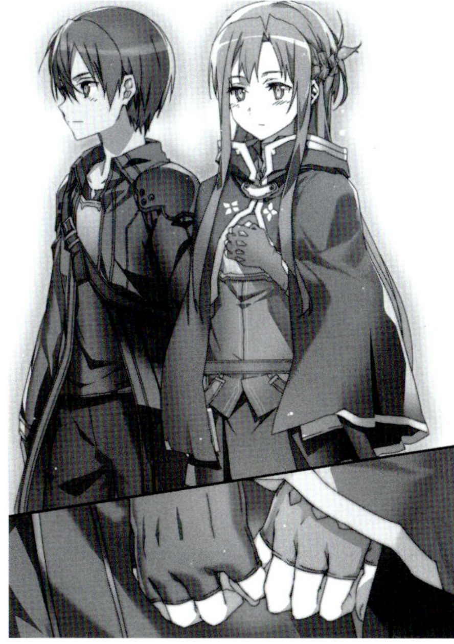

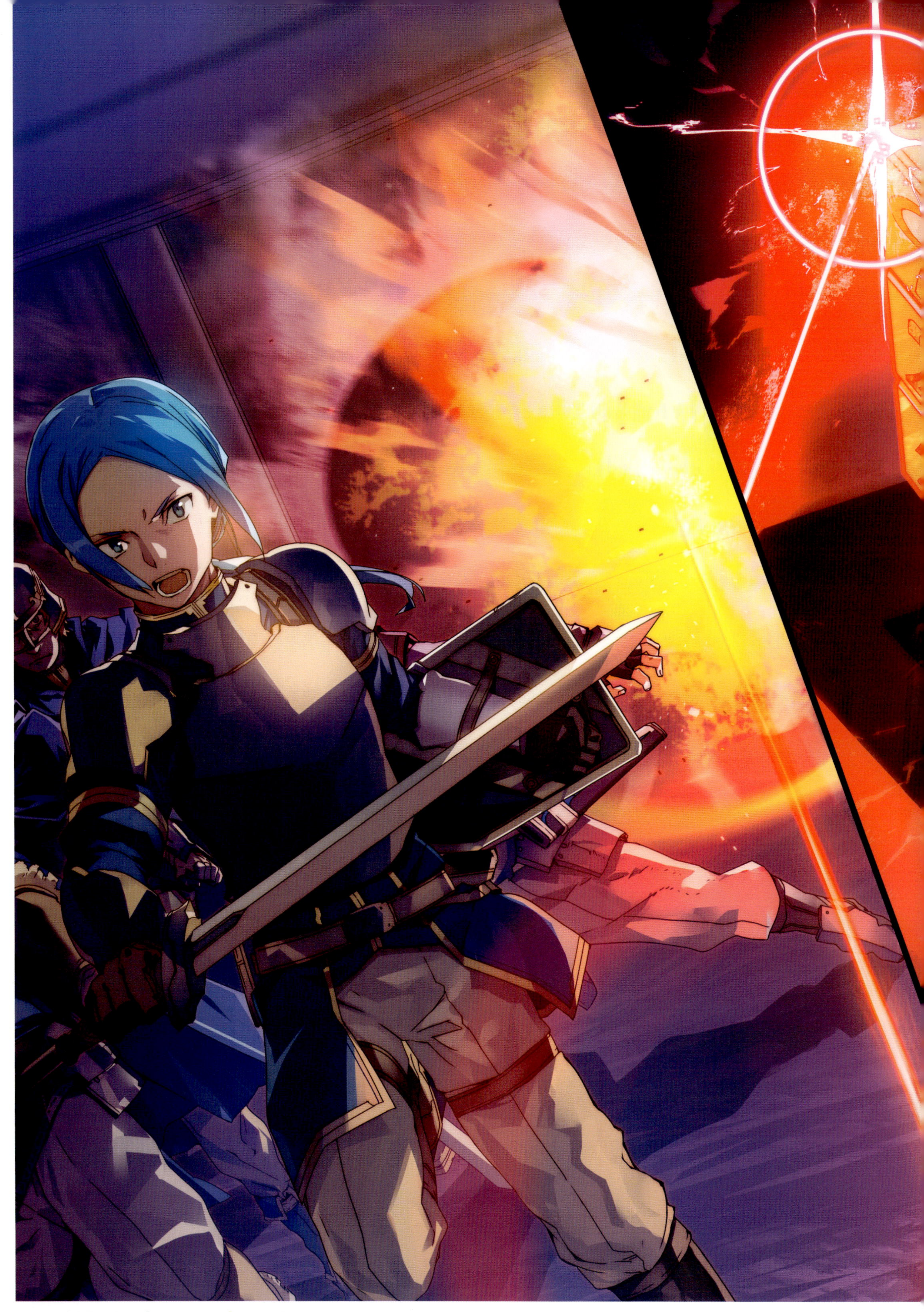

Dengeki Bunko, *Sword Art Online Progressive 6*
Frontispiece: May 2018

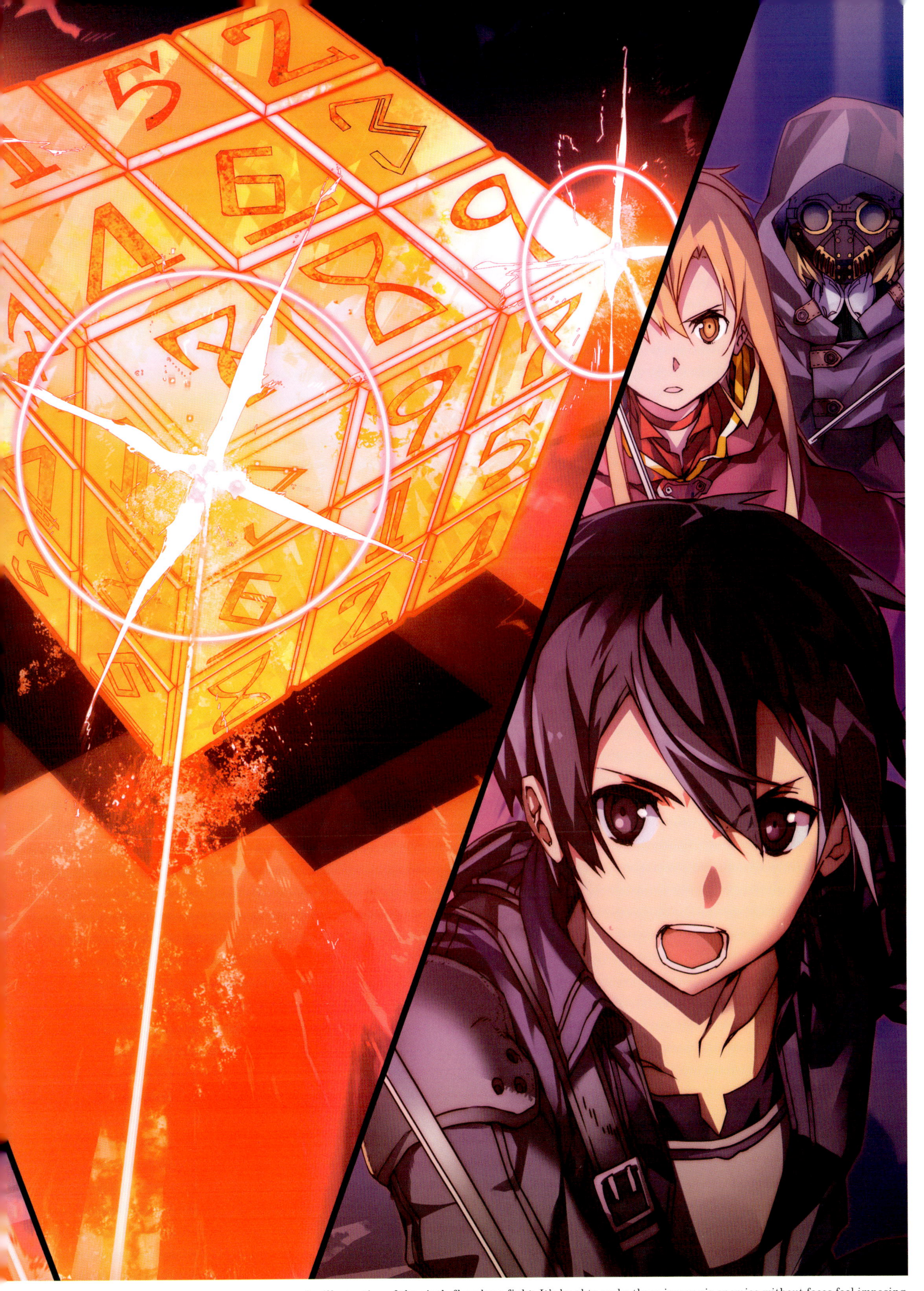

An illustration of the sixth-floor boss fight. It's hard to make these inorganic enemies without faces feel imposing.

SWORD ART ONLINE media mix 4

Here's a grab bag of pieces that I did, including congratulatory messages and art streams. It's a whole variety of stuff.

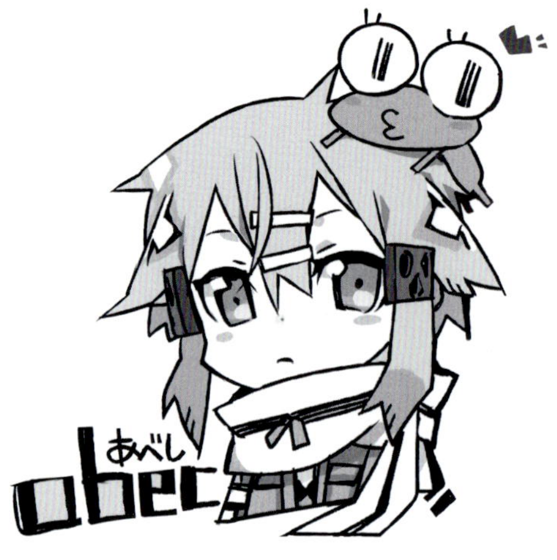

Text: Thank you for 1 million sales of SAO Vol. 1! / Hope you check out the rest of the series too! abec

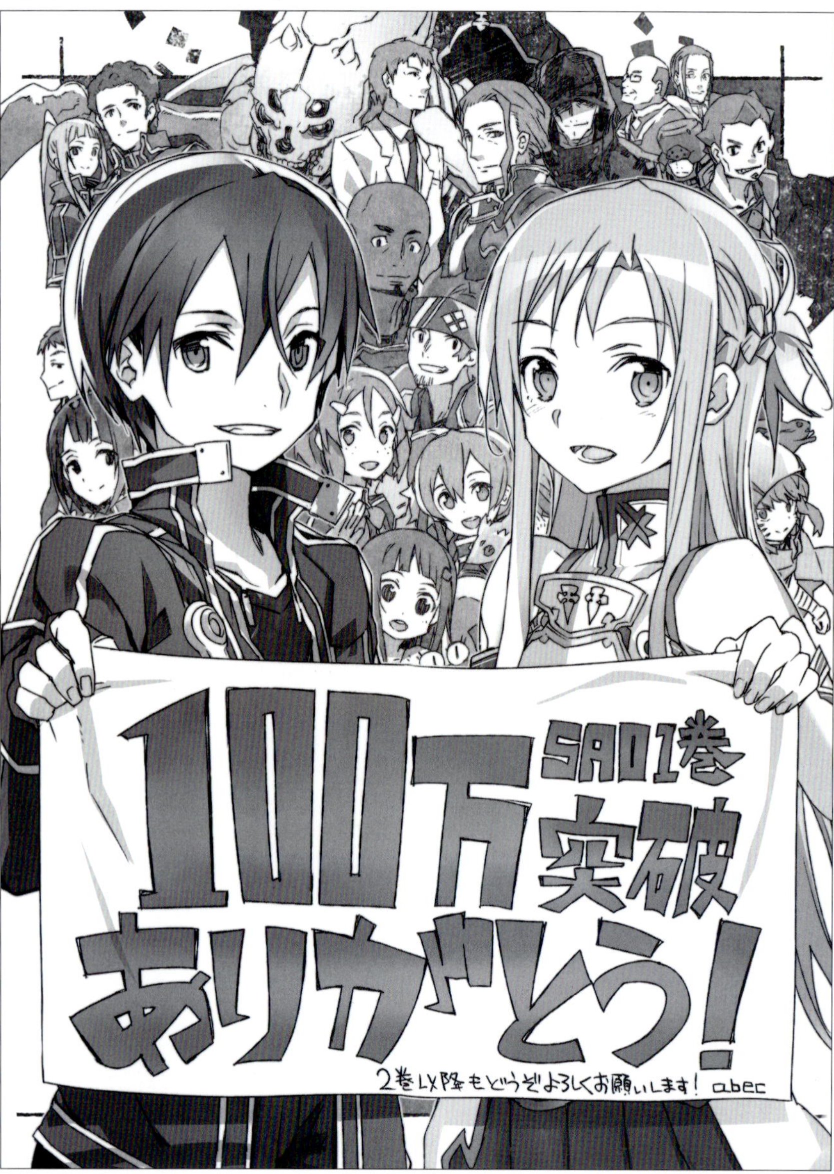

Dengeki Bunko
Sword Art Online
Volume 1 Million Total Sales Illustration: April 2017

One million copies! Thank you so much! Wow!

Dengeki Comics NEXT
Sword Art Online: Phantom Bullet 1
Congratulatory Illustration: September 2014

This was a piece I did for Koutarou Yamada-sensei, who's drawn multiple *SAO* manga, for one of his volumes. My abec avatar is a frog.

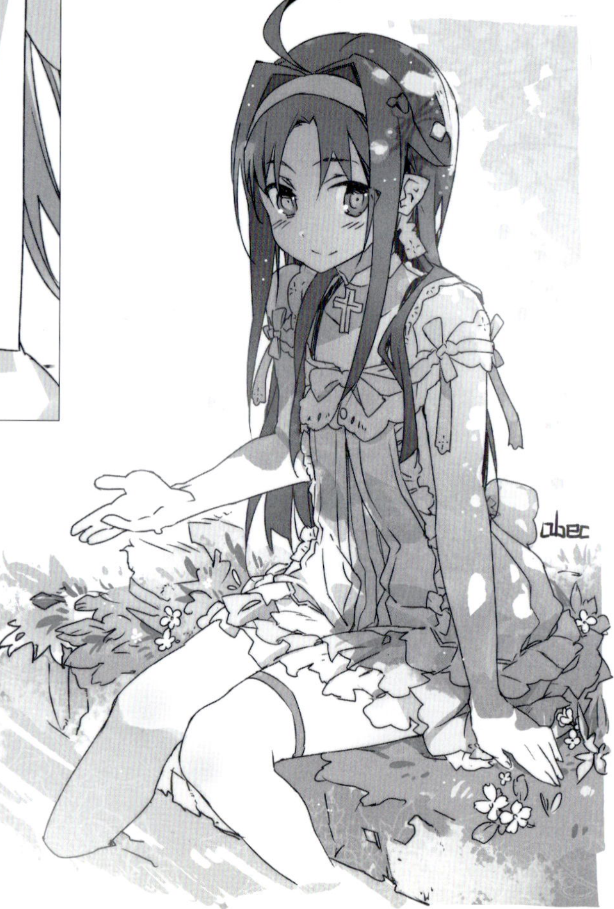

Dengeki Comics NEXT
Sword Art Online: Mother's Rosary 3
Congratulatory Illustration: June 2016

A piece for Tsubasa Haduki-sensei's manga adaptation. I put Yuuki in a frilly outfit that you'd never see in the story.

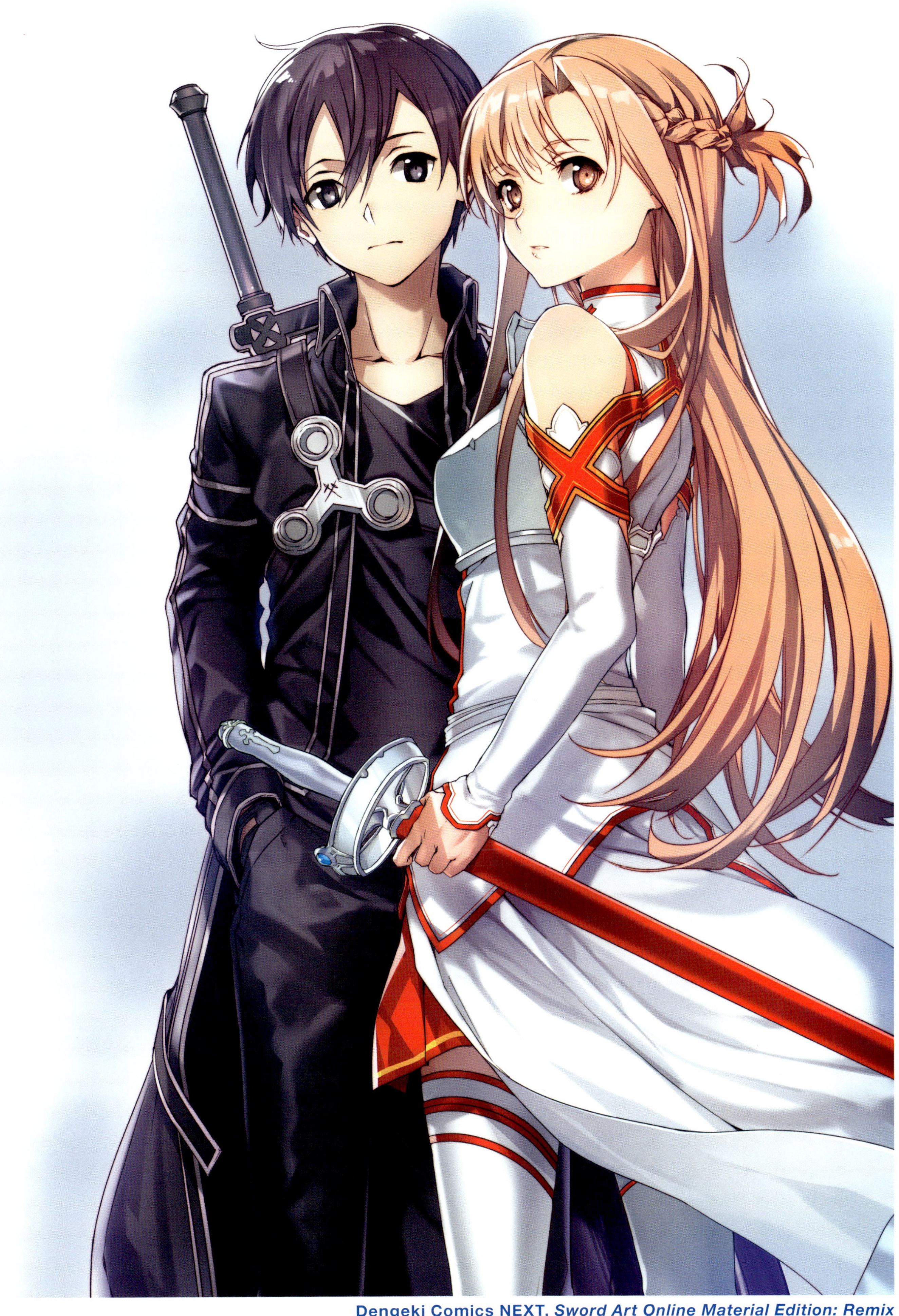

This was originally a series of *doujinshi* created by Kawahara-sensei himself, and the illustration is based on his. That's why the eyes are a bit smaller. The expressions are cool and reserved and different from my usual style.

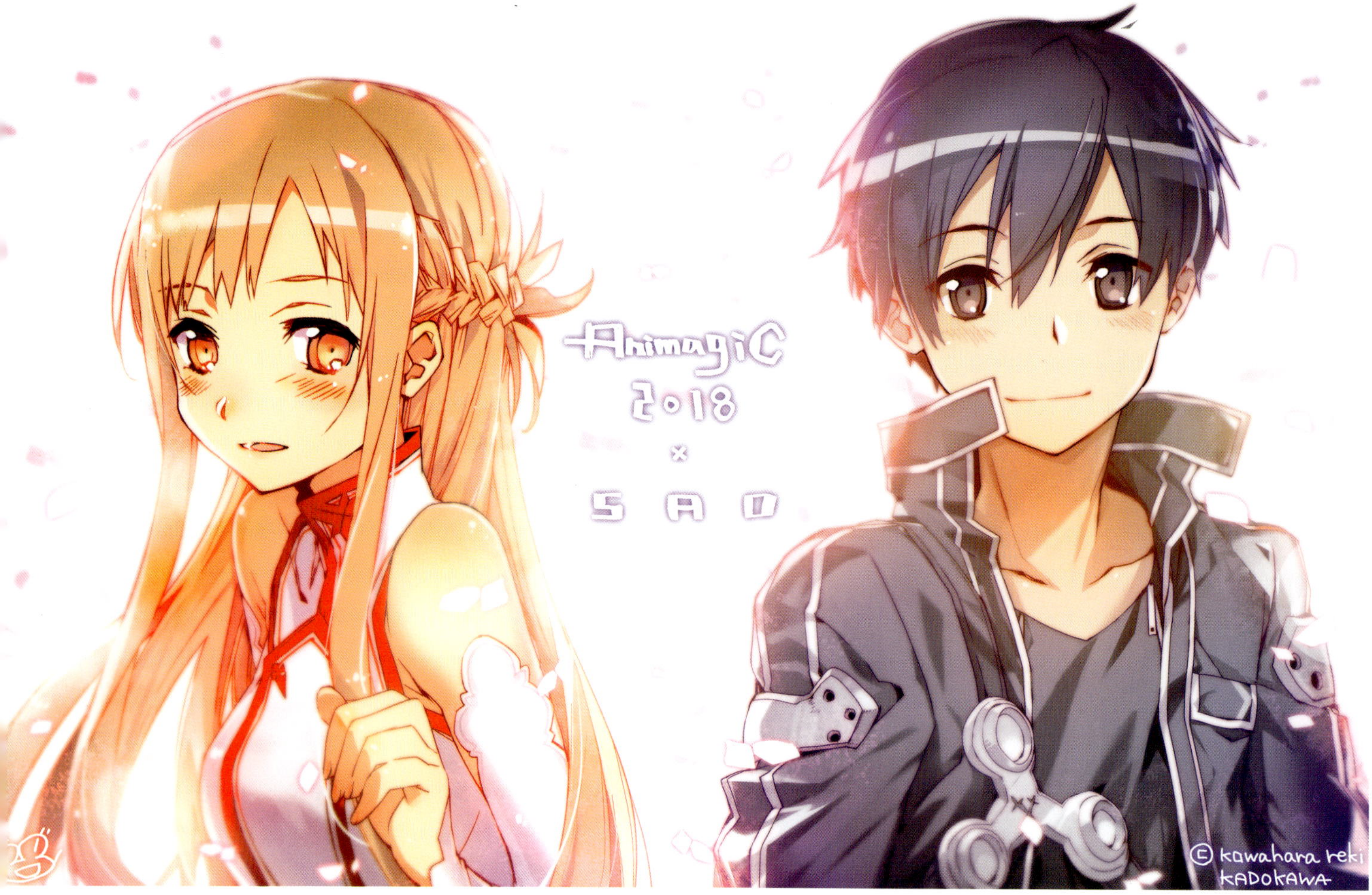

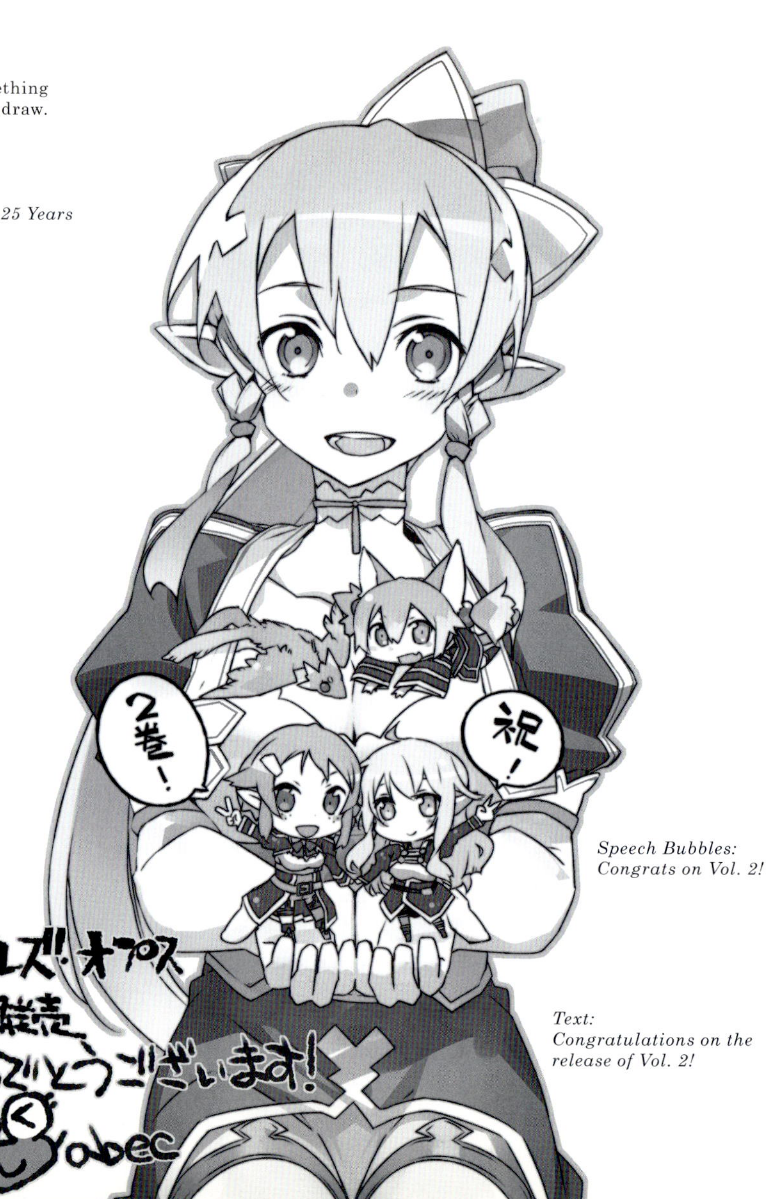

AnimagiC 2018
Live Drawing: August 2018

I drew this at a German anime event. Every now and then, I get to draw something for an event overseas, and it's always a nerve-racking affair trying to talk and draw. In a sense, it's easy, though, because I don't have anything clever to say.

Text:
Celebrating 25 Years

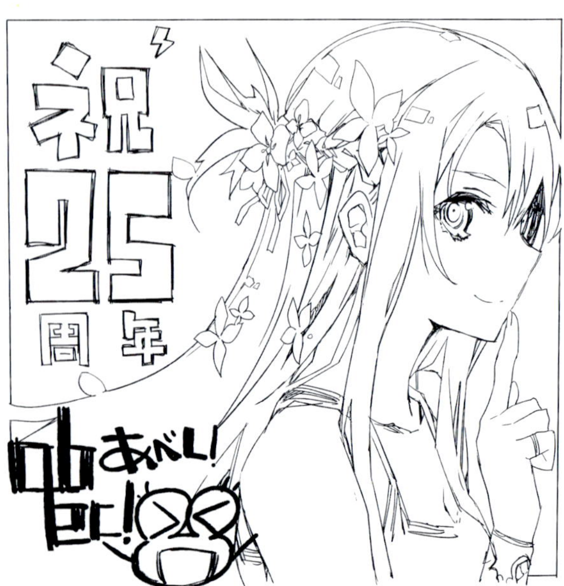

Dengeki Bunko 25th Anniversary
Celebratory Shikishi Illustration: August 2018

An illustration on a *shikishi* board. Sometimes I draw on *shikishi* at events, but they're rarely all that involved, so it's remarkable to have a chance to put one in this artbook.

Speech Bubbles:
Congrats on Vol. 2!

Text:
Congratulations on the release of Vol. 2!

Dengeki Comics NEXT
Sword Art Online: Girls' Ops 2
Celebratory Illustration: April 2015

Neko Nekobyou-sensei's *Girls' Ops* series, known for the "More Scenes" meme, is based on the unfairly left-out trio of Leafa, Silica, and Liz, plus one more original character to round out the group.

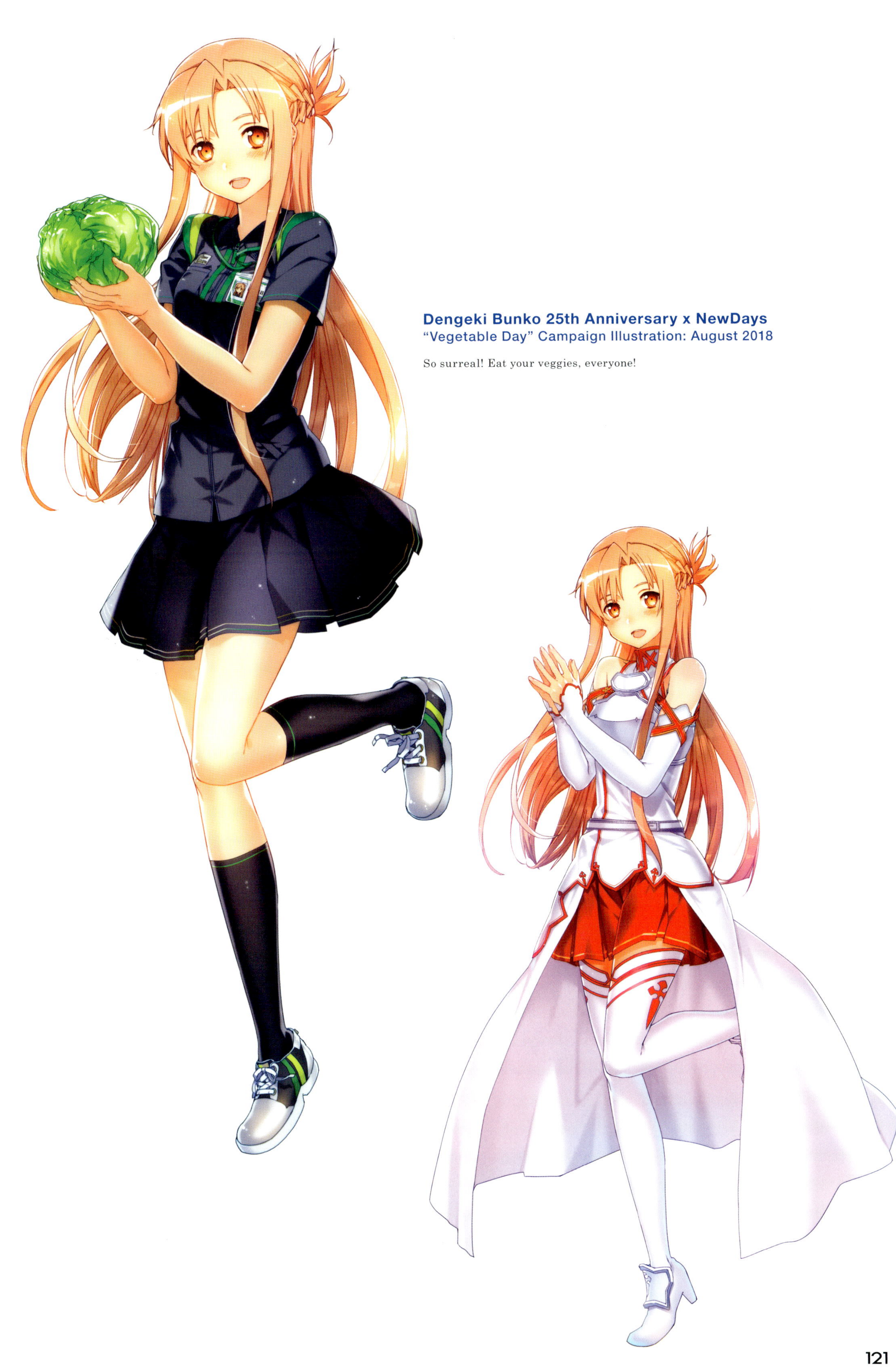

Dengeki Bunko 25th Anniversary x NewDays
"Vegetable Day" Campaign Illustration: August 2018

So surreal! Eat your veggies, everyone!

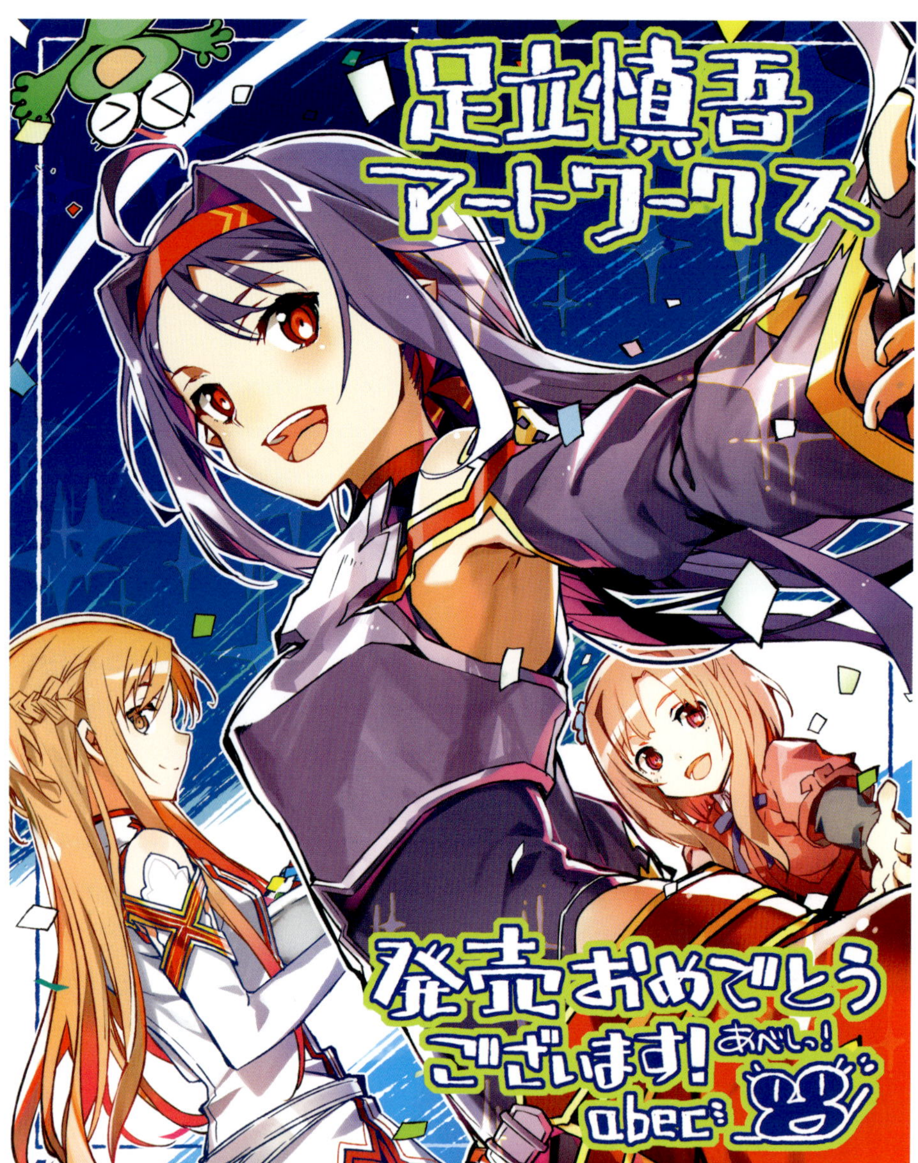

Text: Shingo Adachi Artworks / Congrats on the book! abec

Book, *Shingo Adachi Artworks*
Congratulatory Illustration: July 2019

This piece was to celebrate the artbook from Adachi-san, who was the character designer and director of the first and second season of the *SAO* anime. Check that book out.

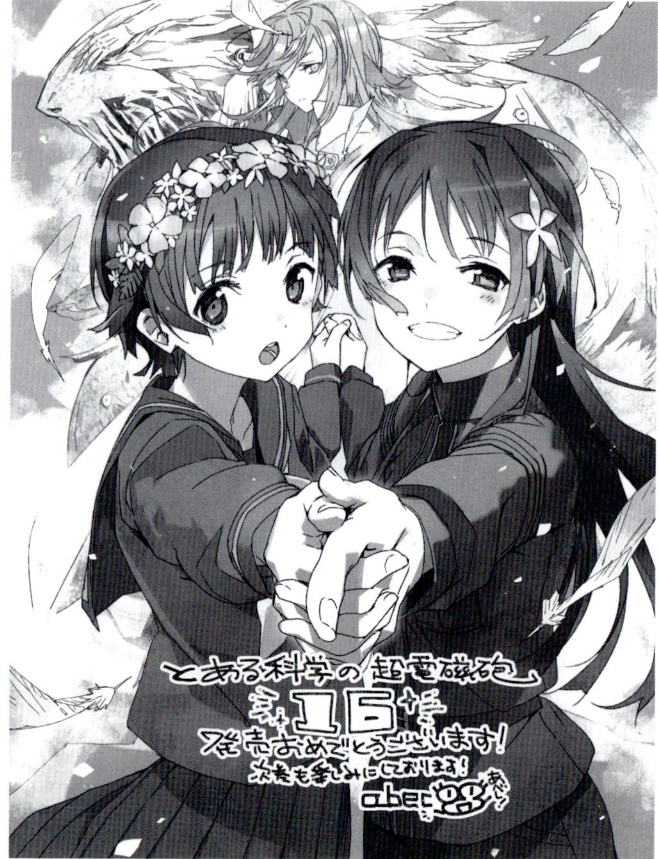

Dengeki Comics
***A Certain Scientific Railgun*, Vol. 16**
Congratulatory Illustration: October 2020

I was always a fan of *Railgun*, so when I was asked about doing this I said yes without a second thought. I love Saten the most.

Text: A Certain Scientific Railgun 16 / Congrats on the release!
I'm looking forward to the next one! abec

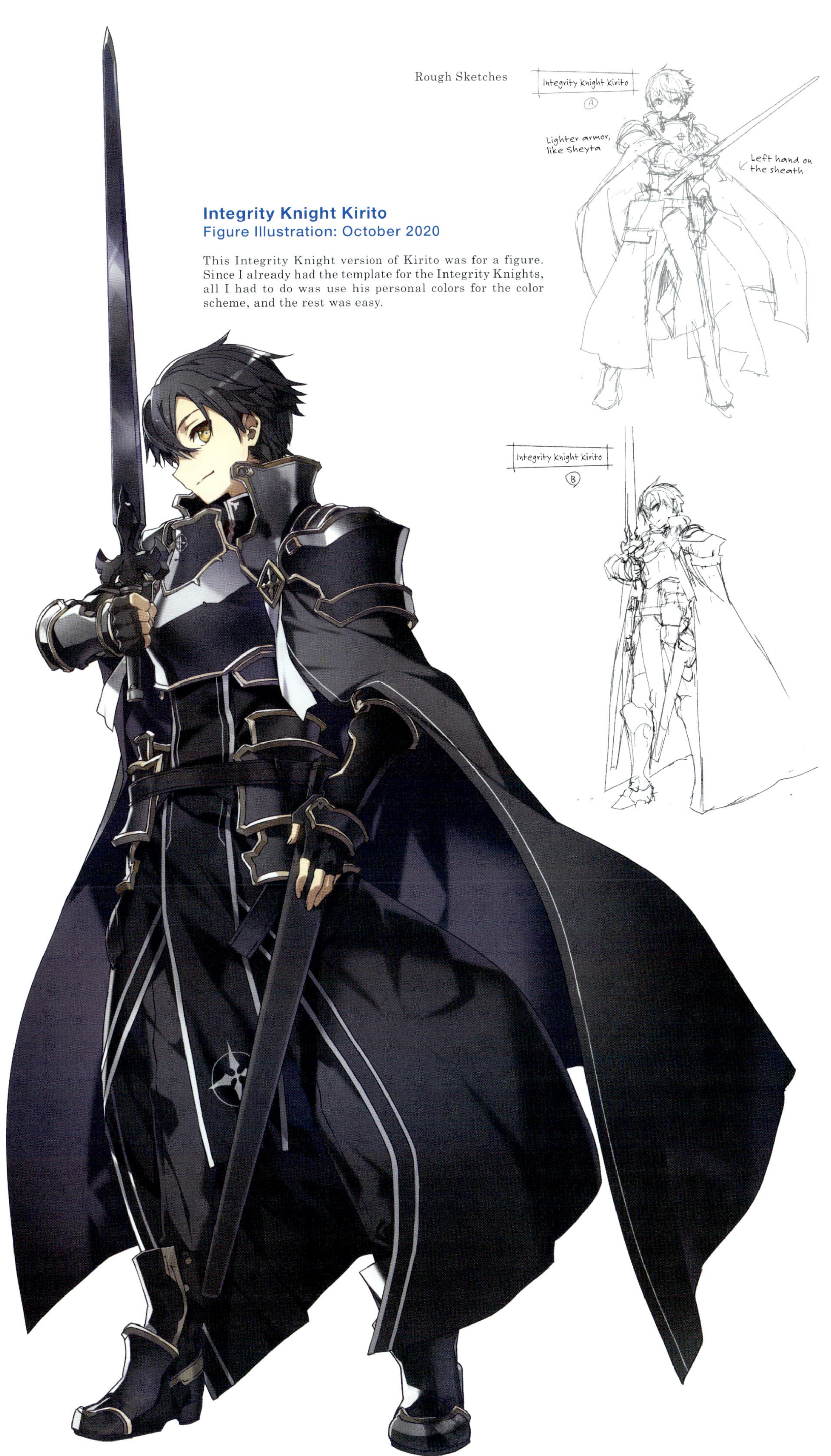

Integrity Knight Kirito
Figure Illustration: October 2020

This Integrity Knight version of Kirito was for a figure. Since I already had the template for the Integrity Knights, all I had to do was use his personal colors for the color scheme, and the rest was easy.

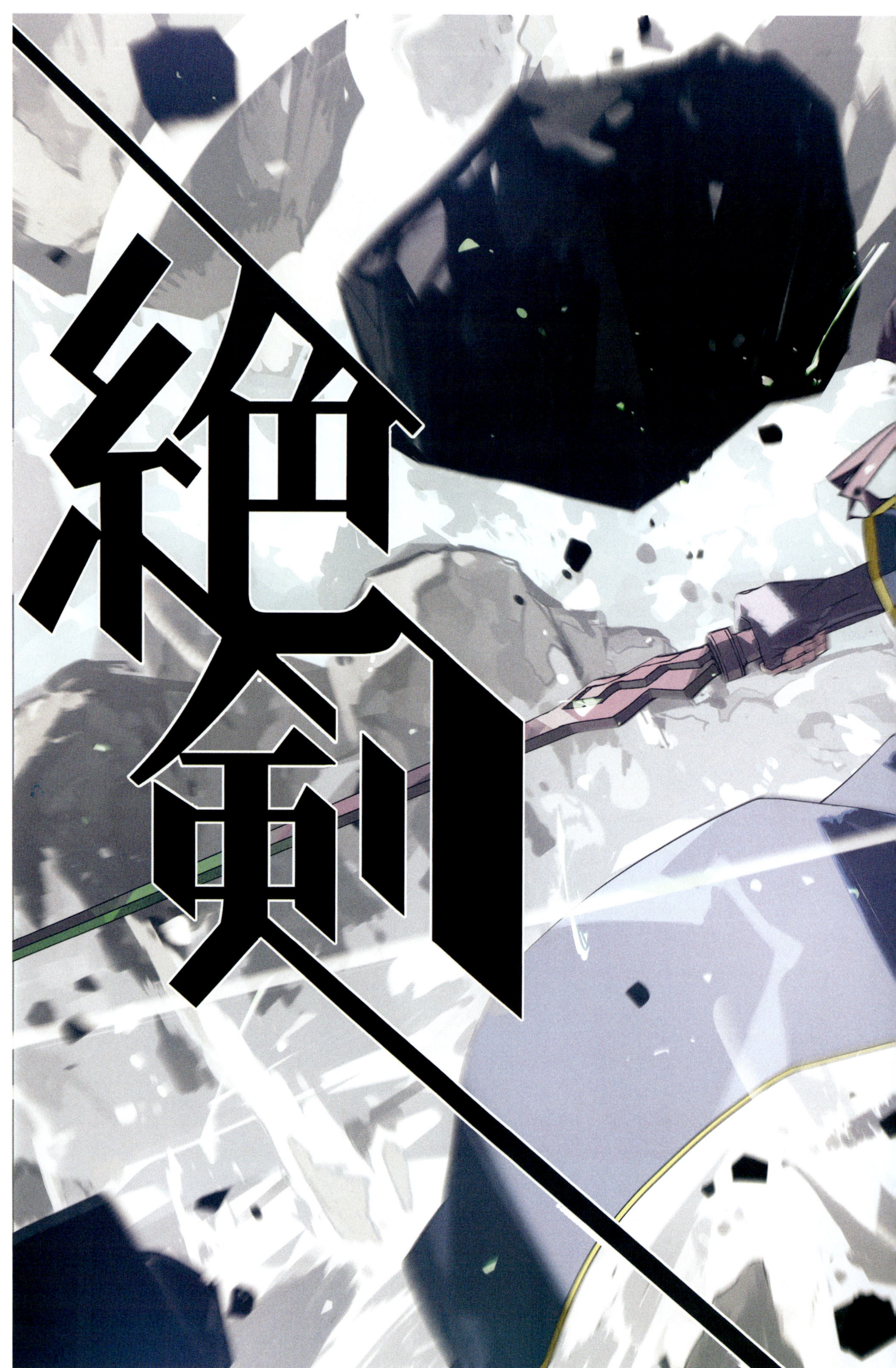

Text: Absolute Sword

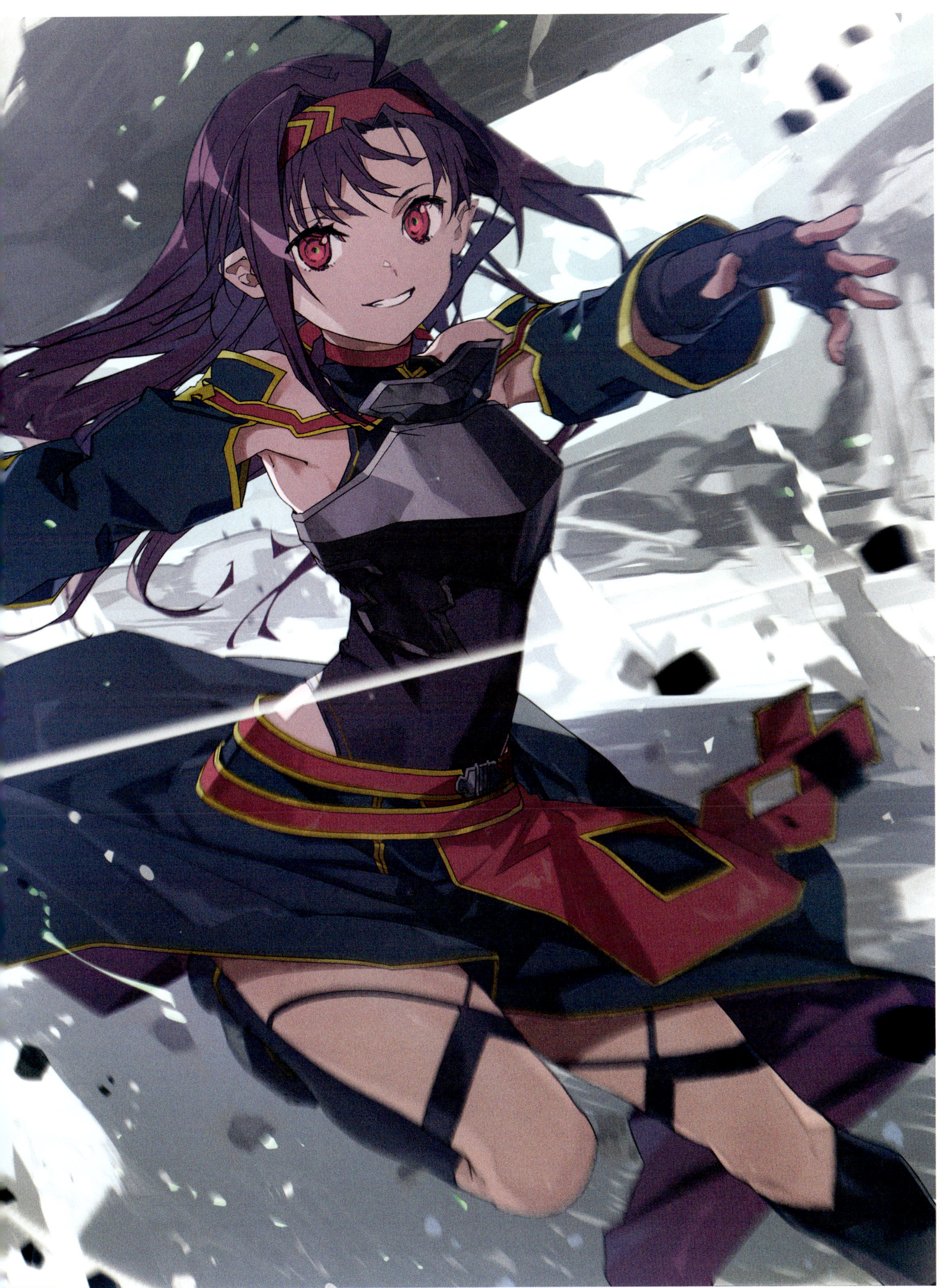

Yuuki
Artbook Exclusive: February 2023

I didn't get to draw Yuuki on the cover because she was 7th in the popularity poll. I was streaming myself as I drew this, and I found it was remarkably easy. The big thing was putting the kanji for Absolute Sword on the image. I love it when you use the name of the attack or whatever as a caption. It's really cool. I like this one.

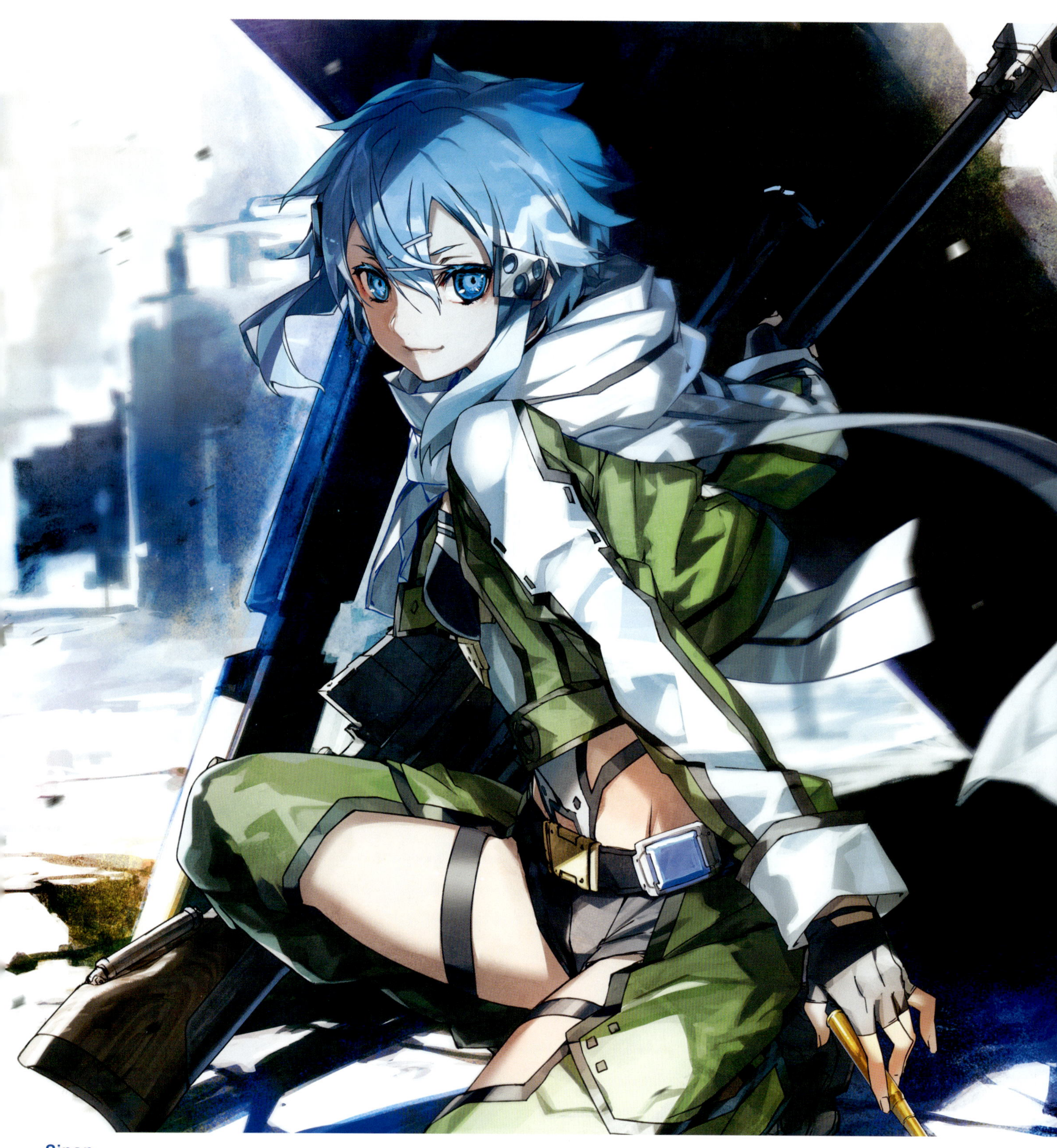

Sinon
Unpublished: September 2020

I streamed myself drawing this illustration, too. I ran a couple of polls on Twitter asking what I should draw, then went online and did it live. I still do that now and then.

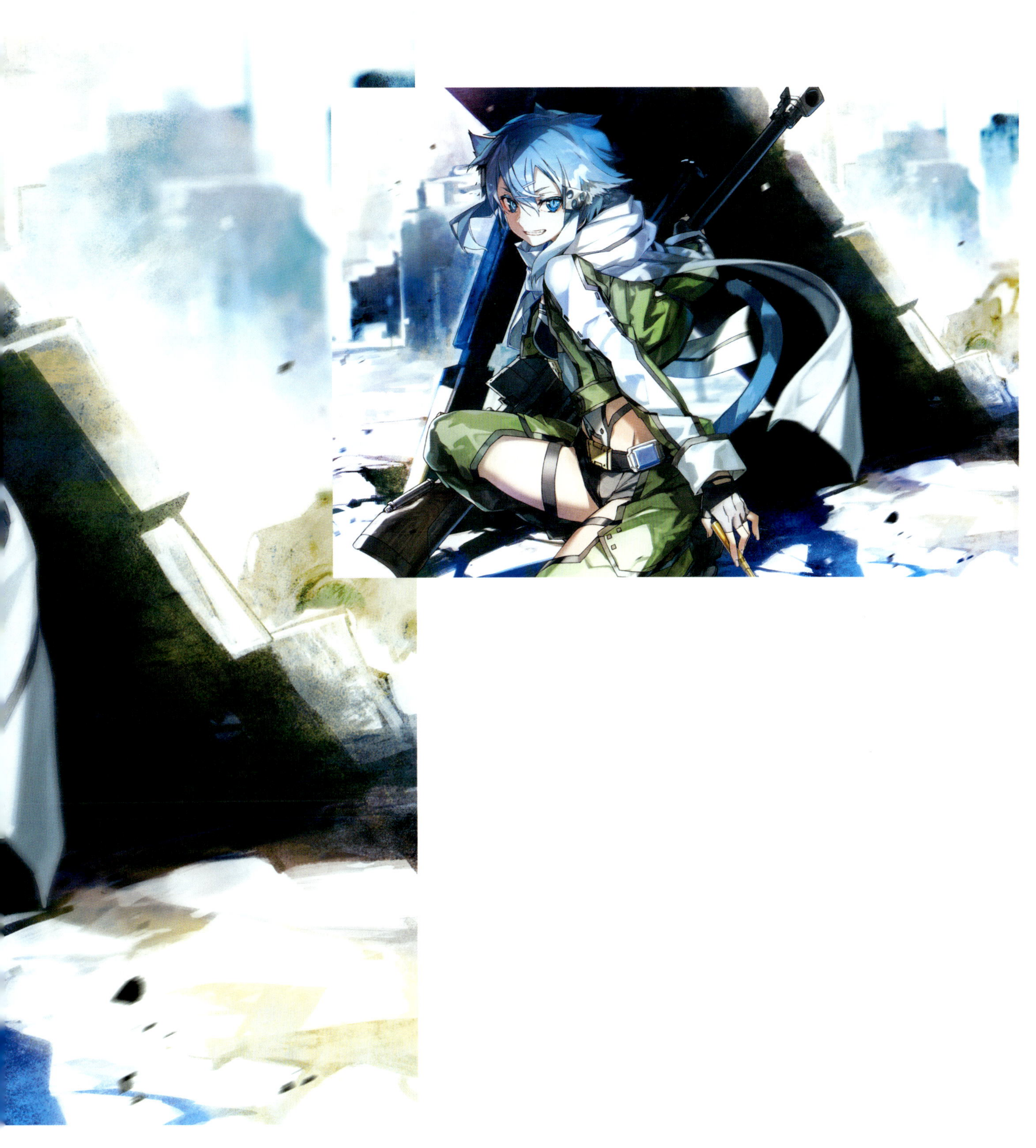

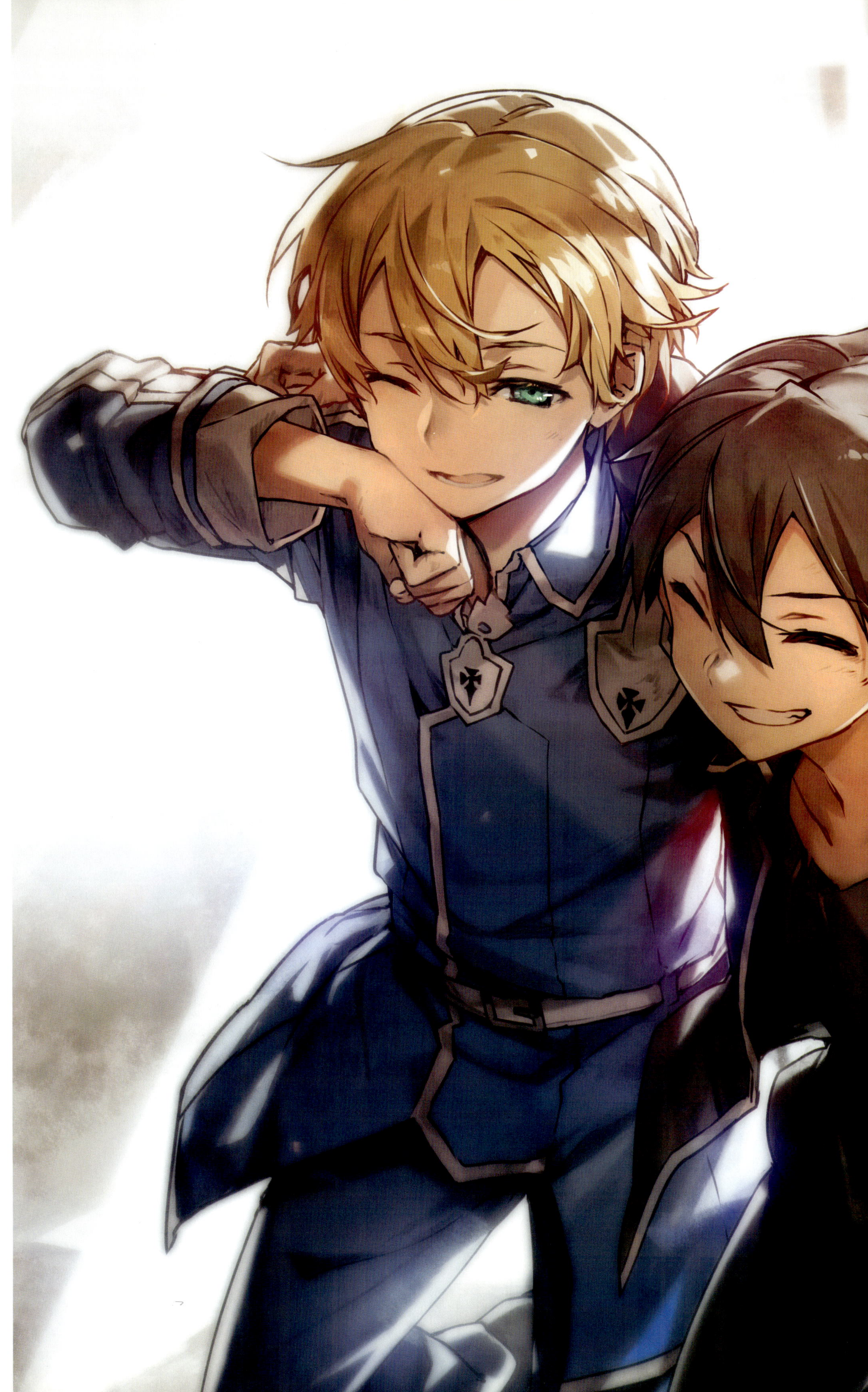

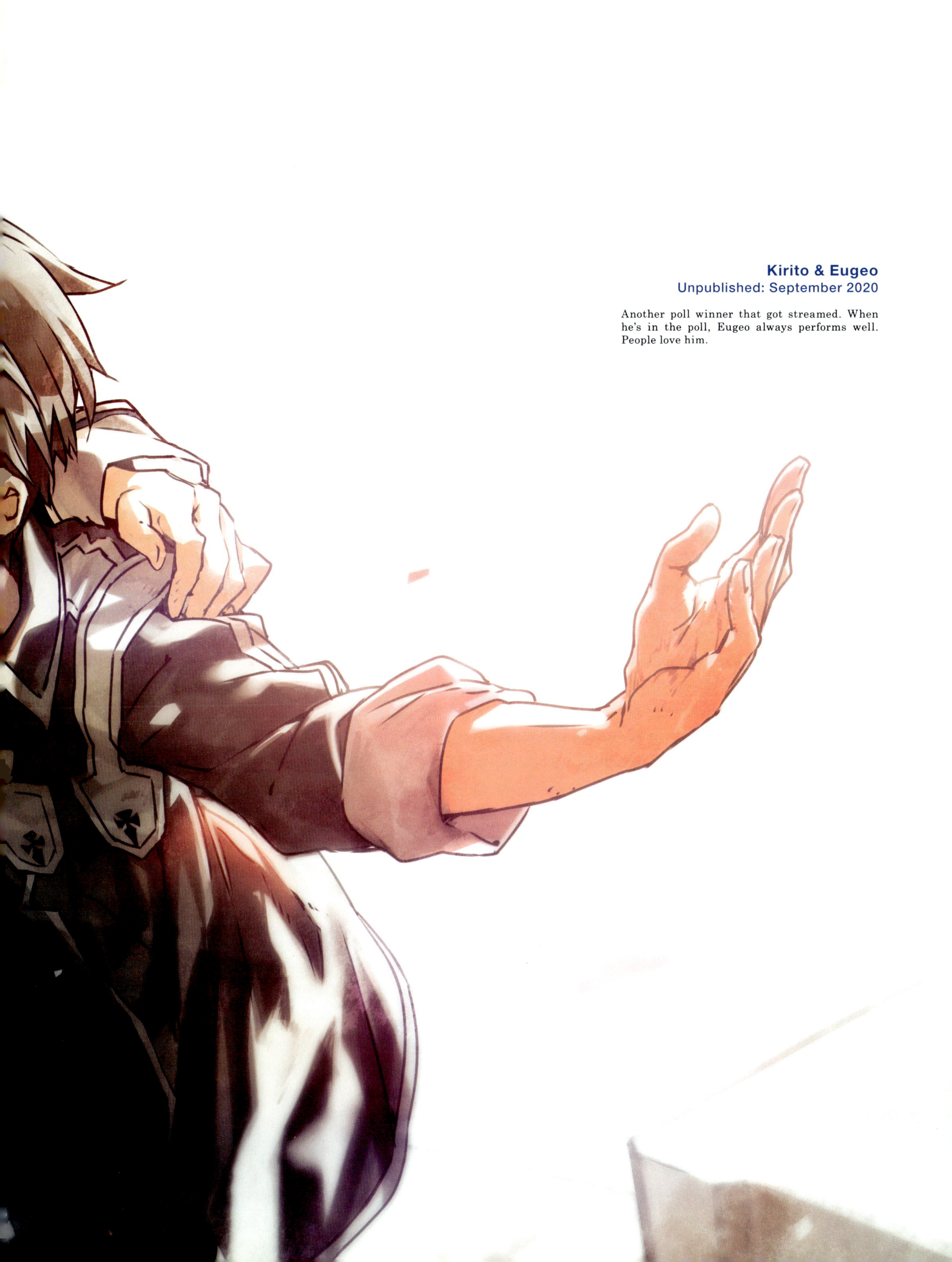

Kirito & Eugeo
Unpublished: September 2020

Another poll winner that got streamed. When he's in the poll, Eugeo always performs well. People love him.

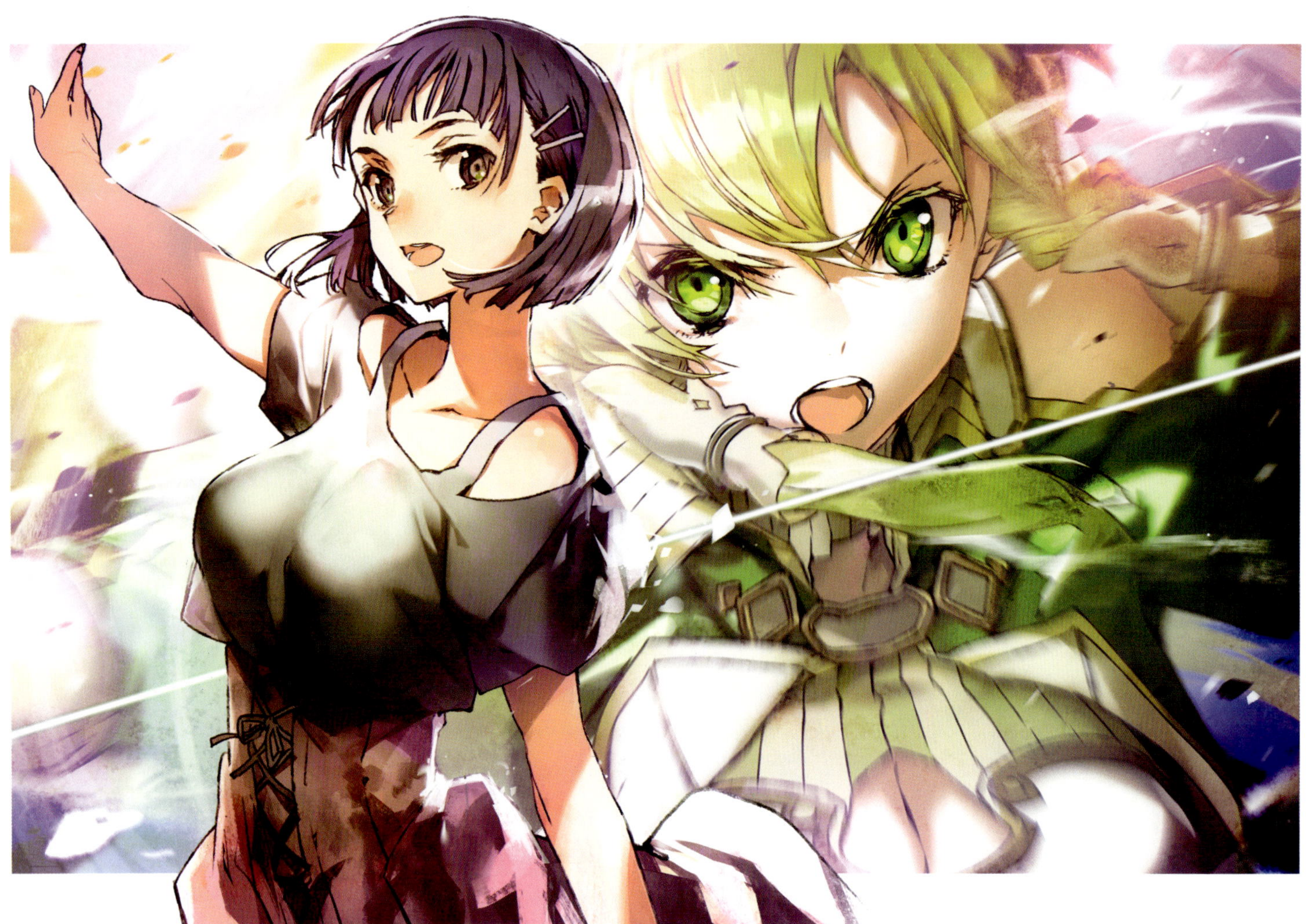

Leafa & Suguha Kirigaya
Unpublished: September 2020

I really wanted to draw Terraria Leafa, but it's
really demanding to do all those little details,
so I settled for a horizontal slice instead.

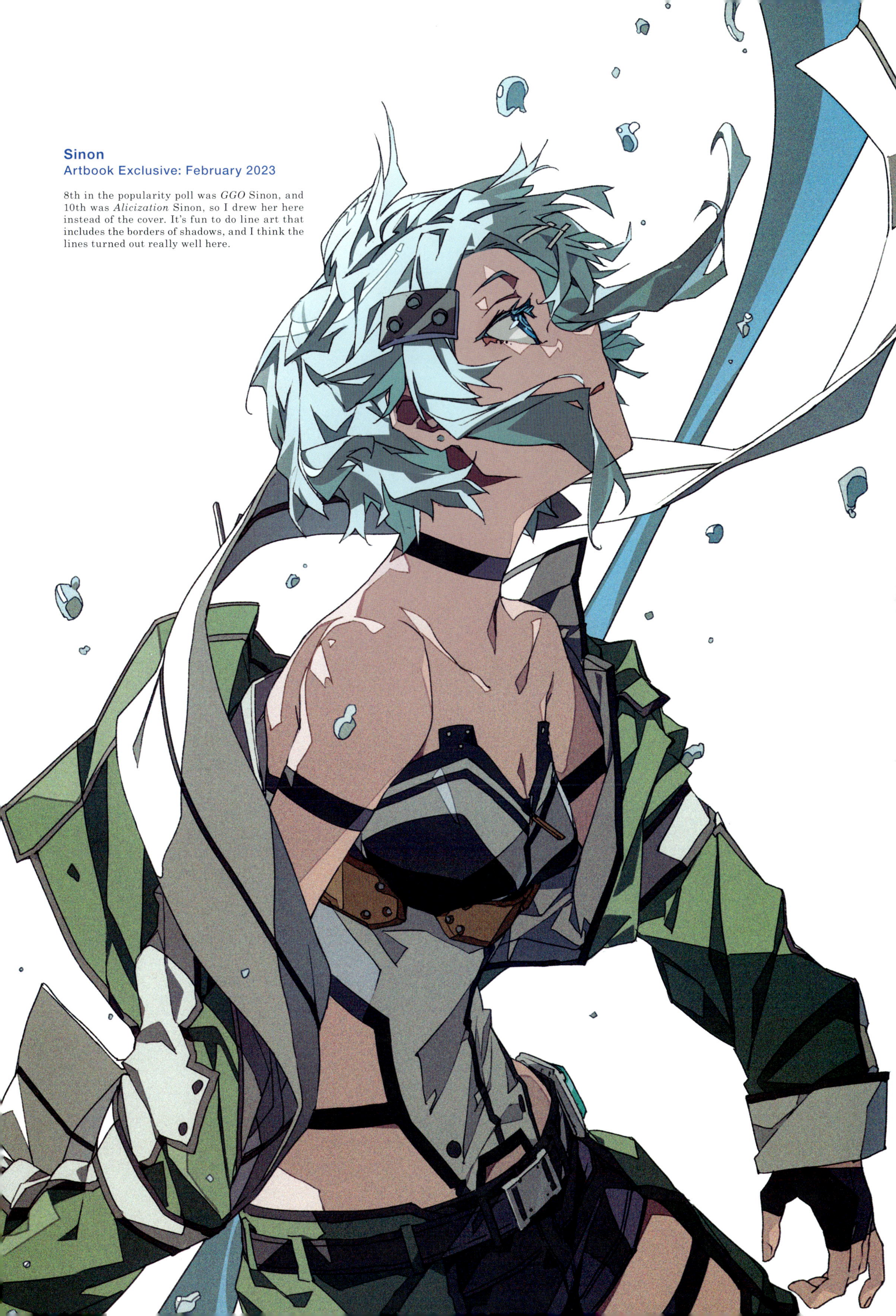

Sinon
Artbook Exclusive: February 2023

8th in the popularity poll was *GGO* Sinon, and
10th was *Alicization* Sinon, so I drew her here
instead of the cover. It's fun to do line art that
includes the borders of shadows, and I think the
lines turned out really well here.

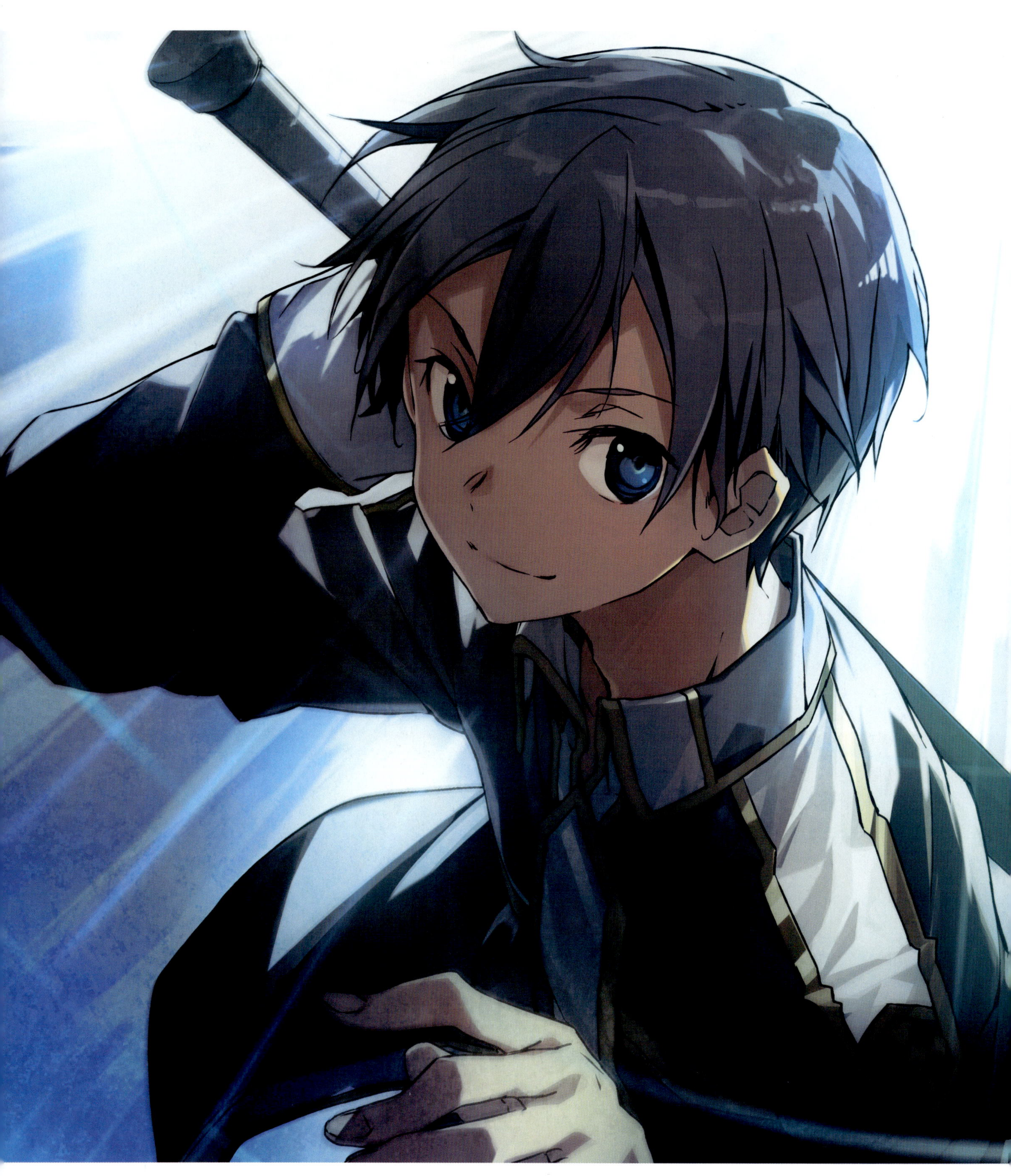

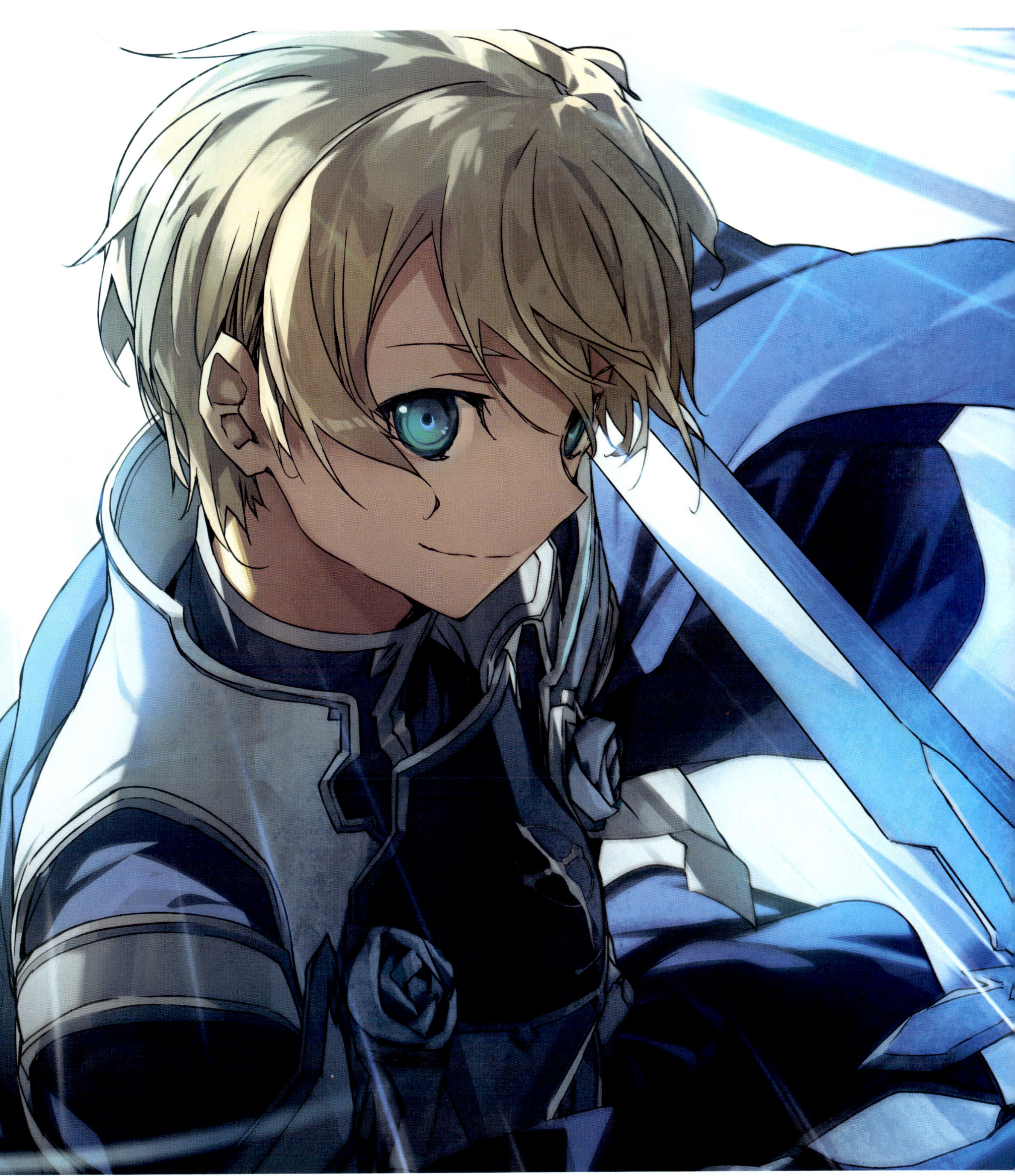

Kirito & Eugeo
Unpublished: September 2020

The cold looks Integrity Knight Eugeo gives are cool...
but for this one, I wanted to draw a softer expression.

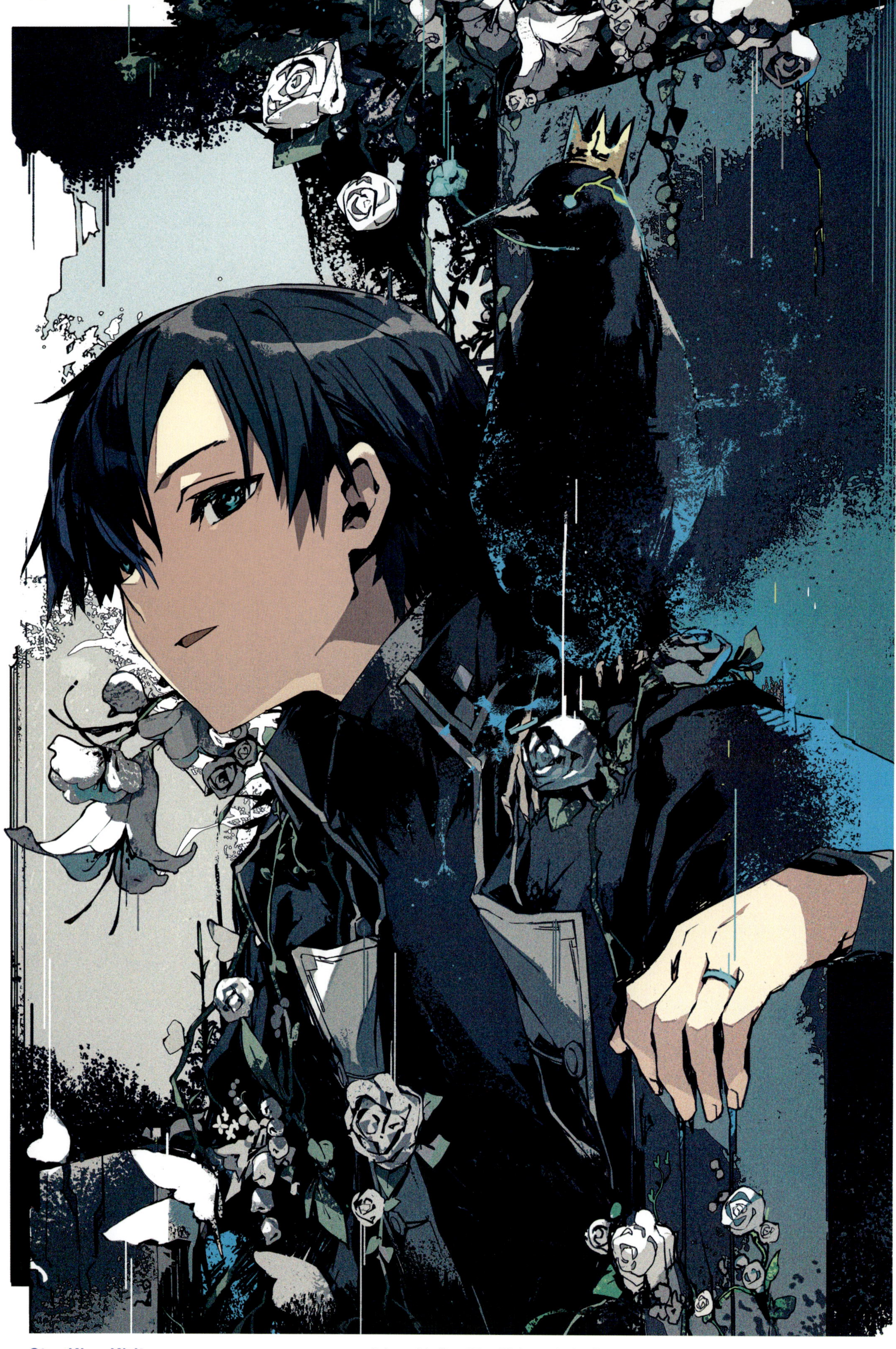

Star King Kirito
Artbook Exclusive: February 2023

I drew this Star King Kirito entirely of my own imagining. I didn't get any specific details from Kawahara-sensei—it's just pure fantasy. If Kawahara-sensei ever gets a chance to draw him, it might turn out to be more like Dance King Kirito who's gotten way into break-dancing while trapped in the Underworld. Or maybe it'll be Funky Grandpa Kirito.

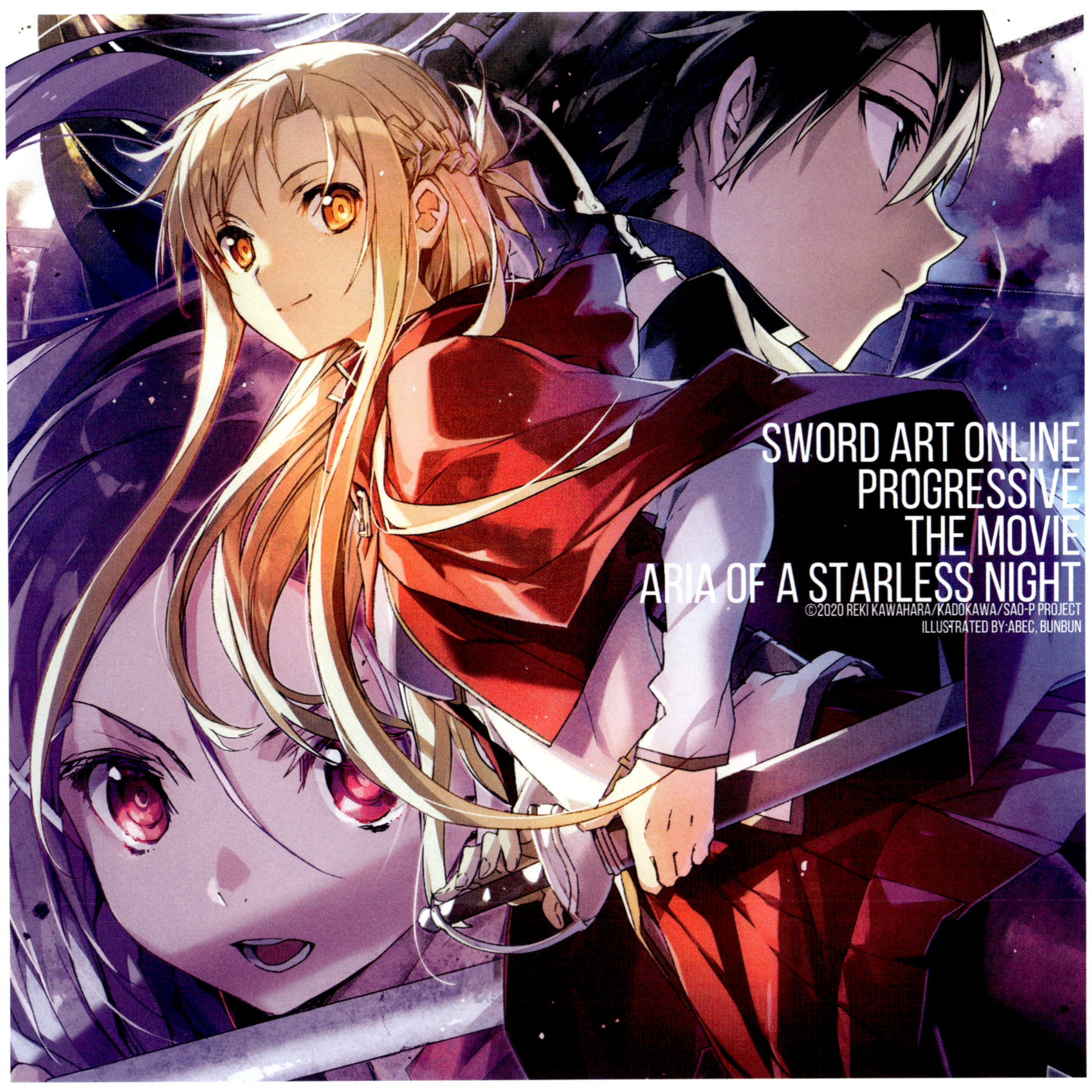

Theatrical Film, *Sword Art Online Progressive: Aria of a Starless Night*
Unpublished: October 2021

This was to commemorate and publicize the animated film being unveiled. The fact that Mito was popular enough to get voted onto the cover in the popularity poll makes me happy. People really love her.

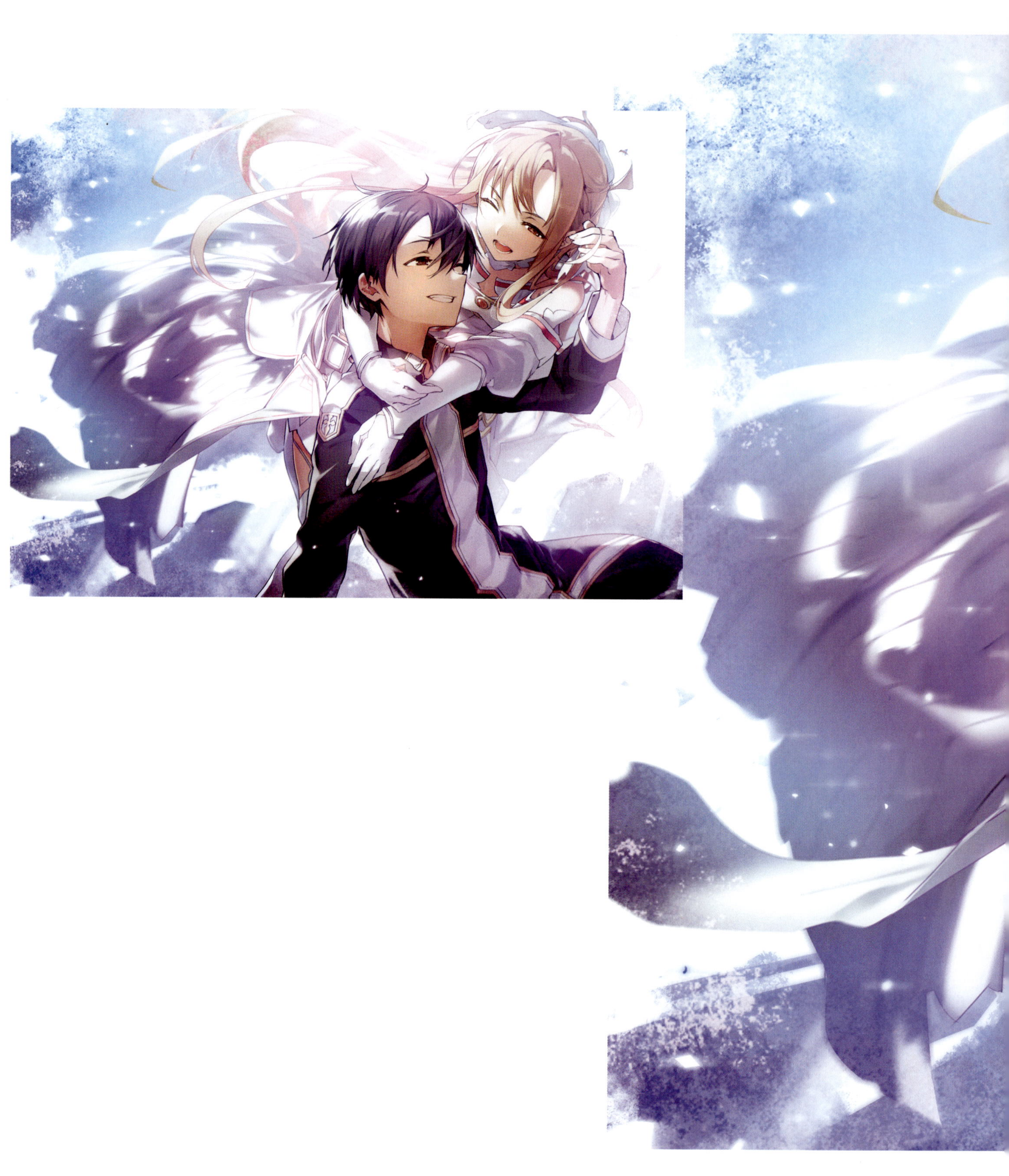

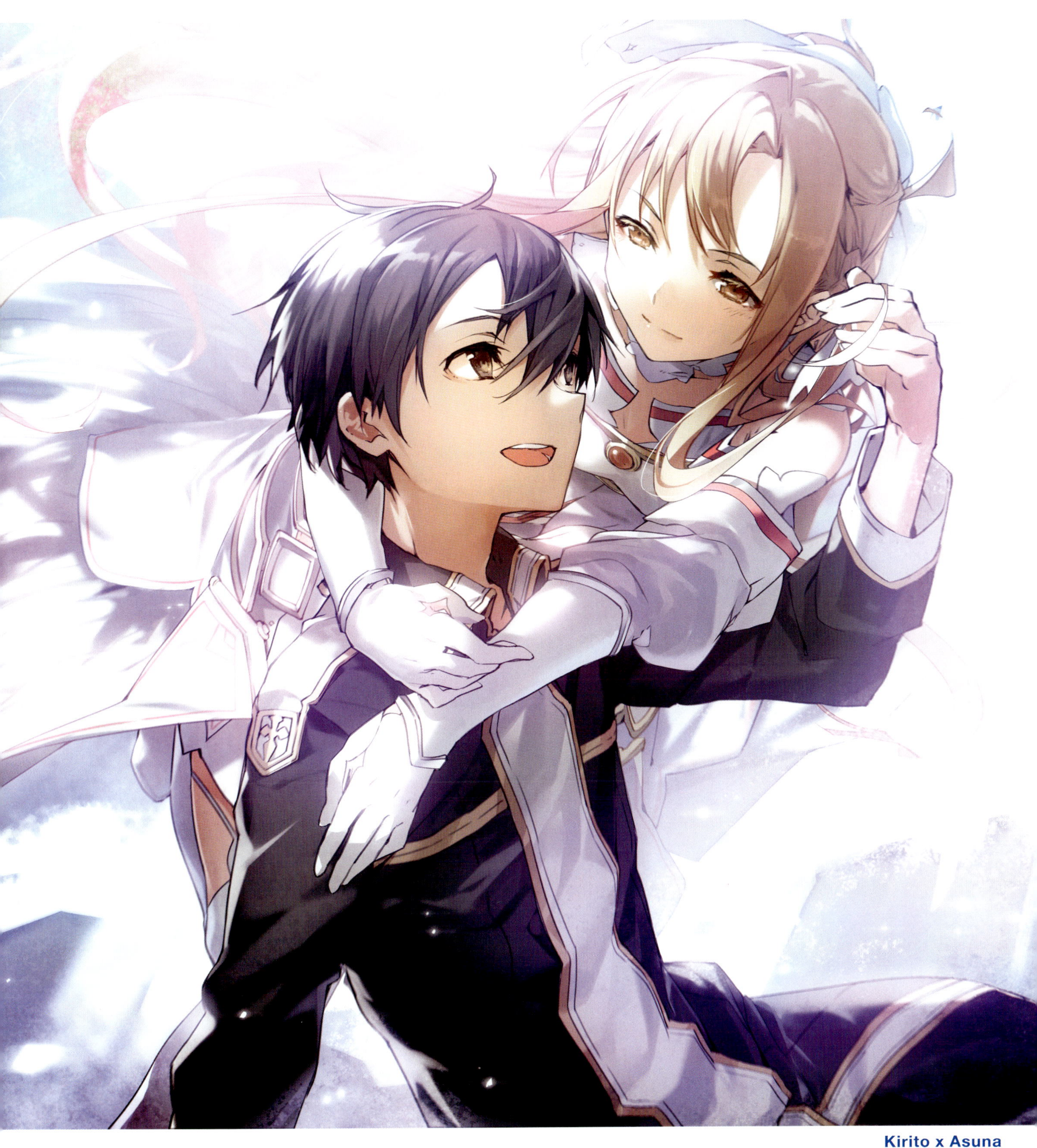

Kirito x Asuna
Unpublished: September 2020

I streamed myself drawing this illustration on my YouTube channel for the final episode of the *War of the Underworld* anime, and put the finished version on Twitter.

These character designs are references I use for the light novel illustrations and for the various needs of the animators. When they're for the light novel, I often just do a very quick and dirty black-and-white piece. I usually go back and work them some more, double-checking them when I do my rough sketch of the novel illustration. Lots of these end up being the final character design sketches, too.

FOR Alicization

For the three goddesses, I whipped up Stacia Asuna first, then used that as the basis for the designs of the other two. They're goddesses, so I wanted to give them more embellished ornamentation, but going any further than this would have been very challenging, and also would've made it impossible to draw them physically interacting with each other. This is pretty much the limit.

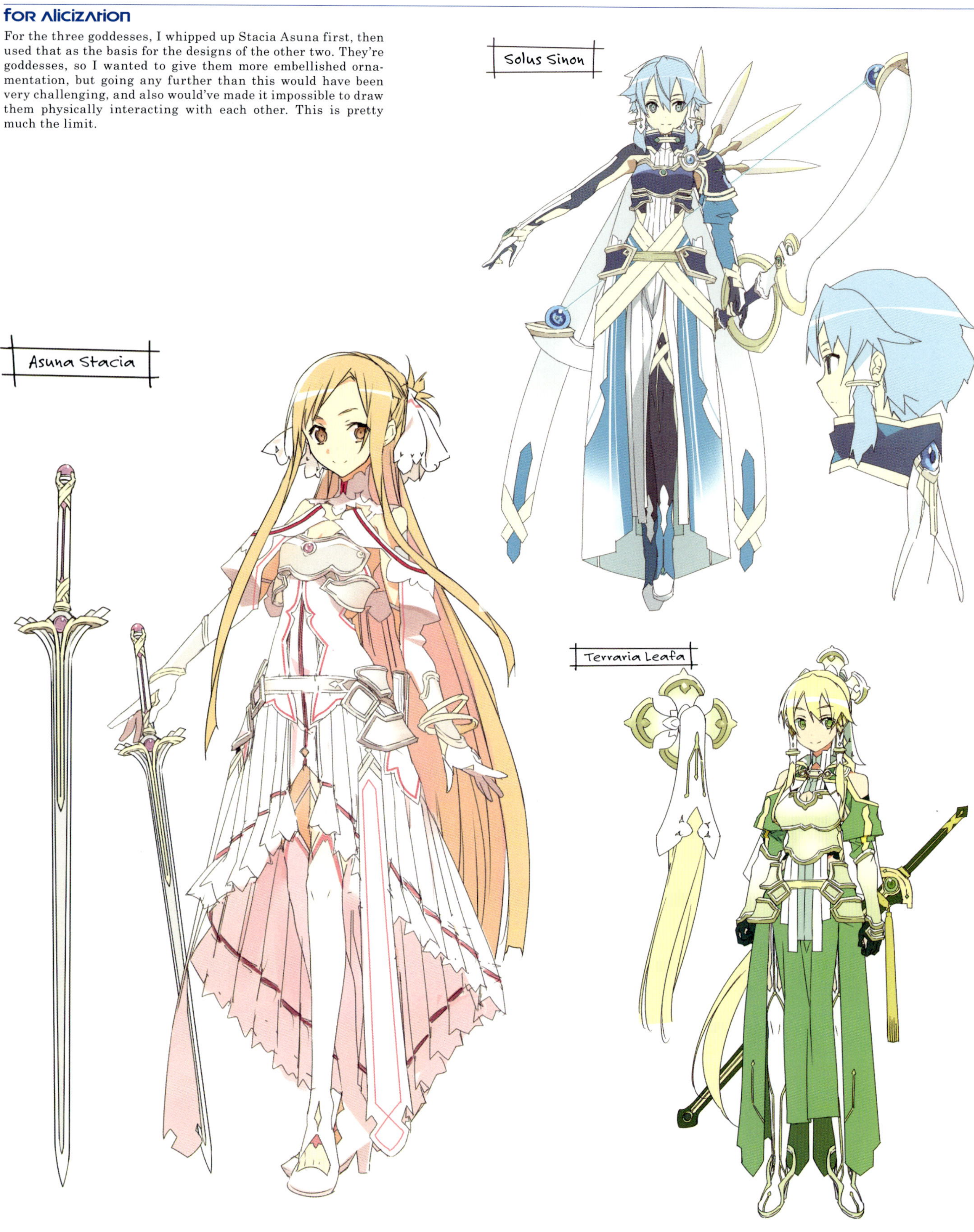

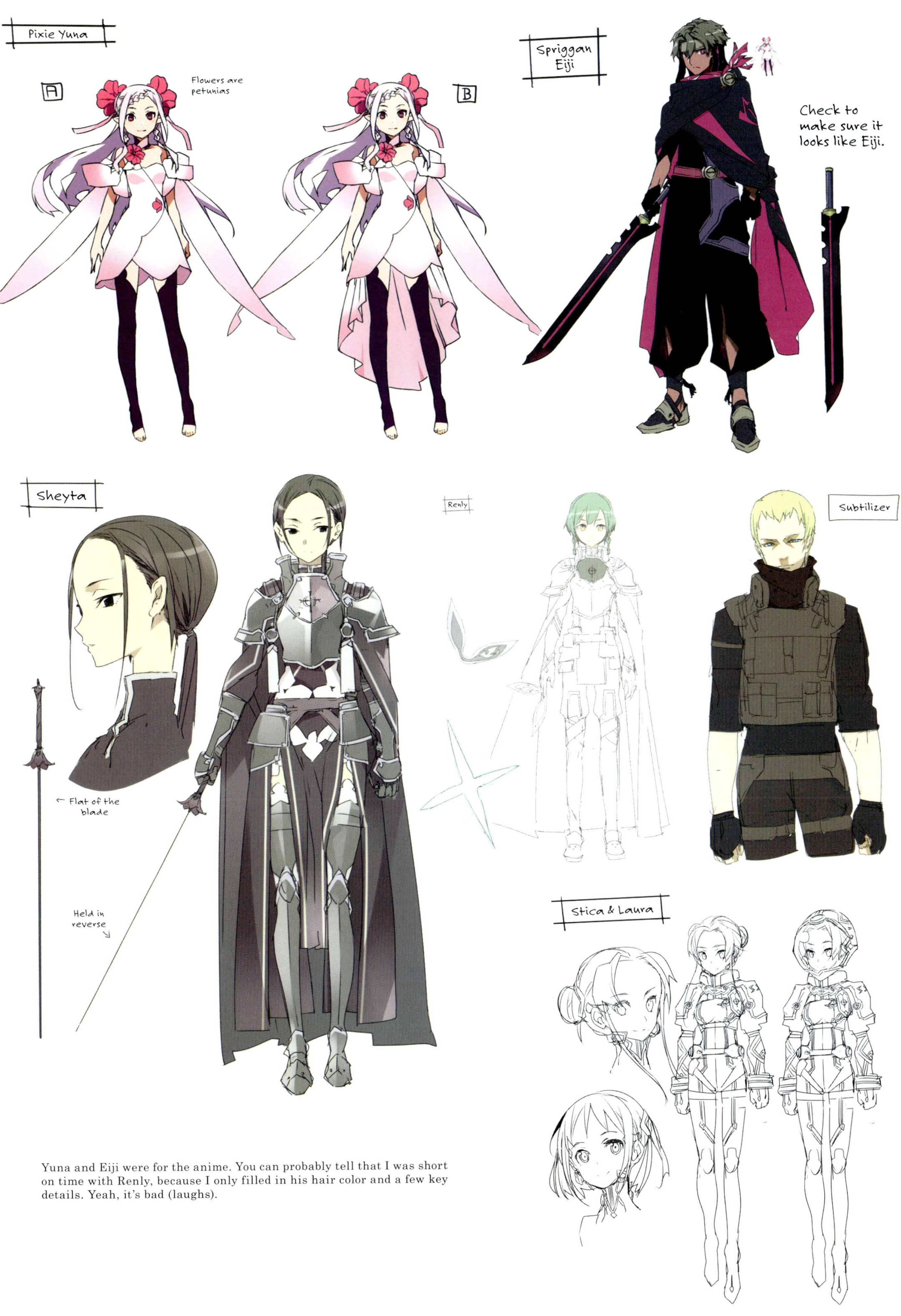

Yuna and Eiji were for the anime. You can probably tell that I was short on time with Renly, because I only filled in his hair color and a few key details. Yeah, it's bad (laughs).

I thought that Kirito and Asuna's jackets should give the impression of people with high status. Kirito's top is designed to be closed, by the way. I also altered his hair a bit to portray the passage of time. So, who's your favorite Tiese?

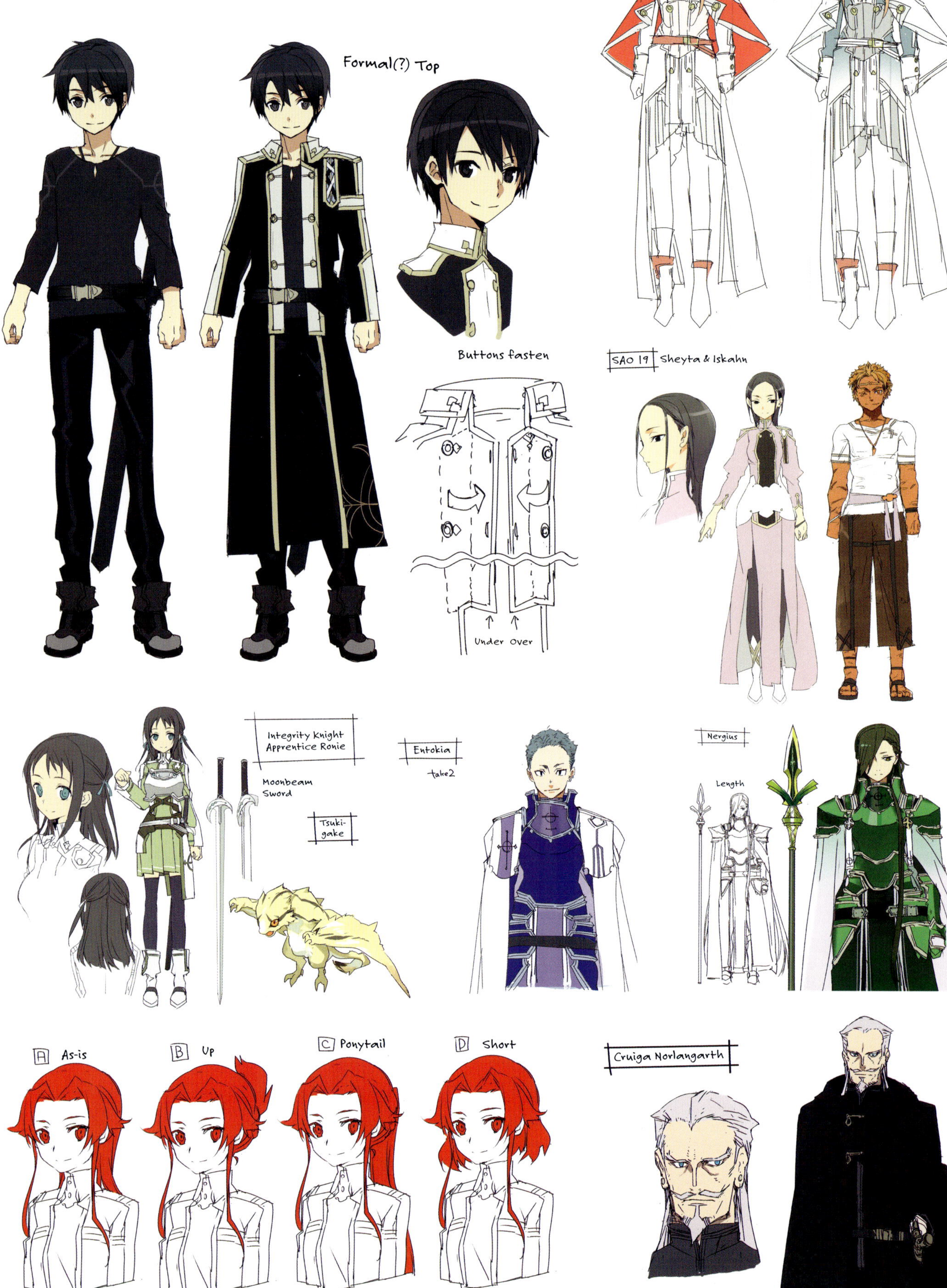

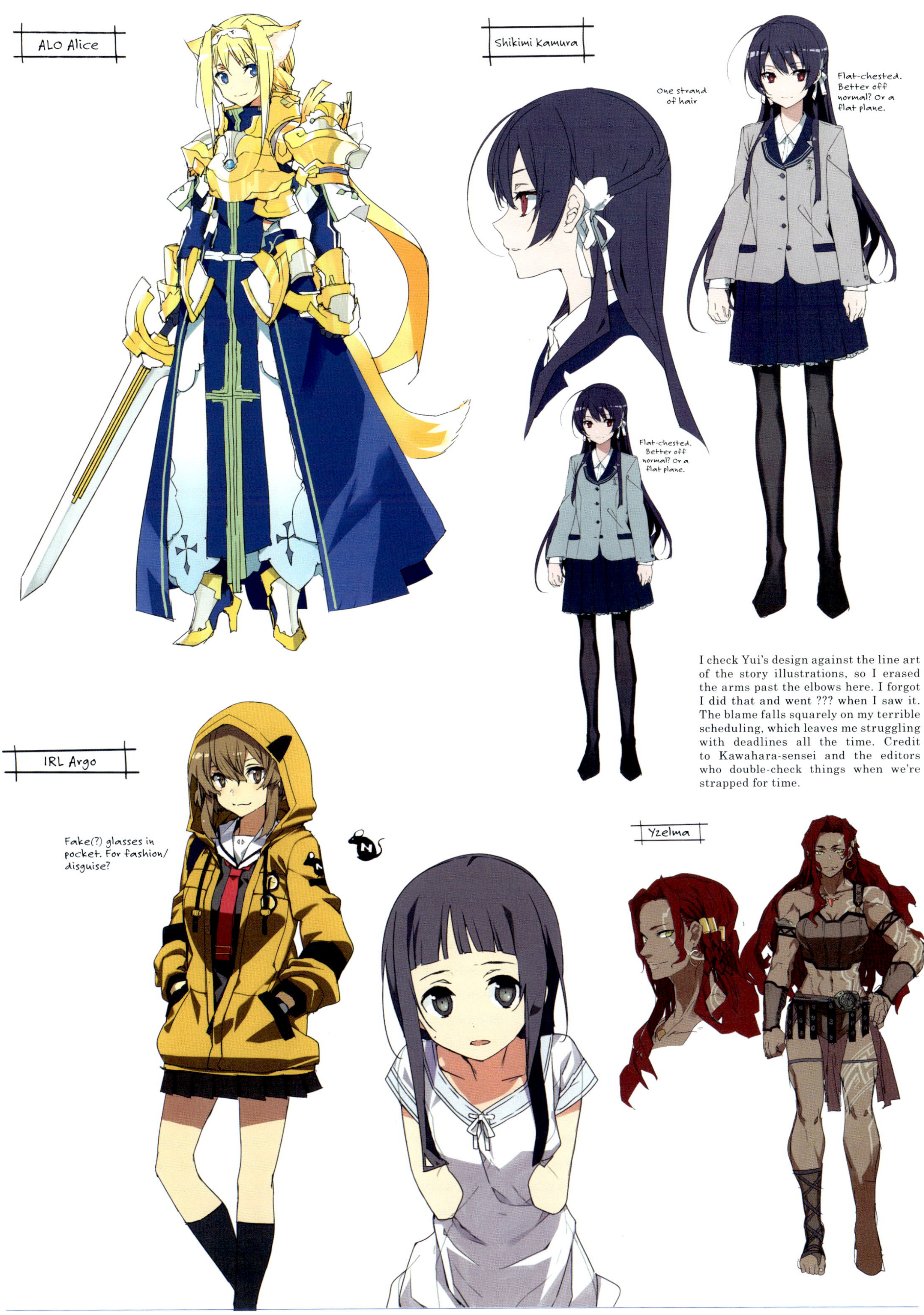

I check Yui's design against the line art of the story illustrations, so I erased the arms past the elbows here. I forgot I did that and went ??? when I saw it. The blame falls squarely on my terrible scheduling, which leaves me struggling with deadlines all the time. Credit to Kawahara-sensei and the editors who double-check things when we're strapped for time.

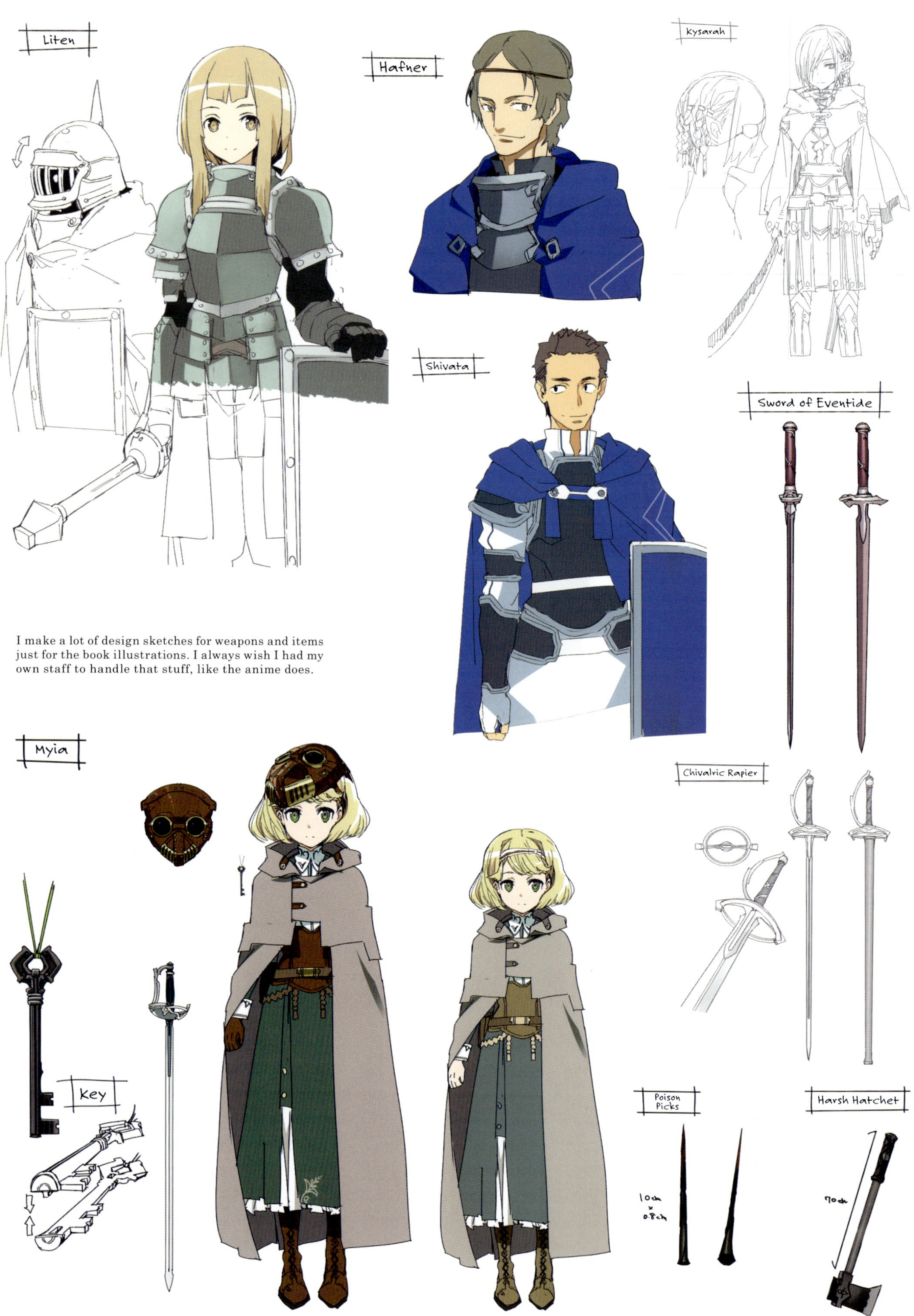

I make a lot of design sketches for weapons and items just for the book illustrations. I always wish I had my own staff to handle that stuff, like the anime does.

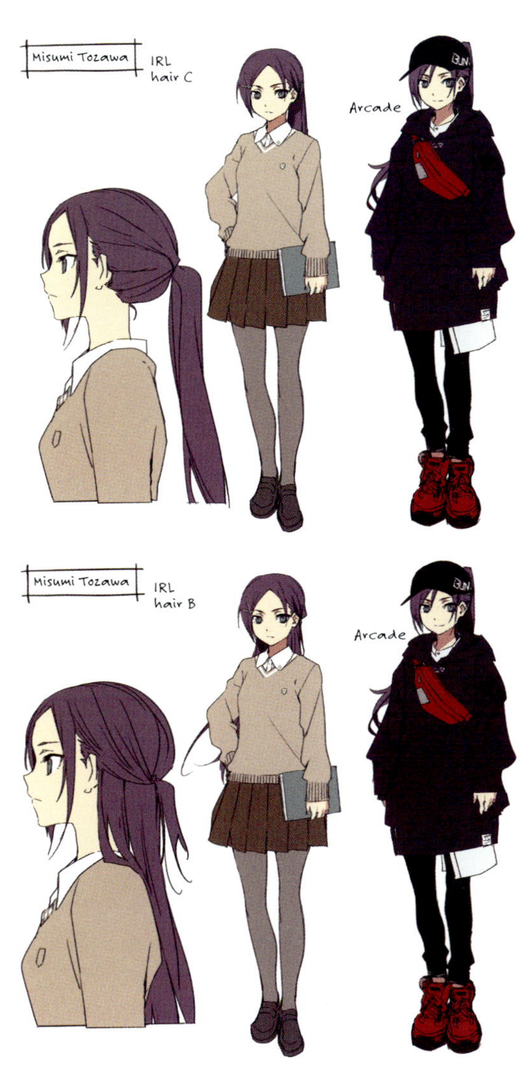

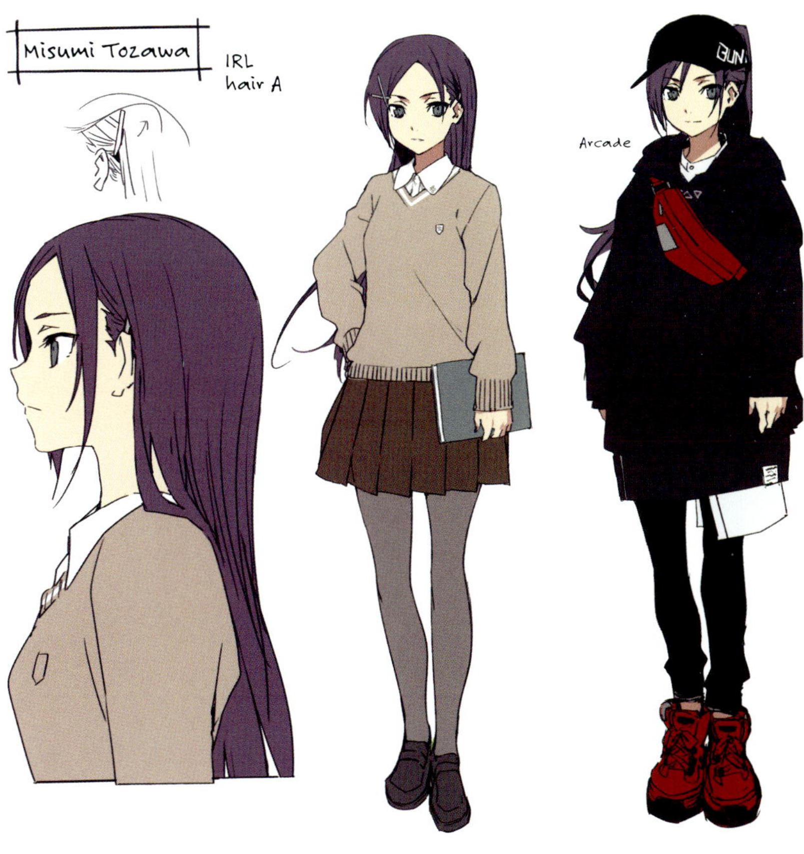

Designs for Mito, Asuna's classmate and an original character for the *SAO Progressive* movie. I really like the real-life Misumi's baseball cap outfit. It's oversized, to mirror today's styles. Also, Mito's male avatar turned out really hunchbacked in the movie, which I thought was funny. If you haven't seen it yet, you gotta check it out.

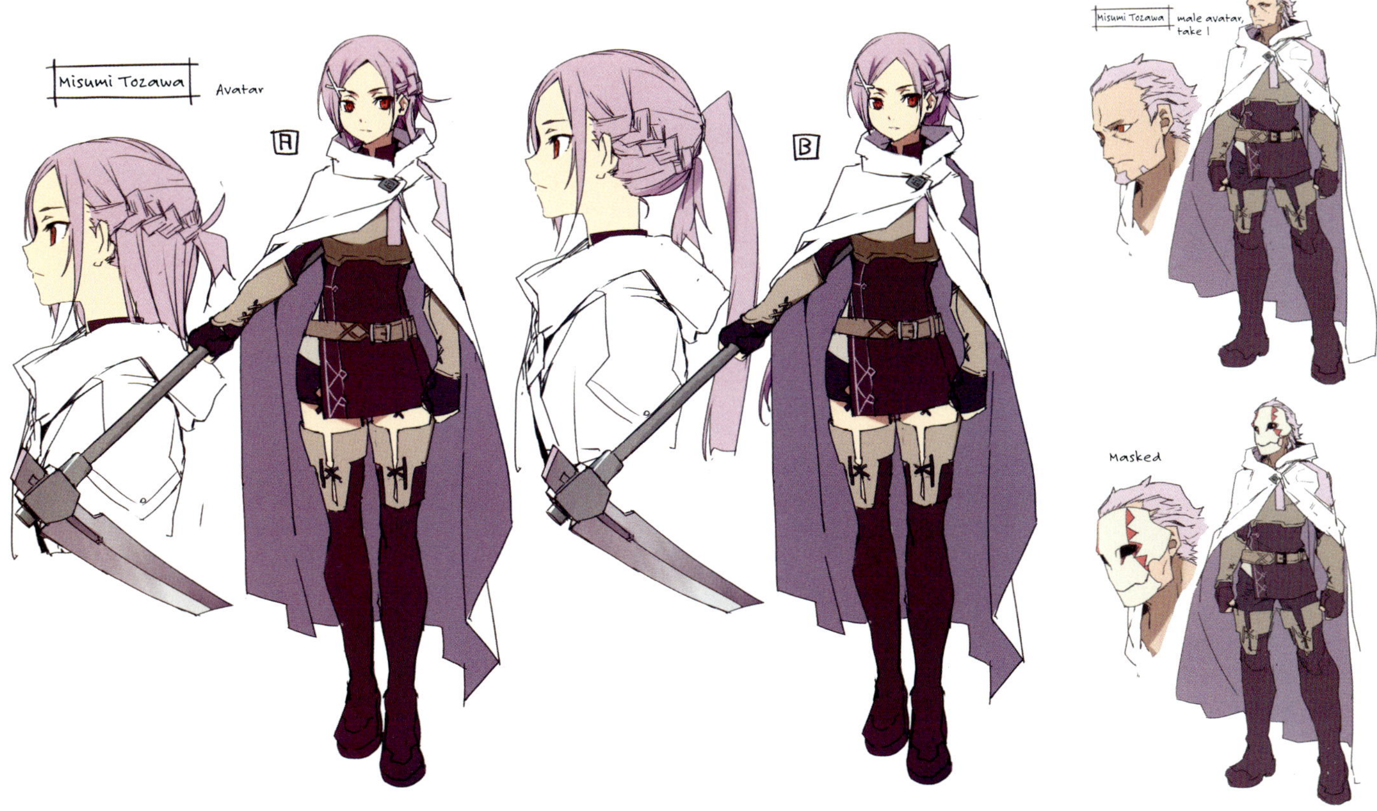

SWORD ART ONLINE
abec Artworks

New World

ILLUSTRATION BY abec

Translation: Stephen Paul
Lettering: Phil Christie

This book is a work of fiction. Names, characters, places, and incidents are the product of the author's imagination or are used fictitiously. Any resemblance to actual events, locales, or persons, living or dead, is coincidental.

SWORD ART ONLINE abec GASHU New World
©abec 2023
©Reki Kawahara 2023
Edited by Dengeki Bunko
First published in Japan in 2023 by KADOKAWA CORPORATION, Tokyo.
English translation rights arranged with KADOKAWA CORPORATION, Tokyo through Tuttle-Mori Agency, Inc., Tokyo.

58-67p
©2017 Reki Kawahara/KADOKAWA ASCII MEDIA WORKS/
SAO-A Project

84p, 86-88p
©2017 Reki Kawahara/KADOKAWA ASCII MEDIA WORKS/
SAO-A Project
©Bandai Namco Entertainment Inc.

85p
©2014 Reki Kawahara/KADOKAWA ASCII MEDIA WORKS/SAO II Project
©Bandai Namco Entertainment Inc.

90-91p
©2016 Reki Kawahara/KADOKAWA ASCII MEDIA WORKS/SAO Movie Project
©2017 Reki Kawahara/KADOKAWA ASCII MEDIA WORKS/SAO-A Project
©2017 Keiichi Sigsawa/KADOKAWA ASCII MEDIA WORKS/GGO Project
©Bandai Namco Entertainment Inc.

92-93p
©2017 Reki Kawahara/KADOKAWA ASCII MEDIA WORKS/SAO-A Project
©2017 Keiichi Sigsawa/KADOKAWA ASCII MEDIA WORKS/GGO Project
©Bandai Namco Entertainment Inc.
©Bandai Namco Amusement Inc.

121p
©NewDays

122p
©KAZUMA KAMACHI/MOTOI FUYUKAWA 2020

English translation © 2024 by Yen Press, LLC

Yen Press, LLC supports the right to free expression and the value of copyright. The purpose of copyright is to encourage writers and artists to produce the creative works that enrich our culture.

The scanning, uploading, and distribution of this book without permission is a theft of the author's intellectual property. If you would like permission to use material from the book (other than for review purposes), please contact the publisher. Thank you for your support of the author's rights.

Yen On
150 West 30th Street, 19th Floor
New York, NY 10001

Visit us at yenpress.com
facebook.com/yenpress | twitter.com/yenpress
yenpress.tumblr.com | instagram.com/yenpress

First Yen On Edition: December 2024
Edited by Yen On Editorial: Ivan Liang
Designed by Yen Press Design: Jane Sohn

Yen On is an imprint of Yen Press, LLC.
The Yen On name and logo are trademarks of Yen Press, LLC.

The publisher is not responsible for websites
(or their content) that are not owned by the publisher.

Library of Congress Control Number: 2024940732

ISBN: 979-8-8554-0725-9 (paperback)
       979-8-8554-0726-6 (ebook)

10 9 8 7 6 5 4 3 2 1

APS

Printed in China

Special Thanks
KOUHAKU KUROBOSHI
GREEN TANUKI
SAO II Project
SAO MOVIE Project
SAO-A Project
GGO Project
BANDAI NAMCO ENTERTAINMENT

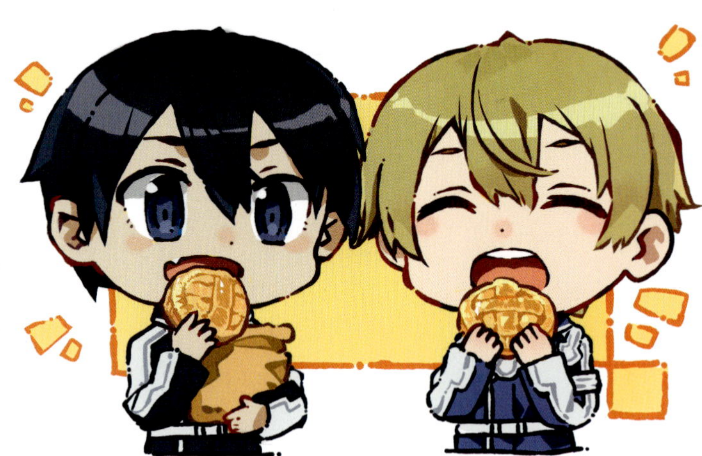